Colonel
JOHN HOLDER

*Boonesborough Defender
& Kentucky Entrepreneur*

COLONEL JOHN HOLDER

Boonesborough Defender & Kentucky Entrepreneur

BY

HARRY G. ENOCH

Acclaim Press
MORLEY, MISSOURI

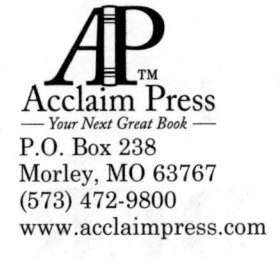

Acclaim Press™
— Your Next Great Book —
P.O. Box 238
Morley, MO 63767
(573) 472-9800
www.acclaimpress.com

Designer: Ron Eifert
Cover Design: M. Frene Melton

Copyright © 2009
Harry G. Enoch

All Rights Reserved.

No part of this book shall be reproduced or transmitted in any form or by any means, electronic or mechanical, including photocopying, recording or by an information or retrieval system, except in the case of brief quotations embodied in articles and reviews without the prior written consent of the publisher. The scanning, uploading, and distribution of this book via the Internet or via any other means without permission of the publisher is illegal and punishable by law.

Library of Congress Cataloging-in-Publication Data

Enoch, Harry G.
  Colonel John Holder:Boonesborough Defender and Kentucky Entrepreneur/ Harry G. Enoch.
      p. cm.
  Includes bibliographical references and index.
  ISBN-13: 978-1-935001-32-4 (alk. paper)
  ISBN-10: 1-935001-32-9 (alk. paper)
  1. Holder, John, ca. 1754-1799. 2. Frontier and pioneer life--Kentucky--Clark County. 3. Pioneers--Kentucky--Clark County--Biography. 4. Soldiers--Kentucky--Clark County--Biography. 5. Landspeculation--Kentucky--Clark County--History--18th century. 6. Land settlement--Kentucky--Clark County--History--18th century. 7. Clark County (Ky.)--Biography. I. Title.
   F457.C56E56 2009
  976.9'5402092--dc22
  [B]
                            2009039863

First Printing 2009
Printed in the United States of America.
10 9 8 7 6 5 4 3 2 1

Royalties from the sale of this book go to the Lower Howard's Creek Nature and Heritage Preserve.

Contents

Foreword 7
Introduction 8
Virginia Beginnings 13
Rescue of the Boone-Callaway Girls 28
Kentucky Frontier 37
In Command at Boonesborough 49
Domestic Relations 68
In Search of Land 90
Holder's Station 104
Land Speculator 129
Yazoo Land Company 139
Business Enterprises 144
Roads Lead to Holder's 175
Howard's Creek Industrial Center 189
Public Service and Local Affairs 212
Journey's End 234
Afterword 254
A Note on Sources 257
Endnotes 261
Index 283

Dedicated to the memory of
Kathryn Owen and C. R. "Pete" Smith,
Lower Howard's Creek "Pioneers"

Foreword

I am pleased to introduce readers to Harry Enoch's profile of John Holder, a noted leader on the Kentucky frontier. Although not as well known as Daniel Boone, Holder's credentials as a pioneer are no less impressive. Holder came to Kentucky as part of a militia force sent to help defend Boonesborough in 1777. By 1779, he commanded that strategic post. His second and permanent home in Kentucky was a large tract of land where Howard's Creek empties into the Kentucky River, located in modern Clark County. Known initially as Holder's Station, this location later developed into an early center of commerce and industry. Enoch's biography of Holder provides an excellent window to better understand the nuts and bolts of settling a frontier.

Holder lived in a world where few records were kept and fewer yet were preserved. Through careful and diligent archival digging, however, Harry Enoch manages to reconstruct Holder's experience in Kentucky to a remarkable degree. He joins the historical documents with direct geographical knowledge of the region. It is a rare combination. The result is an authoritative account that is vivid and puts to rest many mistaken beliefs and suppositions about the Kentucky frontier in the eighteenth century. Readers will enjoy the opportunity to follow the triumphs and disappointments of frontier settlement as encountered by John Holder.

Ellen Eslinger
Professor of History
DePaul University

Introduction

In the course of human history, it seems the politicians and generals get all the books and monuments. Pioneer Kentucky is no exception to the general rule. We commemorate the achievements of Governor Isaac Shelby and General George Rogers Clark, while allowing the important contributions of others to go uncelebrated and unremembered. John Holder is among those who have been overlooked. From obscure origins in Virginia, he rose to prominence in the military, civic and business affairs of early Kentucky. This work tells the story of his life as well as the industrial development he began along the Kentucky River and in the valley of Lower Howard's Creek.

John Holder was one of the Boonesborough defenders whose courage and accomplishments were the equal of any man at that famous fort. His heroic deeds during the great siege were remembered by the pioneers for many years afterwards. When Daniel Boone left Kentucky after the siege, Holder became commander of the fort. He was a military leader who participated in the Revolutionary War in Virginia and, after moving to Kentucky, fought in numerous campaigns during the Indian Wars. Holder's military service began in Dunmore's War (1774) and continued until his death twenty-five years later. He was a trusted officer in the service of George Rogers Clark. The last six years of his life, Holder served as a regimental commander of the Clark County militia at the rank of lieutenant colonel.

Holder was a man of property who claimed thousands of acres of land in Kentucky. His land business connected him to some of the most noted figures in early Kentucky, including Green Clay, John Breckinridge, Matthew Walton, George Nicholas, James Clark and Robert Trimble.

Holder was a commercial-industrial innovator who was involved in far sighted business enterprises. In the 1780s, he founded a settlement in the valley of Lower Howard's Creek, about a mile downstream from Boonesborough on the north side of the Kentucky River. The area was then in Fayette County, Virginia, and later became Clark County, Kentucky. The settlement, which began with a small, fortified station, eventually grew under Holder's leadership to include a store, tavern, boatyard, ferry, warehouse and mill. His landing on the Kentucky River became a major departure point for flatboats bound for New Orleans with Kentucky produce. His enterprises were connected by an extensive network of roads linking them to Winchester, Lexington, Richmond and Paris. Holder's enterprises led to other mills locating in the valley and resulted in Lower Howard's Creek becoming one of the first industrial areas of Kentucky. Much of this area is now enclosed in the Lower Howard's Creek Nature and Heritage Preserve.

Holder was one of Clark County's first county justices, appointed to the court by Governor Isaac Shelby in 1793, and served in that capacity until his untimely death. He was an active participant in the court who was involved in all of the early decisions during the county's formative years. He also served as a deputy county surveyor.

Holder married Frances "Fanny" Callaway, a daughter of Colonel Richard Callaway. Richard was one of the founders of Boonesborough, later commander of the fort, and one of the first justices of the Kentucky County court. He and John Todd were the first burgesses elected to the Virginia legislature from Kentucky County. Calloway County, Kentucky, is named in his honor. Fanny, along with her sister Betsy, and Jemima Boone were captured by the Shawnee in 1776 and rescued by Daniel Boone several days later in what has become one of the signature events on the Kentucky frontier. Fanny and John Holder had eight children, all of whom were still infants when he died in 1799.

John Holder's achievements exemplify the opportunities available on the Western frontier to men born without the trappings of wealth or position. In Kentucky, a man of intelligence, courage and ambition could reach heights of success not possible back in Old Virginia. Many of those who left their mark were military leaders who rose to further prominence through the acquisition of land. Due to the vagaries of land law, early Kentucky was also a place where hard won fortunes could be quickly lost. All of these elements may be observed in the life of Colonel John Holder.

In the interest of historical accuracy, it is important to take a critical look at the life of John Holder, the pioneer, the soldier and the entrepreneur. Although no biography of Holder has been attempted, a considerable amount has been written about him, much of it based on family tradition, legend and folklore. The objective of this work is to tell John Holder's story as factually as possible, relying whenever possible on primary sources. Evidence will be presented to document every phase of his life. Particular pains will be taken to critically examine well-known myths which may or may not be factual.

Lyman Copeland Draper (1815-1891), noted nineteenth century

collector and historian, prepared a brief biographical sketch of John Holder. A patient meticulous researcher, Draper spent many years at the State Historical Society of Wisconsin assembling a vast collection on American frontier life. After his death, the collection was arranged into 491 volumes concentrating on trans-Allegheny frontier history. The sketch below, while focusing heavily on Holder's military achievements, gives a concise but informative picture of the man and remains one of the most accurate summaries of his life.

> John Holder was born on the Blue Ridge in Frederick County, Virginia and went to Kentucky in 1777 as the lieutenant of Capt. William B. Smith's Company raised on the Yadkin [River]. That year made a settlement over the Kentucky River, two miles from Boonesboro. He was in Boone's Paint Creek Expedition and in the big siege of Boonesboro in 1778 and shortly after was raised to the rank of Captain and was stationed at the close of that year at the Falls of Ohio. The following year he commanded a company on [John] Bowman's Campaign and in 1780 in [George Rogers] Clark's Shawnee campaign. On the 14th August 1782 was Defeated near the Upper Blue Licks and served in Clark's Campaign in the fall of that year. He acted as Major on Clark's Wabash Expedition in 1786 and in 1790 was appointed to raise a battalion in Kentucky to settle the Walnut Hills [site of present day Vicksburg] in now Mississippi under the auspices of the Yazoo Company, but never carried out the design. He married Fanny Callaway, one of the captive girls and raised a large family. Colonel Holder was six feet in height, heavily framed and of fine appearance. He died at his residence in Clark County, Kentucky, March 30, 1799 and his widow survived him about five years.[1]

Little has been written about John Holder in his home state of Virginia. Where records can be found, the picture is clouded at times by not knowing which John Holder is referred to. In addition to our Colonel John Holder, there were a number of other men of the same name living in Virginia at the same time. This has proved to be a major obstacle for those trying to piece together Holder's early life. When citing Virginia records in this work, we will try to make it clear if there is any uncertainty regarding which John Holder is referred to.

We would be fortunate indeed if it were only John Holder's origins that are uncertain. However, questionable claims have been made about his military career, his marriage or marriages and ensuing children, his land holdings, and his business practices. There is even mystery surrounding his death: the date and place are uncertain, as are the circumstances.

Biographies of Virginians who did not come from the first families often rely heavily on traditional accounts, which over time take on an air of authority difficult to dispel. The folklore associated with John Holder is extensive. Research documented in this work shows that many of the claims are wrong. Examples abound, from the insignificant (Holder was married at least twice) to the inconceivable (Holder was killed by Indians). The strongly held family tradition, which has Holder marrying 15 year old Fanny Callaway at the advanced age of 42 and dying at age 62, is also inaccurate.

Well known historians have not been able to sort out some of the claims, such as the assertion that Holder was a member of the party who rescued the Boone and Callaway girls after they were captured by the Shawnee. The evidence strongly suggests he was not among the rescuers, but that spoils one of the most romantic stories of the early west: that the three kidnapped girls came back and married three of their rescuers at Fort Boonesborough. Most writers, preferring their histories to read like novels, decline to discuss the evidence and either include the story or leave it out. Of two recent Daniel Boone biographies, for example, one incorporates the version with Holder as a rescuer and groom at a double wedding (John Mack Faragher's *Daniel Boone*), while the other omits it (Robert Morgan's *Boone*).[2] Neither evaluates the evidence pro or con. While Holder's presence or absence is merely a sidelight in Daniel Boone's saga, it would be a key event in the life of John Holder. This claim, as well as many others, will be explored in detail in this work.

* * *

I am deeply indebted to many people who helped me in the course of this work. Anne Crabb was especially generous, not only allowing me the use of her voluminous files of Draper manuscript transcriptions but also critiquing the manuscript at various stages. I am most grateful to the late Robert Coney for our collaboration on a two-year project sorting and cataloging early records stored in the attic of the Clark County Courthouse. Kathryn Owen allowed me complete access to her Clark County research; Larry Meadows provided helpful information on the milling industry; Anne Bowen and Debra Anderson shared valuable documents pertaining to John Holder and his children; Carol Holt and Judy Wilson sent me pertinent records from Franklin County, Tennessee. Thanks to Phil May for permission to include several of his murals painted at the Civil War Fort at Boonesboro, to Ted Hazen for permission to use his drawing of an automated gristmill, to Paula Coney for permission to use her photographs of Colonel Holder's gravestone dedication and to Deidre Scaggs, University Archivist at the University of Kentucky, for permission to use pictures from Joe Kendall Neel's UK thesis. I am also grateful for the assistance provided by Nancy O'Malley, Andy Gary, Phyllis Spiker, Maxine Hobbs (deceased), Mary Alice Farrell, Elizabeth Little, Roberta "Bobbi" Newell, Pat Mount, Michael Drake, Jerry Raisor, Robert Polsgrove, Will Hodgkin, Ellen Eslinger, Clark Circuit Clerk David Hunt (deceased), Clark County Clerk Anita Jones and Clark County Judge Executive Henry Branham. Finally, I would like to acknowledge the continuing support and encouragement of my wife, Clare Sipple. Her helpful suggestions, thought provoking ideas and enduring enthusiasm helped me see this project through to the end.

* * *

Unless otherwise noted, photographs and drawings are by the author.

Chapter 1
Virginia Beginnings

John Holder's father was named Luke, and he had a brother Francis. We learn this from a deed between Luke Holder and Thomas Lord Fairfax, a huge landowner in northern Virginia. In 1773, Fairfax deeded 100 acres of land to Luke "for and during the Natural lives of him the said Luke Holder, John and Francis his sons, and the Longest liver of them." From a marriage bond twenty years later in Clark County, Kentucky, we learn that Luke also had a daughter Margaret, and from one of the pioneer accounts, we know she was called Peggy. That is the extent of our certain knowledge concerning the names of John Holder's parents and siblings.[1]

Prince William County

The first records of Luke are found in Fauquier County, Virginia, in 1759. That year Fauquier was formed out of Prince William County. Tax records establish Luke as a resident the year Fauquier County was formed. Evidence suggests Luke was already residing in the section of Prince William that became Fauquier. His son John may have been born in Prince William County.

The 1759 tithable list for Fauquier County reports Luke living at "G. Hedgman's Quarter."[2] Wealthy Virginia planters often purchased large tracts of land in addition to their manor plantations. These tracts were then divided up into smaller farms called "quarter farms" or simply "quarters." Each quarter was managed by a resident overseer for the absentee landowner.

The Hedgman family— Nathaniel Hedgman with sons Nathaniel Jr. and Peter—owned nearly 5,000 acres on the north side of the Rappahannock River along three small streams known as Great Run, Tin Pot Run and Marsh Run. Mid-eighteenth century maps show a place called "Hedgman" near the mouth of Great Run. Because the family was so prominent in the region, the Rappahannock River for a time was known as Hedgman River. The Hedgman lands were in the vicinity of present day Remington, a small town located where US 15/29 crosses the river. The Rappahannock forms the boundary between Culpeper and Fauquier. Prior to the formation of Fauquier, G. Hedgman's Quarter was in Prince William County.

The six slaves listed with Luke in 1759 may have belonged to one of the Hedgmans. Virginia law required the plantation overseer to list the names of slaves, while the owner was responsible for paying the tax on them. "G. Hedgman" may have been Peter's son George. After Peter Hedgman died in 1765, a dispute arose over his estate. Stephen McCormack, who was an overseer for Hedgman, paid Luke Holder for appearing as a witness in his lawsuit against John Knox, executor of Peter Hedgman's estate.[3]

One other piece of evidence points to Luke being a resident of Prince William. Peter Butler, who obtained a warrant for 292 acres of land on the Rappahannock River, had his tract surveyed in 1757. In a note added to the survey, Butler requested that the deed issue to "Luke Holder of Prince William County."[4] The entry is taken from a list of forfeited plats, meaning the claimant, Luke Holder, never received title to the land.

Formation of Virginia Counties

1731	Prince William from King George and Stafford
1742	Fairfax from Prince William
1743	Frederick from Orange
1749	Culpeper from Orange
1757	Loudoun from Fairfax
1759	Fauquier from Prince William
1836	Clark from Frederick

There were other Holders residing near Luke whose names are shown on the 1759 Fauquier County tithable list: Davis, William and Davis Jr. Davis Holder was appointed overseer of a section of road "from Licking Run to Turkey Run," which places him a little north of present day Germantown, and less than 10 miles from Hedgman's land. Living in such close proximity suggests a close family relationship. The presence of all these Holders in the same area in 1759 suggests that they were living in the part of Prince William County that became Fauquier County. Holder family researchers believe Davis' line migrated to Surry County, North Carolina before the Revolutionary War.[5]

Members of the Rout family owned property adjoining Hedgman's Quarter on Great Run. A landmark there still goes by the name of Rout's Hill.[6] George Rout married John Holder's sister Margaret in Clark County, Kentucky.

Virginia Beginnings

Fauquier County

Fauquier was formed in 1759 out of Prince William County and was situated in the northern tip of Virginia on the east side of the Blue Ridge Mountains. The county seat was called Fauquier Court House until the name was changed to Warrenton. The town is best known as the place where Chief Justice John Marshall began his law practice. The county claims to be the birthplace of Nancy Hanks, the mother of Abraham Lincoln.

In May of 1759, Joseph Settle came into Fauquier County court to request administration of his father Isaac's estate. Luke Holder was his security; both signed a bond to ensure Settle would perform his legal duties. The Settle family lived near Hedgman's Quarter. Their land was on Barrows Run, which was just upstream from Great Run on the Rappahannock.[7]

In March 1761, John Hedgman, gentleman, and Luke Holder were brought before the county court to face a charge of forcible entry. The court "upon hearing the parties and examination of sundry witnesses," voted two to one to discharge Hedgman and commit Holder to jail "until he give Security for his good behaviour, himself in the sum of One hundred pounds, and his two securities in the sums of Fifty pounds each." At the same session, the court recorded that Luke, William Blackwell (one of the justices who voted to convict him) and Thomas Conway committed their "good and chattells, lands and Tenements" on the condition that Luke "shall keep the Peace and be of good behaviour the space of one year and a day."[8] The county minute book does not elaborate on the charges against Holder or explain why they discharged Hedgman, gentleman, and put Holder in jail.

In March of 1765, Luke served on a jury trial in a suit over a debt. Later that same month, Luke himself was sued for debt. He had given a note for £6 to one John Barnes. Barnes assigned the note to Cuthbert Bullitt, who sued Luke to collect. Cuthbert Bullitt was a wealthy lawyer/planter of Prince William County and a political leader during the Revolutionary War. His son Alexander S. Bullitt was an early settler of Louisville for whom Bullitt County was named.[9] The case of *Bullitt v. Holder* was heard in July 1766, when a jury decided in Bullitt's favor and ordered Luke to pay the debt. Luke also had to pay Thomas Howison 155 pounds of tobacco for appearing as a witness for him at the two-day trial.[10]

Luke's other appearances at court in Fauquier County reflect the usual citizen duties such as serving on juries, appearing as a witness and being appointed to appraise a deceased neighbor's estate. He was sued once more,

Colonel John Holder

in 1762 by William Crawford Jr.[a] The cause was not stated and the suit was settled out of court. A court session on August 23, 1768 is of special interest. That day Luke Holder sat on a jury in one trial and Agatha Holder testified as a witness in another trial. It may be no coincidence that they were at court the same day. Luke could have taken her to the county seat to testify, and being available, got selected to sit on a jury. While it seems reasonable to ask if Agatha was Luke's wife, there is no evidence to support it.[11]

Loudoun and Frederick Counties

Luke Holder was listed as a tithable for Fauquier County in 1768. Sometime during the following year he moved to Loudoun County. We find him there, residing in Shelburne Parish, for the next decade or so. Loudoun was formed in 1757 and lies at the northernmost tip of Virginia, adjoining Fauquier and on the east side of the Blue Ridge. The county seat is Leesburg, named for the influential Lee family of Virginia. This part of Virginia began to be settled from 1725 to 1730 with immigrants from Pennsylvania, New Jersey and Maryland. A number of Quakers, Germans, Irish and Scots-Irish settled in the northwest area of the county, west of the Catoctin Mountains. Shelburne Parish was in the western section of Loudoun County, between Goose Creek and the Blue Ridge.[12]

John Holder's Birth Date

In colonial Virginia, taxes were assessed on free white males 16 years old and over and slaves, male and female, of the same ages. These persons were referred to as tithables. The tax was assessed to support the established church of the colony, the Church of England, which became the Episcopal Church of America. The taxes, or tithes, paid the minister's salary, upkeep of the church and rectory, relief of the poor and other responsibilities of the parish. Colonial tithable lists for Virginia still exist only for a handful of counties. Loudoun County records are nearly complete for the period from 1758 to 1799.

Tithable lists serve as a sort of census for white males aged 16 and older. Virginia law divided each county into districts (called parishes) and justices were appointed to collect a list of tithables from each household. The person responsible for paying the tax was required to submit his list to the justice by an appointed date in August. Compiled lists were submitted to the county clerk who made them available for public inspection. Fines were issued for concealing tithables.[13]

---

a William Crawford Jr. married Susannah Holder, daughter of Davis Holder, October 7, 1789. Davis Holder shows up frequently in Fauquier County records.

Virginia Beginnings

Holder in Virginia Tithable Lists[14]

Fauquier County Tithables

1759	Thomas Marshall's list	Luke Holder* (Robin, Ben, Harry, James, Sarah, Grace), 7
1768	Armistead Churchill's list	Luke Holder (Cull), 2

Loudoun County Tithables

1769	Levin Powell's list	Luke Holder (Cull), 2
1770	Levin Powell's list	Luke Holder, John Holder (Cull), 3
1771	Levin Powell's list, SP	Luke Holder, John Holder (Cull), 3
1772	Thomas Lewis' list, SP	Luke Holder, John Holder (Cull), 3
1773	Levin Powell's list, SP	John Holder (Cull), 2
1774	Levin Powell's list, SP	Luke Holder (Cull), 2
1777	Levin Powell's list, SP	Luke Holder, Francis Holder (Cull), 2
1779	Thomas Lewis' list, SP	Luke Holder, Francis Holder (Cull), 2
1783	William Bronaugh's list, SP	Luke Holder, Francis Holder (Cull), 2
1784 & thereafter	absent	

* Reported at "G. Hedgman's Quarter."

Explanation of Table Left column—year. Middle column—name of the person responsible for preparing the list of tithables. Right column—name of each tithable in the household: males 16 years old and above, plus all slaves in the same age range (slave names in parentheses), followed by the total tithables in the household. SP—Shelburne Parish

Tithable lists may be used to establish the exact age of individuals, since free white males appear as tithables for the first time at age 16. Lists were usually completed in August or September. From the tithable lists shown in the table, we see that John Holder was named for the first time in 1770, from which we calculate a birth year of about 1754. He could have been born any time between August 1753 and August 1754, assuming that Luke reported accurately.

There is supporting evidence for this birth year. John Holder gave a deposition in Bourbon County, Kentucky, in September 1798 in which he stated that he was "aged about forty-five." This results in an estimated birth date between September 1753 and August 1754. Kentucky pioneer Daniel Bryan reported that Holder came to Kentucky "in 1777 as a young man between 22 to 23 years old." Holder came to Kentucky in September 1777. This results in an estimated birth date between September 1754 and August 1756.

John Holder Reported Birth Dates and Locations[15]

Source (date)	Birth date	Place from	Basis
Luke Holder (1769, 1770)	c.1754	Loudoun Co.	tithable lists
John Holder (1798)	c.1753		Holder's deposition
George M. Bedinger (1843)		near Winchester	knew Holder
Daniel Bryan (1844)	1754-55		knew Holder
William Sudduth (1845)	c.1750	Frederick Co.	knew Holder
John Rankins (1840s)		on top of the Blue Ridge	knew Holder
William D. Holder (1849)		Culpeper Co.	family tradition
Richard P. Holder (1850)	c.1737		family tradition
George W. Ranck (1901)		Stafford Co.	none cited
Jessie Williams Hart (1934)	c.1736	Clark Co.	family tradition

Looking backwards, we can infer a place of birth for John Holder by locating where his father was living in 1754. The first record for Luke is three years after that, when we find him in Prince William County. If Luke lived in the same place in 1754, John Holder would have been born in Prince William County. Until additional records can be located his birthplace cannot be definitely established.

We can compare these dates with other published claims for John Holder's birth date. Information provided by Holder and his contemporaries support the date calculated from the tithable lists. Dates based on family tradition appear to be in error, a caution, perhaps, for other claims made by similar sources.

John's brother Francis shows up as a tithable in Luke's household for the first time in 1777; however, Luke is missing from the incomplete lists for 1775 and 1776. Thus, Francis' calculated birth date ranges from about 1759 to 1761.

Luke owned one slave, named Cull, and may have been somewhat better off financially than most of his neighbors. Of the 192 households enumerated along with his in 1769, only one-fifth owned any slaves. The Holder neighborhood in 1783, the last year Luke appears on the tithable list, included several men who later lived near John Holder's place on Lower Howard's Creek in Kentucky: Benjamin Rankins; Francis, Henry and John Hieronymous; John and Zealy Moss; and William Sudduth.

Luke Holder's Farm

Land records help locate more precisely the area where Luke Holder lived in Shelburne Parish. In 1773 Luke acquired 100 acres of land from Thomas Lord Fairfax, who controlled over 8,000 square miles of land located between the Potomac and Rappahannock rivers. The Fairfax land

Virginia Beginnings

was known as the Northern Neck because of its long and irregular shape. Fairfax developed his Northern Neck proprietary by leasing rather than selling the land outright.[b] The terms called for payment of a quitrent by the purchaser. Luke's annual rent for his 100-acre farm was 2 pounds, 2 shillings and 6 pence. He was also required to erect a dwelling house at least 20 feet by 16 feet, plant an orchard of 100 apple trees and build a fence around the latter. House, orchard and fence all technically belonged to Fairfax.

The property description gives several clues to the location. Luke's survey began "at a Large white Oak on the South side of the Blue Ridge" and extended one-half mile north-northeast to the north side of the ridge.[16] Thus we see that Luke's farm straddled Blue Ridge Mountain. The deed describes the tract as "lying and being in the County of Frederick." However, since the county line runs along the top of the ridge, Luke's land lay partly in Frederick and partly in Loudoun.

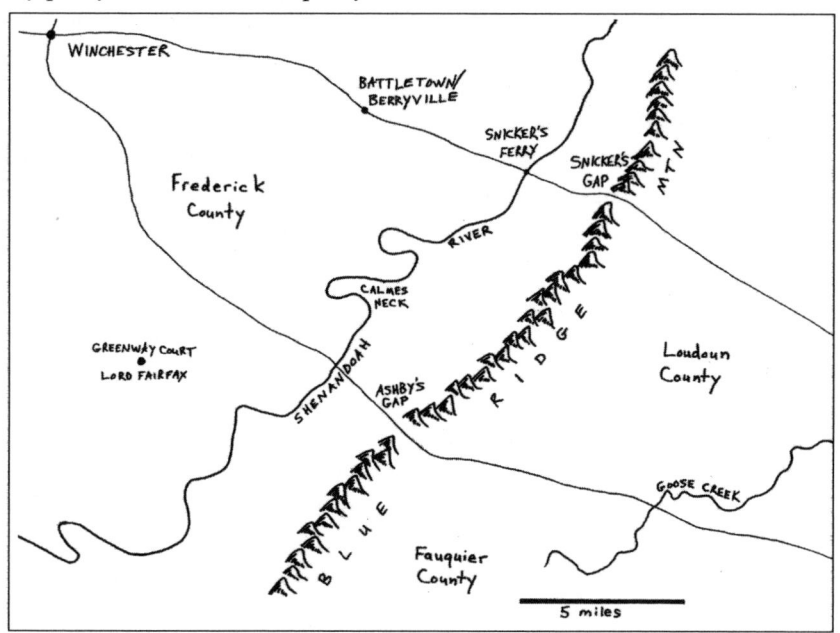

Blue Ridge Mountain, 1773. Luke Holder's plantation was on the Blue Ridge about midway between Ashby's Gap and Snicker's Gap.

---

[b] The Northern Neck proprietary originated as a gift from King Charles II to loyal supporters of the royal family in 1669. By 1719, through inheritance and purchase, the entire property—then embracing about 5.2 million acres—had come into the hands of Lord Fairfax. After Fairfax died in 1781, the Virginia General Assembly dissolved the proprietary, exonerated the landholders from paying quitrents, and the settlers finally received full ("fee simple") ownership of their Northern Neck lands. For a historical sketch of the Fairfax lands, see Josiah Dickinson, *The Fairfax Proprietary* (Front Royal, VA, 1959), pp. 1-11.

Colonel John Holder

Deeds conveying the adjoining property help further refine the location of Luke's farm. In 1770, John Atchison bought 120 acres from Fairfax, "beginning at a chestnut corner to Luke Holder."[17] Atchison family researchers trace their line to the Trapp region of Loudoun County, about midway between Snicker's Gap (Route 7) and Ashby's Gap (US 50) in the Blue Ridge Mountains.[18] By way of confirmation, Edward Snicker was one of Luke's neighbors listed on Levin Powell's tithable list for Shelburne Parish. Snicker also had his feet in both counties. Although he was on the tithable list for Loudoun, he resided in Frederick, where he established Snicker's Ferry over the Shenandoah River in 1766.[19]

The Atchison deed indicates that Luke was in possession of his 100 acres on the Blue Ridge at least three years before Fairfax gave him a formal lease to the tract in 1773. Luke may have moved onto this land when he came to Loudoun County in 1769.

In 1779 Fairfax deeded 100 acres of land to William Bristor of Loudoun County. The survey put the beginning corner at "a chestnut in Luke Holder's line." Tithable lists show William Bristor (Bristow/Bristoe) was a neighbor of Luke's in Shelburne Parish.[20]

The following two deeds appear to involve a related Holder family. In 1766 Fairfax sold James Battson 150 acres of land adjoining John Holder. The tract was on Wankopin Branch[c] and had a corner "near the road corner to John Holder's lot." This small stream is in the area of Middleburg on US 50 near the Loudoun-Fauquier County line. This tract was about 15 miles southeast from where Luke later purchased. Luke's son John was only about 12 years old at the time of the deed (1766). One suspects that living this close, there must have been family ties. In an earlier deed (1755) James Scott sold John Holder, "gentleman," a plantation in Prince William County. The property was conveyed to "John Holder and Cibella his Wife and John his Son." Though not precisely located, in 1755 this could have been in the part of Prince William County that later became Fauquier. The buyer may be the same John Holder of the previous deed. At that time (1755), there were at least three John Holders living fairly close to one another. This gives an indication of the difficulties researchers face when studying John Holder in this part of Virginia.[21]

John Holder's Birthplace

Let us return for a moment to the question of where John Holder was born. As stated above, evidence suggests but does not prove that he was born in Prince William County, in the section that later became Fauquier

---

[c] Now called Wancopin Creek, a tributary of Goose Creek.

Virginia Beginnings

County. Holder's contemporaries spoke of where he "came from" without mentioning anything about his actual birthplace. These men knew John Holder in Virginia and they placed him in the same general area: Winchester, Frederick County and the Blue Ridge. John Rankins, who knew the Holder family well ("Were from our neighborhood."), gave the most specific reference when he stated in an interview, "Old Luke Holder lived on top of the Blue Ridge."[22] At that time, Blue Ridge Mountain formed the boundary between Frederick and Loudoun. With his farm on top of the ridge, Luke had one foot in each county. Luke himself at times was ambiguous about where he lived. The 1773 deed from Fairfax refers to Luke Holder "of the County of Frederick," although he paid his tithe that year in Loudoun. These records are consistent with Luke having a farm lying partly in Frederick and partly in Loudoun. However, they offer no information regarding John Holder's birthplace.

Other accounts have John Holder coming from Clark. Clark County, Virginia, was formed in 1836, when it was separated from Frederick. Clark does adjoin Loudoun, and the western portion of Luke's land on the Blue Ridge was in the part of Frederick that later became Clark. Since John was born about 1754 and Luke did not move to Loudoun until about 1770, it is unlikely that John was born in Loudoun or Frederick/Clark.

There are persistent claims, unaccompanied by any evidence, that John Holder was a Revolutionary War soldier from Culpeper County.[23] That record for John Holder, if it exists, is almost certainly for some other man, not the son of Luke, but it may be why some family researchers place Colonel Holder's birthplace there. No evidence was presented for George Ranck's claim that John Holder was from Stafford County.

To summarize then, evidence suggests that John Holder was born about 1754, possibly in Prince William County. He can be documented in Loudoun County, where he lived with his father Luke and brother Francis through the year 1773. Men who knew Holder claimed that he was from Frederick County or near Winchester, which is in Frederick County. Their statements are consistent with the location of Luke Holder's farm on top of the Blue Ridge. John must have left his family and set out on his own sometime prior to the Revolutionary War. After 1773, we cannot positively document his whereabouts until 1777 when he came to Boonesborough with the Virginia militia. Evidence below suggests that he volunteered for military service in Virginia before coming to Kentucky.

Dunmore's War

Lord Dunmore, Virginia's colonial governor, called out the provincial

Colonel John Holder

militia to put down an uprising of the Ohio Valley Indians. This brief campaign culminated in a decisive battle on October 10, 1774, at Point Pleasant at the confluence of the Ohio and Kanawha rivers. After severe losses on both sides, the Indians, led by Shawnee Chief Cornstalk, withdrew from the battlefield.[24] A John Holder served in this campaign.

Pay roll lists have been transcribed for many of the companies that served in Dunmore's War. A list designated as "Lt. Sigismund Stribling's roll" is found "on the pay rolls at Romney and Winchester." John Holder is listed as a private in Lieutenant Stribling's company. Although difficult to prove, evidence strongly suggests this was the John Holder who later came to Kentucky. In 1789, Stribling received a grant for 1,000 acres of land located on the Kentucky River.[d] His grant included the mouth of Twomile Creek and the present site of Ford in Clark County, Kentucky. The tract is only 2½ miles upstream from John Holder's land.[25]

People who knew each other in Virginia often claimed land and settled near each other in Kentucky. This is a pattern seen over and over in Clark County and elsewhere. We find the Stribling family in Frederick County prior to the Revolutionary War. In the 1770s they owned land just south of the present day town of Berryville,[e] which was less than 10 miles from Luke Holder's farm. One of the Striblings intermarried with a Snicker who lived in Holder's neighborhood. Other members of Lieutenant Stribling's company who lived in this Frederick County neighborhood include Ensign William Frost, Sergeant Thomas Frost and privates Abraham Lindsey and Isaac Frost.[26] Finding these men who lived near Luke's farm serving in the same unit with John Holder is further evidence that this is the same John Holder who came to Kentucky.

John Holder received compensation for a horse he used during Dunmore's War. His voucher was presented at Romney on October 25, 1775 and a certificate for 6 pounds 5 shillings was issued to "Edward Snigarts." This was Edward Snicker who lived on the Shenandoah River at Snickers Ferry about 3 miles from Luke's farm.[27] No evidence has been found to show whether or not Holder's company participated in the battle of Point Pleasant.

Virginia Regiment

A John Holder served as an ensign in the 7th Company of the 2d Virginia Regiment. This company of riflemen, commanded by Capt. Morgan

---

d In 1804, Sigismund sold this tract to William Stribling. William was a Methodist preacher who settled in Clark County. Clark County Deed Book 5:205; William B. Landrum, *The Life and Travels of William B. Landrum* (Nashville, 1878), p. 15.

e Before 1798 Berryville was known as Battletown.

Virginia Beginnings

Alexander, was raised in the Frederick County area and mustered into service in the fall of 1775. Other officers of the company were 1st Lt. George Jump, 2d Lt. Marquis Calmes and Ensign John Holder. Their regiment was sent to meet Lord Dunmore's small Loyalist army composed of the 14th British Regiment, volunteers and runaway slaves. The 2d Virginia Regiment engaged the British forces at the Great Bridge, near Norfolk, on December 9. The battle was a decisive victory for the Americans. British casualties were 102, the Virginians had one wounded. Regimental commander, Colonel William Woodford, sent his report on the battle to Edmund Pendleton, president of the Virginia Convention. The following is an excerpt from the report which was published in the *Virginia Gazette*:

> The defeat of the British regulars at the Great Bridge last Saturday struck the enemy into such dreadful consternation and terror that after abandoning their fort, they thought it most prudent to retire from Norfolk and take refuge on board the ships.[28]

Accounts of battles are rarely sufficiently detailed to determine which units and individuals participated in the action. Fortunately, in this instance, the *Virginia Gazette* published several follow up reports on the Norfolk encounter. We know that Captain Alexander's company did not arrive until several days after the skirmish.

> Great Bridge, December 12
> Capt. Morgan Alexander with his rifle company is expected this day, as fine men we hear as ever were seen.[29]

From ongoing accounts in the newspaper, we learn that Dunmore continued to menace the area with a small fleet of armed sloops and schooners. These boats, referred to as "tenders," were sailing up the coast firing on the towns and looking to pick up runaway slaves to enlist in their cause. Next we read that Alexander's company was dispatched north to intercept them. Their small boat, the Musquetto, carried them to the York River, where they engaged in a daring exploit to capture one of Dunmore's tenders. The account not only mentions Holder's unit but also mentions him by name.

> December 30
> We have just received an account of the taking 14 whites and 2 slaves, which were on board a tender sent out, as it is thought, to plunder the inhabitants on the seaboard and to pick up such other

base wretches as might be found to join in this accursed trade, as they had 8 stand of spare arms besides other military stores on board.

On Friday the 22d instant [December] advice was received at Hampton that the tender was at anchor between the lighthouse point and the mouth of York river. Captain Alexander, with 12 privates of his rifle company, lieutenant Colmise [Calmes] and ensign Holder, as volunteers, together with 6 other gentlemen volunteers from the Musquetto, were detached under the command of the afore-mentioned officer, who found the tender at anchor, as has been reported.

The party continued reconueitreing the coast till about day-light, notwithstanding the great severity of the weather. In the course of the night, which was exceedingly tempestuous, she cut her cable and drifted on shore, when the crew left her, and betook themselves to flight. The party proceeded to examine, and after pursuing some distance, found the crew, whom they took and brought to Hampton. On further examining the vessel, which could only be done by wading as the storm continued, and the breakers were so violent that those in the attempt were frequently beat off their feet. Twenty four stand of arms, some new regimentals, and some other particulars, were found on board.[30]

One of the soldiers, Philip Regan, gave additional details in his pension application. He stated that they were at Yorktown "employed in watching the Bay, and keeping the British from Landing who frequently came up the Bay in small vessels to plunder. On one occasion this Declarant with fifteen others all under the command of Capt. Alexander succeeded in taking twenty four British privates, one lieutenant and two negroes prisoners, who had landed at the Bay in a Small Schooner which they also obtained possession of."[31]

The newspaper article provides a dramatic backdrop to the event: the British were captured "In the course of the night, which was exceedingly tempestuous," and to disarm the boat the men had to wade into surf so high it repeatedly knocked them off their feet. One could hardly wish for a more vivid description of an event or a more specific identification of the participants. With this incident, John Holder gives an indication of the bold character he later displayed in Kentucky, that of a stalwart defender always willing to leap into the fray and do whatever necessary to the occasion.

After Dunmore burned the town of Norfolk, he removed his force to a new base at the mouth of the Rappahannock River called Gwynn's Island. The 2d Regiment was reinforced by several infantry regiments and an

Virginia Beginnings

artillery regiment. Then in July 1776, they drove the British off the island. Dunmore's fleet sailed away and he returned to England.[32]

The Ensign John Holder in Alexander's company and the Colonel John Holder of Kentucky were almost certainly the same man. While there were several John Holders in Virginia, only one, the son of Luke, has been identified in Frederick County. As shown below, Morgan Alexander's company was recruited in Frederick County; Captain Alexander and his fellow officers were all from Frederick.

Morgan Alexander died in the service in 1783. His descendants later applied for back pay he never received. An affidavit of Gen. John Smith stated that he knew Alexander personally and recommended him "as a fit person to bear a captain's commission," which he received in the town of Winchester. We don't know precisely where Alexander lived, but it may have been very near Holder, since he married a daughter of Holder's neighbor, Edward Snicker.[33]

Several men in Captain Alexander's company received pensions for their Revolutionary War service. One of these was Thomas Jones, who later lived in Bourbon County. He stated in his declaration for a pension that he enlisted

> in the fall of the year 1775 in Frederick County, Virginia for the Term of one year. He was commanded by Capt. Morgan Alexander." He marched from Frederick County to Hampden [Hampton] then to Little York, then to Williamsburg at which place his term of service expired.[34]

Philip Regan, John Malone, Solomon Bishop and Marquis Calmes all received a pension for their service in the war, and each served in Alexander's company. They each stated that they were residents of Frederick County when they enlisted in Captain Alexander's company.[35]

Marquis Calmes lived very close to Berryville, which was less than 10 miles from Luke Holder's place in Frederick County. Marquis' grandfather, Marquis I (1705-1775), came to the county early. He was one of the original thirteen justices appointed for Frederick and a vestryman at Cunningham Chapel, one of the earliest Episcopal churches in the Shenandoah Valley. He lived on a 500 acre plantation in a bend of the Shenandoah River still known today as Calmes Neck. The tract is less than 5 miles from Luke Holder's farm on the Blue Ridge.[36] Marquis I had two sons, Marquis II and William. William was the father of Marquis III (1755-1834), a Kentucky pioneer who came out to Boonesborough in April 1775 in search of land with his uncle Marquis II, Benjamin Combs, Cuthbert Combs, Benjamin Berry and others.

Colonel John Holder

Marquis III marked off a 1,400 acre claim at the Indian Old Fields in Clark County, then returned to Frederick County to serve in the Revolution. In December 1776, his unit, the 2d Virginia Regiment, was ordered into the Continental Army. Their regiment fought at Brandywine (September 1777), Germantown (October 1777) and Monmouth Courthouse (June 1778). Marquis III left the army in March 1779. Sometime after the war, he settled in Woodford County, Kentucky. He served for many years in the Kentucky militia and was promoted to major-general in 1809, a rank he held at the time of the War of 1812.[37]

Another officer who enlisted with Ensign Holder in the 7th Company was 1st Lt. George Jump. Jump also lived in Frederick County, near Snicker's Ford on the Shenandoah River. This ford, where Route 7 crosses the river, was about 3 miles from Luke Holder's farm. After the officers recruited the company, Jump died in his home county in the fall of 1776.[38]

In 1780, the Virginia legislature passed a law which allowed the army to pay for materials, supplies, and personal services provided to the militia, State, and Continental troops. Citizens were given certificates or receipts for materials and services, which were later redeemed for payment before specially appointed commissioners. John Holder's public service claim for a horse used during the war was paid in Frederick County where he lived. The following entry appears in the commissioner's book:

> Frederick County
> John Holder for a Horse from the Continent as of Ditto
> [certificate allowed by Court Frederick] two £5, three £10 & two £20 } £80[39]

The entry is dated September 1, 1783. Holder was busy in Kentucky in 1783, but his father could have presented the claim to the commissioners.[f]

---

[f] A roll officers of the 5th Company, 2d Virginia Regiment, dated April 1, 1777, lists George Nicholas, major, and John Holder, lieutenant. The 5th Company was raised in Amelia County, which lies southwest of Richmond. It is not clear that this is the same John Holder who enlisted in 1775 in Frederick County (7th Company). However, the commander, George Nicholas, had raised a company in Hanover County (2d Company) in 1775 and he ended up in the 5th Company. In 1777, the Virginia Regiments were ordered into the service of the Continental Army by General George Washington. It is possible that the units were restructured at that time and George Nicholas was moved to the 5th Company and promoted to major. If so, Holder could have been moved from the 7th to the 5th and promoted from ensign to lieutenant. Holder could have been serving in Virginia in April 1777 and resigned that summer in time to get to Kentucky by September. Or this could have been another John Holder. W. T. R. Saffell, *Records of the Revolutionary War Containing the Military and Financial Correspondence of Distinguished Officers* (New York, 1858), p. 273; H. Levin, editor, *Lawyers and Lawmakers of Kentucky* (Chicago, 1897), p. 215.

Virginia Beginnings

Lyman C. Draper later corresponded with some of John Holder's descendants. Richard P. Holder, a grandson, wrote that

> Colonel John Holder did not perform any military services before leaving Virginia, where he was born, which was near or at Winchester, which I think is now in Clark County, Virginia. He done a good deal of fighting against Indians, was afterwards a magistrate and was a private, a Captain and a Colonel in [Kentucky during] the Revolutionary War. He lived to be 62 years old.[40]

The family had little information about their famous ancestor and some of it was inaccurate. For example, Richard stated that his grandfather lived to be 62 years old, when the best estimates are he died about age 45. It could be that the family was simply unaware of his Virginia military service.

While the above data are suggestive, the evidence is not conclusive. We believe it is likely but not proven that John Holder served as a private in Dunmore's War (1774) and as an ensign in the 7th Company, 2d Virginia Regiment (1775) before coming to Kentucky in 1777.

Chapter 2
Rescue of the Boone-Callaway Girls

On July 14, 1776, there occurred one of the most memorable incidents on the western frontier: the abduction of Daniel Boone's daughter Jemima and two daughters of Richard Callaway, Betsy and Fanny. The event, which is now part of Kentucky folklore, is discussed here because of the alleged involvement of John Holder in the girls' rescue.

The basic story is a thrilling one. On a warm Sunday afternoon, the girls were drifting in a canoe near the north side of the Kentucky River below Boonesborough. As they approached the bank, five Indians rushed out of a thicket and dragged them from their boat. The girls were secured and the Indians prepared to take their prize back to the Shawnee towns in Ohio. The girls' screams alerted the men at the fort, and a rescue party was formed. Two groups set out in pursuit. Daniel Boone led one group which crossed the river to the point where the girls were taken and tracked them from there on foot. Richard Callaway led the other group on horseback. They crossed the river at the ford near Lower Howard's Creek and headed for the Lower Blue Licks. Boone's party camped the first night near some cabin builders a little south of present day Winchester. On Monday, they followed signs left by the girls and closed the gap on the kidnappers. On Tuesday morning, Boone and his men took the small party by surprise, killed two and liberated the girls.[1]

John Holder later married one of the girls, Frances "Fanny" Callaway. The other two girls married men who participated in the rescue: Samuel Henderson to Elizabeth "Betsy" Callaway on August 7, 1776, and Flanders Callaway to Jemima Boone the following year. At some point, the tale was improved by the claim that the three kidnapped girls were betrothed to three of their rescuers. The story was further enhanced by Flanders Callaway and John Holder taking their brides at a double wedding ceremony at the fort.[2]

The tale was told, embellished and retold over the years. It is now part of

Rescue of the Boone-Callaway Girls

Abduction of the Boone and Callaway Daughters. Mural at the Civil War Fort at Boonesboro. Painting by Phil May.

American mythology. To the historian's dismay, some of the details became so embedded in the myth that it is now almost impossible to confirm or disprove them.

Lyman Draper, who was obsessed with every facet of Daniel Boone's life, spent years interviewing family members, writing to participants and their relatives, and gathering all the data he could find regarding this one incident. His account still ranks as one of the most authoritative on the subject. One of the questions Lyman Draper asked over and over was "Who accompanied Boone on the rescue?" In numerous inquiries, he asked specifically whether John Holder was along. The following example is a letter from Draper to Richard French:

> Do you know the names of all the pursuing party? Let me know them if you can. I am anxious to procure references to some friend or descendant of each of the following Pioneers, viz., Col. John Montgomery, Col. William Pope, Major John Holder, Major William Bailey Smith [etc].[3]

In the end, Draper concluded that the evidence did not support Holder's participation, and he did not include Holder in his account of the rescue.

The Evidence

This section reviews the evidence concerning Holder's participation in the famous rescue. There are dozens of different versions and so many conflicting details that it is not possible to reconcile them all. The best place

Colonel John Holder

to begin the search for evidence is with contemporary records and accounts by men who were there at the time.

Known participants in the rescue who left their own accounts include Daniel Boone, John Floyd, William Bailey Smith and Nathan Reid. Reid mentioned that Boone's party consisted of six men, and they were joined on the Clark County side of the river by three men "who were engaged in building a cabbin." Years later the cabin builders were identified as William Bush, John McMillan and John Martin.[a] None of these accounts mention Holder.[4]

John Martin the cabin builder was the John Martin of Boonesborough, who was in numerous Indian engagements on the Kentucky frontier. He came from the state of New York and was known as the "Big Yankee" or "Big John Martin." He established Martin's Station on Stoner Creek and later resided on the Hanging Fork of Dix River in Lincoln County. He has often been confused with the John Martin who settled on Lower Howard's Creek in Clark County. The latter did not arrive in Kentucky until after the Revolutionary War.[5]

Twelve year old John Gass was at Boonesborough when the girls were taken. His father, David Gass, was one of the officers who later served under Holder. John Gass said his father was one of the pursuers. Other rescuers he identified were his cousin John Gass, Samuel Henderson, William Bush and John McMillan. John Gass, who knew Holder personally, said Holder was not along and was not at Boonesborough in 1776.[6]

Richard Callaway Jr. was a six year old boy at the fort when the kidnapping occurred. According to Richard's account, his father led a rescue party that included Jesse Hodges, William Cradlebaugh, William Buchanan, Thomas Brooks, Nathaniel Bullock and Richard Wade. The men were on horseback and headed for the Lower Blue Licks in an attempt to cut off the Indians' retreat. Richard Jr. added that "Boone was not along—neither was John Holder nor was he in Kentucky at the time." Richard Jr. was well acquainted with John Holder and later lived near Holder's children in Tennessee. Since he made such a specific statement about Holder—not being in Kentucky at the time of the kidnapping—we presume he had firsthand knowledge.[7]

Nathaniel Hart Jr. was six years old when he witnessed his father Nathaniel and his uncle David Hart set out on the rescue mission with Richard Callaway's party. Though Nathaniel Jr. knew Holder and lived in the same neighborhood for many years, he made no mention of Holder being one of the rescuers.[8]

---

[a] The cabin builders were identified by John Gass (Bush, McMillan) and Joseph McCormick Sr. (Martin). Draper MSS 31C 2(22-43).

Rescue of the Boone-Callaway Girls

George Bryan came to Kentucky in the company of William Bailey Smith and John Holder in 1777. Bryan named all the men he could recall who accompanied Boone on the rescue: "John Martin, John McMullen, a Big John Guess [Gass], one of the Calloways, I think a Bush, &c." He added that "Holder married the younger Calloway that was taken." George Bryan knew Holder well but did not name him as one of the rescuers.[9]

Elizabeth Thomas (born 1764) was the daughter of William Pogue, who came to Kentucky with Richard Callaway in 1775. Mrs. Thomas was at Harrodsburg when the kidnapping occurred. She stated that "Henderson who afterwards married Betsey was among the pursuers. Holder married Fanny, the other [Callaway sister]." Thus, she mentioned both Samuel Henderson and John Holder, but she named Henderson as one of the rescuers and not Holder.[10]

Daniel Boone's son Nathan (1781-1856) recalled from his father's stories that one of the rescuers was Flanders Callaway. Flanders was with Richard Callaway's company and was not present when Boone's party retook the girls. Flanders later married Boone's daughter Jemima, one of the kidnapped girls. Nathan made no mention of Holder.[11]

Richard French (born c.1792) was the son of James French and Keziah Callaway. Keziah was Fanny Holder's half-sister. Richard's parents lived at Boonesborough, and James French had business dealings with Holder. Richard French lived his entire life in Kentucky and was very close to the Callaway family. Richard gave Reverend Shane a lengthy description of the kidnapping and rescue, but never mentioned Holder as one of the rescuers.[12] Draper wrote to Richard to identify the participants in the rescue and asked about Holder. (Draper's letter to French was quoted above.) In spite of Draper's specific request, Richard's response made no mention of Holder as a rescuer. He simply stated that "Colonel Holder & wife have been long dead" and mentioned that he thought Frances was their only child still living.[13]

* * *

There is considerable evidence that John Holder arrived in Kentucky in September 1777. Other than his supposed participation in the rescue, there is no other support for the claim that Holder was in Kentucky at any time in 1776 or the following year prior to September. The Virginia Land Commission, in awarding Holder a certificate of settlement and preemption, stated:

> We do hereby certify that John Holder is entitled to Four hundred Acres of land in the district of Kentucky on Account of

Colonel John Holder

Settlement made in the Country in the year 1777 & Residing ever since.[14] (emphasis added)

The commissioners' records are a valuable source of information and are often used to determine when an individual first arrived "in the Country." A person received credit for "settlement" by virtue of coming out to Kentucky. He did not have to actually settle on the land he was claiming. Had Holder come to Kentucky in 1775 or 1776 the commission would have so stated.

Septimus Scholl's Statement
With so much evidence indicating Holder was not one of the rescuers, we have to ask how and when such a story could have gotten started. In preparing this section, I reviewed every available account searching for the earliest source to mention Holder's participation.

So far as I have been able to find, Septimus Scholl was the first person to leave a written record stating that Holder was one of the rescuers. Septimus Scholl (1789-1849) was the son of Joseph Scholl and Lavina Boone, a daughter of Daniel Boone. Reverend John D. Shane interviewed Scholl in 1843 or 1844. Shane's note preceding the interview states, "The following is a piece Schull said he had written out for his children, placed it at my disposal." Scholl wrote that Jemima Boone (1762-1829) had been dead about four years, which suggests he may have written the piece in about 1833. Thus, the first written statement that John Holder was one of the rescuers did not appear until nearly 60 years after the event! The following is Scholl's statement regarding the rescue:

> Subsequently, the three girls that were prisoners became the lawful wives of three of their respectable rescuers. . . .
> Calloway, Holder and Henderson, who joined the parents in the pursuit, each married one of the three girls. They, the Indians, had taken them on Sunday Evening and had gotten them by Tuesday morning to Cassiday's Creek. Were breakfasting there. Holder, or Colonel Holder, married Eliza Calloway.[15]

This sounds like a clear authoritative statement, but there are problems. The first is that John Holder married Frances "Fanny" Callaway, not Eliza. Scholl either did not receive or did not pass on information accurately. For example, in his list of Daniel Boone's children, Scholl said son Israel was killed coming to Kentucky in 1773, and son James was killed at the Battle of Blue Licks in 1782, when in fact it was the other way around. There are numerous errors in Scholl's piece, which on the whole is not a particularly useful interview. Reverend Shane's material is most valuable when his subjects described events in which they participated themselves or, at least, were living in Kentucky when the events occurred.

Notwithstanding the above, Scholl's statement about Holder is so provocative we still wonder how he could have made it unless Holder had really been there. One possible explanation suggests itself from the misrecollections of other pioneers. In retelling exploits of the prominent figures at Boonesborough, things that happened in conjunction with one major event were recalled years later as happening in another major event. A pertinent example is the letter written in 1850 by Holder's grandson, Richard P. Holder, in which he states, "Colonel Henderson and Elizabeth Callaway were married immediately after [the] Long siege & returned to North Carolina."[16] Henderson and Callaway actually married shortly after the rescue and returned to North Carolina after the long siege. The writer has conflated the kidnapping and rescue (1776) with the long siege at Boonesborough (1778). Holder was present at the long siege, was one of the leaders in fact. Fanny was there too. They did later marry. Perhaps Septimus Scholl and others made Holder a hero at the rescue by combining parts of these two separate events. In conclusion, Scholl's interview mostly relates information about which he had no personal knowledge. This certainly applies to the rescue which occurred thirteen years before Scholl was born.

William Bransford's Account

The first published account of Holder's participation in the rescue dates to 1848, when William M. Bransford published a fictional version of the event in the *Southern Lady's Companion*, a monthly periodical devoted to literature and religion.[17]

Bransford's first sentence—"The beautiful Kentucky! Ah! whose eye is not brightened when gazing upon it silvery waters?"—gives the flavor of the prose throughout the article. That he is not particularly concerned with historical accuracy is apparent on the first page, where he states that "the fort of Booneslick" was where Daniel Boone "had planted a colony and erected a fort." Bransford told the story of the kidnapping as a romance for young girls with much breathless, invented dialog. The account of the rescue starts off with Fanny Callaway trying to put a curl in her sister Elizabeth's long hair and, finding it "troublesome," wonders aloud why she doesn't cut it off. The dialog continues as follows.

Elizabeth: "Why you know he [Samuel Henderson] is so fond of them, and therefore though inconvenient to me, for his sake I am content to wear them as they are."

Frances: "Well everyone to their own notion. Think you, Lizzy, if Johnny [Holder] liked this, or if Johnny didn't like that, it would in the least influence my conduct? No."

Elizabeth, after a lengthy response, concludes with this obsequious observation: "Yes Fanny, better [to] surrender at once and learn to study the disposition of these lords of creation, so that by agreeably conforming to their tastes and gratifications, we may influence the arm that directs the throne."

Later when they are being held captive by the Indians, Fanny starts crying because their friends have not yet rescued them and her sister tries to cheer her up.

Elizabeth: "Now who knows, Fanny, but that Johnny may be specially delegated to deliver you?"

Jemima: "Johnny Holder may be one of the party, probably, but I take it for certain that your cousin Flanders Callaway will be one of them."

After the article appeared, Draper wrote to the author asking for verification and more details. Bransford replied that he "obtained his materials" from Richard Callaway Jr. but had since destroyed or lost his notes.[18] We have already examined Callaway's statement that Holder was not even in Kentucky at the time.

Holder-Callaway Family Correspondence

Draper wrote to descendants of John Holder asking questions about his life and requesting details regarding the rescue. William D. Holder, a grandson of John, answered Draper's letter in 1849. His statement that Richard Callaway and John Holder "were originally farmers in Culpeper County, Virginia, agreeable to my information and emigrated with Colonel Daniel Boone to Kentucky" is contrary to fact regarding Holder. He gave no information about the rescue but referred Draper to Bransford's published account. William's biography, published in 1891, mentions that John Holder was one of the rescuers. Peter Decherd, married to Holder's granddaughter Frances, a daughter of John W. Holder, wrote to Draper in 1850. He did not mention the rescue. Richard P. Holder, a son of John W. Holder, wrote to Draper in 1850, and gave a lengthy account of the rescue and John Holder's participation. R. G. Williams, married to Holder's daughter Catherine, wrote

Rescue of the Boone-Callaway Girls

to Draper in 1851. He stated that Colonel Holder "was one of the party of three who rescued the girls and to whom they were afterwards married."[19]

Draper also queried Callaway descendants about the rescue. Richard French, son of Keziah Callaway, Colonel Callaway's daughter, wrote a brief answer in 1844, not mentioning the rescue. French also gave a statement regarding the rescue to Reverend Shane but made no mention of Holder participating. Samuel Dixon, son of Elizabeth Dixon, who was a daughter of Betsy Callaway, wrote Draper in 1852. Samuel stated that Holder was one of the rescuers. Eudocia Estill, Betsy Callaway's daughter, wrote in 1852. She mentioned the rescue but did not name Holder, except as the later husband of Fanny. Alfred Henderson, Betsy Callaway's son, wrote in 1853. In response to Draper's question, he replied, "Of the captivity, Mr. Brandifords articles furnishes the particulars and the names of Some of the pursueing party."[20]

From their letters it is apparent that little personal information about their forebear was passed down to the family. They repeatedly told Draper that they did not know the date of John Holder's birth or death and much of what they told him about their ancestor was incorrect. At most they could repeat a few stories they had heard, some of which they had read in the popular press. Several who claimed Holder was one of the rescuers referred Draper to Bransford's fictional account for details. Nothing in their correspondence helps settle the question of Holder's participation in the rescue.

Conclusion

In spite of the shaky foundation described above, other writers and historians have accepted the story of the three girls being rescued by their three future grooms—Samuel Henderson, Flanders Callaway and John Holder. Richard H. Collins[b] incorporated this version into his massive *History of Kentucky* (1874), as did George W. Ranck in *Boonesborough* (1901), R. S. Cotterill in *History of Pioneer Kentucky* (1917), John Bakeless in *Daniel Boone, Master of the Wilderness* (1939), Thomas D. Clark in *The Kentucky* (1942), Goff Bedford in *Land of Our Fathers* (1958) and John Mack Faragher in *Daniel Boone* (1992) — and many others.[21] Of course the mere repetition of a myth does not make it any more likely to be true. None of the above authors provided any supporting evidence for Holder being one of the rescuers.

This much can be stated with confidence: John Holder was not named as one of the rescuers in any contemporary account. Nor was he named in later accounts by any person known to have been in the rescue party. Nor

---

b Richard Collins' father did not mention Holder when writing about the rescue in his earlier history of the state. Lewis Collins, *Historical Sketches of Kentucky* (Maysville, 1847), p. 19.

Colonel John Holder

by anyone known to have been in the fort, or even in Kentucky, at the time of the kidnapping. Nor by anyone who knew Holder personally. The first recorded mention of Holder as a rescuer did not surface until nearly 60 years after the event. The weight of evidence suggests that John Holder was not in Kentucky in 1776 and did not rescue his future bride, Fanny Callaway, from the clutches of her Shawnee captors.

Chapter 3

Kentucky Frontier

The year 1777 — sometimes known as the year of the "Bloody Sevens" — dawned as a fateful one for the western pioneers. At the end of December 1776, Fincastle County, Virginia, was divided into three frontier counties: Montgomery, Washington and Kentucky. The new county lieutenant for Kentucky County was David Robinson, who later resided on Boone Creek. Militia commissions went to John Bowman, colonel; George Rogers Clark, major; and Daniel Boone, James Harrod, Benjamin Logan and John Todd, captains. Richard Callaway was elected to represent Kentucky County in the Virginia Assembly. Richard Henderson had been absent from Fort Boonesborough for a year and a half. He returned home in an unsuccessful attempt to gain approval from North Carolina, Virginia or the Continental Congress for the Transylvania Company's land purchase from the Cherokee. Henderson's brother Samuel and slave London remained at Boonesborough.

With the coming of spring, Native Americans resumed active resistance against the Kentucky settlements. In March, a large party of Shawnee under Blackfish attacked a camp near Harrodsburg and then fell on the fort. Harassment of the Kentucky forts — Harrodsburg, Boonesborough and St. Asaph — continued in April and May. On April 24, Indians attacked Boonesborough, killing Daniel Goodman. Daniel Boone, Isaac Hite, John Todd and Michael Stoner were wounded. Many terrorized settlers went back home; those who stayed retreated to the safety of the forts. If the three forts had been taken by the invaders or abandoned by the settlers, Kentucky and the "West" could have been lost to the British and Indians.[1]

There were less than 300 people in Kentucky at that time. A census taken that spring reported the presence of 201 persons at Harrodsburg, about 50 at Boonesborough and 30 at Logan's Station. Colonel John Bowman organized an expedition of volunteers from Botetourt and Montgomery Counties to come to relief of Kentucky.[2]

One of the Boonesborough defenders during this time was a Virginia officer named William Bailey Smith. In the midst of the turmoil in the summer of 1777, Smith was sent the Yadkin River area of North Carolina to recruit volunteers to aid in the defense of Boonesborough. He raised a full company, including a number of Boones and Bryans. Captain Smith commanded the company. John Holder was elected lieutenant.[3]

William Bailey Smith

William Bailey Smith (1738-1818), who figured prominently in Holder's coming out, was born in Prince William County, Virginia. Recall that evidence indicates Holder was also born in that county. Smith was with Richard Henderson at Sycamore Shoals, when the Transylvania Company bargained with the Cherokees for possession of Kentucky, and was one of the signers of the Treaty of Watauga. Smith came out with Henderson in 1775 and was one of the rescuers when the Boone and Callaway girls were captured in 1776. Smith later claimed he was infatuated with one of the girls at the time. He left an account of the rescue mission that makes himself out to be the hero.[4]

Smith was later promoted to major in George Rogers Clark's Illinois Regiment and was present again at Boonesborough during the great siege in 1778. In 1779 he helped run the boundary line between North Carolina and Virginia. He received at tract of land in Kentucky for his services and settled there near the mouth of Green River (about 16 miles from Henderson) in 1794. Smith never married and some who visited him at his residence thought him a braggart. He died there at the age of 80.[5]

Captain Smith's Company

The most reliable information about John Holder's first appearance in Kentucky comes from his contemporaries, the people who lived with him, worked with him and fought along side him at that time. Many of Kentucky's early pioneers were interviewed by Lyman C. Draper and John D. Shane, two men who collected countless documents and made a major contribution to the history of the Kentucky settlement period. The most helpful of their works concerning Holder are interviews with men who knew him before he came to Kentucky. One of these was Daniel Bryan.

Daniel Bryan (1758-1845) was born in Rowan County, North Carolina. His father, William Bryan, married Daniel Boone's sister Mary. The Boones and Bryans lived near each other in the Yadkin River area. William was killed by Indians near Bryan's Station, the fort he and his brothers established north of Lexington in 1779. Daniel Bryan gave the following statement to Draper, which includes a physical description of Holder:

> Maj. John Holder. He was a Young Man between 22 and 23

Kentucky Frontier

years old [when he] came from Virginia to North Carolina to see his friends at the time and place where Capt. William B. Smith was Raising his Volunteer Company to March to Kentucky. Then and there Holder Joined the company. He was a fine looking young man, full six feet high, of a fair complextion, gray Eyes, &c. After the company Randivoud, Holder was chosen Lieutenant, as was the other under officers, all chosen by the company. Holder Married a Daughter of Colo. Richard Callaway.[6]

Bryan was speaking from memory but with firsthand knowledge. The declaration he submitted in 1833 to obtain a Revolutionary War pension states that he volunteered to serve in Capt. William Bailey Smith's company "about the first of July 1777," then "marched from Rowan County, North Carolina to Boonsborough on the frontier of Virginia." He was stationed at Boonesborough for about six months. He said he was engaged "in guarding the Fort [and] scouting the country around to prevent the depredations of the British and Indians." He said he was discharged the following winter. Bryan's pension declaration also stated that John Holder served as the lieutenant of his company.[7]

In his statement to Draper, Bryan identified Holder as the man who later married Richard Callaway's daughter (Fanny Callaway): the John Holder of this biography. Bryan's constraint rules out his lieutenant being some other John Holder of Virginia or North Carolina. Fortunately, in early times there was only one John Holder in Kentucky.

Samuel Bryan, Daniel's brother, also received a Revolutionary War pension. He stated that he enlisted "about the last of July 1777 for six months with the Virginia state troops under William Bayley Smith who was on his way to Kentucky with about forty men to be stationed as a guard at Boonesborough. John Holder was lieutenant." Bryan provided a description of the route the company took from Rowan County to Kentucky. Starting out, they crossed "the Yadkin River at Scritchfield's ford and New River at Wallings Bottom." Then they marched "up Elk Creek, passing over Iron Mountain to the south fork of Holston, and down the river to the Block House and through Cumberland Gap."[8]

Daniel Bryan was also interviewed by John Shane. Bryan gave him a detailed description of the company's entry into Boonesborough:

> September 2, Captain Smith arrived at Boonsborough with 48 men, all on horseback. They marched into fort in single file, six feet between nose and tail…with fife and drum in military order.[9]

Colonel John Holder

There are several versions of the arrival date of Smith's company. George Rogers Clark's diary contains the following entry for September 23, 1777: "Express resived from Boons and say that on the 13th Captain Smith arrive their with 48 Men, 150 more on the March for this [place], also with an Account that General Washington had defeated. How Joyfull News if true." Clark was at Harrodsburg at the time. After examining various accounts, Draper decided that Clark's diary was more likely to be correct than Bryan's memory of the arrival date.[10]

Further support for John Holder's first coming to Kentucky in 1777 is found in the records of the Virginia Land Commission for the Kentucky District. These commissioners held court during 1779-1780 for the purpose of "adjusting titles of claimants to unpatented lands." They made rounds to the various stations, meeting at St. Asaph (Stanford), Harrodsburg, Bryan's Station, Boonesborough and the Falls of the Ohio (Louisville). At a session held at Boonesborough on December 24, 1779, Holder was awarded 1,400 acres of land "on Account of Settlement made in the Country in the year 1777 & Residing ever since."

Saltworks Petition

In the fall of 1777, John Holder was one of the signers of a petition directed to the Virginia Assembly concerning saltworks. The Kentucky settlers had a pressing need for salt on the frontier. Salt was essential for preserving meat and many considered unsalted food unpalatable. The long distance from Virginia and the Indian presence made it prohibitive to transport large quantities of goods from manufactories in the east. Salt was easily made in Kentucky by boiling water at the many salt springs, the most famous of which was at Lower Blue Licks. More sources were needed, however, and people were impatient with land owners who had salt springs but did not erect their own saltworks or allow others to do so. A petition to the Virginia General Assembly was drafted which stated their needs:

> Now your Petitioneers humbly pray that if the Claimants do not immediately errect Salt Manufactories at the different Springs claimed by them The honourable House would take it into their consideration and Order that the said Springs should be made publick Property and be Manufactored by Government by which Means Government would be profited & your Petitioners have speedy relief.[11]

Kentucky Frontier

The petition was dated November 25, 1777. John Holder signed it, along with Daniel Boone, William Bush, Richard Callaway and numerous others. The General Assembly failed to act on the petition.[12]

* * *

As mentioned previously, John Holder did not neglect to join the land rush in Kentucky. Sometime after he arrived in 1777, he made an improvement on a tract of land on Boone Creek in present day Fayette County. This entitled him to claim a 400 acre settlement and a 1,000 acre preemption.[13] These formed the beginnings of Holder's massive land holdings in Kentucky.

Recruiting for George Rogers Clark

In early 1778, George Rogers Clark was trying to raise an army for an invasion of the northwest frontier held by the British. He obtained permission from Gov. Patrick Henry to raise seven companies and was given secret orders to undertake his Illinois Campaign. His mission would result in the capture of Kaskaskia (July 1778) and Vincennes (February 1779).[14]

About this time, Clark promoted William Bailey Smith from captain to major and dispatched him to the settlements of western Virginia and North Carolina to enlist volunteers for the Illinois Campaign. On March 7, Major Smith wrote to Clark from the Holston River that he had just sent "A Company of forty four men to kintuckey under the Command of Capt. Thomas Dillard" and that within two weeks he expected to send three more. On March 29, Smith, still on the Holston River, wrote Clark to say that only one more company had been raised and he needed more time.[15]

John Holder assisted Smith on the recruiting mission. While Smith was working in the Holston River area, Holder apparently returned to North Carolina. We know the names of two men he enlisted there. Moses Nelson, who later applied for a Revolutionary War pension while residing in Bath County, Kentucky, was one of Holder's recruits. Nelson left the following account in his pension declaration:

> About the first of June 1778, I enlisted in Captain John Holder's Company in Roann County in the State of North Carolina and marched to Kentucky. On the 24th day of June 1778 we arrived at Boonsborough Ky.[16]

Another Revolutionary War pensioner, John Hamlin, stated that he was living in Rowan County, North Carolina, when he enlisted. The county then

Colonel John Holder

encompassed the upper reaches of the Yadkin River. Hamlin also mentions Holder in his declaration, which states:

> That he inlisted in the army of the united states in the year 1778 with Capt. John Holder and served in the Regiment of the North carolina line under the following named officers. He says he inlisted in North Carolina in the Month of February (he thinks the 10th) in the army of the U.S. in Capt. John Holders Company of Regulars for a term of Six Months.[17]

Fort Boonesborough. Drawing of the fort taken from George W. Ranck's, Boonesborough, 1801.

Hamlin added important details concerning their mission. He stated that "the object of the inlistment was to go on to the opost in the state of Indiania for the purpose of dislodging the British and Indians posted at that place." The O'Post was what Americans called the British fort at Vincennes, located on the Wabash River in what is now Indiana. It was originally established by the French as "Poste du Ouabache" and was later known as "Au Poste Vincennes," which was shortened to O'Post. Holder's company did not make it to Kentucky in time to join Clark's mission. According to Hamlin, the company

> commenced our march for the Opost in the above place [North Carolina] and Marched on till we arived at Boonsborough in the then District of Kentucky and when we arived at that place

Kentucky Frontier

where we expected to Join the army destined for the opost, It was gone.[18]

Hamlin stated that his officers, "Capt. Holder and Maj. William Smith thought it advisable to remain at the station above spoaken of [i.e., Boonesborough], which we did."[19] Nelson and Hamlin both said they were at Boonesborough during the great siege in September 1778.

Even though they recruited in North Carolina, Smith and Holder were soldiers of Virginia and were raising companies for their own state. Virginia formed a number of regiments during the Revolutionary War known as the Virginia Line. The state also had several special regiments. George Rogers Clark's was one of the latter and was known as the Illinois Regiment. William Bailey Smith and John Holder both served in the Illinois Regiment.

Another recruit, James McCullough, "volunteered with Capt. William Smith" while on his way to Kentucky in early 1778. McCullough referred to this as the time Smith and Holder were both promoted.

When Captain Smith was promoted to Major and Lt. John Holder Suceeded him as Captain with whom McCullough continued.[20]

This statement implies that Clark promoted Holder to captain at the same time he promoted Smith to major.

Samuel Estill, an early resident of Boonesborough where he was elected first lieutenant of Holder's company, stated that "John Holder was captain in the state troops of Virginia."[21] Little Page Proctor testified that when Capt. John Holder came out from North Carolina, "he was dressed in uniform and said he was authorized to take command of the troops and Capt. [Benjamin] Logan gave up to him the command of the men who had come out under Lt. Hargrave."[22]

Great Siege of Boonesborough

If there is any event on the Kentucky frontier that rivals the fame of the kidnapping and rescue of the Boone-Callaway girls, it would be the great siege of Boonesborough which took place in September 1778. It is hard for us to imagine today the trying conditions faced by those settlers who chose to stay on in Kentucky and face the constant threat of Indian attack. Families were forced to retreat to the safety of the forts and life there could be grim. One of Holder's recruits, who arrived at Boonesborough in June 1778, stated that

Colonel John Holder

we found the people in the garrison in a most distressful situation, in want of almost every thing within, besides the danger they were constantly exposed to from the Indians without lurking in the cane marking an opportunity to take a prisoner or a scalp. In this situation we continued until the month of August. . . .[23]

Another new arrival at Boonesborough that spring said that they "found there a party of poor, desolate and distressed people, almost without provisions and with very little clothing and what added most to their distress was their exposure to constant alarm from the Indians who were very troublesome. They had meat to procure from the forest, always in great danger of losing their lives."[24]

The circumstances surrounding the siege began with the capture of Daniel Boone and his 26 salt-makers in February 1778. The company left Boonesborough to make salt at the Lower Blue Licks. Boone's role was to provide food for the salt-makers. While out hunting in a heavy snow, Boone was captured by a large party composed of 100 to 200 Shawnee under the command of Chief Blackfish. Blackfish informed him they were on their way to Boonesborough. Knowing the fort was in a poor state of repair with few fighting men left to defend it, Boone agreed to surrender his whole company to Blackfish. The men were taken into captivity and led back to Ohio. Boone himself was adopted as a son by Blackfish and for months lived in the Indian fashion with his new family at Chillicothe. Upon learning that the Shawnee were again planning an attack on Boonesborough, Boone looked for an opportunity to escape. On June 16, he took leave of his captors and by traveling day and night made it back to the fort on the 20th.[25]

Paint Creek Expedition

Much work still needed to be done to put the fort in order. The men began repairing the stockade walls, strengthening the gates and building new two story blockhouses at the corners. In late August, Boone arranged a small raiding party and set out for the Ohio towns. The exact purpose of this raid is still not clear, but presumably they sought to learn something of the Indians' plans and perhaps hoped to disrupt their mission by leading them to believe their own villages were in danger of being taken. Richard Callaway was much opposed to the venture. Boone prevailed and set out with 30 men on the last day of August. His party included John Holder, Simon Kenton, Alexander Montgomery, Pemberton Rawlings, Stephen Hancock, John Kennedy, John Logan, Jesse Hodges and others. They crossed the Ohio River and proceeded up the Scioto River. Near Paint Creek Town,

Kentucky Frontier

they engaged a small war party, killing one and wounding two others. The party of 30 or 40 warriors appeared to be headed to Kentucky. Boone and his men made haste to return to the fort.[26]

John Holder was held up on the return to Boonesborough. According to John Gass, "Holder's feet gave out and [Pemberton] Rollins staid with him, and both got in the night before the siege."[27] Daniel Bryan gave a slightly different version of Holder's predicament:

> Boone arrived at Boonesborough at night. Colonel Holder being a fat man, and over fatigued with the rapidity of the journey, was left in the care of William Beasley to bring on next day. In the morning the Indians were before Boonesborough, but the two got in in safety.[28]

These statements suggest that the men were on foot. Bryan, who knew Holder from North Carolina and Kentucky, adds a detail concerning Holder's physical appearance. This description is partly supported by a pioneer from Berkeley County, Virginia, George Michael Bedinger, who knew Holder well. Bedinger said Colonel Holder "was a large, six foot man."[29]

Blackfish's Army

For his Kentucky invasion, Blackfish had assembled an army of 400 Shawnee, Cherokee and Wyandot warriors, along with 40 Frenchmen and Canadians. Blackfish was accompanied by Black Hoof, Moluntha, Black Beard and other chiefs. His principal aide and advisor was Antoine Dagnieau DeQuindre.[30]

On their return from Paint Creek, Boone's party encountered this army at the Lower Blue Licks, and they took a wide detour around them. From Lower Blue Licks, the Indian army followed an old buffalo trace to the Kentucky River near Boonesborough (later called the "Salt Springs Trace"). This trace crossed Strode's Creek several times in Bourbon County (known as the "many crossings") then entered Clark County and turned west along the ridge between Johnson Creek and Hancock Creek (known as the "Sycamore Forest").[31] The trace turned south following Hancock Creek to its head then, after crossing the rise along present day Colby Road, entered the watershed of Lower Howard's Creek. From there the trace went down the North Fork to where the Carroll E. Ecton Reservoir is today.

On Sunday, September 6, Blackfish stopped for the night at a place afterwards called "the Indian Camp."[32] The camp was just below the reservoir in the flat area around Lettie Lane, Waterworks Road and Lower

Howard's Creek. The next day the army continued downstream to the mouth of the creek, where they crossed the Kentucky River at Blackfish Ford,[33] and proceeded on to Boonesborough where they invested the fort in what became known as "the great siege."

The Siege

When the siege began, the defenders had about 75 men in the fort plus a few women and children. Those we know for sure include Daniel Boone's daughter Jemima, Richard Callaway's wife Elizabeth and children, David Gass' wife Sarah and children, and John South's wife Margaret and children. It is probable that there was at least one widow at the fort. This was Margaret Drake, whose husband had been killed by Indians a few weeks before. There were 4 blockhouses at the corners and about 26 cabins. The stockade was about 260 feet long and 180 feet broad, and enclosed an area a little under an acre. Much of the livestock had been brought inside.[34]

Blackfish's army appeared before the fort on the morning of September 7. Over a period of several days, the Indians held conferences outside the fort with the Boonesborough leaders. Blackfish hoped Boone would convince them to accept surrender terms and avoid a battle. Richard Callaway, William Bailey Smith, John Holder and others were strongly opposed. At the last conference, the Indians tried to grab the whites take them captive. Boone, his brother Squire, Callaway, Smith and several others escaped and made their way back to the fort. Both Boones were wounded in the melee.[35]

Great Siege at Fort Boonesborough. Mural at the Civil War Fort at Boonesboro. Painting by Phil May.

Kentucky Frontier

The Indians then spent the next week trying to take Boonesborough and its defenders. They shot into the fort from nearby trees and from the surrounding hills. They tried to tunnel under the fort and tried to set it on fire.

Several accounts of the siege mention Holder's energetic efforts. At night the Indians hurled torches over the walls. Holder helped put the fires out, swearing mightily in the process. His future mother-in-law, Elizabeth Callaway,[a] chastised Holder for cursing.

> For several nights, the Indians attempted to fire the fort by means of branches of scaly bark hickory tied around a stick like a beetle [i.e., a wooden club or mallet], set them on fire, and cast them toward the roofs of the cabins and sometimes clean over into the fort. They never once lodged upon a roof, but on one occasion a torch fell down at the side of an outside door. Holder seized a bucket of water and dashed out the blazing faggot which threatened danger, and in doing it he made use of some rough oaths. When the good Mrs. Colonel Callaway kindly rebuked Holder, intimating that he had better be praying than swearing, Holder said he had then no time to pray. This was the only instance that promised any hope of success by their night attempts to fire the fort by torches.[36]

The above story was told to Lyman Draper by John Gass, who was about 14 years old at the time of the siege. Gass gave John Shane a similar version:

> A torch had been thrown up against the back door of one of the houses, one about half way along [the wall]. Captain Holder was running from one of the bast ends [bastions]. He went in and opened the door and threw a bucket of water on the torch. It had blazed up as high as the top of the house, above the top of the door. Captain Holder swore hard. Mrs. Calloway told him it would be more becoming to pray than to sware. Holder swore it was no time to pray then.[37]

Based on the second version, Holder is sometimes quoted as having told Mrs. Callaway, "I've no time to pray, goddammit!"[38]

On another occasion Holder drew a much remembered remark from

---

a Elizabeth Callaway was the second wife of Col. Richard Callaway and the stepmother of Fanny Callaway, who married John Holder.

Colonel John Holder

Margaret South. The incident occurred during the time the Indians were tunneling into the river bank in an attempt to undermine the fort wall. Holder threw large rocks over the stockade wall in the hope that the rocks would roll down the bank and strike the Indians. Daniel Trabue reported the following:

> Captain Holder, a large strong man, took big stones and cast them from the fort over the bank, expecting they might fall on some of the Indians. One of the woman of the fort said, "Don't Do so, Captain. It might hurt some of the Indians and they will be mad and have revenge for the same."[39]

Draper's account of the siege adds this clarification. He said the Indians "taunted the whites to 'come out and fight like men and not try to kill them with stones, like children.' Old Mrs. South, in the simplicity of her heart, earnestly besought the men 'for God's sake not to throw stones. . .' The good old lady's humane remark evincing her tender regard for the feelings of the Indians became a by-word among the men and a theme for many a gibe and jeer."[40]

When the defenders arose on the morning of September 20, there were no Indians in the vicinity. Only two defenders of the fort had been killed: David Bundrin and Richard Henderson's slave London. While Indian casualties were much higher, they took all the bodies with them precluding a reliable count of their dead.

Chapter 4

In Command at Boonesborough

Following the great siege at Fort Boonesborough in 1778, Richard Callaway brought charges against Daniel Boone for collaborating with the British and Indians. A court martial held at Logan's Station acquitted Boone of all charges, and as a further show of confidence he was promoted to major. Nevertheless, Boone was deeply offended by the attack on his reputation and he left Boonesborough for good. He went back to North Carolina, where his family had retreated when he was captured by the Shawnee. When he returned to Kentucky in 1779, he settled in Fayette County and established Boone Station near Athens.[1] With Boone gone and Richard Callaway off representing Kentucky County in the Virginia Assembly, John Holder was the ranking officer at the fort. Holder retained military command there until he moved downstream to form his own station at the mouth of Lower Howard's Creek in the early 1780s.

Pioneer George Michael Bedinger described the situation at the fort when he arrived there from Virginia in the spring of 1779. Bedinger said that "Boonesborough had been in constant apprehension from Indians loitering around the Fort. They were reduced to great strait. The men few, nor could they risk any great hazard as the life of each was too precious and their families too dear. Stratagems had to supply the place of greater strength. Each night a horse was placed a proper distance from the Fort with one [of] his hind feet securely fastened to the root of a sapling and three good marksmen in ambush near by."[2]

Falls of the Ohio

John Holder's military company was involved in one more mission in 1778. In the fall, volunteers were called out for the purpose of procuring salt, which was still scarce in Kentucky. Volunteers were to meet at the Falls of the Ohio, the site of present day Louisville. James Harrod took a

Colonel John Holder

company of sixteen men from Harrodsburg. They were joined by six men from Holder's company.[3]

Josiah Collins, one of Harrod's men, described the trip to the saltworks "on the Spanish side" or west side of the Mississippi River, near Kaskaskia in the Illinois country. Kaskaskia had been in American hands since that summer, when the British outpost was captured by George Rogers Clark and his small band of men.[4] The saltworks were located in present day Missouri.

> On 15 October 1778 Captain Harrod called out his company and requested that fifteen of his men volunteer and march with him at their head to the salt works on the Mississippi River in the Spanish settlement to procure salt for the use of their own and other garrisons. They had not had any salt from the time of their arrival in Kentucky. [Collins] volunteered and they marched to the falls of the Ohio River, descended to its mouth in a boat, and ascended the Mississippi to the salt works on the Spanish side where they were detained for a considerable length of time, but finally succeeded in getting a load of salt and returned with it to the garrison at the falls of the Ohio a short time before Christmas.[5]

Their transportation was by keelboat, which could be floated downstream and rowed upstream.

Collins said the salt-making venture took place before saltworks were opened in Kentucky at Bullitt's Lick or Mann's Lick. He described the works on the Mississippi: "The saltworks were about 3 miles west of Kaskaskias across on the west side of the Mississippi. They were boiling salt there in leaden as well as iron kettles.... We stayed upwards of three weeks before

A Return for 14 men of Capt holder Company for amanition January 20th 1779
    3½ Powder   *John Holder*
    7 lb lead   *Wm Harrod Capt*[8]

In Command at Boonesborough

we could get any salt." Harrod, he said, "bought the salt and paid for it in continental money."[6]

Quartermaster Daniel Trabue mentioned this salt-making venture in his narrative and suggests it was the initiative of George Rogers Clark. Trabue wrote, "I made some agreement with Clark for some little salt for our Forts...after a while Colonel Clark Did have some Salt made."[7]

Many of the receipts from this mission — for ammunition and provisions — are preserved in the George Rogers Clark Papers of the Illinois Regiment. Receipts from November 1778 to mid January 1779 refer to "six men of Captain Holder's company" and were signed by Capt. William Harrod or his lieutenant, James Patton, both of whom served in the garrison at Louisville. The receipt below was for rations for an unidentified volunteer who was headed down the Ohio River on his way to Illinois.

> falls of the ohio November 16th 1778
> A provision for one man of Capt holders Company on his way Down the ohio to the Eyeloynis [Illinois] for Eight days givin under My hand att the falls.
> Wm Harrod, Capt[9]

Holder joined the company at the Falls sometime in January, after their return from the saltworks. Receipts after this time list fourteen men and are signed by Holder, indicating that Holder brought out eight men to help bring the salt back to the forts.

Josiah Collins mentioned John Holder and his men in his account of the mission:

> [We] remained at the falls until the river was cleared of ice in February 1779 [when] Captain Holder came from Boonsborough for the salt with a small party of men. He returned to Boonsborough with them and assisted in taking the salt in a boat which was designed for that place and arrived at Boonsborough about 1 March 1779.[10]

Daniel Trabue described the quantity as "a bout 2 bushels to each Fort" which seems a small amount for all the effort, but he said "With that salt we saved a vast quanetety of Beare Meat."[11]

Boonesborough Reinforcements, 1779

In 1779, large numbers of Virginians came out in search of Kentucky land. Many of those who traveled overland on the Wilderness Trail through

Colonel John Holder

Cumberland Gap eventually passed through Boonesborough. One of the most useful observers of events that year was George Michael Bedinger, who ventured out with a party from Berkeley County. They arrived in early April with a dozen men and found that neither "Boone nor Calloway were at the fort.[a] Holder was then in command."[12] Bedinger, never one to understate his importance, said he and his party

> reached Boonsboro to the infinite gratification of the inhabitants. The loss of their late companions was now fully replaced and this was a sufficient cause for extravagant expressions of joy. With Holder were some 15 or 20 men only; and next in point of influence to Holder were Capt. David Gass and Capt. James Estill and Lt. Samuel Estill.[13]

Within hours of their arrival at the fort, young Jacob Starnes came in with the news that his father's party had been attacked 20 or 30 miles from Boonesborough and "all save himself had doubtless fallen a prey to the Indians."[14] Problems with Indians persisted throughout the year. Bedinger added:

> When we arrived at Boonesboro the distress of the Fort induced me to join Captain John Holder's Company, who was in command of the Fort at that time, in which company and service I served seven months. A part of the time I acted as an Indian spy, scout and hunter, always taking my turn with the other men of the Fort as hunter.[15]

At this time, families were cloistered in the fort for safety. Men had to leave the protective walls to hunt, tend gardens and search for vacant land to mark and improve. They went out in well armed groups by day and usually returned to the fort at night. Food was shared among all the residents. Ralph Morgan came to Boonesborough that spring with his father William, George Michael Bedinger, and the other Berkeley County men. Morgan later recalled how well everyone got along with each other during hard times:

> Think there were between 20 and 30 white men there generally during the spring and summer of 1779. There was a remarkable

---

[a] In April 1779, Boone had left the fort for good and Calloway was escorting British prisoners captured by George Rogers Clark to Virginia. Beginning in May 1779, Calloway was at Williamsburg representing Kentucky County in the General Assembly. Young, *Narrative of Daniel Trabue*, p. 173.

In Command at Boonesborough

degree of friendship, harmony and affection existing among the people of Boonesboro. The whole station lived nearly as one family. It was common when we would take in a load of meat, to put it down near the middle of the station for all who wanted to come and take freely.[16]

Bedinger gave Draper a list of "the defenders and hunters of Boonesboro" he recalled from that summer:[17]

John Holder	old Nicholas Proctor
James Estill	son Joseph Proctor
Sam Estill	son Reuben Proctor
Capt. David Gass	old John South
Maj. Thomas Swearingen	son Tom South
Benoni Swearingen	son Jack South
Col. William Morgan	John South, distant relative
Ralph Morgan	John Martin
John Taylor	John Calloway
Samuel Duree	James Bathe
John Strode	James Berry
James Duncan	John Baukman [Baughman]
John Constant	John Harveson [Harbison]
Jesse Hodges	Charles Lockhart
Lawrence Thompson	Edward Lockhart
John Gass	Aquilla White
William Cradlebaugh	Joseph Doniphan
Jacob Stearns [Starnes]	

Corn was the one essential crop for early Kentucky. With the coming of spring, nearly everyone at the fort would have been involved in some fashion with planting corn. A "corn compact" was signed on April 15 by nineteen men[b] who agreed to raise their crop on the south side of the Kentucky River as a cooperative venture. Several others, including Holder, put in a crop on the north side of the river at Bush's Settlement. Bedinger made a brief mention of it in his interview:

Bedinger and all his companions [*illegible*], together with Capt.

---
b The compact included Nicholas Anderson, James Anthony, John Cartwright, Robert Cartwright, Whitson George, Edward Hall, Thomas Hall, William Hall, John Harper, Peter Harper, Nathaniel Hart, William Johnson, Beale Kelley, John Kelley, George Madden, Jesse Oldham, Jesse Peake, Benjamin White and Edward Williams. Draper MSS 29CC 59.

Colonel John Holder

John Holder, went out early in May and commenced preparing for raising a crop of corn at Bush's settlement.[18]

This was a few miles north of Boonesborough in present day Clark County on land claimed by William Bush. That summer, several men from the fort went out in search of land. On their return, they were ambushed by Indians near this corn field. Bedinger described the incident.

> Sometime in July 1779, three men from Virginia were at Boonesboro. Wished to locate good land. A young Calloway[c] went with them to Elkhorn [Creek]. When within a few miles of Boonesboro on their return on the trail up Howard's Creek, Callaway advised them to leave the path for safety. They scouted the idea. They didn't fear Indians and boasted concerning their bravery. Callaway left them. When within three miles of Boonesboro, and in ambush opposite to a five acre field of corn…were fired on by a party of Indians.[19]

Bedinger described the corn field as being three miles from the fort and further stated that it was "known as Bush's Settlement, abandoned two or three years before and grown over with cane and reclaimed that year [1779]." He added that the field "covered the corn right preemption of ten persons [in] Bedinger's company of emigrants."[20]

Two of the men were captured by the Indians, and a man named Smith escaped. Bedinger continues:

> Smith escaped and came dashing and halloeing into Boonesboro, lost his overcoat in his flight. Captain James Estill, with Bedinger, Holder, young Calloway and some dozen others seized their rifles and dashed off, first failing to get Smith to accompany and show them the spot.[21]

The company discovered the ambush site and estimated the party had consisted of about 21 Indians. Pursuit was called off as it was too near dark to safely follow. The next morning, they found the Indian party, now gone, had been hiding about 100 yards or so from the first ambush site in hopes of waylaying the pursuers. The company recovered some things the Indians had left behind: "buffalo tugs and other small articles lay scattered about

---

[c] Bedinger's interview mentions only one Calloway at the fort in the summer of 1779 and that was John.

and some slippery elm bark which they generally carried with them for use in case of wounds." They also found the Indians "had eaten and destroyed cucumbers in the corn field."[22]

The two captured by the Indians were identified in Daniel Trabue's narrative as the men who had recently helped him bring powder and lead out from Bedford County, Virginia. Moses McIlwain and Ambrose White had lived near Col. Richard Callaway in Bedford. Trabue said

> they stopt at Boonsbourough and in a few Days Mr. Muckilwain and Mr. White went to the woods with some other men to explore and see the rich land on the other [north] side of the Kentucky River. A party of Indians found them out and way laid them. Mr. Muckilwain was took prisoner, also Mr. White was taken prisoner and badly wounded.[23]

Trabue went on to describe their lengthy captivity and eventual escape.

Bowman Expedition

In February 1779, Boonesborough received the surprising but welcome news that George Rogers Clark's small force had captured the British outpost at Vincennes in the Illinois country. While an important victory, it was so far away that it did little to stop Indian incursions into Kentucky.

In May, Colonel John Bowman, commander of the Kentucky County militia, ordered an expedition into the Ohio country to subdue the Shawnee, whom they blamed for most of the attacks on Kentucky settlements. Bowman was noted for his girth — he was said to have weighed 300 pounds — as well as a powerful set of lungs: "a man of great voice. Could be heard a mile." One of the pioneers recalled that Bowman "was the swiftest man of his size I ever saw. He was a jolly man, mighty funny man."[24]

Bowman's small army of nearly 300 men was composed of volunteers recruited from the Falls of the Ohio, Logan's Station, Whitley's Station, Ruddle's Station, Lexington, Harrodsburg and Boonesborough. The companies included those of John Holder (58 men), William Harrod (99), Benjamin Logan (48), Levi Todd (28), Silas Hardin (43) and John Haggin (19).[25] According to Bedinger

> Holder commanded a company. Not over 20 or 25 belonged to Boonesboro, the remainder in neighboring stations if any then settled. Marched to Lexington then to the mouth of Licking.[26]

Colonel John Holder

John South, who was with Holder, said the company got lost on the way from Boonesborough to Lexington.

> Capt. John Holder told me he had orders from Colonel John Bowman to meet him at Lexington, now so called. The first night we missed our way to Lexington and encamped; the next morning, we sent out spies to hunt where Lexington now stands; thence we marched towards the mouth of Licking.[27]

They met Levi Todd[d] and his company along the way and joined the others near present day Newport.[28]

Battle at Old Chillicothe

The army crossed the Ohio River and proceeded to the Shawnee stronghold at Old Chillicothe (or Old Town).[e] This town was on the Little Miami River about 60 miles into Ohio, between present day Xenia and Springfield. The army, apparently undetected, stopped near the town at twilight on May 29. Bowman divided his army into three divisions headed by John Holder, Benjamin Logan and William Harrod. His plan was to surround the town during the night and attack at daybreak.[29] Bedinger, who was with Holder's company, reported that

> Logan with his own and William Harrod's company was [to] go to the left of the town, Harrod, with Bowman, to the right and Holder in front [and] take their respective positions as early in the night as they could reach. Between Logan's and Harrod's command a space [was] to be left through which for the Indians, when raised from their cabins by Holder's party, to escape. It deemed the better policy to suffer them first to get out of the town and then fall upon them, rather than completely surround them and compel to keep their cabins or take to their council house, from which, as the sequel proved, they might make a successful stand. These arrangements made, the march resumed with proper care and secrecy. Each party posted itself as originally designed: Logan on the left between the town and the Miami, Harrod on the right and Holder directly in front of the town, in the high grass.[30]

Holder's division was situated on the south side of the town and waiting

---

d Levi Todd later served as the commonwealth attorney for Clark County.

e This was where Daniel Boone had lived as the adopted son of Chief Blackfish after he was captured in 1778.

In Command at Boonesborough

for dawn. However, the battle started prematurely — in the dark — in front of Holder's line. Colonel Bowman gave an account of what happened in a letter he wrote to his uncle.

> About an our Before Day an Indian came to see what was the cause of the Dogs barking at such a Rate and came within five feete of the line [Holder's line] where I had placed the men. I had given orders not to fire a gun till day lite without we should be discovered. this Indian discovering us Raised the Shout and Immediately was Shot down by one of our men. this gave the Indians time to Get into sume Block Houses the[y] had Bult to Defend themselves.[31]

Josiah Collins was in Holder's company and stated that he was "within two or three men of him" when the battle began. "An Indian man came running out of town with a gun on his shoulder as though he was going out hunting. One of our party, Hugh Ross, shot that Indian down. The crack of the gun alarmed the Indian town. I was close to Ross when he shot the Indian. The Indians immediately came out of their huts and gave us battle."[32]

Bedinger's report is similar. He said that the Indian, "as he neared Holder's party, puffing and blowing, and seeming to suspect or sense the trap into which he was running, he suddenly stopped...when one of the party of the name of Ross shot him, upon which Jacob Starnes ran up, scalped and tomahawked him.... In the hurry of the moment, Holder's men maked into the town, killed a few dogs and may have shot [an] Indian."[33]

The town was burned and looted, with the exception of one fortified log house where many had gathered, which Bowman called a "block house" and Bedinger called a "council house." When word came that Simon Girty was approaching with reinforcements, Bowman ordered an immediate retreat. Some of Holder's men got separated from their company. They found themselves pinned down by the Indians and could not get away when Bowman gave the order to withdraw. According to Bedinger, "a little party of 15, among whom were Major Bedinger, Jesse Hodges, Thomas and Jack South and one of the Proctors, had screened themselves behind a log not over 40 paces from the council house and there awaited the approach of day break. [Thomas] South was shot in the forehead. His young brother John, or Jack as he was familiarly called, then a lad of about 17, who was on Major Bedinger's left, was affected at the fate of Thomas.... By that time, seven of the fifteen behind the log were killed, besides Hickman[f] at

---

f William Hickman who was killed was with Harrod's company. Draper MSS 17J 26.

the corner of the cabin, and still the survivors awaited a regular attack from their friends. But they hoped in vain."[34]

Josiah Collins blamed Holder for the retreat and for their losses.

> I believe Holder was a coward, what caused him to leave. We never went any farther round than we had done, when the firing commenced. Holder and all his company but 12 of us had left that side. They retreated, and then we retreated and with them joined Logan in the prairie. Had a run to get from our log to where Holder had gone to.... We left seven men laying there, at that place we retreated from, dead, for the Indians to do what they pleased with.[35]

Collins was a man of strong opinion but, like most privates, he did not always have good information about the decisions that commanders made during battle. It was actually Colonel Bowman who called for the retreat, not Holder. It was Holder's responsibility to get the word to all his men, which he did. Bedinger, who was behind the log with Collins, stated that they got the order but could not withdraw. Bedinger's lengthy account of the battle had plenty of blame for Bowman but only praise for Holder.[36] As for their comparative military records, Collins served in two campaigns (Bowman's 1779 and Clark's 1782), while Holder served in those and countless others. It is not to Collins' credit that he falsely impugned the honor of his departed comrade.

According to Colonel Bowman's account, "the[y] Returned into their Block Houses. by their cryes their appered to be many wounded amongst them but at daylight finding that the[y] had fortified themselves, that we could not storm the Place without sacrificing many a man, I ordered them to withdraw at a convenient Distance and cept [kept] the fort in action till we gathered up wards of 200 horses. we Packed up what Plunder we could and Sat fier to the greatest Part of the Town."[37]

Battle on the Little Miami River

Colonel Bowman hurried his army down the valley of the Little Miami River. They brought with them a sizeable herd of the enemy's horses. The Shawnee pursued, caught up with Bowman and engaged them in a fierce battle for nearly three hours. Bowman arranged his division in a rectangle with the horses in the middle. During the battle, the horses became agitated and many escaped through the lines. After the Indians withdrew, Bowman continued the march to the site of present day Cincinnati, where they

In Command at Boonesborough

crossed the Ohio River. They stopped there for two days to auction off the horses and other plunder.[38]

The militia usually received no pay for their services. To encourage volunteers, commanders often offered to share the spoils of war — horses and other booty — as an inducement. An auction was held and the proceeds of the sales were divided equally among the men.

According to Josiah Collins, "We then came on to the Ohio and crossed at the mouth of the Little Miami, bringing with us 163 head of horses, besides some other plunder gotten from a trader's store, which was broken up, etc.... After we had crossed the Ohio, right on the river bank on this side, the plunder was divided equally among officers and soldiers according to the agreement under which we had volunteered."[39]

Collins said he and his brother Elisha got a small mare, a yearling colt and a three year old mare and stated that "this amounted to 15 pounds more than our share." Then he took another dig at his former captain.

> Holder, two or three years after, asked me for that mare, but I knew it didn't belong to him. It ought to be divided among the whole company and [I] wouldn't give it to him.[40]

Collins admitted to getting more than his fair share of the loot, and then attempted to blame Holder for his transgression.

According to Bedinger, Bowman's campaign "was well nigh a total failure." His conclusion is somewhat exaggerated. Although Shawnee losses were small, Chief Blackfish was wounded and died soon after. Their town was also destroyed and the Shawnee were put on the defensive, which prevented some 200 warriors from participating in a campaign led by British Captain Henry Bird against the Americans at Fort Laurens in northeastern Ohio. At the same time, however, Bowman's campaign prevented 300 Kentuckians from joining George Rogers Clark in his planned attack on Detroit. Clark had to cancel the attack due to lack of volunteers.[41]

Bowman's campaign made the newspapers back in Virginia. One account was published in July in the *Virginia Gazette*.

> By a Gentleman from the frontiers we are informed, that Captain Bowman with 200 volunteers marched from Kentucky against Chillacothie, the lower Shawanese town, and surrounded the 29th of May last (being the night the moon was totally eclipsed) without being discovered. At day break the next morning he made an attack, and after a short engagement, the Indians, with a number of British

troops, fled to a small blockhouse which the red coats had provided for a safe retreat. Captain Bowman burnt the town, with a great quantity of corn, ammunition, and stores. He has taken from the enemy 163 valuable horses, loaded with goods to the amount of 32,000£. The Indians had five killed at the town, and were repulsed with loss in two attacks they made on our party on their return. We had seven men killed in this expedition.[42]

Holder's Company

One of Holder's men, who later filed a declaration for a Revolutionary War pension, recalled the other officers in the company. James Bunton was lieutenant, Thomas South was ensign, Nathaniel Bullock and Page Proctor were sergeants and Bland Ballard served as commissary. Reuben Proctor was appointed ensign after South was killed.[43]

The names of the seven men with Holder who were said to have been killed at Chillicothe were not given in any of the accounts of the campaign. We do know that not all the casualties were from Fort Boonesborough. In the company Holder commanded only 20 to 25 men were from Boonesborough, the rest came from other stations. Also, at Chillicothe Bowman assigned Holder a division that may have contained men from several other companies. From Bedinger's account, we know Thomas South was killed (he was the father of John South, the younger). Draper listed two men killed in William Harrod's company — William Hickman and John Murdoch. Pioneer accounts mention Elisha Bethy, who was "killed in Bowman's Campaign in 1779 in a battle at Chillicothe," and John Denton, who was "brought off mortally wounded."[44]

John Holder was tardy submitting his pay roll list to Colonel Bowman. He finally sent it to him on June 10, along with a letter requesting payment of his company's share from the auction of the Shawnee plunder.

> To Col. John Bowman
> at Harrod's Town
> Sir, As I cannot conveniently call on you at this time, I have sent a list of the men of my company who were on the late expedition against the Indian towns, and beg you will favor me with the amount of the sale of the plunder by the bearer, John Martin, to enable me to settle with them. I am, Sir, your most obedient Humble servant.
> John Holder[45]

This suggests that the men who volunteered had not yet been paid their

In Command at Boonesborough

share from the auction of the horses. It appears that Bowman held the money awaiting a list of names from each of his companies.

Lyman Draper made a copy of the letter and attached a list of names on the pay roll.[46] The original list is in the John B. Bowman Papers.[g]

Capt. John Holder's Company on the Bowman Expedition
June 10, 1779

Uriel Ash	Thomas Bailey	Bland Ballard
Henry Baughman	John Baughman	George Michael Bedinger
James Berry	James Bryan	James Bunton
John Butler	John Callaway	William Collins
Elijah Collins	Josiah Collins	William Combs
John Constant	David Cooke	William Cradlebaugh
John Dumford	James Estill	Edward Gear [Fear]
David Gass	Stephen Hancock	William Hancock
John Harbison	William Hays	Jesse Hodges
Jeremiah Horn	Robert Kirkham	Samuel Kirkham
John Lee	Charles Lockhart	John McCollom
William McGee	Ralph Morgan	William Morris
Moses Nelson	James Perry	John Plick
Samuel Porter	Nicholas Proctor	Reuben Proctor
Pemberton Rawlings	Hugh Ross	Bartlett Searcy
Reuben Searcy	John South Jr.	John South Sr.
John South, younger	Thomas South	Barney Stagner
John Stapleton	Jacob Starnes	Benoni Swearingen
John Weber	Daniel Wilcoxen	

Total - including myself - 57

Richard Callaway Killed

Richard Callaway returned from Williamsburg in the fall of 1779 after representing Kentucky County in the legislature. While there, he secured a lucrative prize for himself: the exclusive license for a ferry at Boonesborough. Ferry permits at that time were issued by the General Assembly, and this

---

[g] Draper's list differs in several respects from those later published by Richard H. Collins in his history of Kentucky and George W. Ranck in his history of Boonesborough. Draper's list includes 57 names, Collins' and Ranck's have only 56; the latter two omitted Henry Baughman. Collins and Ranck incorrectly list Uriel Ash as Uriel Ark, John Harbison as John Hawiston, Moses Nelson as Moses Wilson, and Benoni Swearingen as Benoni Vallandingham. Collins' and Ranck's versions have been widely reprinted with these errors in other histories and on the Internet. Collins, *History of Kentucky, Vol. 1*, p. 13; Ranck, *Boonesborough*, p. 255.

Colonel John Holder

was the first one established in Kentucky. When up and going, Callaway could collect three shillings for each person, three shillings for each horse and eighteen shillings for each wagon and driver. He could sell the ferry if he wished and upon his death the ferry would pass to his heirs.[47] That winter, however, Callaway was killed near Boonesborough while hewing logs for a ferry boat. Lyman Draper's account of the tragedy was pieced together from many sources:

> On the 8th of March, 1780, while Colonel Callaway and others were at work about a mile above Boonesborough, engaged in constructing his ferry boat, they were fired on by a party of Shawanoe Indians, the colonel killed on the spot, Lt. Pemberton Rawlings badly wounded, who, after running a quarter of a mile, was overtaken, tomahawked in the back of the neck, and scalped.[48]

When the alarm came to the fort, Holder led a rescue party that soon arrived on the scene. There they found Callaway's remains. He had been stripped, scalped and his body cut up and mangled. One of the pioneers later recalled, "Colonel Calloway was the worst barbecued man I ever saw. Cut his head bones up. They stripped him stark naked and rolled him in a mud hole." Two slaves were captured and carried off. Callaway and Rawlings were buried in a common grave near the fort. John Holder was appointed administrator of Callaway's estate at one of the first sessions of the Lincoln County court.[49]

Bird's Raid

Based on the reports of two escaped prisoners, word spread in Kentucky that a "number of the different tribes of Indians in conjunction with some of the troops belonging to the King of Great Britain" were preparing an attack "with cannon" on the settlements at the Falls of the Ohio. On May 27, Col. John Bowman wrote to Col. Daniel Broadhead at Fort Pitt asking for "assistance of men, amunition and provisions together with artillery in order to relieve us from the approaching danger." No assistance was received.[50]

With arrival of summer 1780, the attacks came but not at the Falls of the Ohio. Capt. Henry Bird led a raid into Kentucky with 150-200 British regulars and 500 Shawnee. They were the first invaders to bring artillery. They took Ruddle's Station on June 24 and Martin's Station the next day. Knowing the cannon would destroy their wooden forts, both stations were surrendered. About 160 captives were taken. The Indians murdered many of the prisoners on the spot. After taking Martin's, Bird, who had promised to treat the captives well, terminated his raid. The surviving prisoners were taken to Detroit.[51] Martin's Station was on Stoner Creek, about 3 miles north of Paris in present Bourbon County. Ruddle's Station was on the South Fork of the Licking, 3 miles below the junction of Hinkston and Stoner creeks in present Harrison County.

Clark's Ohio Expedition

Fear spread quickly on the frontier. George Rogers Clark arrived at Harrodsburg within a few days of the attacks. At his urging, a large muster of the Kentucky County militia turned out. One of Holder's men later stated, "General George Rogers Clark came on with a considerable body of troops, and called to his aid Captain Holder's Company and the militia of the neighborhood."[52]

A force of nearly 1,000 men under George Rogers Clark crossed the Ohio River at the mouth of Licking on the first of August. Companies were on their own getting to Licking, at which point they were provisioned by Clark at Virginia expense. Food turned out to be in short supply on the whole expedition.

The army marched up the Little Miami River to Old Chillicothe which they found abandoned by the Shawnee. They burned the town and destroyed the corn in the fields. Clark then moved his force to Piqua (sometimes called "Pickaway"), a Shawnee village on the Great Miami River near present day Springfield, Ohio. Here the Indians joined them in battle from behind a small stockade. Clark then brought out his cannon and destroyed their fortification. Although the Indians were routed and fled, Colonel Benjamin Logan's encircling column allowed most to escape. The Americans suffered 27 casualties. Clark's men burned and destroyed Piqua and its corn fields. According to one account, they "cut down and destroyed 600 acres of corn" at Piqua. According to another, they "burnt the corn fields" at the "Pickaway Towns." With provisions running low, Clark discontinued the expedition and the army returned to Kentucky.[53]

John Holder's Company

John Holder had the largest company (54 men) reported in the return for Benjamin Logan's battalion. The other companies under Colonel Logan were commanded by Levi Todd, William McAfee (wounded at Piqua and died), Thomas Denton, William Hays, William Hogan, John Logan, John Kennedy, John Boyle and Eli Cleveland.[54]

A list of Captain Holder's men is found in the George Rogers Clark papers. A previously published copy of this roll is shown below with identifiable names rendered in their more common spelling.

Capt. John Holder's Company[55]
July 12-August 25, 1780

James Anthony	Jonathan Anthony	Peter Banta
Thomas Bell	[*illegible*] Brooks	William Buchanan
John Bullock	[*illegible*] Callaway	Jesse Copher
Ambrose Coffee	John Colefoot	Peter Cozart
William Cradlebaugh	Zachariah Crews	Daniel Duree
Samuel Estill	Albert Forie	Enoch Furr
William Goggans	Higgison Grubbs	James Hamilton
Nathaniel Hon	Jesse Hodges	John Holder
Henry Hoover	Thomas Howell	William Hoy
Samuel Huff	William Hughs	[*illegible*] Hupp
Christopher Irvine	Abram Kieler	Charles Lockhart
David Lynch	Joseph Proctor	Nicholas Proctor
Reuben Proctor	William Smith	John South Sr.
John South Jr.	Jacob Starnes	John Pleak and Stalver
John Taylor	Benjamin White	

Holder is the only officer listed on the roll. In his Revolutionary War pension declaration, Samuel Estill stated that he was elected first lieutenant of Holder's company after the fall of Martin's and Ruddle's stations.[56]

Holder's pay roll was not prepared until several months after the expedition returned. It was witnessed by David Gass and certified by Colonel Logan.

> October 20th 1780
> This Day came Capt. John Holder before me Justus of the Pece of Kentucky County and made oath that the within Role is just.
> Certify by me   David Gass
> I do certify the above pay role to be just.
>   Benjamin Logan, Colo.[57]

There is a discrepancy between the number of men in Holder's company reported on Holder's list (44) of October 20 and the number reported in Logan's return (54) of August 1.

Holder submitted a number of vouchers to reimburse those who supplied

In Command at Boonesborough

livestock for the use of his company on the expedition. One was for £220 for a beef steer belonging to David Gass:

> I Do Certify that I Received of David Gass one Beif Stier for the Use of My Company of Militia of Kentucky County in Actual Service Under the Comand of Col. George R. Clark Appreased to Two hundred & twenty Pounds by John South Senior & John South Junior, Sworn Appreasers. Given Under My hand this 16th Day of July 1780.
>
> John Holder Capt.[58]

Holder submitted vouchers for Richard Callaway's widow Elizabeth for one beef (£220) and for Nicholas Anderson for one horse lost on the expedition (£700).[59] Another was prepared for Jesse Hodges for one horse "killed in action":

> Kentuckey county Boonsburrough we the subscribers being first Sworn do praise one bay mare branded LH the property of Jessey Hodges To fifteen Hundred pounds for the use of Capt. John Holders company under the command of Colo. Benjamin Logan on Shawney Expedition he ware killed in action certified by us
>
> the appraisers
> John South Junior
> John South Senior
>
> Lincoln County July 12th 1780
> I do Certify that the Appraisers here mentioned were first sworn by me John Cowan a Justice of Peace for County £1500
> John Cowan[60]

The amounts paid for a beef (£220) and horses (£700-1,500) sound surprisingly high. In fact, it reflects wartime inflation, Virginia's deteriorating credit and the devaluation of her paper currency. At that time, a hundredweight of tobacco was selling for £45 in Virginia paper money.[61]

John Holder also submitted vouchers for provisions drawn during the Clark expedition. The following example is a photographic copy of the original:

Colonel John Holder

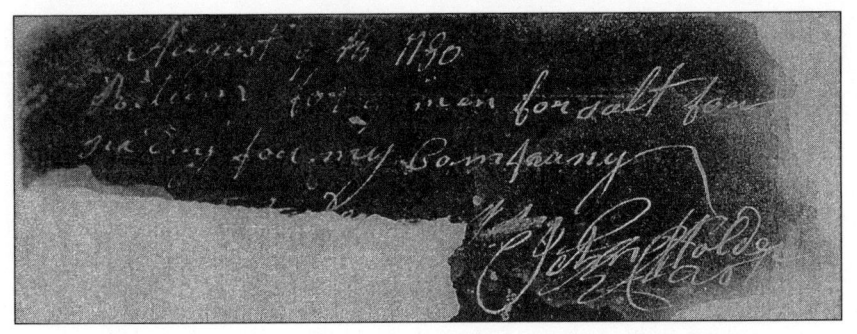

August 9th 1780 Return for 9 men for salt for six days for my Company John Holder Capt[62]

At least one of the men in Holder's company was not happy with his compensation. William Clinkenbeard said that Holder "was our Captain in the 1780 campaign. Got all the money due to us in 1780 [and] bought up land warrants. We never got a cent." In his interview with Reverend Shane, Clinkenbeard proved himself to be an irascible old man who had sharp opinions about many of his fellow pioneers, especially those who came out from North Carolina, whom he referred to generally as "Tories" the term for British sympathizers during the Revolutionary War. Clinkenbeard said Holder "was another Carolina chap, and as grand a tory as ever lived."[63] This is a curious charge to make against the man who led him into battle against hostile Indians.

* * *

On November 1, 1780, Kentucky County, Virginia, ceased to exist, and three new counties were created — Fayette, Lincoln and Jefferson. Boonesborough was situated in Lincoln County. Land north and east of the Kentucky River was in Fayette County.[64]

Benjamin Logan was appointed county lieutenant for Lincoln, with the rank of colonel. In Logan's position, he was responsible for the Lincoln County militia. He was assisted by George Adams, major, and captains John Holder, James Estill and Nathaniel Hart.[65]

Strode's Station Attacked

After Clark's expedition, the Indians did not molest the stations again in 1780. They resumed their raids with the coming of spring the following year. In the early morning of March 1, Indians attacked Strode's Station. Daniel Sphar, who was nine years old at the time, described the event in an interview with John Shane.

In Command at Boonesborough

Jacob Spohr, my Uncle, was out in the morning and, alarmed by the Indians, started to run and was fired on and fell within 40 yards of the Fort, where they scalped him. He had gotten into the midst of them without his knowing of it. They were all around the fort. And with that the attack commenced.[66]

Sixteen year old John Judy, later one of the founders of Mt. Sterling, was also out in the field. He was shot but made it back to the fort and lived. Patrick Donaldson was shot and killed while inside the fort. The Indians, said to number about 100, taunted the inhabitants to come out and get their livestock. Sphar said they "made a dreadful slaughter among the cattle. Killed them all up about the Fort." He added that the Indians camped within hearing that night and left the following morning.[67]

Before the three counties were created, John Holder had regularly sent men from Boonesborough to provide protection at Strode's and McGee's stations. There were no militiamen present at Strode's during the attack. Boonesborough where Holder commanded was then in Lincoln County. Since Strode's Station was in Fayette County, their militia was responsible for garrisoning and "spying" (scouting) around the fort. William Clinkenbeard told Shane that he and seven others had been ordered from Strode's to Boone Station and they were absent during the attack.[68]

Chapter 5
Domestic Relations

At this point in the story, we turn from Holder's military exploits to focus on his personal life. It is well known that Holder married Frances "Fanny" Callaway, daughter of Col. Richard Callaway. Many sources put their wedding at Fort Boonesborough shortly after Fanny was rescued from her Shawnee captors, along with her sister Elizabeth and Jemima Boone. Before he married Fanny Callaway, however, Holder had a liaison at the fort with a widow named Margaret Drake. Some family histories describe this as his first marriage. This seems not to be the case. The relationship with Margaret produced a daughter prior to his marriage to Fanny. Evidence suggests he fathered a second and perhaps a third daughter with Margaret after his marriage to Fanny. This chapter attempts to shed some light on John Holder's relationships with Margaret Drake and Fanny Callaway.

* * *

A few months before the great siege of Boonesborough began, Indians killed Joseph Drake, one of the fort residents. His widow, Margaret Drake (nee Buchanan), remained at Boonesborough with her two small children. Sometime later Margaret had two daughters, named Rhoda and Sabrina. Both girls, born without the benefit of a formal marriage, were fathered by John Holder. John Holder took Rhoda into his household and raised her. Rhoda remained with her father's family until her marriage to Eli Vaughn. Sabrina, who was handicapped in some manner, was raised by her mother. Margaret eventually moved to Tennessee with her second husband, William Jones. She died there, a widow, in March 1827. Evidence will be presented to document the paternity of Rhoda and Sabrina. The chapter also discusses the paternity of Euphemia, another of Margaret's daughters.

Margaret Buchanan

Margaret Buchanan (1755-1827) was the daughter of Colonel John Buchanan, a prominent citizen of Virginia's western frontier. He was

Domestic Relations

a wealthy landowner who lived at Anchor and Hope plantation on Reed Creek, a tributary of the New River, in present day Montgomery County. In 1756, he moved to Cherry Tree Bottom plantation at Looney's Ferry on the James River (just west of the Blue Ridge, near the present day town of Buchanan in Botetourt County). He was a surveyor and land trader and operated a ferry and gristmill. Colonel Buchanan also had a distinguished military career, culminating with his appointment as county lieutenant in command of the militia.[1]

Margaret was born on December 28, 1755. She was named after her mother, who was the daughter of another western Virginia icon, Colonel James Patton. Patton was killed in an Indian massacre at Draper's Meadows the same year Margaret was born. This was during the French and Indian War. The following year, George Washington, in his capacity as commander of Virginia's military forces, visited the Buchanan home on a tour of the western forts.[2]

John Buchanan died in 1769, leaving a widow, a married daughter, three sons, and three young daughters. Buchanan's will directed that the land remaining after paying his debts was to be reserved for his three youngest daughters, Ann, Margaret and Jane. They were to receive their inheritance at age 21 or when they married with the consent of their mother and older brothers. William Preston, a noted political figure of western Virginia, was one of the executors of Buchanan's estate. The three youngest girls all wed Kentucky adventurers. Sister Jane married Colonel John Floyd in 1775. He was one of the Fincastle County surveyors for Preston and ran some of the first surveys in Kentucky. Sister Anna married Ephraim Drake in Kentucky. Margaret married Joseph Drake, older brother of Ephraim.[3]

Joseph Drake

Joseph Drake was a son of Samuel Drake, who lived on Reed Creek in the same neighborhood as Colonel John Buchanan. Joseph was one of the Long Hunters who came to Kentucky prior to its settlement, hunting and exploring. Drake was out with Michael Stoner in 1767 and again in 1768 on the Cumberland River. In 1769, one of the largest and best known groups of Long Hunters came to Kentucky, spending more than a year in the Cumberland Country. This company of twenty or so men included Joseph Drake, Kaspar Mansker, Obediah Terrell, James Dysart, Uriah Stone and the Bledsoe brothers, Anthony, Abraham and Isaac. They set out from Reed Creek, came by Abingdon and Powell's Valley, went through Cumberland Gap and then broke up into smaller parties in Kentucky.[4]

Drake was along on a tour of the Barren River country where someone

Colonel John Holder

in the company carved the names of thirteen men, including "J. Drake," in a beech tree that stood about 3 miles east of present day Bowling Green. Nearby Drake's Creek and Drake's Pond take their names from Joseph.[5]

Drake saw extensive military duty, served in militia companies under William Christian and John Floyd, and participated in several campaigns in the area that later became Ohio and West Virginia. Lyman C. Draper prepared a brief biography of Drake:

> Joseph Drake early settled on the frontiers of West Virginia, and was one of the leaders of the "Long Hunters" (1770-71). He served as a private in Bouquet's Ohio expedition (1764); married Margaret (1773), daughter of Colonel John Buchanan; and served the next year in Christian's regiment on the Point Pleasant campaign. Among the early adventurers he visited Kentucky in the spring of 1775, and in June aided to pilot a party to explore the region of Green River; and the same year he settled on a tract of land six miles below Abingdon, Virginia. He was a rough, fearless man, well-fitted for frontier life and hardships.[6]

In 1773, Drake married 18 year old Margaret Buchanan. They were wed "agreeable to the established custom by Mr. Woolsey,[a] a Baptist preacher," at Town House, the home of her cousin James Thompson,[b] about 17 miles east of Abingdon. For a time Drake showed some indication of settling down. In 1774, he purchased 326 acres of land in the Holston River valley (near present day Chilhowie in Smyth County, Virginia) and obtained a tavern keepers license. Western Virginia and all of Kentucky were at that time part of Fincastle County, created in 1773. Drake appears in Fincastle court records for the usual matters: he was ordered to view a road and fined for skipping jury duty; he provided a security bond for his brother-in-law William Buchanan; sued a neighbor for debt and was sued himself.[7]

In the summer of 1774, the Drakes' domestic tranquility was interrupted by preparations for Dunmore's War. Fearful that a full scale Indian war was about to break out, Col. William Preston sent Daniel Boone and Michael Stoner to Kentucky to warn the land surveyors there of the danger. In July, Col. William Christian wrote Preston that had not heard from Boone and

---

[a] Thomas Woolsey served as a Baptist minister for many years in Washington County, Virginia.

[b] James Thompson (1755-1811) was a justice and militia captain of Fincastle County, Virginia. He lived on the Holston River. His mother, Mary Patton, and Margaret's mother, Margaret Patton, were sisters. Warren Skidmore and Donna Kaminsky, *Lord Dunmore's Little War of 1774* (Bowie, MD, 2002), p. 157.

Domestic Relations

"thought of sending Drake alone, and engaging to give the pay of two Scouts; he is very willing to go." Christian decided to give Boone more time and did not send Drake out.[8]

In August, Joseph was engaged to help his brother-in-law, John Floyd, raise a company of volunteers, which apparently drew criticism from some of the local political figures. Floyd wrote to William Preston, commander of the Fincastle County militia, defending Joseph:

> August 28 from Town House
> I wrote you yesterday that I made no doubt of raising my company, but when I came to enquire particularly of Drake, I find he has engaged but few, I imagine about 15.... There are several men engaged with Drake who did not live in Mr. [William] Campbell's bounds, and others that did not live in the colony, but I have sent them all along.... I have heard every man's sentiments with regard to Joseph Drake's conduct and upon the whole when you are made more sensible of it, I hope you will not be of the same opinion.... Drake wants to see you he says to clear up his character.[9]

Floyd was captain of the company that included 60 men on the pay roll. Joseph Drake was the lieutenant, his brother Ephraim was a private. Floyd and Drake set out with the company for the Ohio River. They were "about 12 or 15 miles from the Ohio [when] news met us that the army was attacked that morning early by a large body of Indians." When the company reached the river about midnight, the battle of Point Pleasant had ended.[10]

In 1775, Drake again visited Kentucky. He was mentioned in Richard Henderson's Boonesborough diary on May 3:

> Finished the magazine. Capt. John Floyd arrived here conducted by one Joseph Drake from a camp on Dicks River where he had left about 30 men in his company from Virginia, and said he was sent by them to know on what terms they might settle our lands.[11]

That summer, Drake visited Col. William Preston at Preston's home in Fincastle County, where he had been appointed colonel of the militia and county surveyor. Preston was an executor of John Buchanan's estate, and Drake went to see him "to settle the legacy bequeathed to his wife." Drake made an agreement to take a tract of 1,150 acres on the Holston River that Buchanan had claimed. He moved his family onto the land that summer, put up a cabin, cleared some land and raised a crop of corn. A neighbor named Jacob Young, who also claimed the tract, "proved troublesome and vexatious." On one occasion, Young came to Drake's cabin and fired off a pistol. Due to Indian excursions in the summer of 1776, "the inhabitants left their homes and forted." Drake left the land to Young and never returned. He relocated for a time back at Reed Creek near his father's place.[12]

In the spring of 1778, Joseph removed to Boonesborough. He brought with him his wife Margaret, their two small children and a slave girl named Aggy. Like other new settlers, he found time to stake out a land claim. The tract he picked was located on the Ohio River, 2 or 3 miles below the mouth of the Little Kentucky River (in present day Trimble County).

Tragedy struck the family that summer. One witness recalled that "Joseph Drake was killed at Boonesborough in sight of the fort" and went on to add that he "was killed in August 1778 I think."[13] A more specific account was provided by William B. Jones, a son of Margaret Drake by her second marriage:

> Mr. Joseph Drake...was a Gentleman, much distinguished for his courage and sagacity, qualities which gave character and influence in those troublesome times. He was killed by the Indians on the 6th day of August 1778 near Boonsborough, the place he had selected for the better security of his family.[14]

Following Drake's death, John Floyd filed a claim for the tract on the Little Kentucky River in the name of Drake's son John. As John was a small child at the time, the land commission issued a certificate for 400 acres to one James Drake. John Drake received the patent for this land in 1797.[15]

Widow on the Frontier

Her husband's death placed Margaret in a precarious situation. Joseph left her with a son John, a daughter Mary and a slave. In similar circumstances, having small children to support, most women on the frontier remarried quickly. Margaret did not. She was still unmarried thirteen years later, when she appeared on the Fayette County tax rolls as a single woman in 1791. She may have had resources of her own to draw on, as her wealthy father left a sizeable inheritance to his three youngest daughters. The promise of an inheritance would have made her an attractive catch, but it may also have allowed her a means of independence.

Margaret had some of her kin to call on at Boonesborough. Her brother William came to Kentucky about the same time she did. William Buchanan was in the great siege of Boonesborough in September 1778. He served in

Domestic Relations

John Holder's company at the fort and was killed in Holder's defeat at the Upper Blue Licks in 1782.[16] Margaret had two other brothers, John who was killed at the battle of Saratoga in 1777 and James who was still living in Kentucky in 1807. Margaret's sister and brother-in-law, Anna and Ephraim Drake, were nearby for some time. So were her sister Jane and husband Colonel John Floyd, until his untimely death in 1783.[17]

Margaret was resourceful enough to file a petition to the Virginia General Assembly asking compensation for horses the Indians carried off when they killed Joseph:

> November 21, 1778
> Also a memorial of Margaret Drake; setting forth, that her husband, who was a lieutenant of militia ordered to Kentucky, was killed by Indians, and several valuable horses, which accompanied him at the time of his death, taken in consequence thereof, whereby the petitioner is left in great distress; and praying relief.[18]

The legislature allowed her £350 "for horses lost or taken by enemy."[19]

Margaret also managed to stake a claim to 400 acres for herself during the great land grab of 1779.[c] With the help of friends and family at the fort, Margaret obtained 400 acres of land in her name, for which she paid £160 to the Virginia Treasury. In December 1779 at Boonesborough, she placed her claim before the Virginia Land Commission. She was issued a certificate based upon an "actual settlement" made in March of that year. "Actual settlement" would have meant that she (or others in her name) made an improvement of some kind on the land. The law did not require her to actually live on the land as long as she was residing in Kentucky. Her tract was located on the waters of Drowning Creek[d] in present day Madison County. The tract was surveyed by Christopher Irvine in 1785 and patented to Margaret Drake in 1787.[20]

After her husband's death, Margaret continued at Boonesborough until late 1781 or early 1782, when she moved across the river to Holder's Station. She resided there for two or three years, then moved a ways north of there to "the ponds." This place, referred to several times in county court orders, appears to have been in the Becknerville area, about 4 miles north of Holder's Station.[21]

---

c The Virginia Land Law of 1779 resulted in hundreds of men heading for Kentucky in search of a claim.

d Drowning Creek forms part of the boundary between present day Estill County and Madison County.

Colonel John Holder

Additional detail about Margaret Drake is provided by the testimony recorded in a lawsuit filed many years later. Margaret's grandson filed the suit to recover some slaves in the possession of Rhoda and her husband, Eli Vaughn. Testimony in the lawsuit reveals the following sequence of events. Joseph Drake died in 1778 without leaving a will. In 1783, Margaret applied to the Fayette County court for administration of her husband's estate. This indicates she was living in Fayette at that time. The court appointed her administrator; Flanders Callaway and Bartlett Searcy signed a bond as her securities. Joseph had owned a slave named Aggy, who by this time had several offspring. Since Joseph was "considerably indebted" when he died, Margaret sold one of these slaves, Celey, to pay off his debts. John Holder was the purchaser. Holder later gave Celey to his daughter Rhoda when she married.[22]

Margaret Drake appeared on the tax roll for Fayette County in 1787—she was assessed for four slaves and four head of cattle. She was on the rolls again in 1789, 1790 and 1791. In 1791 she was listed with one slave and three horses. After that we do not find Margaret listed again under her name in either Fayette or Clark. Clark's first tax list was in 1793.

Margaret Drake Jones

We know that Margaret married again. Her second husband was William Jones, but we have little information about him. The tax rolls indicate that he was a resident of Clark County from 1793 through 1796 and resided in the Becknerville area. He may have been kin to Richard Jones who lived in the same area. William and Richard both served as deputies under Sheriff John Martin.

Margaret was widowed again by October 1810. A document filed that month in Washington County, Virginia, listed Margaret Jones "now living in Franklin County, Tennessee, widow and relict of William Jones, deceased, also of Joseph Drake."[23] Franklin County is located in southern Tennessee on the Alabama border. This was the same county where two children of John Holder and Fanny Callaway — John W. and Frances Holder — lived as adults. The children of Samuel Henderson and Elizabeth "Betsy" Callaway also resided in Franklin County.

In 1813, Margaret gave her power of attorney to "my friend and beloved son-in-law Presla Anderson," for the purpose of selling the 400 acres she still owned in Kentucky. The land was "about six miles from the town of Richmond on Drowning creek." Her signature was witnessed by John W. Holder and James Estill. In 1815, Presley Anderson conveyed part of her 400 acre tract to Samuel Williams of Madison County for $262 in horses and

74

Domestic Relations

$285 in cash. Presley married Euphemia Jones, who was born in Kentucky in about the year 1786. If the birth date is correct, Margaret was still a single woman when Euphemia was born.[24]

Margaret died in Franklin County, Tennessee. Her will, signed in October 1826, was proven at May court 1827. The will names only five of her seven known children: John Drake, deceased, and Mary Stovall—children of Joseph Drake; William B. Jones and Jane B. Sims—children of William Jones; and Sabrina Jones, a child of John Holder's. The will did not list Margaret's other two daughters, Rhoda Drake Vaughn and Euphemia Jones Anderson. Julius Sims was to be be paid for the expenses he had incurred on Margaret's behalf trying to recover "the Legacy due me in the State of Virginia, Botetourt County, from John Buchanan, my father, Deceased." The will states that Margaret still had not received all the legacy from her father, who had been dead for nearly sixty years.[25]

Rhoda Drake

Sometime after Joseph Drake was killed by Indians, Margaret gave birth to a baby girl she named Rhoda. The identity of Rhoda's father comes from many sources, including Rhoda's own recorded statements. For example, she gave a deposition in support of Benjamin Rankins' application for a Revolutionary War pension in which she stated that

> she was acquainted with Benjamin Rankins. Rankins and Jane his wife lived on Colonel John Holders farm, the deponents Farther, which is well known as Colonel John Holders boat yard—[they] lived on my Fathers farm the year of 1789 or 1790.[26]

Another source is James Stonestreet of Clark County who, following a visit with Rhoda, wrote, "She says her father Colonel Holder died on the 30th of March 1799."[27]

We also have a deposition filed by Eli Vaughn stating that he married Rhoda Drake, "a daughter of the said John Holder." Margaret's grandson produced testimony to the same effect—that "the widow Drake" sold her slave Celey to Colonel Holder, who had given her to Rhoda, when Eli married "Rhody, the said Holder's natural daughter by Mrs. Drake."[28] There is no record indicating that Holder was married to Margaret Drake. As unusual as this event must have been—an unmarried woman having a child within the small community around Fort Boonesborough—no pioneer account has been found that mentions it.

Rhoda Drake grew up in John Holder's household and was apparently

Colonel John Holder

close to her father. Court records state that "Colonel Holder took to his own house the defendant's wife [Rhoda] when she was a small child and that she resided there until she was married."[29]

On June 12, 1797, Rhoda and Eli Vaughn obtained a marriage license in Clark County. John Holder gave his consent. Enos Vaughn[e] signed the surety bond. Eli and Rhoda were married on June 15 by Rev. Robert Elkin of Providence Baptist Church. Her name was listed as "Rhoda Drake" on the marriage license and the minister's return. Neither Rhoda nor Eli was a member of Providence Church then or later. Eli and Rhoda lived near Lower Howard's Creek for many years.[30]

In 1826, Rhoda and Eli still had Celey along with nine of Celey's children. That year, John D. Stovall sued Eli in Clark County circuit court to obtain possession of these slaves, who had been in their possession for 29 years. The background of *Stovall v. Vaughn* is as follows:

For their inheritance, John and Mary Drake had been given Joseph and Margaret Drake's slave named Aggy and several of her other offspring. Years later, John D. Stovall, Margaret's grandson who lived in Franklin County, Tennessee, decided that he had a claim to Aggy's daughter Celey and her increase, which he testified "are of the value at least of $3500," a substantial sum in those times. Margaret had sold Celey to John Holder to satisfy some of her late husband's debts.

In 1824, 46 years after Joseph Drake's death, John Stovall came to Madison County, Kentucky, and got the county court to appoint him administrator of his grandfather's estate. He argued that Joseph Drake died in Madison and his estate had never been administered there. He then filed suit in Clark County Court for the slaves in possession of Eli and Rhoda Vaughn. There he argued that Fayette County erred in giving Margaret administration of the estate and, thus, she had no right to sell Celey. Stovall lost the case in Clark County, and took it to the Kentucky Court of Appeals, which agreed with him and sent the case back to Clark for retrial. The case was then moved to Montgomery County. That county's court records were destroyed during the Civil War. That Stovall eventually lost is inferred from the fact that Eli still had Celey in his possession in 1846. Though it is dangerous to form judgments in hindsight, Stovall appears to have been motivated by greed. He knew Rhoda and Eli were nearly destitute and so stated in his suit, "Eli

---

e There were four Vaughns who married in Clark County between 1797 and 1802—Eli, Elijah, Enos and Nancy—who may have been siblings from Frederick County, Virginia. Rev. John Shane wrote, "While at Mr. Niblick's [in Clark County], I met with Elijah Vaughn of Madison, from whom I got the following. He was born in Frederick County, Virginia. Came to Kentucky the year before Con Jackson's defeat. Con Jackson's defeat 1780." Draper MSS 11CC 84.

Domestic Relations

Vaughn has no property of any description in his possession, except a very little personal property, besides said slaves." Perhaps it is fitting that Stovall eventually lost his lawsuit. Testimony in the case provides much valuable information regarding the John Holder-Margaret Drake relationship.[31]

From census data, we learn that Eli and Rhoda had nine children. Sometime between 1830 and 1840, they moved to Athens in Fayette County. In 1846, Eli mortgaged his house and "one old negro woman Celia and one negro girl Harriet." Celia was the slave Celey named in *Stovall v. Vaughn*.[32] Eli died in Lexington in 1849 when a cholera epidemic swept through the town.

> Eli Vaughn, of Lexington. Died of cholera at the home of John O. Sprakes on Main Street, Lexington, July 11, 1849. He was 79 years of age.[33]

Rhoda Vaughn died in Lexington in June of 1863. She is buried in an unmarked grave in the Old Episcopal Cemetery on East Third Street. *The Guardian*, a monthly magazine "Devoted to the Cause of Female Education on Christian Principals," published a brief account of her life in 1873.[34] George W. Ranck in his *History of Lexington* essentially reprinted the text word for word. Ranck's version is copied below:

> The first white woman born in the savage wilds of Kentucky lived for many years in Lexington. Here she died, and here she sleeps. Many now living still remember the venerable Mrs. Rhoda Vaughn, the first born of the wilderness. She was the daughter of that Captain John Holder, spoken of by Boone in his narrative, as the man who pursued the Indians who had attacked Hoy's station in August, 1782. Captain Holder was one of the old pioneer's earliest companions. He assisted in building and defending Boonesborough fort; and within the palisades of that noted stronghold, and about the year 1776, his daughter, afterward Mrs. Vaughn, was born. Her earliest recollections were of savages, sufferings, alarms, and bloodshed; and she passed her infant years in the midst of memorable sieges and desperate conflicts. When she grew to womanhood, and was married, her father started her in life with a home and servants, but she lost both in a few years, by her husband's mismanagement, and after his death, times with her grew worse and worse.
>
> At a very early day, she settled in Fayette county, and subsequently made Lexington her home, and here she remained and raised her children. One of her sons was the gallant adjutant, Edward M.

Colonel John Holder

Vaughn, a Lexington volunteer, who fell upon the bravely contested field of Buena Vista, in 1847. His blood-soaked gauntlets were carried reverently to his mother, and they told at once, to her stricken heart, the same tragic and eloquent story that the armless and battered shield expressed to the Spartan mother in the classic days of old. Other afflictions and misfortunes followed; and destitute and desolate, the brave old lady struggled on through a life, not unfrequently made brighter by kind and sympathetic friends. Mrs. Vaughn lived for some time in the residence lately occupied by Rev. J. D. Matthews, on Winchester street, between Limestone and Walnut. She died, however, at the residence of Mrs. Susan Craig, on the south side of Short Street, between Georgetown and Jefferson street, in the month of June, 1863, aged about eighty-seven years, and was buried in the Whaley lot, in the Episcopal Cemetery, where her remains still repose. . .

Mrs. Vaughn was a woman of excellent mind, warm heart, and sincere piety; and neither her true pride, nor the beautiful characteristics of her christian life, were abated by her poverty and misfortunes. How strange were her experiences. The fate-star of sorrow, which beamed upon her birth, seemed ever to follow her with its saddening influence. She was born when the tomahawk and the torch were busiest; the hope of her declining years died upon a field of battle, and she breathed out her own life in the midst of a terrible civil war. Her parents helped to reclaim and settle an empire; their daughter died without a foot of land that she could call her own. Will justice, even now, be done to her memory? Will the state appropriately mark the spot where rest the mortal remains of the first white woman born in the now great Commonwealth of Kentucky.[35]

Rhoda's grave was and still is unmarked.[36]

When Was Rhoda Born?
When we try to determine when Rhoda was born, the available information leads to conflicting dates that cannot be completely resolved. Excluding some statements shown to be inaccurate, we can come close but perhaps not close enough. For there is another question which cannot be answered exactly and that is, Did John Holder marry Fanny Callaway before or after Rhoda was born?

The Guardian biography of Rhoda Vaughn opens with the statement that

Domestic Relations

she was "the first white woman born in the savage wilds of Kentucky" and gives her birth year as 1776. George Ranck, historian of Boonesborough and Lexington, added the following paragraph to his biography of Rhoda:

> That Mrs. Vaughn was the first white woman born in Kentucky, there can not be the slightest doubt; the fact is placed beyond dispute by the frequent declarations of many of the earliest settlers of this state to persons still living. Mrs. Vaughn, herself, always declared that she had never heard a statement to the contrary.[37]

In spite of Ranck's assertion, the issue was very much in dispute. Surprising as it may seem, by the mid nineteenth century, no one knew for certain who had been the first native white child born in Kentucky. Definitive evidence is still not available. Historian Richard H. Collins examined claims for ten individuals, Rhoda Drake among them. He concluded that Rhoda was unlikely the first born:

> Mrs. Rhoda Vaughn, a daughter of Capt. John Holder, of Boonesborough, is claimed in Ranck's History of Lexington as the first white child born in Kentucky. It is probable that she was born early in 1777, but not probable that she was the first native child.[38]

In Collins' judgment, Fanny Henderson, the daughter of Samuel Henderson and Betsy Callaway, probably preceded Rhoda. Fanny was born May 29, 1777, and named after her aunt, Fanny Callaway. Samuel and Betsy moved back to North Carolina, and Rhoda may not have known about them. Collins' date for Rhoda's birth, "early in 1777," is problematic on several counts: it predates Joseph Drake's death not to mention the arrival of the Drakes or John Holder to Boonesborough.

Since she was described as a sincere and pious Christian woman, it seems reasonable that Rhoda would have had some basis for her claim of being the first white child born in Kentucky. She may have arrived at the conclusion on her own from the legends that developed in the mid 1800s regarding the rescue of the Boone-Callaway girls. One of these myths was that the future husbands of all three girls were among the rescue party. Further embellishments had the three rescuers already engaged to the girls and had their three marriages occurring soon after the rescue.[39] Rhoda, knowing she was born before John Holder married Fanny Callaway, might have inferred that she was also born before any of the Samuel Henderson-Betsy Callaway children or the Flanders Callaway-Jemima Boone children. Both couples

Colonel John Holder

left Kentucky and would not have been present to confirm or deny her conclusion.

Another version of Rhoda's birth maintains that the widow Drake went to live with or near her brother, William Buchanan, at Holder's Station and that Holder took up with Margaret there.[40] This is supported by a statement in *Stovall v. Vaughn* that Margaret lived at Boonesborough

> until the fall of the year 1781, when she moved from there across the Kentucky river to a place called Holder's Station, where she resided for several years and during her residence there had a natural female child by the name of Rhoda of whom Colonel Holder was the reputed father.[41]

Margaret was reported to have lived there for two or three years before she moved a few miles north to "the ponds."

John Holder was living at Boonesborough during the period following Joseph Drake's death. He may have helped Margaret obtain her land claim. At that time, he was personally engaged in locating lands on the Kentucky River to the south and east of Boonesborough. Margaret's claim was in this area. Holder purchased a slave from Margaret, which reportedly helped her settle her deceased husband's debts.

Whatever brought John Holder and Margaret Drake together, a romance must have followed. Given that he was an eligible young bachelor and she an attractive widow, this part of their relationship is not surprising. If Holder's attentions aiding and consoling Margaret occurred in 1778 or 1779, then Rhoda could have been born at Fort Boonesborough. If their liaison began in 1781 or 1782, Rhoda could have been born at Holder's Station.

Rhoda provided her age to the census taker five times between 1820 and 1860.

Census Records for Rhoda Vaughn[42]

1820, oldest female with Eli Vaughn, age 26-45	born 1775-1794
1830, oldest female with Eli Vaughn, age 40-50	born 1780-1790
1840, oldest female with Eli Vaughn, age 60-70	born 1770-1780
1850, Rhoda Vaughn, age 70	born 1779-1780
1860, Rhoda Vaughn, age 79	born 1780-1781

Calculations lead to a best estimate for Rhoda's birth year of 1780, with a range between 1779 and 1781. These estimates assume that Rhoda

Domestic Relations

knew her birth date and reported it correctly in the census. The weight of evidence slightly favors Rhoda Drake being born about 1780 at Fort Boonesborough.

Sadly, Rhoda died in poverty in Lexington during the Civil War. She was not mentioned in her mother's will, and there is no indication that her half brothers or sisters ever contributed anything to her support. In fact, one of Margaret's grandchildren tried to take away from Rhoda and her husband the only legacy she received from her parents — the gift from John Holder of a slave girl named Celey.

That John and Margaret did not marry after the birth of their daughter is also difficult to explain. One may speculate that the Holder-Drake liaison was a brief one. They may have quarreled or she may have lost interest in him or she simply may not have wished to marry him.

We do know that sometime after 1780 Holder turned his attentions to young Fanny Callaway.

Fanny Callaway

Frances "Fanny" Callaway was the daughter of Richard Callaway, one of the pioneers of Boonesborough and a leading figure in early Kentucky. Richard Callaway (1722-1780) was born in Virginia. As a young man, he moved with his older brothers to Bedford County in the western part of the state. Callaway fought in the French and Indian War, rising to the rank of major in the militia. He married Frances Walton, the daughter of Richard and Frances Walton. The couple had twelve children. After Frances died, Richard married the widow Elizabeth Jones Hoy, and they had three children.*f*

In 1775, Richard came out with Richard Henderson's party of road cutters to help establish the settlement at Boonesborough. Callaway was appointed one of five justices of the Kentucky County court and was elected to represent the county in the Virginia House of Burgesses. In 1777, he was appointed to the rank of colonel and assumed command at the fort where he was a participant in all the major events. He was one of the first trustees of the town of Boonesborough and received a permit to operate a ferry there, the first in Kentucky. He was killed by Indians in 1780. Calloway County, Kentucky, was named in his honor.[43]

Fanny was named for her mother, Frances Walton. Fanny's birth date, supposedly found in a bible record, is given as June 16, 1763.[44] She came to Boonesborough in September 1775 when Richard brought the family

---

f Children by Frances Walton were Sarah, George, Zachariah, Mary, Nancy, Mildred, Isham, Elizabeth, Caleb, Frances, Lydia and Theodosia. Children by Elizabeth Hoy were Keziah, Richard Jr. and John "Jack."

Colonel John Holder

out from Virginia. Fanny, her older sister Betsy and Jemima Boone were captured by Indians in July 1776 and saved two days later by Daniel Boone's rescue party. Lyman Draper reported that the 13 year old Fanny beat one of the Indians over the head with her paddle when he tried to drag her from the canoe.[45] There are similar family legends for Betsy and Jemima hitting the Indian with a paddle.

According to family tradition, Fanny also participated in the fort's defense during the great siege of Boonesborough in 1778. One of Holder's daughters later recalled often hearing stories about her mother Fanny and Aunt Betsy "moulding bullets at the Fort at Boonsboro whilst the men were discharging them at the Indians. The young ladies themselves repeatedly fired at the Indians themselves from the fort." It was two years after the siege, when she was about 17 years old, that Fanny's father was killed and mutilated. The court named John Holder administrator for his estate.[46]

Fanny must have been a spirited lass. Her character must have been partly defined by the harrowing experiences she endured as a child. It is unfortunate that we have only the slightest description of Fanny. A Richard Callaway granddaughter stated that "She was a common sized woman." A somewhat more vivid picture comes from a statement made by George Michael Bedinger who came to Boonesborough in 1779. In commenting on John Holder's wife, Bedinger said, "She was a pretty, lively girl."[47]

Holder-Callaway Marriage

If we set aside the myth that John Holder and Fanny Callaway married shortly after he helped rescue her from her Shawnee captors, what information are we left with concerning their marriage date? A statement by David Crews, a contemporary of Holder, sheds some light on the date. Crews was asked to name the people at Boonesborough with whom he was acquainted in the years 1780-1782. He answered

> I was acquainted with Colonel Calliway and his family that lived there, John Harper and Edward Williams and his family and several others, but it has been so long I have forgot their names. There were Nicholas Anderson and his family [and] Colonel Holder, but he was not married.[48]

According to Crews' recollection, Holder was still unmarried up until 1782. Another piece of evidence comes from John D. Shane's interview with John Rankins, who knew Holder back in Virginia. Rankins stated

Domestic Relations

Colonel Holder that lived down by Combs' landing, mouth of Howard's Creek, married Colonel Calloway's daughter that was taken [by the Indians]. Jack Calloway, a younger brother that was taken out of the watermelon patch at Hoy's Station, I saw when he was exchanged and brought in, the same summer we came. His sister [and] Holder had been married a year or two say before we came.[49]

Rankins added that he "came to Kentucky in 1784. Got to Boonsborough in May and spent the first summer there." From these statements we estimate a marriage date for John Holder and Fanny Callaway of 1782 or 1783. This puts the marriage sometime after Holder left Boonesborough to settle his own station at the mouth of Lower Howard's Creek. These dates also suggest that Rhoda was born before Holder and Callaway were married.

Assuming the couple was wed in 1782, Holder would have been about 28 years old and Fanny about 19, if we accept the Callaway bible version for Fanny's birth. This is a significant age difference, but nowhere near the family tradition that Holder was 42 when he married 15 year old Fanny.[50]

Fanny must have been an understanding wife to have accepted Holder's illegitimate daughter into their household and raised her as one of her own. We recall the testimony stating that Margaret Drake moved out of Fort Boonesborough and went to live at Holder's Station for two or three years, then moved a few miles north of there, to an area known then as "the ponds." The testimony went on to state that, while residing at Holder's Station, "the widow Drake lived in 150 or 200 yards of Colonel Holders."[51] Sometime after Holder moved to Holder's Station, he and Margaret had another daughter. She was named Sabrina.

Sabrina Jones

In 1841, Margaret Drake's grandson, John D. Stovall, filed another lawsuit against his family, this time in Franklin County, Tennessee, where Margaret died. The case was styled *Stovall and Marshall v. Sims et al.* One of the defendants named in the suit was "Sibby Jones otherwise called Sibby Holder of the State of Missouri." Stovall's complaint states that Margaret had two children by William Jones (William B. and Jane) and "another daughter by a supposed marriage at a former period named Sibby Jones, otherwise called Sibby Holder." Stovall said Joseph Drake was dead, "as was also Holder the father of said Siby."[52] Although his given name is not stated in the suit, Sibby's presumed father was John Holder.

Most of what little we know about Sibby comes from this lawsuit. She filed her answer from Montgomery County, Missouri, and signed it Sabrina

Colonel John Holder

Jones by "her cross." She stated that Margaret left her a legacy of $1,000, "no part of which has been paid to her although from her poverty and very helpless and infirm condition She has much needed it." Sabrina's half brother, William B. Jones, made several references to Sabrina's condition, stating that she "was laboring under great Phisical disability, even from her infancy." He said, "The destitute Situation of that much infirmed and helpless female is not by any means to be attributed to her who was the kindest and best of Mothers," and called Sabrina "an afflicted child, dependant upon her [mother] from her very infancy."[53] Sabrina was able to provide her attorney with detailed information with which to make her case, and the depositions were signed by her rather than a guardian. This suggests that she was mentally competent and that her handicap was only a physical one.

William B. Jones further testified in the case that each of Margaret's children, "got a portion of her property, chiefly of Negroes," when they left home, "except in the solitary case of his sister Sabrina, whose ill fortune it has been never to have inherited a negro or anything of value belonging to her Mother's estate except a bed and some few other things of no great value." He said that his mother had "one very likely Young Negro fellow" intended for Sabrina "which Sims managed to get out of her hands" after Margaret died.[54] Julius Sims was the executor of Margaret's estate. From the answers of Julius Sims and Sabrina in this case, we learn that Sabrina filed suit against Sims in Franklin County court accusing him of collecting part of Margaret's legacy and refusing to pay Sabrina. Sims confessed to receiving from Margaret's estate notes worth $1,700 (of which he claimed he could only collect $610), a horse valued at $80 and $100 in cash. The court issued a decree in August 1841 ordering Sims to pay Sabrina $1,175 with interest.[55]

Sabrina lived with her mother, until her mother died in 1827. At the time of her death, Margaret was residing in the home of her daughter Jane and son-in-law Julius Sims. Sims had no intention of caring for the invalid daughter. He got the slave "out of her hands" and then shipped Sabrina off to Missouri to live with relatives she hardly knew. According to Sabrina, "without consulting her feelings or wishes," Sims "hurried her away to a distant country in the care of an entire Stranger without bed or bedding, poor and pennyless, to live upon the charity of whomsoever she might fall in with."[56]

Little information is available to determine Sabrina's date of birth. Margaret Jones was listed in the 1820 census of Franklin County, Tennessee, with a female aged 16-26 in her household. This suggests that Sabrina was born between 1794 and 1804.

In the 1840 census for Montgomery County, Missouri, there are two

Domestic Relations

adult females living in the household of Presley Anderson, one aged 40-50 and the other 50-60. Presumably, one is Euphemia and the other Sabrina.

In the 1860 census, we find "Siebrna Jones," age 70, indicating a birth date of 1790. The entry lists Siebrna as a male, but this is almost assuredly Sabrina. She was living with her nephew William Anderson, a son of Presley Anderson Jr., in Montgomery County, Missouri. If Sabrina was born in 1790 or later, it would have been after John Holder married Fanny Callaway.

Margaret Drake was listed as a single woman on the Fayette County tax roll in 1791. Sometime after that she married William Jones. Sabrina was raised in their household and adopted the surname of her stepfather. Margaret bore William Jones two children — a son William B. and a daughter Jane.

Stovall's reference in the 1841 lawsuit to "another daughter by a supposed marriage at a former period named Sibby Jones, otherwise called Sibby Holder" bothered William B. Jones, who regarded it as an insinuation that Sabrina was born out of wedlock. William's answer went on at length to defend his mother:

> Defendant begs leave most respectfully to state that his Mother was the daughter of Colonel John Buchanan, of Augusta county, Virginia. She was born in 1755, connected to some of the most illustrious families of that State, her father being rich. She was well raised and educated. She married young, and was among the first emigrants to Kentucky.
>
> [After her husband was killed] she was left in the Fort, without a single relation except two infant children — many hundred miles from her father's house and connections; where subsistance could not be had without the imminent hazard of life; and when widows, and those without competent protection, were in a most deplorable condition.
>
> It was under circumstances of this kind that her connection with Mr. Holder was formed. This defendant believes that it was in accordance with such regulations as the moral sense of an isolated community were under the necessity of establishing for their own protection and common welfare; and though it may have differed in form from the customs which obtained in the old and well-organized counties of Virginia, this defendant has yet to learn that it was no less obligatory on the parties, no less respectable in the eyes of all righteous and honorable men on that account.[57]

William went on to state that he made his answer "with a mind oppressed

Colonel John Holder

and Melancholy. He feels resentment, wounded family pride and every emotion which a transaction so Shockingly depraved is calculated to produce."

Despite William's noble defense of his mother's honor, there is no evidence that Margaret and John Holder were ever married. One could make a case for such a frontier marriage in the case of Rhoda, born circa 1780, but it becomes untenable in the case of Sabrina, if she was truly born in 1790 or later. By that time, Holder and Fanny Callaway were married and had a number of children. Census data are notoriously unreliable, however, and Sabrina could have been born earlier. Although it would be a bit of a stretch, there was time for John Holder and Margaret Drake to have had Sabrina after Rhoda was born (c.1780) and before Holder married Callaway (1782-83).

Jane Jones, Sabrina's half sister, married Julius Sims in Franklin County, Tennessee. Margaret Drake Jones died in 1827 while living with her daughter Jane. Jane and her husband made arrangements for Sabrina to go live with someone else. A likely candidate would be a closer relative than a half sister, a full sister perhaps. Old letters and Anderson family histories suggest that Sabrina went to Missouri to live with her sister Euphemia, wife of Presley Anderson.[58]

Euphemia Jones

We have even less information about Euphemia than we have for Sabrina. The 1850 census for Montgomery County, Missouri, lists Presley Anderson, farmer, age 64, born in Kentucky, and his wife Euphemia, age 64, also born in Kentucky. They had two children living at home: William, age 26, and John, age 24, both farmers. A pioneer history of Missouri has a biographical sketch of Presley Anderson Jr. Presley married Euphemia Jones and, in 1814, "brought his family to Missouri on pack horses." They moved into a house near Marthasville, soon after a family was murdered there.

> The blood was still upon the floor when they went into the house and Mrs. Anderson scoured it up before they put their furniture in. During the Indian war, Mr. Anderson served as a ranger in Capt. Hargrove's company in Illinois. He was a devout Methodist.[59]

The biography lists the names of nine children, including William and John.

Presley was the son of Presley Anderson Sr., who owned land and resided for a time on Lower Howard's Creek in Clark County. In 1789, Presley Sr.

Domestic Relations

purchased 250 acres of James Speed's 1,000 acre patent on Lower Howard's Creek. Anderson sold off portions of this tract in 1796 and 1800.[60]

William Clinkenbeard, a pioneer of Strode's Station, came out from Virginia with Presley Sr. in 1779 and knew him well.

> Pressly Anderson was bare footed and bare legged coming out, rolled up his pantaloons. His wife was walking and carrying her child. They passed us pretty nigh every day.[61]

Clinkenbeard went on to describe all the residents he recalled living at Strode's Station in 1779-1780:

> Old Pressly Anderson, I think, lived on the one side of that gate in the north till he got afraid and went back to McGee's, way inside. [Indians] never troubled them there as they did at Strode's.[62]

Presley Sr. knew John Holder, and Clinkenbeard recounted a story about the two men:

> Holder and Pressly Anderson were riding out together. Holder had his gun swinging by a strap over his shoulder, the barrel in his hand, the muzzle before. It went accidentally off and took his mare right in the jaw. Pressly Anderson was before. He just laid whip, and Holder could hardly get him to stop. The horse died.[63]

Presley Jr. may have met Euphemia while his father was living in the Lower Howard's Creek neighborhood and Euphemia was living with her mother, Margaret Drake Jones. The connection of Euphemia with Margaret comes from a document in Madison County, Kentucky. In 1813, after she had moved to Tennessee, Margaret gave a power of attorney to "my friend and beloved son-in-law Presla Anderson," in order to sell the 400 acres she still owned in Madison County.[64] This establishes Euphemia as a daughter of Margaret.

It would be logical to assume that Euphemia Jones was a daughter of Margaret and her second husband William Jones. That this is not the case is suggested by testimony in *Stovall and Marshall v. Sims et al*. Stovall's complaint stated that William and Margaret Jones had two children, William B. and Jane. None of the defendants challenged the statement, and in fact, William B. Jones made the same assertion in his answer. He also made the statement that her property was divided among "the whole of his Mother's Children, *Seven in number*," and went on to add:

Colonel John Holder

> Though three times married, she spent much the greater part of her life in the State of widowhood, consequently, the cases of her family, *consisting of three sets of children*, devolved mainly upon her.[65] [emphasis added]

This indicates that, to the best of the children's knowledge, Margaret had seven children by three different fathers. If Margaret had only two children by William Jones (William B. and Jane) and only two by Joseph Drake (John and Mary), then perhaps she had three by John Holder — Rhoda, Sabrina and Euphemia. This would explain why Sabrina was sent to live with Euphemia after Margaret died.

Euphemia's age (64) in the 1850 census indicates a birth year of about 1786, at which time, according to the tax rolls, Margaret was still a single woman and John Holder was married to Fanny Callaway. While conclusive proof of Euphemia's paternity is absent, the evidence suggests John Holder was the father.

* * *

We could argue that the census evidence is incorrect, that Margaret Drake and John Holder had a frontier marriage without benefit of clergy, that she had three children by him, then they divorced and he married Fanny Callaway. Numerous Boonesborough pioneers stated that John Holder married Fanny Callaway. None mentioned another wife, much less a divorce. One recalled that Holder was still a single man as late as 1782 and another that he married Fanny in 1782 or 1783. The "supposed marriage" to John Holder came from family members attempting to spare their mother any perception of dishonor. We can admire their concern for Margaret's reputation without accepting their claims.

A more likely scenario has Holder fathering Rhoda before his marriage to Fanny. Given the circumstances—Margaret was left a young widow at the fort and Holder was the fort commander—their attraction for each other is easily imagined. Holder openly acknowledged Rhoda and took her in to raise with his own children. His other daughter or daughters appear to have been the result of an extramarital affair, and there is no evidence that their paternity was publicly acknowledged by Holder. We would not know about them at all were it not for an obscure lawsuit filed long ago in Tennessee.

It is now time to return to the chronological sequence and pick up Holder's story at Boonesborough in 1779.

Domestic Relations

Children of Margaret Buchanan Drake Jones

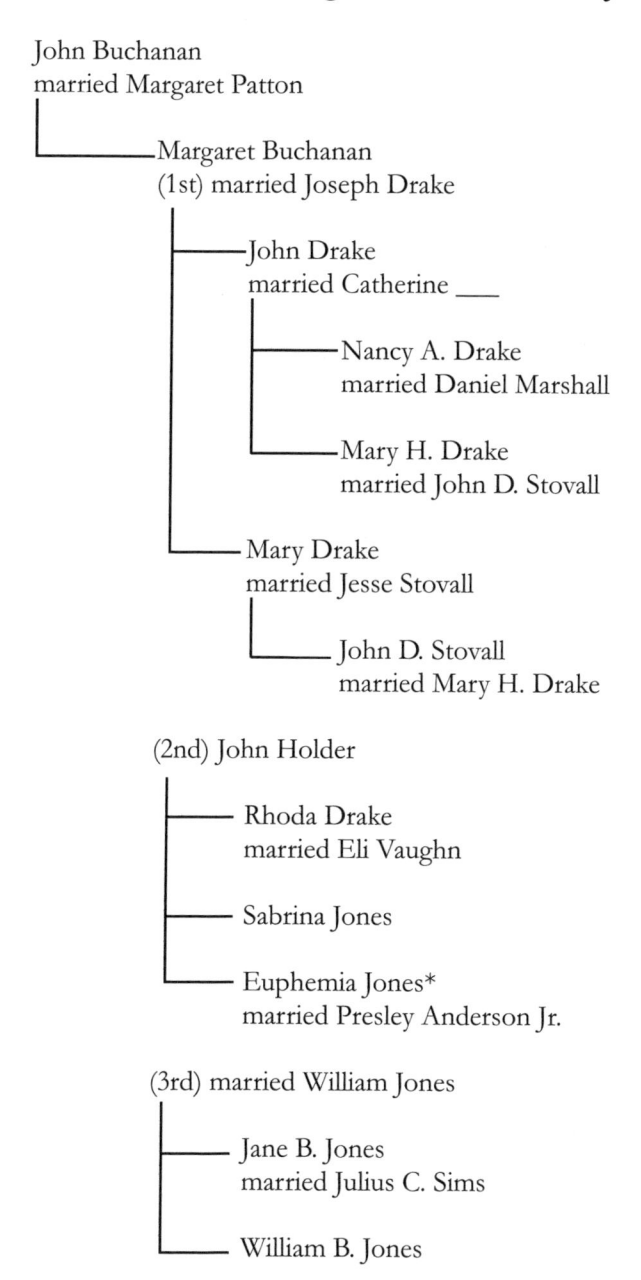

John Buchanan
married Margaret Patton
└── Margaret Buchanan
    (1st) married Joseph Drake
    ├── John Drake
    │   married Catherine ___
    │   ├── Nancy A. Drake
    │   │   married Daniel Marshall
    │   └── Mary H. Drake
    │   married John D. Stovall
    └── Mary Drake
        married Jesse Stovall
        └── John D. Stovall
            married Mary H. Drake

(2nd) John Holder
├── Rhoda Drake
│   married Eli Vaughn
├── Sabrina Jones
└── Euphemia Jones*
    married Presley Anderson Jr.

(3rd) married William Jones
├── Jane B. Jones
│   married Julius C. Sims
└── William B. Jones

* not positively confirmed as John Holder's daughter

Chapter 6

In Search of Land

The quest for land occupied nearly everyone at Boonesborough in the summer of 1779. John Holder accompanied the Berkeley County men in a cooperative venture. Ralph Morgan described how this party of men had gathered at Boonesborough "to go out and improve land." He said that they

> Agreed to make improvements until we had one apiece and then ballot for choice. John Holder, our pilot, being a resident of the country before we came. The names of the improving party were Thomas Swearingen, Benoni Swearingen, John Holder, John Constant, Joseph Doniphan, Samuel Duree, William Morgan, Ralph Morgan, John Taylor and George M. Bedinger.[1]

This company went out the first time in early May, locating lands in now Madison County on Muddy Creek and Silver Creek. Many of the same men went out again later that summer to make improvements in the area between Lexington and Paris. On South Elkhorn Creek, they encountered a bear in a tree. Benoni, who was 6 feet 5 inches tall, tried to poke the bear out of its tree with a long stick. The bear "gave the pole a spiteful knock with her paw" and sent it flying then retreated into her hole. They shot her, cut the tree down and found her four cubs "which they killed for food."[2]

While on this trip, the party located and marked a number of claims in the area of present day Bourbon County, west of Paris. They made one improvement on a tract of land they called "Lydia's Mount," which Thomas Swearingen named after his youngest daughter. Lydia's Mount was located at the head of Cooper Run, about 7 miles west of Paris. William Beasley ended up with this claim. Holder later gave a deposition that mentioned this tract. When he was asked, "Did you not make an entry at Lydia's Mount?" he answered "Yes. I made a settlement entry in the name of Beesley, of which I had a part." The party continued making improvements in the area,

In Search of Land

including some on Houston Creek, which they called "Holder's Creek" at that time.[a] At the land office in May and June of 1780, eleven claims were entered on "Holder's Creek."[3]

Holder must have received a good education from the men in his party. Not only were they knowledgeable in the legal process for obtaining land, but also their number included three surveyors—Thomas and Benoni Swearingen and George Michael Bedinger. Holder, who would later receive appointments as deputy surveyor in the counties of Fayette and Clark, may have learned the craft from them. We know that young Ralph Morgan learned the surveying trade from them.[4]

Petition from the Distressed Inhabitants of Boonsfort

By 1779, the residents at Fort Boonesborough were highly displeased with the way the Transylvania Company had divided up the land around the fort. First, the trustees were appointed by the company, not elected, and they included three men "that were intire strangers to us [and] not even settlers in the country." The trustees, after allowing the best lands to be taken up by Richard Henderson and Nathaniel Hart, were requiring other lot holders to build a cabin within one year. This imposition applied to poor widows and those who had lost all their horses to the Indians and could not obtain timber. The residents had called upon Richard Callaway, one of the trustees, and asked "that a fair Election should be held and that he would still serve as a Trustee, but he utterly refused." The petitioners requested that Virginia establish a "Township by the Name of Boonsborough" and that they appoint the following men as trustees: John Holder, James Estill, David Gass, John South, Pemberton Rawlings, Stephen Hancock and John Martin. The petition also listed the names of 55 men, women and children who had been killed or captured by the Indians near Boonesborough.[5]

The General Assembly acted upon the petition at its October 1779 session. They set aside 640 acres for the town of Boonesborough, the first established in Kentucky. Lot holders were given three years to build "a dwelling house, sixteen feet square." They also appointed the following trustees for the town: Richard Callaway, Charles Minn Thruston, Levin Powell, Edmund Taylor, James Estill, Edward Bradley, John Kennedy, David Gass, Pemberton Rawlings and Daniel Boone.[6] By that time, however, Boone had left Boonesborough forever.

---

[a] In 1804, Henry Clay wrote that he thought Houston Creek had been widely known as Holder's Creek but that Lydia's Mount was not so well known by the "early adventurers." James F. Hopkins, editor, *Papers of Henry Clay, Vol. 1, The Rising Statesman, 1797-1814* (Lexington, 1959), p. 131.

Colonel John Holder

Petition from the Distressed Inhabitants of Kentucky

The settlers in Kentucky had held on for four years withstanding the hardship of the wilderness and the dangers of the Indians. They felt Virginia had done little to support them in their constant war with the Native Americans. Many had been killed, others had lost all their property. With passage of the Virginia Land Law, enacted in early 1779, settlers feared they could lose their land as well. In a petition to the General Assembly, they complained that they were well aware that many speculators, who had contributed nothing to the defense of the frontier, were coming out to lay off land for profit. The "Destressed Inhabitants of the county of Kentuckky" face the possibility of "becoming tennants to private gentlemen who have men employed at this junction in this country, at one hundred pounds per Thousand [acres], running round the land, which is too rough a medicine ever to be dejested by any set of people that have suffered as we have." Others came out just long enough to mark a 1,000 acre claim and went home. These men "only raised a small cabbin [and] perhaps never stayed three weeks in the country [and] never lost to the amount of one shillings worth, yet they are intituled to their choice of one Thousand Acres at State price." The petitioners complained that if no changes were made, it would have been better "for us if we had all been such cultivators and never come to settle in the country untill there had been a peace." They also suggested that if they did not "get speedy redress," they might be forced to go "Down the Mississippi to the Spanish protection."[7]

The petition was signed by John Holder, David Gass, James and Samuel Estill, John South Jr. and Sr., and many other residents of Boonesborough. There were over fifty signatures in all, two of them by women, Margaret Drake and Catherine Baughman, both widows. The petition was referred to the Committee on Propositions in October, but resulted in little legislative relief. There was a provision added to the Land Law in May 1781 allowing indigent persons to obtain land without paying the state price. This "poor right" provided up to 400 acres, but claimants still had to pay land office fees and had to pay the state 20 shillings per 100 acres of land within two and a half years from the date of survey.[8]

Virginia Land Commission

The Virginia Land Law of 1779 changed the whole game for those seeking land in Kentucky. The law not only legitimized the claims of those already settled, but also laid out the process by which any person could acquire land from the state through the purchase of treasury warrants. A land office was to open in Kentucky the first of May 1780 for entry of

In Search of Land

these treasury warrants for specific claims.[9] Many Virginians, realizing that land in Kentucky could soon be valuable, rushed out to make their claims. Speculators ranged from wealthy aristocrats, who obtained rights to tens of thousands of acres, to poor yeomen, who were fortunate enough to acquire a few hundred acres. At times it must have seemed like everyone in Kentucky was trying to obtain land in hopes of getting rich—or richer.

John Holder was one of many who ended up with vast acreages. Holder did not begin as a wealthy man. He started out acquiring land by buying the claims of others at low prices. Then he began locating land for those who were too fearful or too busy to do it themselves. A locator would find a tract of vacant land, mark it and get it surveyed for the eventual owner. The new owner would then assign an agreed upon share to the locator.

The Virginia Land Law also established the process by which persons who settled before 1779 could obtain title to their lands. Bona fide residents could get a settlement certificate for 400 acres of land and a preemption warrant for 1,000 acres adjoining the settlement. Those who had not resided in Kentucky for a year or grown a crop of corn prior to 1778 could still obtain 1,000 acres on a preemption warrant. These settlement certificates and preemption warrants were issued by special commissioners sent out from Virginia to hear the claims of settlers. They were referred to as the Virginia Land Commission, and they held their land court at the various forts and stations during the winter of 1779-80.[10] The complete record of their judgments and awards is found in the *Certificate Book of the Virginia*

John Holder's Settlement & Preemption[12]

At a Court continued & held at Boonesboro for adjusting titles of claimants to unpatented lands by the Commissioners of Kentucky district the 24th day of December 1779.
Kentucky County Sct.

We do hereby certify that John Holder is entitled to Four hundred Acres of land in the district of Kentucky on Account of Settlement made in the Country in the year 1777 & Residing ever since, lying about one and a half Miles from the Mouth of Boons Creek on the west side thereof to include Russells Spring & that the said John Holder is also entitled to the Preemption of one thousand acres of land adjoining the said Settlement. Given under our hands at Boonsborough this 24th day of December 1779.

Test.	William Fleming
John Williams jr [clerk]	Stephen Trigg
	Edmund Lynn

Colonel John Holder

Land Commission, 1779-1780. The original certificates issued by the commissioners are housed at the Kentucky Land Office in Frankfort. Through the wonders of technology and the diligence of Kandie Adkinson, the certificates may now be viewed on the Internet.[11]

The first session of the land court was held at St. Asaph in October 1779. The court met at Boonesborough from December 18 through 29. Holder presented the claim for his settlement and preemption on the west side of Boone Creek, which was approved on the 24th. Part of this 1,400 acres is now included in the Raven Run Nature Sanctuary in Fayette County.

Holder kept busy during the session at Boonesborough presenting the claims of others. On the 22d he submitted three claims. One was for John Beasley, heir of William Beasley who was killed by Indians. This was for the claim Holder had helped locate at Lydia's Mount. He also submitted a claim for Major Beasley. The third was for Daniel Dumpard on Holder's Creek (now Houston Creek in Bourbon County). Daniel was the heir of John Dumpard or Dumford, who was killed by Indians in July of that year. Daniel sold his rights to the tract to Holder. Holder paid the fees on the preemption — £400 for 1,000 acres — at the land office in May 1780.[13]

One of the last claims presented at the Boonesborough session was by Margaret Drake. She was awarded a 400 acre preemption for residing in the district of Kentucky prior to 1779. The cost was £160, which she paid in May 1780.[14]

Holder followed the commissioners to their next meeting at Bryan's Station. There he was awarded certificates for claims that he bought from two men who had served in his company on Bowman's Campaign. One was for 400 acres on Silver Creek, in present day Madison County, which he purchased from Moses Nelson. The other was for 1,400 acres on Houston Creek purchased from Edmund Fear. Holder bought the latter claim in partnership with John Martin.

Hard Winter

The winter that year was so bad it became known simply as the "Hard Winter." It was the coldest weather anyone alive had ever experienced. The snow fell early and persisted. Rivers froze solid from bank to bank. Settlers lost their livestock and much of the wild game perished as well. According to one observer, "This hard winter began about the first of November 1779 and broak up the last of Feberary 1780. The turkeys was almost all dead. The buffeloes had got poore. People's cattle mostly Dead. No corn or but very little in the country. The people was in great Distress."[15]

The land commissioners had difficulty writing out certificates because

In Search of Land

their ink kept freezing. One of them, William Fleming, kept a journal that winter. On January 24th, he reported, "I had one of my toes bit with the frost and some of my fingers frozen." Fleming penned the following description of Boonesborough:

> Dec. 31st
> Boonesburg has 30 houses in it. stands in a bottom that is surrounded by hills on every side that commands it. the hills over the Kentucky opposite as indeed all along the River is very very steep and [one] discovers the Rock at no great depth under the soil. the Fort is a dirty place in winter like every other Station.[16]

Fleming did not elaborate on the "dirty place," but later he did describe the foul conditions at Harrodsburg, which may have been similar to Boonesborough.

> The Spring at this place is below the Fort and fed by ponds above the Fort so that the whole dirt and filth of the Fort — putrified flesh, dead dogs, horse, cow, hog excrements and human odour — all wash into the spring, which with the Ashes and sweepings of filthy Cabbins, the dirtiness of the people, steeping skins to dress, and washing every sort of dirty rags and cloths in the spring perfectly poisons the water and makes the most filthy nauseous potation of the water imaginable.[17]

Fleming became so ill at Harrodsburg that he had to delay his return home to Virginia.

Food began to run short in places during the Hard Winter, but Boonesborough residents had grown accustomed to a nearly constant diet of meat. Daniel Trabue later recalled how people subsisted at the fort.

> [It was] about 2 o'clock when we got to Boonsbourrah on the Kentucky River. The people all ran out over Joyed to see strangers come to their town or Fort. They Give us something to eat.... The people in the fort was remarkable kind and hospetable to us with what they had. But I thought it was hard times — no bred, no salt, no vegetables, no fruit of any kind, no Ardent sperrets, indeed nothing but meet.[18]

In the fall of 1779, settlement began in what would later become Clark County. Two fortified stockades were erected: McGee's Station, established

Colonel John Holder

by David McGee, and Strode's Station by John Strode.[19] McGee's was located near the head of Jouett Creek. Evidence suggests it stood on the south side of present day Jones Nursery Road on property now owned by Harkness Edwards. Strode's was situated on a creek by the same name and stood on the north side of US 60 at Caudill Drive, about where Applebee's® restaurant is today. No trace of either station remains.

Kentucky Land Office

The state of Virginia had a four step process for obtaining previously unpatented land. These steps are usually designated as warrant, entry, survey and grant. A person had to first obtain a warrant, which was a legal entitlement to a specific quantity of land. There were several kinds of warrants. Military warrants were given for service in the French and Indian War and, later, for service in the Revolutionary War. Treasury warrants were purchased in Virginia at the rate of £400 per 1,000 acres. Finally, there were the settlement certificates and preemption warrants issued by the Virginia Land Commission. After selecting a tract of land and marking the corners and lines, the tract had to be entered on the books at the land office. The entry had to state the specific location of the land so that others could avoid claiming the same tract. And the claim was required to be on "vacant and unused land," meaning land where no one else had yet marked or registered a claim. Of course, the surveyor at the land office usually had no way of knowing if this condition was met. The surveyor would then send one of his deputies out to survey the tract and return with a plat, or map of the claim. The survey description was in "metes and bounds" and contained language such at the following from David McGee's survey of his station tract:

> Beginning at two White Oaks and Sugartree in Hickman's line, thence south 70 degrees east 230 poles, crossing two branches to a White Oak and sugartree in a Cane break.[20]

The survey and warrant were then sent to the governor of Virginia who issued and signed the grant.

In April 1780, the Kentucky land office opened at Wilson's Station near Harrodsburg. The office was superintended by George May, the surveyor for Kentucky County. Hundreds of men gathered to enter their claims. From April 26-29, over 600 entries were recorded. These first entries were for military claims and the settlements and preemptions awarded by the Virginia Land Commission. In May, the office was open for entering

In Search of Land

treasury warrants. There were so many waiting by then that a lottery system had to be devised to handle them all.[21]

Holder did not show up at the land office for the first time until the end of May 1780, when he entered 400 acres near the mouth of Silver Creek in Madison County.

> John Holder assee [assignee] &c Enters a Preemption Warrant of 400 acres on Silver Creek about ½ mile from the mouth including Spring.[22]

This was Moses Nelson's tract, awarded to him on a settlement certificate, which Holder had purchased. In June, Holder entered two more claims, for 1,000 acres each, on Houston Creek. One of these was for the claim he and John Martin acquired from Edmund Fear.[23]

Holder did not have to appear at the land office in April to enter his settlement and preemption on Boone Creek, since he had by then sold the rights to Alexander Cleveland. Alexander sold the tracts to his brother Eli Cleveland, who later established a ferry, warehouse and gristmill on Boone Creek. The controversial Eli was involved in a suit over the Holder tracts. Another brother, Oliver Cleveland, described in a court deposition what happened.

> [Oliver] was living and resided with his brothers Eli and Alexander Cleveland in Fayette County Kentucky, at or about which time Eli purchased of Alexander entries of settlement and preemption, which said Alexander had purchased of John Holder on Boons creek and that the settlement was entered in the name of John Holder and to include Russels spring. [Oliver] was present when the Contract was made between said Alexander and Holder, and between said Alexander and Eli. [Oliver] said Alexander was to receive 20,000 pounds or 20,000 dollars from Eli.[24]

Oliver added that his brother had to bring suit to get his money from Eli Cleveland.

Lincoln County Court

At their first session in February 1781, the Lincoln County court appointed John Holder administrator of Richard Callaway's estate. Holder married Callaway's daughter Fanny around that time (between 1781 and 1783). The court recorded Holder's appointment as follows:

Colonel John Holder

Leave of Administration was granted to the following persons, to wit, John Holder upon the Estate of Richard Callaway, deceased.[25]

At the same session, the court appointed three men to appraise Callaway's personal estate — Nicholas Anderson, John South Sr. and John South Jr. A number of people owed Callaway money when he died. In pursuance of his administrator duties, Holder later (1784) brought lawsuits against John South and Thomas Oder on behalf of Callaway's heirs.[26]

Richard Callaway's will was eventually produced, and the Virginia Supreme Court recorded it in March 1784, appointing his son Caleb Callaway as executor.[27]

Years later, the Madison County court awarded the ferry license at Boonesborough to Richard Callaway's heirs. At a session in March 1788, the county justices ordered that

> the Ferry on the South side of the Kentucky River at Boonsborough unto the opposite shore be vested in Caleb Callaway, Fanny Holder, Lydia Irvine, Doshia [Theodocia] Callaway, Cuzza [Keziah] French, Richard Callaway and John Callaway, to them their heirs or assigns forever to hold as Tenants in Common and not as Joint Tenants.[28]

The heirs must have leased the ferry operation, since we find at the same session of court, "Matthew Walton, James French and William Irvine Enter into Bond with sufficient security at the next Court for keeping the Ferry at Boonsborough in such repair as the Law requires."[29] Matthew Walton was a cousin of Richard Callaway's first wife, Frances Walton; James French was the husband of Keziah Callaway; and William Irvine was the brother of Christopher Irvine (died in 1786), who married Lydia Callaway. Keziah and Lydia were daughters of Richard Callaway.

Returning to Lincoln County, in November 1781, Nathaniel Hart was named administrator of Thomas Marshall's estate. The court appointed John Holder, James Buchanan and John South to appraise Marshall's personal goods.[30]

Lower Howard's Creek

By 1781, John Holder had selected the tract of land he planned to settle on. It was located just over a mile downstream from Boonesborough on the north side of the Kentucky River at the mouth of a stream called Lower Howard's Creek. The site had many advantages — fertile upland plains, over a mile of river frontage and an entrenched creek with water power potential

In Search of Land

— all of which Holder eventually put to good use. This tract, like many others in Kentucky, was surveyed for more than one owner and resulted in a long drawn out lawsuit to establish who had the superior claim. This particular suit, *Jouitt v. Holder*, provides a wealth of information regarding the history of this land. Some of the most valuable testimony is in Holder's own words. We will begin with a brief recitation of events, which will be followed by a more detailed review.

Holder's interest in the land dates back to at least 1779 or 1780. That is when he said he learned about Matthew Jouett's claim of 1,000 acres between Lower Howard's Creek and Jouett Creek, based on an improvement Jouett made in 1775. When Jouett returned to Virginia, William May purchased the claim. May's application to the Virginia Land Commission for rights to the improvement was rejected. Holder went to May and asked if he was going to enter the tract on a treasury warrant. May suggested that Holder enter the land himself. Holder testified that he made an entry "on the said Howards creek in the year 1780 and settled on the said land in the year 1782."[31]

Holder then learned that John Howard also claimed 1,000 acres between Lower Howard's Creek and Jouett Creek. Howard had presented his claim to the Virginia Land Commission and had been awarded a preemption warrant for it. Holder worked out an arrangement with Howard and purchased the tract from him for "a valuable consideration" on August 1, 1783.[32] We shall learn more later about the "valuable consideration."

John Howard's Claim

John Howard (c.1731-1834) was born in Goochland County, Virginia, and married into the influential Preston family of Augusta County. His wife Mary was the sister of Col. William Preston. Howard settled on a military claim in Fayette County and became a prominent citizen of central Kentucky. His plantation, known as "Howard's Grove," is the site of the now legendary Gainesway Farm. Howard served in the Revolutionary War and fought in the battle of Guilford Courthouse. His son became governor of Missouri, and one of his daughters married Robert Wickliffe, one of the wealthiest men in Kentucky. Howard died at the age of 103 and was buried at Howard's Grove.[33]

During his visit to the western country in 1775, John Howard staked out land claims at the mouth of two Kentucky River tributaries. One site was a few miles upstream of Fort Boonesborough, the other was just downstream of the fort. The streams came to be known in early times as Upper Howard's Creek and Lower Howard's Creek. He made his improvement on Lower Howard's Creek in June 1775.[34] In spite of the fact that his name is attached

Colonel John Holder

to two creeks in Clark County, John Howard's name is little known there today.

Howard returned to Kentucky in 1779 to present his claim to the Virginia Land Commission. He was awarded a 1,000 acre preemption for the tract below Boonesborough. His certificate stated that he obtained this right

> by building a Cabbin & making other Improvements on a Tract of land lying on the North side of Kentucky [River] at the mouth of Howards Creek to extend up the Creek and Westward for quantity in the year 1775.[35]

One of the documents filed in the suit with the Jouetts states that Howard's improvement was "within a few yards of the creek and not more than forty poles from its mouth."[36] The statement is too vague to determine a more precise location.

By virtue of the preemption warrant he obtained from the commissioners, Howard entered his claim with the Fayette County surveyor on June 14, 1783.

> John Howard Enters 1000 Acres of Land on a preemption Warrant No 1048 lying on the Kentucky Beginning on the said River at the upper side of the Mouth of Howards lower creek, and Running agreeable to the Commissioners certificate down the River about 1½ Mile, thence out from the River Including the lower part of the next creek below, called Duets creek, and extending [north] along near that creek as is necessary to make the complement, when the back line is Run [east] across to the upper side of Howards creek, so far as thence to Include the said creek to its mouth, or to a line that shall be agreed upon between the said Howard & William Bush, who has an adjoining preemption.[37]

On the same day, on the same page in the entry book, John Holder withdrew his entry covering the same tract in the following words: "John Holder assignee etc. withdraws his Entry of 2000 Acres made on part of a Treasury Warrant No 6328, and Reserves the same again, on Howards creek adjoining an Entry of 100 acres of said Holders (which lies at the Mouth of said Creek) on the upper side where it Joins Bushes line then to Run West to Mays line then to extend up Howards creek between Mays and Bushes lines for quantity."

The wording of Howard's entry — not being specific whether it ran down

In Search of Land

Howard's Creek to the mouth or followed an agreed upon line between Howard and William Bush — would later cause problems for John Holder.

Justinian Cartwright, a deputy surveyor for Fayette County, surveyed the 1,000 acre tract on September 20, 1785. John Holder was the marker; Edward Hall and Henry Hieronymous were chain carriers. The tract began "at a forked Dogwood and a sassafras on the bank of said River and corner to William Bushs land."[38] This landmark corner, marked "A" on the survey plat, was still known to surveyors many years later. The corner was located "about Ten poles[b] above the low water mark and 36 poles above the mouth of Lower Howard's creek."[39] The fact that the beginning corner was 594 feet upstream from the mouth of the creek indicates that Howard's claim included the small bottom where Hall's Restaurant is located today.

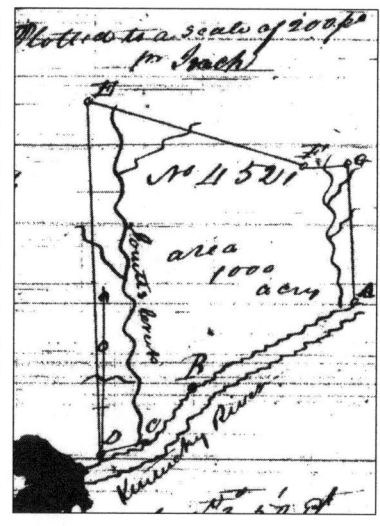

John Howard's Survey.[40]

Howard transferred his survey to John Holder. Selling a survey was an early means of conveying legal interest in a property. Howard added the following notation to the plat before returning it to the land office:

> I Hereby assign the within plot of one thousand acres of Land unto John Holder and desire the patent may Issue in said Holders Name. Witness my hand this 18th day of November 1785. John Howard

A grant for 1,000 acres in Fayette County was issued to John Holder "for a certain tract of land…lying on the Kentucky River, Howards Creek and Jouetts Creek and beginning at a forked dogwood and sassifrass on the bank of said River." The grant was signed by Beverly Randolph, Lieutenant Governor of the Commonwealth of Virginia on May 28, 1787.[41]

Matthew Jouett's Claim

Matthew Jouett (c.1753-1777) was born in Charlottesville, Virginia. He came to Kentucky in search of land in 1775. He was in Boonesborough for the first meeting of the "House of Delegates or Representatives of the

---

b 1 pole = 16½ feet.

Colonel John Holder

Colony of Transylvania," on May 23. At that meeting he was elected clerk of the convention. Sometime while he was out, he went to the north side of Kentucky River in company with David McGee and others. He marked a tract and made an improvement near a large spring on the creek that still bears his name. The creek has been spelled many different ways in county records; the more common include Jouett, Jouitt, Jewitt, Duit and Dewit. The nature of his improvement was not specified but in most cases it was a small cabin, which was sufficient to secure a land claim under the laws of Virginia. Jouett then returned to Virginia, raised a company in the Virginia Regiment, and was mortally wounded in the battle of Brandywine.[42]

The efforts by the Jouett family to complete this claim were extraordinary — including litigation that was still being pursued more than fifty years after Matthew's death — but ultimately futile. After learning that the Virginia Land Commission had rejected Matthew's claim ("there being no proof that an improvement had been made there"), John Jouett came to Kentucky in order to acquire rights to the land as the heir to his slain brother. Jouett stated that he did not arrive until the 5th or 6th of May 1780, at which time he learned that the commission "had finished their sitting." Jouett enlisted the aid of a number of influential men, including Humphrey Marshall, Caleb Wallace, William May and Harry Innes, the federal judge for the district of Kentucky.

In 1786, Judge Innes personally traveled to the contested property with David McGee, who showed him Matthew Jouett's beginning corner, and Innes marked a tree there. That September John Jouett went to Fayette circuit court and obtained a certificate for 1,000 acres between Lower Howard's Creek and Jouett Creek. With the certificate in hand, Jouett arranged a meeting with John Holder and William May. Holder by then was living on Howard's claim, and May had an entry of 200 acres near the mouth of the creek. The May brothers — John, William and George — were recognized as the most active land speculators in Kentucky at that time. John Jouett ("Repondent") described the outcome of their meeting.

> William May, John Holder, and this Respondent met together in Danville, and a proposition having been made between the said Holder and this Respondent respecting a compromise of the dispute, this Respondent applied to the said May to know what he should take from the said Holder, who [May] answered not less than three hundred Pounds. And the said Holder having offered 500 Acres of land, the said May refused to have any thing to do with the land, in consequence of which the treaty of a compromise about the said land was put an end to.[43]

In Search of Land

The Mays, judging that "the dispute was likely to be tedious and expensive," extricated themselves from further actions in the matter. Jouett pressed on and filed suit in Fayette County in a case styled *John Jouitt, heir at law of Matthew Jouitt v. John Holder*. The case was before the courts for 37 years, and went through numerous interim decrees, final judgments, appeals, and re-filings. One of the decrees held that John Howard's entry was defective because it did not state precisely whether the easternmost boundary ran along Lower Howard's Creek or along an agreed upon line between Howard and William Bush. The circuit court judge threw out the entry, and with it Holder's grant, but the ruling was overturned by the court of appeals. The case of *John Jouitt's heirs v. John Holder's heirs* finally ground to a halt in 1830, when it was decided in Holder's favor. For all their trouble, the Jouetts were awarded 17 acres out of Holder's original claim. The award would not have paid a year's worth of expenses in the case.[44]

John "Jack" Jouett (1754-1822) achieved lasting fame during the Revolutionary War for his "midnight ride" in 1781 to warn Williamsburg that the British were coming, allowing Governor Thomas Jefferson and most of the legislature to escape just ahead of Banastre Tarleton's horsemen. Jouett later moved to Kentucky and settled first in Mercer County, then Woodford County, and represented both in the Kentucky General Assembly. The home he built in Woodford is now a local landmark. He was the father of Kentucky's most famous portrait painter, Matthew Harris Jouett.[45]

Chapter 7
Holder's Station

John Holder planned to live on the valuable tract of land he acquired at the mouth of Lower Howard's Creek. In *Jouitt v. Holder*, he testified that he "settled on the said land in the year 1782." Pioneer accounts refer to a fortified settlement there widely known as Holder's Station. The station must have been built shortly before or soon after Holder moved onto the land. Joseph Berry gave a deposition which states, "In year 1782 he came to this country and resided at Holder's station on the Kentucky River."[1]

After Capt. James Estill and six others were killed near Mt. Sterling, a burial party returned to the battlefield. Joseph Proctor later testified that they

> collected a body of men together from the different stations, to wit, from Boonesborough, Magee's, Strode's, Holder's and Estill's stations, to the amount of 50 or 60. Then we started to this place again in order to bury the dead.[2]

This indicates that the station was settled before March 22, 1782, the date of Estill's Defeat. In August of that year, Holder was serving as a captain in the Fayette County militia, which means he must have been living on the north side of the Kentucky River.

No description of Holder's Station survives, but we do have one statement that alludes to the number of people living there. Aquilla White was an early hunter who settled at Boonesborough in 1779. White recalled the station in a deposition.

> Deponent thinks there was above 130 people, old and young, who lived at McGee's station in 1780 and about thirty families who lived at Boonesborough and nearly as many at Strode's Station, and about twenty families at Boonesborough and about eighty people at Holder's, and thinks the trace named aforesaid [Boonesborough to Lower Blue Licks] was well known by most of the men that lived at the above mentioned stations in 1782 and 1783.[3]

Holder's Station

The wording is a little confusing, since there are two numbers reported for Boonesborough. It appears that the first figure refers to the year 1780 and the second figure to 1782-83. This suggests that there were about 80 people living at Holder's Station shortly after it was established. Robert McMillan gave the following deposition in the same suit.

> Deponent thinks there was between 20 and 30 families living at Boonesborough in latter part of 1782 and in the year 1783, and between 15 and 20 families living at McGee's station at the same time, and about the same number living at Boon's station, and about 5 or 6 families living at Holder's station, and about 20 families at Stroud's station, and a great number of unmarried men that lived at said stations at that time, and most were hunters.[4]

McMillan's testimony indicates that most of the residents of Holder's Station at that time were single men whom he called "hunters"; however, these hunters, like almost everyone else in Kentucky, were probably also out in search of land.

The historical marker for Captain John Holder on Athens-Boonesboro Road stands in front of Hall's Restaurant on the east side of Lower Howard's Creek. It has long been believed that Holder's Station was located on the site where the restaurant stands today. The testimony of early settlers, however, proves that the station was on the west side of the creek, along with Holder's residence, ferry, boatyard and warehouse. Nathaniel Hart Jr., son of the pioneer killed by Indians, gave a deposition in *Jouitt's heirs v. Holder's heirs* that refers to the station in passing. He and several others were questioned about the trails that led up the cliff on the west side of the creek. Nathaniel said he resided at Boonesborough and Lower Howard's Creek from December 1780 until the summer of 1786. He stated that he was

> well acquainted with the trace that crossed the Clift of Lower Howards Creek. That it was the usual Way from Boonsboro to McGees Station, Boons Station, Holders Station and Morgans Mill [and] he frequently passed along said trace across Howards Crick and Clift aforesaid from Boonsborough to McGees Station.[5]

According to Hart, in traveling from Boonesborough, one had to cross Lower Howard's Creek and ascend the cliff to get to McGee's Station (near the head of Jouett Creek), Boone's Station (near Athens), Holder's Station and Charles Morgan's Mill (on Boone Creek). Ambrose Bush also testified

Colonel John Holder

regarding the trails up the cliff. He stated, "I used to ride up and down them to mill and knew them most intimately," since these trails were the ones "leading from McGees and Holders Stations to Boonsborough and Bush's Settlement." Whitson George and Eli Vaughn made similar statements.[6]

These depositions prove that Holder's Station was on the west side of the creek. Hart's statement that one had to traverse the creek and the cliff on the way to Holder's Station suggests the station was up on the bluff rather than in the river bottom. This places the station on what used to be called the "Hieronymous farm" and, until recently, was known as "Colonel William Strong's place." The Benjamin Hieronymous family lived there in the 19th century, and the graveyard on the place has legible tombstones that date back to the 1850s. The area is poorly watered today and hauling water up from the river would have been tiring, time consuming work. There is a hillside spring located on the small branch north of the intersection of Amster Grove Road with Athens-Boonesboro Road. The spring was shown on an 1844 map of the road to Combs Ferry[7] and is still flowing today. This spring, and perhaps others, would have made the bluff a desirable location for settlement.

There is no indication that Holder's Station was ever bothered by Indians. There was a well used buffalo trace and Indian trail that followed along Lower Howard's Creek. It was the route used by Chief Blackfish and the Shawnee on their way to the great siege of Boonesborough in 1778. The trail followed the creek down to the Kentucky River and crossed at the ford. A station on the bluff above the cliff may not have been detected.

Another explanation follows the line of thinking espoused by William Clinkenbeard, early resident of Strode's Station which did have problems with Indians. He said, of McGee's Station, the Indians "never troubled them there as they did at Strode's" because McGee's was "way inside."[8] The Indians usually focused their attacks on exterior stations that were more exposed than those on the interior of the settlements. By the time Holder's Station was built, it was "inside" of McGee's and Strode's.

An interesting letter from this period survives in the Draper Collection at the Wisconsin Historical Society. It was written by Richard Henderson to "Captain John Holder at Kentucky, or to any other Persons who has my Books in possession." The former proprietor of the Transylvania Company was trying to recover some fifty volumes he left behind.

> Sir, The above mentioned books with some others, which I cant now recollect, I left at Boonsborough and am informed that they may have since fallen into your hands. Therefore, desire that you will deliver them to Colonel Daniel Boone, and if any of them

should be scattered to other places, shall be much obliged if you would assist in collecting them.[9]

Henderson enclosed a list of the books he was seeking: "Church Bible, Common Prayer Book, Blackstones Commentaries, Smollets letters, Johnstons Dictionarys, Two Sets, Virginia Laws, Voltairs works."

In January 1782, George May sent the following notice to Colonel Robert Patterson and five other officers:

> Gentlemen, you are required to meet this Day at Some convenient place & hold a Court of inquiry into the Conduct of Captain John Holder against whom complaint is made to me. Report your opinion of the same.[10]

It is uncertain if the inquiry was regarding Holder's military duties, his land business or some other complaint. No documents pertaining to this action have been found.

Estill's Defeat

After more than six years of war, George Washington and his Continental Army had lost most of its battles, and in 1781 they were in danger of being rolled up and crushed between British troops converging on Virginia from the north and the south. In October, however, General Washington seized an opportunity to trap the British army at Yorktown and thereby forced the surrender of Lord Cornwallis. The victory signaled the end of the Revolutionary War in the east. But the Ohio Indians had not been subdued, and they continued their attacks on the Kentucky settlements.

In March 1782, a Wyandot war party made a raid into Kentucky. After signs of the Indians had been spotted, Capt. James Estill led a company in pursuit. The next day the Indians attacked Estill's Station, located about 5 miles east of present day Richmond. They killed Jennie Gass, daughter of David Gass, and captured Monk, a slave of Estill's. Estill's company soon caught up with the Wyandot a few miles north of present day Mt. Sterling and a fierce battle ensued that became known as Estill's Defeat. The numbers were about equal on both sides and the combat was hand to hand. Estill and five or six in his company were killed. Several of the men in the engagement had served previously under John Holder at Boonesborough: James Berry, John Colefoot (killed), David Cook, William Cradlebaugh, James Estill (killed), David Lynch, Reuben and Joseph Proctor and John South Jr. (killed).[11]

Colonel John Holder

Caldwell's Invasion of Kentucky

In the summer of 1782, British captains William Caldwell and Alexander McKee began assembling a large army of Indians for an invasion of Kentucky. They recruited among the Shawnee, Delaware, Mingo and Huron. The main body of 300 Indians crossed the Ohio at the mouth of Licking. Scouts were sent to Louisville and other points before a decision was made to attack Bryan's Station. Their strategy was to lure a large number of militia to a predetermined ambush site, thereby destroying Kentucky's defensive capabilities. The plan, which culminated in the Battle of Blue Licks, nearly succeeded. Some historians believe that the attack on Hoy's Station and the subsequent ambush of John Holder's militia at the Upper Blue Licks were coordinated elements of the invasion. Neal Hammon, in his book *Daniel Boone and the Defeat at Blue Licks*, discusses preparations for the invasion in some detail. Hammon argues that the attack at Hoy's Station and Holder's Defeat were not conducted by Caldwell's army.[12]

Incident at Hoy's Station

In early August, a party of Wyandot attacked William Hoy's Station, located about 6 miles southwest of Boonesborough. They kidnapped two boys — Jones Hoy and Jack Callaway — near the station. Jack Callaway's son later described the scene:

> My father...was taken prisoner by the Indians...he said him and his cousin by the name of Hoy was going from home to whare some persons was cutting out a race track and they stopped in a water melon patch to get some mellons.[13]

Jones was a son of William Hoy, and Jack was a son of Richard Callaway.[14]

Holder's Defeat

When notified of the raid on Hoy's Station, John Holder gathered a company and started off in pursuit. Daniel Boone's "Narrative" in John Filson's *Kentucke* includes a brief but oft quoted statement regarding Holder's Defeat.

> The Indians continued their hostilities; and, about the tenth of August following, two boys were taken from Major Hoy's station. This party was pursued by Capt. Holder and seventeen men, who were also defeated, with the loss of four men killed, and one wounded.[15]

Holder's Station

The Kentucky historical highway marker closely follows this version.

> Upper Blue Licks. Aug. 12, 1782, Capt. John Holder and 17 militiamen overtook band of Wyandotte on Great Salt Creek (Licking River) six miles N.E. The Indians had captured two boys, Jones Hoy and Jack Calloway, near Boonesborough. In the skirmish that took place Holder lost four men, and being outnumbered he withdrew without the boys. Hoy held captive seven years, Calloway not so long.[16]

There is some uncertainty concerning the number in Holder's company and the number killed and wounded. Several other versions will be considered below.

Most accounts of Holder's Defeat state that the battle occurred the same day as the attack at Hoy's Station, August 10. The highway marker puts the defeat on August 12. Both are incorrect. Pay vouchers and receipts, issued shortly after the battle, show the event occurred on August 14. This date is verified by a letter written shortly afterwards by Benjamin Logan to the governor of Virginia, Benjamin Harrison.

> Sir, I beg leave to present your Excellency and Council with one of the most melancholy events that has happened in all this western Country. On the 14th instant Captain Holder from Fayette pursued a party of Indians who had made prisoners of a couple of boys in his neighborhood; he overtook them and was repulsed with the loss of four men. On the 16th a considerable army appeared before Bryants station under the command of the noted Simon Girty...[*remainder of the letter deals with Bryan's Station and Battle of Lower Blue Licks*][17]

Logan refers to "Captain Holder from Fayette" which provides another indication that Holder had moved across the Kentucky River from Boonesborough to Holder's Station at the mouth of Lower Howard's Creek.

One of the participants, Samuel Boone, later stated that pursuit did not take place until the morning following the kidnapping of the boys.

> Arrangement was made as quick as the natur of [the] case woude admit to persue the next morning. All men that could be got started in persuit and the command was given to Captain Holder. They pursued the trail of the Indians till they crossed Kentucky River

Colonel John Holder

and not long before the trale became more plainer, by Being joined by more Indians. They pushed on and soon discovered that another party had joined them, and the indians went on till they came to what is called the upper Blue licks.[18]

Holder did not write up his version of events, but we have a secondary account from pioneer Fielding Belt, who owned the land where the defeat occurred. Belt told John Shane, "About 30 maybe 31 years ago, Captain (Colonel) Holder came here to see if he could designate the battle ground. Was commander in the battle fought on Battle run." At first, Holder thought he recognized the spot on the north side of Battle Run, about 1½ miles from Fleming Creek. Fleming Creek lies north of Battle Run and flows from east to west to Licking River. Holder then brought Michael Cassidy to the site and they agreed on another location: a hill "just to the south side of Battle run, 150 yards from its mouth, where it empties into Licking, and 1½ miles below the salt Lick of the Upper Blue Lick."[19] Belt went on to tell Shane what else he learned from Holder.

> Col. Holder's statement was that the Indians had been to Hoy's Station, over the Kentucky river, and taken Hoy's son and two or three horses. Col. Holder raised a party and pursued. At Strode's Station they received an additional supply, among which were captains [Michael] Cassidy and [John] Fleming. The company was increased to 63 men...Col. Holder judged there were four or five hundred Indians.[20]

Presumably Belt was quoting Holder when he put the number in the company at 63. That figure is much larger than Boone's 17. Pioneer James Wade reported another number: "About 35 men from Stroud's [Strode's] pursued to the Upper Blue Licks, where they were defeated in 1782.... There were not more Indians than there were white men." [21] There is a significant discrepancy between Wade's estimate of the Indians' strength and that reported by Belt (400-500). Historian R. S. Cotterill,[a] in an article he wrote on Holder's Defeat, used the figure of 63 men and stated, "All Holder's men were mounted." Cotterill put the Indian strength at about 70 men.[22]

The Wyandot war party did not hurry back to Ohio with their captives but rather left a plain trail for Holder to follow. The company caught up with the war party at the Licking River crossing known as Upper Blue Licks.

---

a Robert S. Cotterill grew up in the village of Battle Run. He graduated from Kentucky Wesleyan College (1904) in Winchester and later returned there to teach history.

Holder's Station

In an article on Holder's Defeat, Professor Cotterill provided a colorful description of the area where the battle took place:

> In the extreme western part of Fleming County, about a mile from the Licking River, where Fleming and Nicholas County meet in mutual reluctance, lies the dispirited little village of Battle Run. It is only a straggling collection of tumble-down houses shambling along a flea-bitten street and lying in the midst of a geography, which seems perennially ambitious of standing on its head. There is a 'run' through the village, which in the summer time is most inordinately dry, and which in the wet season swells to a raging torrent in its course to the Licking River. The village gets its name from the fact that on this 'run' there was fought one of the three or four big Indian fights of our pioneer days.[23]

The village of Battle Run is still shown on maps (on Route 57), but the small stream is now known as Sap Branch.

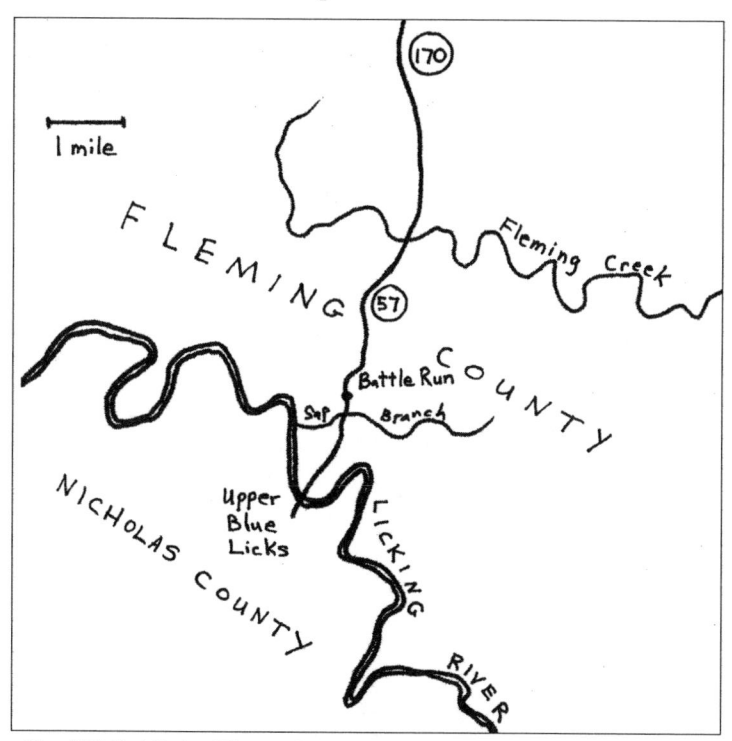

Site of Holder's Defeat, Fleming County. The battle took place on Sap Branch (formerly called Battle Run) in a ravine about where the word "Sap" appears on the map.

Colonel John Holder

Accounts of the subsequent action are confusing and conflicting. All are derived from second hand reports of what the participants said and rely on intermediaries to recount accurately what they heard. The following is the generally agreed upon sequence of events.

Upon reaching Licking River, the men observed "the rocks still wet where the Indians had passed over." Holder's company saw the Indians come into plain view making it obvious to all that they wished to be followed. At that point, they expected the Indians were trying to draw them into an ambush somewhere on the north side of the river. Holder then divided his men. He sent one group under John Constant down the south side of the river. Holder led the other group across the river in pursuit of the Indians who were demonstrating.[24]

Thomas Jones was in Holder's company, and his son wrote down Thomas' recollection of events.

> John Fleming[b] loosened his hunting shirt and clothing, and when asked why he did so, replied, seeing the pains the Indians took to court pursuit, "If we go across, we shall get badly whipped." Holder, Cassidy, and the majority were for meeting the enemy, it was in their estimation what they came for. The brave and spirited Fleming calmly replied, "I can go where any of you dare to go," and all dashed across the stream.[25]

Fleming's statement, if accurate, is conspicuously similar to the officers' response at Lower Blue Licks a few days later to Hugh McGary's reputed challenge, "All who are not damned cowards follow me." Whether McGary ever made such a statement has been called into question.[26]

John Fleming, Thomas Jones, Jerry Poor, John Wilson and others were with Holder. A little over a mile north of the river, they encountered the expected ambush near Battle Run. John Fleming was shot from his horse, and the others dismounted "so as to fight after Indian style, with trees and logs to protect their bodies as much as possible."[27] The fight was brief, as the whites were badly outnumbered, and Holder ordered a hasty withdrawal.

Constant's men, hearing the guns, immediately crossed the river and followed the small stream to the battle site. They arrived to find Holder's

---

[b] John Fleming was appointed one of the first deputy surveyors for Fayette County and ran a number of surveys on Lower Howard's Creek in what later became Clark County. R. S. Cotterill, "John Fleming, Pioneer of Fleming County," *Register of the Kentucky Historical Society* (1951) 49:198.

Holder's Station

men had fallen back. With the Indians now firing on them, Constant's party helped several of the wounded off the field as they retreated back down Battle Run and across the Licking. John Fleming and William Buchanan were among those rescued. It turned out Buchanan's wounds were too painful for him to continue and they left him concealed in a thicket. That night the men camped near present day Sharpsburg, at a place known ever since as Fleming's Pond. Dispatches were sent to nearby stations requesting assistance, but by the time the messengers arrived, Caldwell's army of Indians was already besieging Bryan's Station.[28]

Samuel Boone, one of Holder's men mentioned the battle in his declaration for a Revolutionary War pension:

> He remained in garrison [at Boone's Station] until the 2d of August, when he was again detached under the command of Major John Holder in pursuit of a party of indians, who had taken two boys, named Jones Hoy son of Major Hoy and John Callaway son of Col. Richard Callaway. They overtook the Indians at the upper Blue licks, and in the battle which insued they were defeated and returned to Boone station.[29]

Other pioneers commented on the defeat but were not among Holder's company. Several told their stories to Rev. John Shane. Isaac Clinkenbeard provided his version of the battle:

> At Holder's defeat, John Douglass, George Johnson and one Clemens were killed, and Captain Fleming and Jim Harper wounded. Jim Harper lived several weeks and then died. From Strode's to McGee's Station was about 6 or 7 miles. All the killed and wounded in this battle were from those two stations. Indians had taken Hoy's son. I was down at Boone's Station when the news came, and when I got back they were gone....
>
> When the pursuers came to the place and found the Indians were there, the forces were divided, and Holder led on one the one way and Constant the other down a different way. Holder and his party happened to get a sight of the Indians and found they were so many, and they run. Don't believe any of Holder's men were killed. Constant and his party clapped to and fought. Joe and Richard Proctor were in that battle. Joe Proctor, if living, on Muddy Creek in Madison County.[30]

Colonel John Holder

Clinkenbeard's brother William named some of the participants:

> Clemens lived at McGee's. Harper had a might slighty wound, just across the elbow. Captain Fleming was shot just above the bone in the pit of the stomach. Had married, or did, [Patrick] Donnalson's widow. Joe and Page Proctor.[31]

Josiah Collins gave several additional details in his account:

> A party of Indians had come to the south side of Kentucky and taken Hoy's son and young Dick Calloway prisoners. Colonel Holder and Captain Fleming raised a number of men, don't know how many, and then on Fleming Creek were defeated. Captain John Fleming was wounded and John Clemms was killed. Holder was defeated.[32]

James Wade recalled the following participants:

> Bill Buchanan from Holder's station, and John Clemens from McGee's station were all that were killed, or even hurt. Clemens was left on the ground; but Buchanan was brought off by Manuel Kelly. They killed Douglass at [from] Stroud's.[33]

William Sudduth, who came to Kentucky the year after the battle, wrote Lyman Draper telling what he had learned about the defeat:

> When Holder's party arrived the Indians fired on them and Holder's party returned the fire and retreated. John Harper,[c] John Clemens and John Douglass were killed on the ground. John Fleming, Squire Boon and William Buckhannon were wounded, the latter of whom died of his wounds on his return, about 8 or 10 miles from the battle ground and the balance of the party returned to their respective homes, and the Indians continued on their rout and took the prisoners with them.[34]

Fielding Belt said the men went back to get Buchanan the next morning. "He had drank some water and it had ran out of the wound. They gave him some milk and that ran out too." Buchanan died on a litter while they

---

[c] Sudduth must have meant James Harper instead of John. James' brother John Harper lived for many years a little south of Mt. Sterling. Enoch, *In Search of Morgan's Station*, p. 183.

Holder's Station

were bringing him home.[d] He had been living at Holder's Station and was Margaret Drake's brother.[35]

Belt also told a story about Fleming. After he fell from his horse, "the Indian that shot him then came running towards him to scalp him. Cassidy was near by Fleming, behind a tree loading his gun. Fleming called to him to drive that Indian off that was coming to scalp him. Cassidy said his gun wasn't loaded. Fleming told him that made no difference, the Indian wouldn't know that. So Cassidy ran out with his gun and the Indian took off."[36] Cassidy helped Fleming on his horse and they both got away.

When Lyman Draper visited Upper Blue Licks in 1866, he interviewed as many locals as he could about the battle. Michael Cassidy's son Francis told Draper that there were graves near the battle site "of three or four persons who fell there." Francis added that "William Clemens, who lived and died in Fleming County, died about 40 years ago, was in Holder's Upper Blue Lick fight — an old bachelor." James Jones told of a man named Constant who was killed in the battle. Though Jones said the man was buried on the battle ground and that he had often seen his grave, no other report is known of a Constant being killed there.[37]

The engagement at Upper Blue Licks immediately preceded the disastrous defeat at the Lower Blue Licks on August 19, which took place only 10 miles to the northwest. Two days before, Levi Todd wrote to Stephen Trigg to tell him of Holder's Defeat: "I last night [August 15] Received an Account from Colonel Boon of Captain Holders defeat at the Blue Licks and agreable to his desire ordered twenty men to Join others and go to the Blue Licks."[38] Just as Todd's men were ready to leave, an express arrived telling him that Indians were attacking Bryan's Station and he was needed there. Todd's brother, Colonel John Todd, led a company of 180 men from Bryan's Station in pursuit of the Indians. In the ensuing engagement at Lower Blue Licks, 77 Kentuckians were killed and many wounded. It was the most costly defeat Kentucky had ever suffered.[39] The two bloody battles, occurring within days of each other, stunned frontier residents. Several months would pass before George Rogers Clark could organize a retaliatory raid upon the Ohio tribes.

---

[d] John Floyd later provided another version of his brother-in-law William Buchanan's death. "Poor Billey Buchanan was wounded a few days before the defeat at Licking. He went with a party in pursuit of some Indians who had captured a boy to near the upper Salt Springs where they were attacked by a superior number of enemy and obliged to retreat. His dastardly company all left him in the woods, where he lay several days before his brother [James Buchanan] found him then alive, but he expired before he could carry him home." John Floyd to William Preston, March 28, 1783, Draper MSS 17CC 144-148.

Colonel John Holder

* * *

Pay vouchers, submitted shortly after the battle at Upper Blue Licks, provide some additional information. We learn from a number of documents that Holder's engagement was initially referred to as "Constant's Defeat." This suggests that most of the victims were in Constant's group, as Isaac Clinkenbeard stated in his account. One of the documents, "a list of appraisments of horses etc. lost at Capt. Constants Defeat on the 14th of August 1782 at the Upper Blue licks," mentions several names that do not appear in any other accounts: James Buchanan, Aquilla White, William Stevenson and John Long. The same list also includes the names of John Douglas, Emanuel Kelly and Elizabeth Clemons, presumed widow of John Clemons.[40]

The following is a tentative list of men in Holder's company. Though far short of 63, it does include four who were killed on the field. The names Finley and Vaughn are from Professor Cotterill, but their accuracy cannot be determined as his sources were not stated.[41] (Abbreviations are k, killed; w, wounded; and d, died from wounds.)

Partial List of John Holder's Company at Upper Blue Licks

Capt. John Holder	Capt. John Constant
Samuel Boone	Squire Boone
James Buchanan	William Buchanan (d)
Michael Cassidy	John Clemons (k)
William Clemons	John Douglas (k)
____ Finley	John Fleming (w)
James Harper (d)	George Johnson (k)
Thomas Jones	Emanuel Kelly
John Long	Jeremiah Poor
Joseph Proctor	Little Page Proctor
William Stevenson	____ Vaughn
Aquilla White	John Wilson (k)

Several of the men killed at Upper Blue Licks have mistakenly been included in some accounts of the casualties from Lower Blue Licks. These include John Clemons/Clements, John Douglas/Douglass and John Wilson.[42]

Clark's Campaign, Fall 1782

Less than two weeks after the Blue Licks defeats, Indians attacked and burned Kincheloe's Station, about 7 miles northeast of present day

Holder's Station

Bardstown. On their retreat the Indians killed several settlers at McAfee's Station on Salt River. Several other stations, including Squire Boone's at Painted Stone, were abandoned at that time.[43]

Kentuckians looked to George Rogers Clark to lead an army against the Ohio tribes in an attempt to finally subdue the Indians and end the raids on the settlements. When volunteers did not turn out in sufficient numbers, others had to be drafted. Clark sold 3,500 acres of his own land to finance the expedition. There were 39 companies totaling 1,128 men, mostly from Jefferson and Lincoln. Only five or six companies were raised in Fayette County, which was still reeling from the losses at Blue Licks. The army crossed the Ohio in early November and marched up the valley of the Little Miami River, the same trail followed in 1780. After reaching the site of Old Chillicothe, they turned west towards the Great Miami River. Their objective was the Shawnee village of New Chillicothe, also known as New Piqua or the Standing Stone. Clark sent 500 men under Hugh McGary to take Alexander McKee's Town and 100 men under Daniel Boone to take Willstown, both just a few miles away. The Indians had nearly completed their evacuation of all these towns when Clark's men arrived. His army plundered and destroyed what was left. Clark also sent 150 men under Benjamin Logan to take Pierre Loramie's trading post. Loramie escaped but all his goods were captured and his cabins burned. While few Indians were killed, their towns and large stores of provisions were destroyed. The intent was to force the Indians to spend their time seeking food and building shelter in the hopes they would have little time to annoy the white settlers. One of the few casualties on the mission was Capt. William McCracken. He suffered a minor wound which became infected, and he died on the journey home.[44]

Lyman Draper's biographical note on John Holder states that Holder was along on this campaign. His name is not found on the rolls listed for Fayette County companies; however, it is quite possible that those rolls are incomplete. Draper's conclusions are usually based on sound information. At this time, however, we cannot confirm Holder's participation on the expedition.[45]

Holder Family Comes to Kentucky

In 1784, John Holder returned to the Blue Ridge of Virginia for his family. He brought them out by way of the Ohio River. They departed by boat from Redstone Old Fort, a popular port of debarkation for immigrants coming to Kentucky. Redstone (now Brownsville, Pennsylvania) was located about 30 miles up the Monongahela River from Pittsburgh. The Reuben Rankins

Colonel John Holder

family — Blue Ridge neighbors in Virginia — came out with Holder's party. What we know about the trip comes from an interview many years later with Reuben's son, John Rankins. He told Reverend Shane, "We Came to Kentucky in 1784. Got to Boonesborough in May and spent the first summer there." Rankins then gave a brief description of their journey.

> Took water at Red stone old fort and came down the Ohio. Landed to take in wood and graze our horses every day. There were five or six boats before us that we were to have been in company with, but they had gotten a little start from the very first in Virginia. Were from our neighborhood. Pretty much the same neighborhood. Old Luke Holder lived on top of the Blue Ridge.
>
> We went by Strode's and McGee's in our first coming out. We had talked of going to Louisville, but we had Holder along, bringing out his father's family, a brother and sister, and he piloted us through. We didn't go by Bryant's Station. There was but a little clearing in the cane at McGee's and one or two cabins. Cane very thick all around it.[46]

We conclude from Rankins' description that Holder brought out his father Luke, brother Francis and sister Margaret. All three show up in Kentucky records after that time. Whether or not his mother came out, or whether she was even living at that time, is uncertain. Holder's family probably lived with him at the station.

While the Indian threat had subsided somewhat, there were still isolated raids and most of the settlers in the area were still forted at Boonesborough, Strode's or McGee's. When not hunting or working on their land, most settlers lived within the security of the small stockaded stations and forts. William Clinkenbeard, one of the first settlers at Strode's Station in 1779, told Reverend Shane, "We were seven years in the fort before we got out."[47]

The Fayette County clerk's office was destroyed in a fire in 1803, so we have few court records for this period to document the activities of Holder, his family and others living at Holder's Station. Some of their dealings can be gleaned from other sources.

Luke Holder

After John Holder brought his father to Kentucky, Luke eventually moved into his own house on his son's land. There are no deeds in Fayette or Clark for Luke buying or selling real estate. The tax rolls listed his property as horses and cattle but no slaves or land. If Luke was 20 to 25 years old when

Holder's Station

John was born, then he would have been between 50 and 55 when he came to Kentucky and between 65 and 70 when he appeared for the last time in Clark County records (1799).

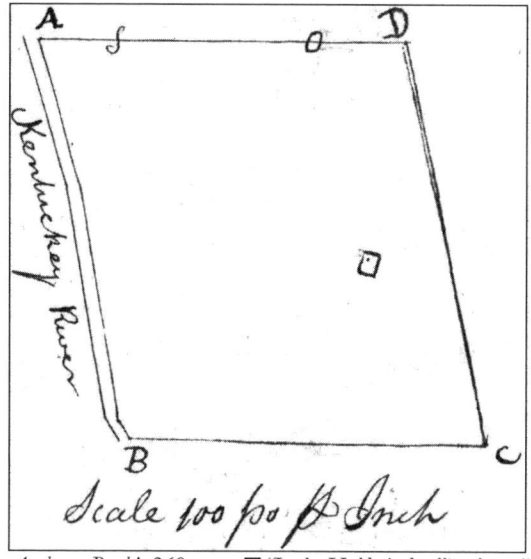

Ambrose Bush's 260 acres. ☐ *"Luke Holder's dwelling house"*
C *"walnut on Jewits creek."* [48]

In January 1799, the sheriff auctioned about 260 acres of John Holder's land to satisfy a judgment rendered against him in Clark County court. Ambrose Bush Jr. purchased this tract which lay on the Kentucky River and Jouett Creek. It seems a little surprising to learn that Holder put up for sale the tract where his father was living at the time. Not surprisingly, a month after he bought the land, Ambrose Bush filed a suit "in ejectment" to have Luke put off the property. John Holder was made a defendant in the case and was represented by Henry Clay, who was then practicing law in Clark County. The suit was settled out of court. Bush moved to discontinue the action, and the court ordered him to pay the defendant's costs. Bush must have come to some arrangement with Luke but no further information was given in the record, except that Bush had to pay the court cost in the case, which was 30 shillings plus $2.32. The survey map made during the suit shows Luke's "dwelling house" north of the Kentucky River and west of Jouett Creek.[49]

Luke's wife may have died the year before the above lawsuit. A jury was convened by the county coroner, Benjamin Dod Wheeler, in August 1798 to conduct an "Inquest on the body of Mrs. Holder, deceased." Coroners

Colonel John Holder

were charged with investigating the deaths of "any person slain, drowned or otherwise by misadventure suddenly dead." They were to determine if a crime had been committed and, if so, to prosecute the offender.[50] A copy of the inquest was found among the loose papers in the Clark County courthouse attic:

> An inquest on the death of mrs. Holder
> a Jury being Sworn & witnesses being Sworn to wit
>   James Morrow, Caleb Browning, John Blackwell, Eli Vaughn, Daniel Burch, Edward Gillespie, Sam R. Combs, William Young, Zealy Moss, Lenard Hill, Moses Parrish, Enis Vaughn
>   We of the Jury Called upon for the Examnation in to the death of mrs Holder by witnesses & the best emformiation we can git beleave her to be accessary to her own death
>   Samuel R Combs, Foreman
> august the 4th 1798
>   as signed by me Benjamin Dod Wheeler, Coroner[51]

The jury concluded that Mrs. Holder's death was a suicide. John Holder's wife Fanny was still living at that time. The only other Holders on the tax rolls for Clark County were Luke and Francis — Mrs. Holder was probably the wife of one of them.

There is no record of Luke's death in Clark County. He left no will and no administrator was appointed for his estate. No grave has been located. Since no record of him is found after 1799, Luke may have died soon after the suit with Ambrose Bush. John Holder's grandson, William D. Holder, wrote that Luke, after coming out from Virginia, "lived and died near the Kentucky river."[52]

Francis Holder

Francis Holder left even less of a trail to document his life than his father had. He was probably born in Fauquier County, Virginia, between 1759 and 1761. There are no records of him serving in the Revolutionary War or in any military engagements on the Kentucky frontier.

Although no marriage record has been found for Francis, he may have married a daughter of Josiah Jackson. John Holder had a number of close associations with the Jackson family. Josiah Jackson and his son Francis lived at Holder's Station for a time. Josiah Jackson's will, written in 1821, listed a daughter named Edah Holder.[53] The name of Edah's husband is not known. Josiah Jackson married in 1769, so his first child could have

Holder's Station

been born about 1770. If Francis and Edah married in Kentucky sometime after Francis came out with his parents (1784) and before Clark County was formed (1793), then their marriage record would have been lost. (Fayette County marriage records prior to 1803 were destroyed in a fire.) This is speculation, however, and is only supported by the fact that there were no other known Holders in Kentucky in early times for Edah to have married.

Edah Holder was still living in 1821 when Josiah Jackson listed her as a daughter in his will.[54] If she was the wife of Francis, then the Mrs. Holder who committed suicide in 1798 could have been Luke's wife.

Francis Holder always lived near his brother John and never bought or sold property in Fayette or Clark. He shows up repeatedly as a witness on John Holder's land transactions and signed his name with a trained hand. We also find his signature on a number of petitions to the Virginia General Assembly: to create a new county with the seat at Boonesborough (1787), to create new seats of the supreme court at Lexington and Baird's Town (now Bardstown), to create a new county out of parts of Bourbon and Fayette (1789), and to create new warehouses for tobacco inspection, one on William Bush's land and one on John Holder's land (1789). In 1792, Francis placed a notice in Lexington's newspaper, the *Kentucky Gazette*, stating that he "found a mare near Colonel John Holder's in Fayette County." He signed a petition in Clark County for a new road down Boone Creek to the Kentucky River.[55]

Francis appeared regularly on the tax rolls. From 1792 through 1796 he was taxed for one slave under age 16, several horses and cows, but no land. He was not listed in the 1810 census, but he may be the male over age 45 living with his nephew John W. Holder (the son of Colonel Holder) in Clark County.

A possible clue to Francis' lack of success comes from the trial of Jacob Smith, who was accused of stealing a silver watch from Edmund Callaway. Callaway, a brother of Flanders who married Jemima Boone, kept a tavern in Winchester. The trial took place in 1805. In the course of his testimony, Callaway happened to state that "F. Holder was at my house Drunk."[56]

The Clark County delinquent tax roll for 1816 lists Francis Holder "gone to Missourie." However, he may have only gone across the river to Madison County. He is found there in the 1820 census, his household consisting of one male over 45 years of age and fourteen slaves. Francis would have been about 59-61 years old in 1820. The number of slaves is difficult to explain, unless he was listing them as overseer for someone else.

Colonel John Holder

If Francis did not go to Missouri, perhaps one of his children did. A Luke Holden/Holder married Elizabeth Bryan on January 13, 1814 in St. Charles County, Missouri. Luke served as a private in the Missouri militia under Lt. Col. Dodge during the War of 1812.[57]

Margaret Holder

John Holder's sister Margaret rounds out the known family members who came to Kentucky in 1784. George Rout may have come out with the Holders on that trip. The Routs were also from Loudoun County, and the Holders must have known them there. George was living at Holder's Station in 1787. Margaret married George Rout on June 11, 1793. Luke gave his consent which indicates that Margaret was under age 21 at the time. Her brother John signed as a witness, and brother Francis was the surety. The ceremony was performed by Robert Elkin, minister of the Lower Howard's Creek Baptist Church. Church records indicate that neither George nor Margaret were members of the congregation.[58]

Margaret married with the permission of her father Luke, meaning she was not yet 21 years old, the age of consent in Kentucky at that time.[59] Her marriage bond was dated June 9, 1793, so she was born after June 9, 1772. Thus, she would have been at least 18 years younger than her brother John (born about 1754). Family researchers have suggested that Margaret and John had different mothers, because of the great age difference; however, they were assuming John was born about 1736 and, thus, was more like 36 years older than Margaret. While evidence is inconclusive, John and Margaret could have had the same mother.

In 1798, Rout paid £30 for 100 acres of land on Jouett Creek. His brother-in-law John Holder put the land up for sale to satisfy a judgment against him in a lawsuit. The tract was on the west side of Jouett Creek, less than a mile from the Kentucky River, near the area where Luke Holder lived. George appeared irregularly on the tax rolls. In 1801, he was charged for one slave and four horses. In 1806 George and Margaret, along with Benjamin Grimes were subpoenaed to appear in court to testify for the plaintiff in a case of debt. It is uncertain when George died. He left no will in Clark County and no administrator was appointed for his estate.[60]

Margaret married Randolph "Randle" Bivion in May 1816. Bivion was a widower and had a number of adult children when he married Margaret. It is uncertain if Margaret had children with either of her husbands. In 1812, Randle paid $400 for a piece of land that became his homeplace: 100 acres on Snow Creek, a tributary of Lulbegrud in present day Powell County. He later purchased 11 acres adjoining this tract. Randle worked as a farmer but

Holder's Station

also made and sold whiskey, though not always legally. He paid a ten dollar fine in 1813 "for Retailing Spiritious liquor without license." An 1824 court order refers to a road that goes by "Bivions old still house."[61]

Randle Bivion died in August 1839. His will left Margaret the plantation "on which we now reside." The remaining property, including one slave, was divided among his children: Bazell Bivion, Charles Bivion, Betsey Bivion, Hannah Corbin, Polly Rogers, Rachel Mitchell, Nancy Fish and Sally Eaton (deceased). Bazell received 65 acres of land. The delinquent tax list for 1843 shows Margaret owing $3 and Bazell, then residing in Bath County, owing $3.90.[62]

A court record dated August 1844 gives an indication of the unhappy circumstances Margaret faced after the death of her husband: "Ordered that the keeper of the poor house take into his charge Peggy Bivin, a poor person of this county." A voucher submitted to the county court reveals that Arthur Everman was paid $4 for "Taking care of Margaret Bivin four weeks" and another $3 "For taking Margaret Bivin to the poor house."[63]

Sadly, it appears that none of the family members were willing or able to provide for Margaret in her declining years. In 1841, three years before she went to the poorhouse, Randle Bivion's surviving children sold Margaret's homeplace to James Wood. Randle's will gave Margaret a life interest in the land and she obviously still was living. The circumstances surrounding this transaction are unknown.[64]

The Clark County poorhouse, which provided care for indigent residents, was located on Ironworks Road where the county fairgrounds are today. The cemetery there, where Margaret was probably buried, is still in use.

Gary Holder

Gary Holder lived for a number of years on Lower Howard's Creek and later moved to the Lulbegrud area. An 1813 court order lists Gary Holder, along with Francis Holder, Eli Vaughn, Samuel R. Combs and others, as hands assigned to work on the road from Combs' Warehouse to Jouett Creek. He was the right age to have been a son of Francis. His signature is found on a deposition he gave in *Jouett v. Holder's heirs*.[65]

Gary Holder was the surety on Randle Bivion's marriage bond in 1816. Gary and Mary Everman were joined in matrimony on December 7, 1817, by the Baptist minister, Thomas Boone. She may have been a member of the large Everman clan who lived on Lulbegrud Creek near Red River. One of these Evermans (Arthur) took Margaret Bivion to the poorhouse. By 1819, Gary was living in the Lulbegrud area and was listed as a road hand there, along with neighbors Jacob, John and James Everman. During this

Colonel John Holder

period, Gary's name appeared on Clark County's delinquent tax rolls with "no effects," meaning he had no taxable assets.[66] Although his presence in the county can be documented between 1810 and 1820, he was not listed in the Clark County census for either of those years indicating that he may have resided in a family member's household, possibly with Margaret Bivion or one of the Evermans. His fate is unknown.

A Gary Holder was listed in the Montgomery County census from 1810 through 1850. This Gary Holder was born about 1784 in Kentucky and was a cooper by occupation. One would expect that there was actually only one Gary Holder, but there is no good explanation for him being a resident in both Montgomery and Clark during the same period (1810-1820).

Other Holders

The only other Holder in early Clark County who cannot be placed is Benjamin Holder. Benjamin was listed as "insolvent" on the delinquent tax list for 1818. He appeared on the 1820 census for Fayette County, where he was living in the Boone Creek area. Living nearby was Elijah Holder. Both were married; Elijah's household included six children and Benjamin had none. Benjamin and Elijah could have been the children of Francis, but there is no evidence to prove it.[67]

Descriptions of John Holder

From bits and pieces of old interviews and letters, we can put together a composite description of Holder's physical appearance and other characteristics noted by the early pioneers.

From Daniel Trabue (knew Holder personally) description of the great siege at Boonesborough in his memoir:

> Captain Holder, a large strong man, took big stones and cast them from the fort over the bank....[68]

From Daniel Bryan (knew Holder personally) interviews with Draper and Shane:

> He was a fine looking young man, full six feet high, of a fair complextion, gray Eyes, &c.[69]
>
> Colonel Holder being a fat man, and over fatigued with the rapidity of the journey [on the Paint Creek expedition], was left in the care of William Beasley to bring on next day.[70]

Holder's Station

From George M. Bedinger (knew Holder personally) interview with Draper:

> He was a large, 6 foot man, not brilliant, yet useful. Dark complexion.[71]

From Richard P. Holder (grandson) letter to Draper:

> He lived to be 62 years old.[e] His height was about ordinary, weighed generally 160 to 170. Was a man of very fine appearance. Said to be when in his prime very handsome and a man of a good deal more than an ordinary share of agility & strength.[72]

Richard G. Williams (married Holder's daughter Catherine) letter to Draper. He quotes Samuel R. Combs, who knew Holder personally:

> S. R. Combs, somewhat conspicuous in the War of 1812, now dead, who was also Son in law to Col. Holder & Brother to Leslie, has informed me that Col. Holder was a man of rather uncommonly commanding appearance with great energy of character.[73]

From Lyman C. Draper (historian) collection of frontier materials, which included all the above descriptions:

> Colonel Holder was six feet in height, heavily framed and of fine appearance.[74]

We are faced with several difficult to resolve contradictory statements ("dark complexion" versus "fair complextion" and "being a fat man" versus "weighed generally 160 to 170"). Overall, however, we get the impression that John Holder was a tall, physically imposing figure, and that he was a strong, energetic man of action.

Clark's Wabash Expedition

By the year 1786, Kentucky was far along in her effort to separate from Virginia. Three statehood conventions had been held and a petition sent to the Virginia Assembly requesting "Sovereignty & Independence" for the district of Kentucky. One of the major issues was Virginia's inability to

---

[e] Since this is known to be inaccurate, Richard P. Holder's comments must be given less credence than others.

Colonel John Holder

provide adequate defense against Indian attacks on the frontier. Hostilities worsened during the early part of that year, especially in Jefferson County. One of the victims was Colonel William Christian, Patrick Henry's close friend and brother-in-law. Raids were coming from tribes on the Wabash River, in addition to the traditional rivals, the Shawnee. The Wabash River forms the boundary between present day Illinois and Indiana.

A military convention was held at Harrodsburg that August to decide on Kentucky's defense. George Rogers Clark was asked to lead a campaign to destroy the Indian towns. The plan was to draft 2,500 militia men for a campaign to the Wabash. They were to rendezvous at the Falls of Ohio in September. Only 1,200 men showed up by the appointed date. Clark sent an officer from each county back to round up additional troops and ordered Benjamin Logan to lead this contingent against the Shawnee towns in Ohio. Clark took the army collected at the Falls and marched them to the Illinois country. While Logan's mission was relatively successful, Clark's campaign was fraught with difficulties. Provisions were low to start with, so he went first to Vincennes to await his supply boats, which were subsequently delayed. By the time the boats got to Vincennes, some thought the supplies were too low to mount an assault on the Wabash towns. In spite of Clark's pleading, the Lincoln County men refused to proceed on short rations.[75]

At this point, Clark was forced to change his strategy. He proposed to occupy Vincennes with a body of troops, which would screen Kentucky from attack by the Wabash Indians, and he made overtures to the Indians to conclude a peace treaty. Needed supplies would be impressed from locals. In addition, he intended to confiscate by court-martial goods belonging to some Spanish and French merchants. The plan was accepted by his council of officers. John Holder was elected to head the garrison.

> Post Vincent, October 8, 1786
> Pursuant to the General Orders the field Officers assembled and are unanimous of opinion that a Garrison at this place will be of essential Service to the District of Kentucky and that Supplies may be had in the District more that Sufficient for their Support by Impressment or Otherwise under the direction of a Commissary to be appointed for this purpose pursuant to the authority vested in the field Officers of the District by the Executive of Virginia.
> Resolved as our Opinion that two field Officers with 250 Men (exclusive of the Company of Artillery to be commanded by Capt. Valentine T. Dalton) be recruited to garrison Post Vincent.

Holder's Station

That Major John Holder act as a field Officer over the Troops in this Service. Resolved That the Inhabitants of St. Vincent ought to be paid for the Damage done them by the Army and that the Magistrates ascertain the amount and the offenders in this instance ought to be punished.

Isaac Cox[76]

From this document, we also learn that John Holder had been promoted from captain to the rank of major. Typically, a captain commanded a company, while a major commanded a regiment composed of a number of companies.

Upon Clark's return to Kentucky, the statehood convention, then sitting at Danville, agreed to the plan to garrison Vincennes but censured Clark for the confiscation of goods by court-martial.[77]

Clark reported in December that "the garrison now at Post Vincennes is about one hundred strong." The Wabash Indians agreed to peace in the spring of 1787. Presumably, Holder and his garrison returned home at that time.[78]

Six years later, the French merchants at Vincennes were still trying to get satisfaction for their losses. They sent a petition to President George Washington praying for relief and charging that

> General Clarke embodied a number of his followers and stationed them at this place under the command of a John Holder, and compelling the Inhabitants to supply them with Provisions and Fuel…Your Suppliants were arrested and imprisoned on the 17th of October [1786] and their Effects seized by the said General George Clarke, John Holder and other officers, who at a Court-martial tried and condemned your Suppliants, forfeited their Effects to the United States and appropriated the whole as they thought most proper.[79]

Charges that Clark acted illegally were filed with the Virginia government and Congress, but restitution was never made by either.

It has been written that Holder received a certificate for his services on the Wabash Expedition based on an act of the Kentucky legislature. A possible document to that effect, an "Act for the Relief of Henry Brock," is confusingly written.

> He was proprietor of a certificate for about 30 pounds, granted to John Holder, for services in the Wabash expedition, and had lost

Colonel John Holder

it. This act authorized the renewal of it. Approved December 20, 1802.[80]

One can interpret this one of two ways. Either Holder was awarded the certificate and he assigned it to Brock who lost it, or Brock was awarded a certificate which was issued to Holder (perhaps as his commanding officer) who lost it. The wording seems to favor the former meaning but we cannot be certain.

* * *

John Holder was promoted to major sometime after his move from Boonesborough to Holder's Station. He held that rank during George Rogers Clark's Wabash Campaign in 1786. Documents dated 1789 and later refer to him as colonel, indicating another promotion. An example is the petition submitted to the Virginia Assembly requesting establishment of a tobacco warehouse. Robert Todd, a county justice for Fayette, attached a note to the petition stating that the warehouse would be located "on Colonel John Holder's land on the Kentucky River." In June 1792, prior to the formation of Clark County, a notice in the Lexington newspaper announced that a stray horse had been found, "a mare near Colonel John Holder's in Fayette County."[81] This indicates that Holder had been promoted to colonel but no record of the promotion has been found.

Military Career
By the time Clark County was formed in 1792, John Holder had been in active military service for 18 years. He had fought against the Indians (Dunmore's War, 1774), then against the British (Revolutionary War in Virginia, 1775-1777) and finally against the Indians again (Revolutionary War and Indian Wars in Kentucky, 1777-1792). He participated in most of the important campaigns of his times. There is no indication that he ever ducked service for personal gain or fear for his own safety. That he served with distinction is indicated by his steady rise through the ranks. Many of his compatriots spoke highly of him. Although he was for periods of time totally engrossed in land speculation and other business enterprises, he still managed to accept additional military duties. He became the first regimental commander of the Clark County militia, with all of its attendant responsibilities, and continued in that post until his untimely death in 1799. His demise brought to an end 25 years of service. With little risk of exaggeration, we can say that John Holder belongs on the list of Kentucky's most notable military figures.

Chapter 8
Land Speculator

Much of the narrative to this point has focused on Holder's military career, his family and the settlement of his station on Lower Howard's Creek.

In 1781, John Holder took a major step in the direction of land speculation. On September 11, he purchased six Virginia treasury warrants authorizing him to 6,100 acres of land for which he paid £9,760. These sequentially numbered warrants (#6448 to #6453) were paid for in full that day with "continental money."[1] It is not clear where Holder came up with so much ready cash. There does not seem to have been enough time or opportunity on the frontier to acquire that amount. It is quite possible that he had backers who put up the money.

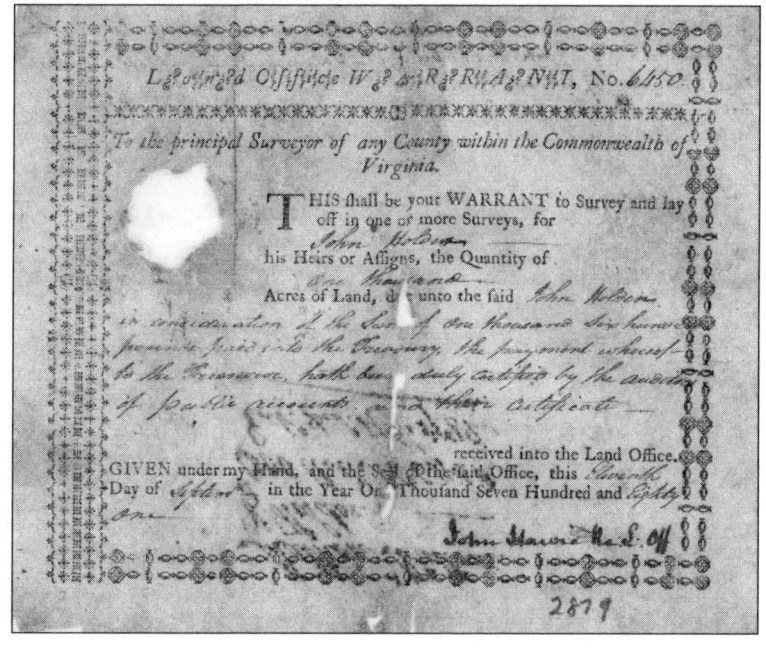

John Holder's Treasury Warrant. Virginia treasury warrant issued to John Holder on September 11, 1781, for 1,000 acres for which he paid £1,600.

Colonel John Holder

Over the next few years, Holder partnered with others to enter, survey and patent numerous tracts. (The terms "patent" and "grant" were used interchangeably.) Men who performed this service were called "locators" and many found the business lucrative. They were responsible for finding vacant land, marking the tracts, making the entry at the surveyor's office, accompanying the surveyor to the land as his pilot and marker, and paying the surveyor and office fees. For this service the locator received an agreed upon portion of the land, which could be up to half the acreage. It was recognized to be a risky occupation, as the threat of Indians was always present and the work involved a small group far from the safety of the stations. Many surveyors were killed by Indians.

Matthew Walton Partnership

In tracing two of the 1,000 acre treasury warrants Holder purchased in September 1781, we find that he assigned 500 acres of each warrant to Matthew Walton. The wealthy Walton was a serious land speculator himself. General Matthew Walton (1759-1819) came from a noted Virginia family. His cousin George Walton was one of the signers of the Declaration of Independence. Matthew Walton was educated at the College of William and Mary. He was a soldier in the Revolution and fought at the Battle of King's Mountain. Walton was in Kentucky early surveying and later acquired title to over 200,000 acres. Walton is recognized as the founder of Washington County, Kentucky, and the county seat of Springfield. The courthouse was built on his land. He was a delegate to Kentucky's statehood conventions of 1785, 1786 and 1787, a member of the Virginia Convention that ratified the U.S. Constitution, and a member of the convention that formed Kentucky's first constitution in 1792. He saw long service in the Kentucky militia, eventually rising to the rank of major general. Walton was one of the first justices of Washington County, was elected a representative and senator to the Kentucky legislature and served two terms in the U.S. Congress. He was reputed to have been the richest man in Kentucky when he died.[2]

Walton also happened to be a first cousin of Holder's wife Fanny. Matthew Walton's father (Sherwood) and Fanny's mother (Frances) were brother and sister. Holder and Walton eventually became joint owners of nearly 8,500 acres. Holder later formed other partnerships with other wealthy speculators, which helps explain how he was able to acquire large acreages of land for himself.

By late 1782, Holder must have been completely occupied in the land business. We find him making Fayette County entries on November 29 and 30, December 3, 17, 18, 21 and 30, 1782, January 17 and February 19,

Land Speculator

1783. He also made an entry in Lincoln County on January 10, 1783.[3] We learn from a deposition in a lawsuit that Holder visited the Fayette County surveyor so often he became a recognized face at the land office:

> Deponent thinks that John Holder, Joshua Bennett, Col. Daniel Boon, Thomas Swearengen, James Parberry, Timothy Peyton and John Fleming attended surveyors office of Fayette county in January 1783, as this deponent saw these men at said survey office frequently in January and February 1783 or the most of them, and this deponent saw entries of land in said office said to have been made by these men at about that time.[4]

Another pioneer said that in the winter of 1782 and spring of 1783 he often saw Holder, John McIntyre, William Calk, Jesse Cartwright, and Bartlett Searcy at the surveyor's office.[5] All the above men were deputy surveyors at the time for Fayette or Lincoln, except for Holder and Parberry.

Based on information provided in his entries, we can discern two of Holder's objectives. The first was to acquire speculative land holdings in partnership with Matthew Walton. The second was to secure ownership of the land north of Kentucky River lying between the mouth of Boone Creek and the mouth of Lower Howard's Creek, which he had settled on.

In the partnership with Walton, we find Walton purchasing the treasury warrants and Holder locating, marking and entering the tracts. Holder's 25 entries during that period (November 1782-March 1783) covered 23,566 acres; of that total nearly 20,000 acres was entered jointly with Walton. While these entries were made over a four month period — twelve of them on December 17-18 — locating the land must have taken much longer. The tracts were spread over a large area, being located in the counties of Fayette, Clark, Bourbon, Fleming, Mason and Campbell. Some of these claims cannot be tracked further after the entry was made; however, it appears that most of the entries proceeded to surveys and resulted in grants to Holder and Walton as joint owners.[6]

Holder's other objective was to acquire the land north of Kentucky River where he built his station. There was some urgency to this task since he had already relocated from Boonesborough and was living on the tract. In contrast to his work with Walton, the efforts on his own behalf appear singularly unsuccessful. None secured the land where he was living. Of the eight entries he made for himself during this period, none were even surveyed. One was amended, four were withdrawn. His entries on land between Boone Creek and Jouett Creek were trumped by William Triplett's

Colonel John Holder

superior claim. On the entries between Jouett Creek and Lower Howard's Creek, Holder made several attempts to work around the claims of George May, Richard Hickman and William Bush. He then learned that this whole area had been awarded to John Howard by the Virginia Land Commission.

Finally, on June 14, 1783, the Fayette County entry book shows Holder withdrawing his most recent claim on Lower Howard's Creek. On the very next line, John Howard's entered 1,000 acres that Holder made a deal to purchase. While Holder's efforts seem awkward, if not inept, it should be recalled that land so close to Boonesborough was much more likely to be subject to conflicting claims than land some distance away. Another obstacle was the fact that John Howard was awarded his claim by the commissioners in the winter of 1779 then he returned to Botetourt County, Virginia. Howard did not move out to Fayette County until about 1786. He also delayed entering his preemption for more than three years after the land office opened. When the grant was issued in 1787, Holder finally made good on his efforts to gain title to the land he had settled on.

Holder must have learned his skills as a locator from others. He had some experienced men to train him, including Matthew Walton himself, George Michael Bedinger and the Swearingens, Thomas and Benoni. Holder spent the summer of 1779 in the company of the latter men and others from Berkeley County, Virginia, who came out for the sole purpose of securing land. These men were surveyors as well, and Holder must have acquired this skill while working with them.

Holder also was well acquainted with the surveyors at Boonesborough and Strode's Station, including William Bailey Smith, Enoch Smith, William Calk, James French, Jesse Hodges, James McMillan, Bartlett Searcy, John South, John Fleming, William Sudduth and others. He managed to have himself appointed a deputy surveyor for Fayette County in 1783 and later was a deputy surveyor for Clark County after it was formed. I have never found an official survey that he performed. He used various surveyors on land he located, most frequently Justinian "Jesse" Cartwright. Except for his Lower Howard's Creek tract, Holder, surprisingly, does not even appear as the pilot or marker on land surveyed for him. Perhaps, his busy schedule precluded that task, which he found others to perform for him.[7]

In late 1783, Holder again changed the focus of his land business. He ended the collaboration with Matthew Walton and began locating for other speculators. He made only a handful of entries during this period, but they were for extraordinarily large tracts. In December he entered 10,687 acres with Thomas Swearingen and John Fleming. The tract was on the south (now Levisa) fork of Big Sandy River, near the head of Licking River. Holder's

Land Speculator

other entries were closer to home: He claimed tracts of 49,665¼ acres with John Taylor as well as 50,612½ and 6,212 acres for himself. Holder also located 33,815 acres for Richard Graham, and he obtained title to 16,125½ acres of this tract as his share. These four contiguous tracts were in the present day counties of Clark, Montgomery, Powell and Estill. It took a number of years to carry all of these claims to survey and grant.[8]

These four large tracts totaled over 140,000 acres. Such large patents were made on what were called "covering surveys," meaning the patentee knew the area included many prior claims. By covering these other claims, the patentee hoped to end up with all the land in between. Although this sounded good in theory, especially while Virginia treasury warrants were selling so cheaply (£160 per 100 acres), the practice produced questionable results. Other speculators had the same idea, which resulted in overlapping covering surveys. For example, Holder's 50,612½ acres and Holder and Taylor's 49,665¼ acres were shingled over by two huge patents: 108,344 acres of Thomas Franklin and 60,000 acres of William Fitzhugh et al.[9]

We know that Holder received a good title to a little over 16,000 acres of Graham's patent, but he had a mixed record on the other three. Holder assigned his 6,212 acre survey to Benjamin Grayson, who received the patent. Grayson was a deputy surveyor for Fayette County. The assignment did not show how much Holder was paid for the tract.[10] Regarding the Holder and Taylor survey, Taylor assigned his interest to Robert Trimble, who then gave James Clark and James Sympson one-third of his interest. No record could be found showing the disposition of Holder's share.

Holder's 50,612½ acre survey had a more complex history. He sold three-quarters of it off prior to receiving the patent. The buyers, whose names appear with him on the patent, were John Cape, Daniel Gano and Andrew Holmes. Each was assigned one-quarter of the acreage. These men were noted figures in early Kentucky. John Cape was a Lexington architect and builder who erected Kentucky's first capitol building. He was later involved with Holder in the Yazoo affair. (see Chapter 9) Capt. Daniel Gano was an officer in the Revolutionary War and was with General Montgomery at Quebec. He was one of the first settlers of Frankfort, which he laid off in 1787. Andrew Holmes was a Frankfort capitalist and promoter. In 1793, the legislature met at his house, which he later sold to Thomas Love. Holmes may have had more influence than anyone else on Frankfort being chosen the capital.[11] In 1795, Holder sold 6,000 acres of his remaining share of the tract to George Nicholas and John Breckinridge, two of Kentucky's most influential political leaders, both of whom had counties named after them. Holder received £1,000 "to him in hand paid."[12] Holder's heirs lost

Colonel John Holder

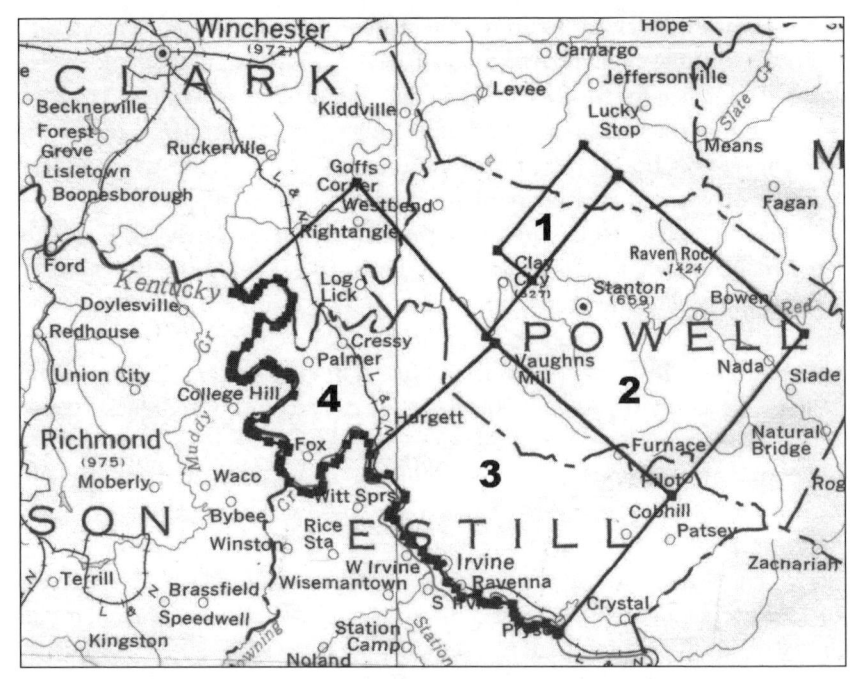

Holder's Large Grants in the Clark County Area. 1 – Holder's 6,212 acres; 2 - Holder's 50,612½ acres; 3 – Holder and Taylor's 49,665¼ acres; 4 – Graham's 33,815 acres.

the remaining interest in the tract (approximately 6,650 acres) in a later lawsuit.

Holder also located a tract for David Irvine in Clark County on the Kentucky River: 3,812 acres near the mouth of Indian Creek. Irvine did not receive the patent until 1798, and Holder's heirs applied for a locator's share of the land. Out of Irvine's patent, Commissioners William Sudduth and Achilles Eubank surveyed and deeded 1,720 acres to the heirs in 1803.[13]

Upper Howard's Creek

John Howard transferred his survey at the mouth of Lower Howard's Creek to John Holder on November 18, 1785.[14] By this date Howard had already commenced what turned out to be a fairly long business relationship with John Holder. Howard's agreement to sell Holder the land on Lower Howard's Creek required Holder to make a 1,000 acre survey for the land Howard most wanted which was at the mouth of Upper Howard's Creek. Holder assumed responsibility for resolving all conflicting claims at that location. While this agreement was reached in 1783, it was many years before Howard obtained a clear title to the land.

Land Speculator

On his first visit to Kentucky in 1775, John Howard found a desirable area near the mouth of Upper Howard's Creek, where he built a cabin at the first fork of the creek to help establish his claim. According to the testimony of Edward Hall at a land trial:

> He [Hall] became acquainted with Howard's Upper Creek in 1780. It empties into Kentucky River on the north side. The creek was known in many states by Hunters. The creek took its name from John Howard. He built a cabin on it. I saw cabin in 1780.[15]

Howard entered his claim for 1,000 acres at the land office in March of 1783.[16] Cuthbert Combs[a] told a story about the dramatic manner in which Howard later tried to prove his claim:

> Howard had a claim…at the mouth of Howard's Upper Creek. He lived in Lexington. I was present when he established his claim. He made a square & said if they would dig in that square, they would find the broken glass of a green bottle, that if they didn't find it, it wasn't his land & he didn't want it.[17]

Howard was unsuccessful in getting the title due to the fact that there were prior claims on the land that were superior to his. Thomas Maxwell had two military grants of 200 acres each running up the creek from the Kentucky River.[b] The survey was made by John Floyd in 1775. Military claims took precedence over all others, and Maxwell received a patent for his land in 1780. Joseph Combs entered 1,000 acres in the same area, part of which overlapped Maxwell's claim. Combs had his tract surveyed in 1783 and later received a patent for it.[18]

While it may seem surprising that Virginia issued patents to both Maxwell and Combs for the same land at the mouth of Upper Howard's Creek., this was in fact a common occurrence. The practice led to years of litigation between thousands of persons who had been granted the same tract of land. Some of these suits dragged on for several generations.

In order to get the land he wanted, Howard used a more direct method than suing: He struck a deal with John Holder to obtain the land for him, and

---

a This was Cuthbert Jr. The Combs brothers—Cuthbert Sr., Benjamin, Joseph and Fielding—were all involved in Upper Howard's Creek land.

b Maxwell made his claim on a military warrant issued for service in the French and Indian War. Warrants for Revolutionary War service were not used for land in the Bluegrass region; these warrants were used on land reserved below the Green River.

Colonel John Holder

the two signed a formal contract. Howard gave Holder the land on Lower Howard's Creek. In exchange, Holder was to survey a tract at the mouth of Upper Howard's Creek for Howard's benefit. The contract called for "Colo. Daniel Boon [to] survey at his own Discretion, paying Regard to the said Howards advice so far as he sees fit." Then Holder was to extinguish all other claims to the land, namely those of Maxwell and Combs. In the words of the contract, "the said Holder or his heirs shall clear out of the way of such survey all prior surveys, entrys & claims, so that the said Howard shall have clear Title for the Land." Holder was to do all this at his own expense. If he should fail, Holder was to quit "all Claim & Pretentions to the thousand acres of Land included in the said Howard's preemption Claim which includes the mouth of Howard's lower Creek & Juets Creek & whereon the said Holder now lives, [and] in that Case he will then remove from it, leaving it to be possessed & peaceably enjoyed by the said John Howard." Howard and Holder signed the contract on August 12, 1783.[19]

In 1785, however, it was Jesse Cartwright, not Daniel Boone, who surveyed the 1,000 acres with little or no input from Howard, who was still living in Botetourt County.[20] In July 1786, while on a visit to Boonesborough, Howard sent a note to "Major John Holder." First he chided Holder for taking so long to complete their agreement: "I presume you know that Mr. Joseph Combs has a Preemption Warrant not only entered, but also surveyed on Howard's upper Creek, including the Mouth of it...where you was to have let me have one thousand acres of Land."

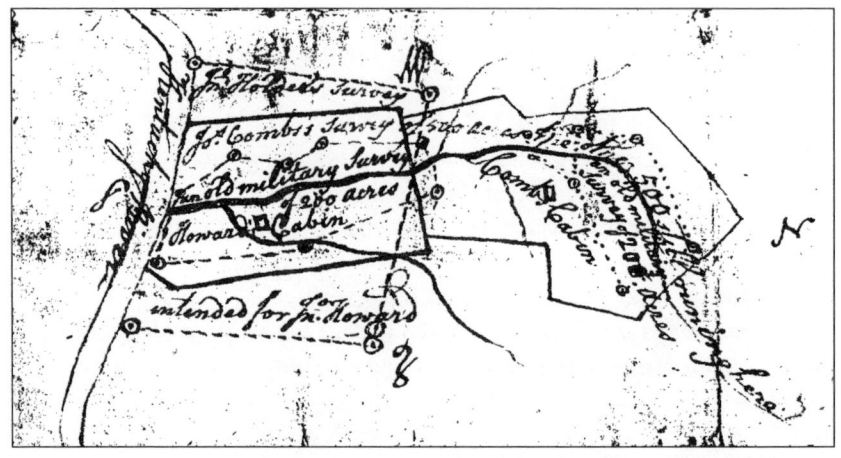

John Howard's Sketch of Upper Howard's Creek Surveys. Shows two 500 acre surveys of Joseph Combs, two 200 acre military surveys of Thomas Maxwell, and the survey Holder had made for Howard. ☐ *John Howard's Cabin. North is to the right of the page.*[21]

Land Speculator

Howard then complained that the tract Holder had surveyed was not at all suitable. Daniel Boone, who was "by your agreement with me to have surveyed the Land," had recommended running the survey up the creek "as you may observe Combs has done," and "not in a right Square, taking in broken Hills, as you have got a Survey made for me." To make his point to Holder, Howard drew a detailed map of the interfering surveys.

Howard requested Holder to "let me know what I may depend you will do on this affair." Holder responded immediately, "Please to Com by on your Return from Boonsborough & I will satisfy you that I intend nothing Else but to Comply with our agreement."[22]

In 1795, Howard obtained the rights to 501 acres at the mouth of the creek. The conveyances were recorded as deeds of purchase: 200 acres from Thomas Maxwell of Madison County, Kentucky, for which Howard paid £100, and 301 acres from Joseph Combs[c] of Stafford County, Virginia, for which he paid £226.[23] While there is no indication in these deeds that Holder arranged and paid for the transactions, it seems almost certain that he did. Howard still held a contract that could have put Holder out of business and off the land at Lower Howard's Creek. On the property at the mouth of Upper Howard's Creek, John Howard eventually established several commercial enterprises, including a tobacco warehouse and Kentucky River ferry.

Later in 1795, Howard's son Benjamin pursued the remainder of his father's claim, the nearly 500 acres still owed on the contract. It appears that Holder came through on this part of the bargain as well. On November 30, Benjamin left a note at "Holders Store" for Phillip Detherage, a deputy surveyor of Clark County, requesting his services:

> I would thank you to attend here tomorrow morning if possible with your Instruments to do some surveying for me. I shall take it as a favour if you will certainly attend early in the morning.[24]

On December 7, Detherage ran a survey for 1,000 acres on the Kentucky River between Upper Howard's Creek and Bull Run. Detherage recorded the metes and bounds, and on the same document, Holder added and signed the statement, "I do Certify Mr. Datherage has surveyed the above measured survey to my satisfaction."[25]

That same day John Holder wrote out an order for Benjamin to purchase land within this survey belonging to John Graham for which Holder agreed to pay:

---

[c] The property was conveyed to Howard on Joseph's behalf by his brother, Benjamin Combs of Clark County, "his attorney in fact."

Colonel John Holder

Capt. Benjamin Howard will please to buy from John Graham the land that Lays within his thousand acre survey at the mouth of Howards upper Creek by Exchanging Land for it or upon the Best turms he can for me, which Bargan I oblige myself to Comply with.[26]

Thus did John Howard finally obtain his 1,000 acres on the Kentucky River at Upper Howard's Creek. Well, almost 1,000 acres. When Howard sold all of this land in 1828, his four parcels totaled 937 acres.

Chapter 9
Yazoo Land Company

One of the most unusual episodes in John Holder's eventful life may have been his involvement with the South Carolina Yazoo Company and its agent, Doctor James O'Fallon. At one time, the state of Georgia claimed all the territory encompassed by the present states of Alabama and Mississippi. Holder, with his long history in land speculation, was a natural fit for the companies formed to settle this western country. In 1785, the Georgia legislature established Bourbon County and authorized its proprietors to settle the land along the Yazoo and Mississippi rivers. The proprietors engaged John Holder to take four hundred families down to settle near the Walnut Hills, now Vicksburg. Nothing came of these plans, and the company failed before the mission got underway.[1]

In 1789, the company reorganized as the South Carolina Yazoo Company. The owners were three influential men in Charleston, Alexander Moultrie, William Clay Snipes and Isaac Huger. Upon being falsely informed that "part of the territory has already been settled," the legislature approved a grant of five million acres for the purchase price of $66,964. The company hired Kentuckians John Holder and John Cape and wrote enthusiastic letters to them in October urging them "to take instant possession, establish friendly relations with the Indians and make overtures to the Spanish officials." In another letter to Holder they wrote, "We consider their [the Spanish] interests and ours as intimately connected and inseparable. We confidently flatter ourselves that we shall form a highly advantageous rampart for Spain, and that we shall ourselves feel that such should be the case." The company then hired James O'Fallon as its general agent.[2]

Born James Fallon in Ireland, he studied at the University of Edinburgh and immigrated to North Carolina in 1774. He served as a surgeon in the Continental Army, after which he settled in Charleston and began a series of intrigues with the Spanish government. He adopted the cognomen "O'Fallon" while corresponding with Spain's chargé d'affaires, Don Diego de Gardoqui. O'Fallon's scheme was to convince land hungry Americans to relocate in Spanish territory where they would become subjects of Spain.

Colonel John Holder

He expected these colonization plans to appeal mostly to families of trans-Allegheny Kentucky and Tennessee.[3]

With this background, O'Fallon was well prepared to serve as an agent for the South Carolina Yazoo Company. In a letter from Moultrie, dated March 9, 1790, the company directed O'Fallon "to proceed to Kentucky, get an accounting of goods from Holder, recruit and initiate the colony at the mouth of the Yazoo, conciliate the Indians, and visit New Orleans for the purpose of establishing relations with the Spanish Governor." In addition to these written instructions, O'Fallon reportedly received a set of "secret orders."[4]

Doctor O'Fallon arrived in Lexington in April, where he began planning the colonization venture and "the collection of goods from Holder." Though not stated, these likely included flatboats from Holder's Boatyard for the transport of colonists. At one point, O'Fallon announced a version of his plans in a lengthy letter to the *Kentucky Gazette*. He wrote to Esteban Miro, governor of Louisiana, laying out his plans for establishing a colony independent of the United States. O'Fallon was soon befriended in Kentucky by General James Wilkinson, an even more adept intriguer than himself. Wilkinson offered his complete cooperation but immediately set out to wreck O'Fallon's plans by informing President George Washington of his schemes and poisoning his relationship with Miro.[5] It should be recalled that General Wilkinson was in the secret employ of the Spanish at this time.

When informed of Miro's resistance to his plans, O'Fallon began preparing for a military invasion of Spanish territory. On September 16, 1790, the Yazoo Battalion of about 650 men was "filled, mustered, and enrolled." The battalion consisted of one cavalry company, one artillery company and eight infantry companies. John Holder was appointed "Colonel Commandant," and Thomas Kennedy of Madison County was the lieutenant colonel. Another noted scoundrel, Ebenezer Platt, was the captain of a cavalry company. Holder's associate in the boatyard, Andrew McCroskey, was a lieutenant in the artillery company. In all, thirty-three officers were named on O'Fallon's list. According to the "Military Articles of contract, &c" drafted by O'Fallon,[a] Holder and Kennedy were to receive 6,000 acres each for their services. Presumably, the "Military Articles of contract" were intended to stimulate enlistment with the offer of land: 200 acres for infantry privates, 250 acres

---

[a] O'Fallon's pretentious plans extended even to the uniforms. Cavalry were to be outfitted with "a light horseman's cap, covered with bearskin; a short skirted coat of blue, faced with buff, and yellow metal buttons." Artillery uniforms "are to consist of yellow hunting shirts, bound about the waist with broad, black, leathern belts; of a hat, with its leaf flapped up behind, and the crown thereof covered with a piece of bearskin; with overalls of blue." U.S. Congress, *American State Papers, Indian Affairs, Vol. 4* (Washington, DC, 1832), p. 117.

Yazoo Land Company

for privates of horse and artillery. "Female adventurers" who accompanied the troops were to receive 100 acres; 500 acres would be awarded the first woman to reach the settlement and 500 more "to her who shall bring forth in it the first live child, bastard or legitimate."[6]

O'Fallon even wrote a presumptuous letter to President Washington boasting that he expected to obtain "from the Spanish and Indian borders, intelligence of vital import to transmit to your Excellency." He then suggested that, due to the remoteness of the new colony from the president and the official Indian superintendent, Washington should give him full authority to treat with the Choctaw and Chickasaw nations.[7]

O'Fallon's grandiose plans soon began to unravel. Wilkinson sent word to the South Carolina Company accusing O'Fallon of misusing funds and general incompetence. He was thereby able to get O'Fallon's battalion reduced to about 50 men.[8] Miro began military preparations of his own in anticipation of O'Fallon's arrival. By now, the Western caper was receiving national attention; a Philadelphia newspaper reported that

> Late accounts from the Mississippi positively mention That the Spaniards have erected a fort at the Walnut Hills and garrisoned it with a considerable number of troops, and that they are determined to oppose the settlement intended to be made there by Colonel Holder and a number of Kentuckians under the auspices of the Georgians. That, in consequence of this, many of the Kentuckians are rendezvousing and intend marching down, shortly, to dispossess them of that valuable situation, and, that this being the case, it was the general opinion that war with our neighbors must inevitably be the consequence.[9]

O'Fallon repeatedly delayed plans to embark for the new settlement. In November, he reported to the company that he planned to send the first 300 within the week, with himself to follow with 300 troops and 600 families in February. O'Fallon spent some time in Louisville where he was able to briefly convince George Rogers Clark to head his venture. Then in February 1791, O'Fallon married Clark's younger sister Frances. Ominously, George Washington issued a proclamation warning the West against O'Fallon. The president's proclamation was eventually published in the *Kentucky Gazette*:

> Whereas it hath been represented to me that James O'Fallon is levying an armed force in that part of the State of Virginia which is called Kentucky, disturbs the public peace and sets at defiance

Colonel John Holder

the treaties of the United States with the Indian tribes...that those who have incautiously associated themselves with the said James O'Fallon may be warned of their danger.[10]

Orders were sent to the attorney of the district of Kentucky to proceed against the doctor.

Meanwhile, the South Carolina Company itself was disintegrating. They made their first installment payment with depreciated state currency and had not paid a penny since. And about that time one of the founders of the company was hanged at Charleston for counterfeiting.[11]

O'Fallon himself was deeply in the hole from his own expenditures as agent for the company. To reimburse himself, he spent the next several years trying, without success, to obtain the goods Holder had been contracted to deliver. After exchanging letters with Holder (see "Boatyard" in Chapter 10), O'Fallon sent directions to his associate, Philip Buckner, in a letter full of tirades against Holder and the company.

> I am sorry from engagements which I have tomorrow and on the following day to attend the Sick at the garrison[b] where I am engaged, that I cannot see you before you go up to Lexington. I, in the meantime, send you Holder's Bond, which you will recover as you think fit. No part of its amount has been ever paid, but 30 Hogsheads of Tobacco and a Small order in favour of Mr. Moore of Louisville. There are 20 Hogsheads or thereabouts still due, two hundred & fifty pounds for provisions, Some paints, Boats &c. He was [*illegible*] to send the Tobacco to the Wilmit Shelhy what he never did, althoug my Agent, little Nolan,[c] attended there at the time. I have his, Holder's, letters promising to send it &c to the falls, but he clandestinely gave it to little Spring on some darke compromise, this being to evade his Bond to me. The Company is deeply in my debt; and beside this, I am still the general Agent of that body, and yet personally in, for some of their contracts. The property out here was the whole Company's property, consisting of 20 Gentleman; and not Snipes's or Huger's, who were but two, and the most inconsiderable of them. Snipes & Huger acted clandestinely with the Company, and for this purpose [*illegible*] as Spring. My Commission, my Secret & general Instructions from the Company, to all which Snipes & Huger

---

[b] O'Fallon was employed by General Anthony Wayne as a physician to the garrison at Fort Steuben, located in present day Steubenville, Ohio.

[c] This was Philip Nolan, who was actually an agent of General James Wilkinson.

Yazoo Land Company

have signed, and the Director's repeated Letters to me, and Snipes & Washington's powers of attorney to me, all declare & announce the goods and every other effect out here to belong to the whole Company only. This I can establish beyond contradiction, when I see you, or in court. Holder has no subterfuge to escape by that reason, Justice, or Law can give him. This Bond (as you know) had long since been made over to you; and on the day after Holder had passed it to me. Foreseeing Snipes's tricks against the Company, and thinking then I might [*illegible*], I addressed it to the acting Director, or the Company's agent, whoever he should be. I still continue that agent, as yet unrecalled. On your return, you will give a receipt for the Bond. Keep a copy of it for me in case you sue Holder.[12]

Soon after this, O'Fallon's wife left him, and he was involved in a physical altercation with George Rogers Clark. O'Fallon died in Louisville in 1794. Of O'Fallon's hectic and flawed career, the scholar John Parish noted that that "the Yazoo Company failed to support him, Kentucky friends deserted him, Wilkinson betrayed him, the President of the United States denounced him in a proclamation, the King of Spain issued orders for his arrest, he came to blows with George Rogers Clark, his wife left him, and early in 1794 he died, with no obituary in the newspapers and apparently little mourning over his departure."[13]

Holder's involvement with the Yazoo Company apparently ended with little harm to his pocketbook or reputation. He saved his commission and worthless land certificates, which were passed down several generations. His grandson, William D. Holder, wrote to Lyman Draper:

> I have in my possession an old paper which purports to be a commission of colonel to John Holder, bearing date the South Carolina (Charleston) 1st September 1790 & signed by Alexander Moultrie, Director, Isaac Huger, T[homas] Washington, as a majority of the grantees of the South Carolina Yazoo Company & a grant, a certificate of right, was afterwards issued to said Holder of 100,000 acres of Land in view of his raising a batallion of well organized Troops for the defence of the territory belonging to South Carolina.[14]

Speculators continued to beseech the Georgia legislature for access to Western lands until the state finally ceded the Yazoo territory to the federal government.

Chapter 10
Business Enterprises

After he established his station at the mouth of Lower Howard's Creek, John Holder turned his attention to a variety of business enterprises that took advantage of this location. On his place he would establish a boatyard, inspection warehouse, store, tavern, ferry and gristmill, and he may have been the proprietor of a distillery and quarries located on his land. Holder did not build and operate all these himself. He recruited individuals with the needed skills to locate on his place.

Pioneers who erected frontier stations often attracted settlers with the promise of cheap land or the free use of land for a specified period. For example, a resident of Strode's Station said he came there "because Strode gave us all a chance to clear what we pleased and we were to have it rent free till the close of the war."[1] We don't know what Holder's business arrangements were with the men who came to settle at his station and who stayed on to build and operate the various enterprises. He did not give away land, however, and sold very little.

John Holder in Kentucky Tax Lists

Year	County	Tithables	Slaves	Horses	Cattle	Land (acres)
1787	Fayette	7	20	9	28	
1788	"	14	11	13		
1789	"	12	10	11		
1790	"	no tax list exists for the Clark County area				
1791	"	11	8	7		
1792	"	1	19	38	30	2,150
1793	Clark	1	18	6	25	1,150
1794	"	1	19	6	25	2,000
1795	"	1	22	6	35	18,400
1796	"	1	27	10	50	24,000
1797	"	Holder failed to list his property				
1798	"	no tax lists exist for Clark County				
1799	"	Holder died before the tax list was prepared				

Business Enterprises

The 1787 tax roll for Fayette County lists John Holder's household with seven taxable white males over age fifteen. Although some of them probably were not living with Holder's family, Holder was charged for the tax on all seven. No one else in the county was listed with so many tithables. The seven included Holder himself, his father Luke and brother Francis, future brother-in-law George Rout, former Loudoun County neighbor Benjamin Rankins, plus Adam Hartford and Griffin Taylor. Little is known of the latter two men, as they soon left the area.[a] The number of tithables at Holder's peaked at 14 in 1788. One explanation for paying the taxes for so many non-relatives could be that they were hired men. It was during this period that Holder commenced his commercial-industrial activities. His enterprises were all located at his tract on Lower Howard's Creek.[2]

As a sign that Holder was beginning to prosper, the 1787 tax roll shows Holder as the owner of 20 slaves, 9 horses and 28 cattle. He was among the larger slave owners in Fayette County. In 1792, Kentucky began to list real estate holdings on the county tax rolls. That year Holder reported owning 2,150 acres. Four years later, he reported 24,000 acres.

Panoramic View of Holder's Plantation. Looking southwest from Lower Howard's Creek Nature and Heritage Preserve.

Plantation

Holder's land, on a bluff overlooking the Kentucky River, was beautifully situated for a country estate and manor house. The farms in his day were referred to as plantations. The limited data available in tax records suggest that Holder, like nearly all Kentucky residents at the time, was involved in agricultural pursuits to some degree. Fayette County tax rolls show Holder with as many as 38 horses and 30 head of cattle. Clark tax rolls show the

---

[a] Taylor may be the Griffin Taylor who was born in Frederick County, Virginia, son of William and Catherine (Bushrod) Taylor. Mary Taylor Brewer, *From Log Cabins to the White House* (Wooton, KY, 1985), p. 80. Taylor signed petitions to the Virginia Assembly in 1785 and 1786; he is on the Bourbon County tax list in 1791 and on the Harrison County list for 1800. Adam Hartford signed a petition to the Virginia Assembly in 1787.

Colonel John Holder

number of his horses decreased to 10 and the number of cattle steadily increased to 50.

A letter written by William Dunbar Holder to Lyman Draper in 1849 states that his grandfather John Holder was a farmer. "Col. Richard Callaway & Col. John Holder were originally farmers in Culpepper County, agreeable to my information, and emigrated with Col. Daniel Boon to Kentucky...Col. John Holder married Frances Callaway, daughter of Col. Richard and settled after marriage in Clark County near Boonsboro as a farmer, also had a stock of goods &c."[3] Holder certainly would have found his place suitable for a plantation—the land has been farmed continuously for over 200 years.

Store and Tavern

One of the businesses Holder operated was a store. From his location, he could supply goods not only to residents along the river and creek in Clark County, but also across the river in Madison. The first reference we find to the store dates to November 1795: Benjamin Howard left a note addressed to John Holder at "Holders Store."[4]

Indirect references to Holder's Store go back much earlier — to 1784. Holder sued several men in Madison County court for debt, apparently for goods they purchased at his store, a significant portion of which was whiskey. In April 1787, the court ruled for the plaintiff in *John Holder v. Reuben Proctor*, and *John Holder v. Talbot Arthur* was settled out of court.[5] One piece of evidence produced was a copy of Proctor's account with Holder.

Mr. Reuben Proctor in account with John Holder[6]	
1 quart of whiskey July 1784	0.4.0 [pounds.shillings.pence]
1 Bushel of Corn July 1784	0.5.0
1 quart of whiskey	0.2.6
1 quart of whiskey	0.2.6
4 Gallons & a half of whiskey	1.7.0
2 Buck skins at 6/pr Skin	0.12.0
Note to Anthony Hundley Dec 25 1786	2.13.0

Holder must have opened the store while residents were still forting at his station, captive customers so to speak. He may have operated a still as well, but there is no evidence of it except for the whiskey sales. Holder also went after Aquilla White and won a judgment from him in 1789.[7] There is a copy of a note in the court records, a joint obligation from Reuben Proctor and Aquilla White to John Holder for "Sundry Goods" totaling "the sum of 3 pounds 6 shillings."[8]

Business Enterprises

Holder also had a tavern at his place. In November 1793, upon Holder's motion, the county court awarded him a license to keep an ordinary "where William Harris now lives in this County." Harris lived on Holder's place on Lower Howard's Creek and was involved in the boatyard (see below). The tavern license was good for one year; no renewal was found in 1794.[9]

Boatyard

John Holder began building boats on the Kentucky River in about the year 1788. Our informants for this period are Francis F. Jackson and his father Josiah, who were closely associated with Holder. The Jackson family resided on Lower Howard's Creek for a time, and Francis' sister Edah married a Holder. Francis and Josiah both got into the business of producing tar from pine trees. They made the tar in present day Powell County and floated it down the Red River to boatyards on the Kentucky River. The tar was used for caulking flatboats. Francis said the "tar shoals" on Red River, took its name from a load of tar they spilled.

> Tar shoals on Red river, 3 miles above iron works [at now Clay City]. My father run a canoe of tar against a log and upset the canoe and tar, and years after that a quantity of tar was turned up in the shoal. My father had learned to burn tar—burnt tar hundredweight [equal] 20 gallons. I burnt tar. Put it in the canoe, made bulkheads of clay, took it down, and walked back. [James] Wilkinson took two boats of tar down the river.[10]

According to Powell County historian, Larry Meadows, the tar shoals is still a known location on Red River between Clay City and Stanton.

Gen. James Wilkinson, the famous scoundrel and intriguer, is generally credited with opening the Mississippi River as a trade route to Spanish held New Orleans. In 1787, Wilkinson shipped a flatboat load of tobacco, hams and butter from Frankfort to New Orleans, and while there entered into a secret alliance with Spain. His triumphant return to Kentucky spurred a furious race to get into the business of "trading down the river."[11]

As soon as early Kentuckians were able to produce a surplus from their farms and small industries, they began looking beyond their borders for markets. Goods could not be profitably carried over the mountains to eastern cities. As Dr. Thomas Clark wrote of this period, "Not one of the farm products of Clark County could pay its transportation costs overland, not even whiskey." Westerners were counting on using the Ohio-Mississippi

Colonel John Holder

waterway as an economical shipping route to New Orleans. At the close of the Revolutionary War, the Spanish were in control of the city as well as the lower Mississippi River. Spain essentially shut down river traffic while negotiating a treaty with the newly formed United States.[12]

Wilkinson arranged for a second, larger venture in the spring of 1789, but by then a number of market hungry entrepreneurs had decided to make the trip on their own. Holder was in on this business at the outset, but the niche he chose was building the flatboats. According to Francis Jackson, Holder was the first in the boat building business.

> The first boat built in Kentucky was at Holder's landing, now Comb's ferry. Took 20 gallons tar. William Harris was the foreman in building it. Built in 1788. Thompson and McCroskey. Both Scotchmen. They took 25 hogsheads of tobacco to New Orleans. It was the first tobacco and the first boat.[13]

Jackson's statement can be read a number of ways. Since Wilkinson's boat (1787) preceded Thompson and McCroskey's made at Holder's Boatyard (1788), one interpretation would be that Holder's boat was the first one built on that end of the Kentucky River. But that is at odds with Jackson's statement that Holder's was the first in Kentucky. It is possible that Jackson's 1788 date is incorrect and that he meant to say that Holder's boat did get to New Orleans before Wilkinson's. Jackson was doing business with both Holder and Wilkinson at the time and one supposes he had firsthand knowledge of their activities. The latter interpretation is supported by his statement that "the second set of boats were built for General Wilkinson."[14] If Holder's boat was the first to break the embargo, the fact has been lost in history. Wilkinson was at his best molding favorable public perception about himself. His taking the first flatboat to New Orleans could be another example.

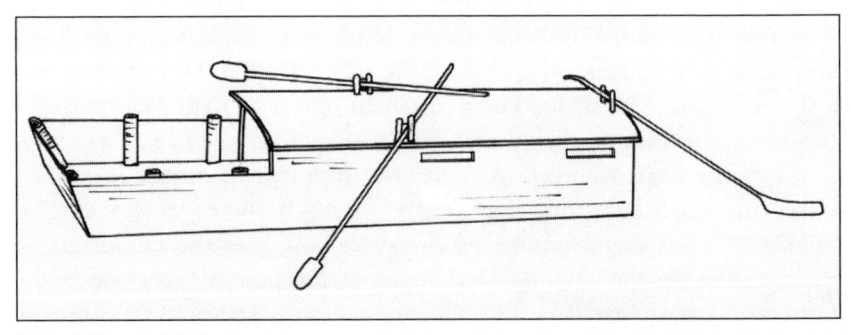

Typical Kentucky Flatboat

Business Enterprises

New Orleans bound flatboats were similar to the ones used to transport settlers from Pittsburgh and Redstone Old Fort down the Ohio River to Kentucky. They were made for a one way trip downstream. While they mainly floated with the current, the boats were equipped with a pair of sweep oars for maneuvering and usually carried a sail to take advantage of favorable winds. At the end of the journey, in Natchez or New Orleans, after the produce was taken off, the boat was sold for its timbers. The design below was typical:

> Specifications called for gunwales "fifty feet long and six inches square, the bottom planks two inches thick, twelve boards to be put across the boat, the side planks to be one and one-half inches thick. The stanchions or studs to be three by six, five feet high and five to a side. The boats to be finished in a workman-ship-like manner, to be pinned with seasoned white oak pins and bored, and the sides to be five feet high and the whole to be of oak timber." This was the structural description of the "Kentucky boat." A stout cabin, a pair of ornamental deer horns, a pair of side sweeps, and a long steering oar topped off the equipment.[15]

Flatboats might vary in length from 20 to 100 feet long. Boats 12 feet wide cost about one dollar per foot, and a typical boat could carry 40 to 50 tons of payload packed in barrels of different sizes.[16]

We have no indication that Holder was in the shipping business. All evidence points to him being the boat builder, that is to say, the proprietor of a business building boats for the New Orleans trade. The shipper was exposed to far more financial risks. He had to buy a flatboat, pay for all the produce loaded on it, and then had to hire a pilot and crew to take the boat down river. Boats could sink or goods could be stolen on the trip down; money could be stolen on the trip back. Of course, the financial rewards were higher for owners.

Francis Jackson stated that Holder's first boat was built for Thompson and McCroskey. There were too many Thompsons in early Kentucky to know which Thompson this was. In 1790 Andrew McCroskey was appointed lieutenant of an artillery company in Holder's Yazoo Battalion. He was on the Bourbon County tax rolls from 1792 through 1796. He was a Scot who married Nancy McDougal in that county. We know little else of him, except what Jackson added: "After he came he married. McCroskey had a bag pipe which he used to play."[17]

Other boats, Jackson mentioned, were built for James Wilkinson and

Colonel John Holder

William Theobalds. Wilkinson arranged for a second, larger venture in the spring of 1789. That April he placed the following notice in the newspaper:

> I wish to engage a number of hands to conduct my boats to the city of New Orleans in the course of the next month, to whom I will give ten Dollars Per month, and a bounty of twenty Dollars, or thirty five Dollars for the trip.[18]

William Theobalds came from Virginia and settled in Georgetown where he kept a hotel on Main Street. He may have gotten early experience in the run to New Orleans, as everyone called him "Captain Theobalds." In 1793, the *Kentucky Gazette* ran an advertisement "regarding a boat to sail from Frankfort to Pittsburgh under William Theobalds, master." He and his wife, the daughter of Judge William Brown of Harrison County, raised a large family. Theobalds died on his farm near Stamping Ground in 1820.[19]

The men who built the boats would have included carpenters, laborers, and others Holder persuaded to come to Lower Howard's Creek. Francis Jackson mentioned two of them. "William Harris was the foreman in building" Thompson and McCroskey's boat. For Wilkinson's set of boats, "Harris the superintendant and Caj. Hall go under the boat." No telling what "go under the boat" means. Micajah Hall was a Clark resident when the county was formed in 1793. He married Milly Powell there in 1806 and later moved to Estill County. Jackson listed several other Harrises — Tom, Billy, Archy, John, Daniel and Webber — who may have comprised a family group. William Harris lived near the boatyard and kept a tavern for Holder.

Holder's Boatyard. Mural at the Civil War Fort at Boonesboro. Painting by Phil May

Business Enterprises

He was appointed a constable of Clark County in 1793. Harris later sued Holder for £40 in Clark County court but the case was dismissed.[20]

Numerous market hungry entrepreneurs decided to run the river in 1789. One set of boats making the run belonged to John Halley of Boonesborough. Halley was another of the energetic business minded men on the Kentucky frontier. He came out in 1780 and eventually acquired most of the original town lots of Boonesborough. He had a gristmill on Otter Creek and grew great quantities of tobacco. Family tradition credits him with building the first tobacco barn and shipping the first tobacco to London. The latter claim, perhaps, derives from the boat he piloted to New Orleans in 1789. Two years later he took four boats down with a cargo of tobacco, flour, bacon and lard. On both trips, Halley kept a journal, which has been transcribed and annotated for modern readers.[21] Holder's Boatyard would have been the nearest known source for Halley's boats but no proof exists of their construction there.

The boatyard stood on Holder's land on the north side of the Kentucky River, but the precise location is unknown. The flat land on the east side of the creek, where Hall's Restaurant is today, might seem an ideal level spot for such a business. However, the original contour of the site would have been much different and perhaps not so level. It is more likely that Holder built his boatyard on the west side of the creek, adjacent to his warehouse and

Site of Holder's Landing on Kentucky River. The tributary at the lower right is Lower Howard's Creek. Joe Kendall Neel, University of Kentucky Master's Thesis, 1938.

Colonel John Holder

ferry, as well as the terminus of the wagon road to the boatyard. It would have been more practical and much more convenient for Holder to manage his operations if all were located on the same side of the creek. During times of high water, it would have been impossible to cross the creek at the mouth on foot or horseback and time consuming to cross by boat.

Similarly, it would have been impractical for roads to the boatyard to terminate on the opposite side of Lower Howard's Creek rather than ending at the boatyard itself. In fact, evidence proving the boatyard was on the west side of the creek has been found in Clark County road orders. (See "Winchester to Holder's Boatyard," Chapter 11)

The presumed site of the boatyard is on the narrow plateau now occupied by Hidden Grove Lane, in the area near Holder's landing, ferry house and warehouse. An 1938 photo of the mouth of Lower Howard's Creek shows how Holder's Landing looked before Hidden Grove Lane was developed.

Holder's boat building business could have started as early as 1787, the year of Wilkinson's first trip to New Orleans. The business was a going concern by 1790, the year Holder's Boatyard appears for the first time in county records. In March of that year, the Madison County court issued a directive to view a road to the river opposite the boatyard.

> Ordered that John Sapington, Peter Evans, Benjamin Persley & William Calk be appointed to View the way for a Road from opposit to Holder's Boatyard to intersect the road from Boonsborough to Madison Courthouse &c.[22]

The county established the road, and it continued to be mentioned in court records for at least the next ten years.[23] The road in Madison began at the Kentucky River opposite the boatyard and connected to the road from Boonesborough to Richmond. In later years, when the boatyard was long gone, the road was one segment of the highway from Paris to Richmond.

There are several communications from John Holder himself regarding his boatyard. The first is an undated note written to James French, who was then residing at Boonesborough.

> Sir, Was Over to See you yesterday to Know what was to be Dun with your Boat left word with Mrs. French for you to meet me this Morning at the Boatyard sir if possable must Get and order from you on Capt. Robert Craduck for about three pounds will pay you the Cash for it in few weeks I want the order on Craduck for to

Business Enterprises

Rejister sum platts or if the Rejister are owing you and order on him will do your Compliance will much oblije me
                    your Frind & Humble servant
                    John Holder[24]

James French married Keziah Callaway, half-sister of Holder's wife Fanny. Robert Craddock of Danville was a wealthy landowner who held a patent to 325 acres on Lower Howard's Creek.[25] Holder's request to borrow money indicates that he planned to submit several survey plats to the Land Office, where they would be recorded by the Register. Holder may have been locating land for Craddock. This is confirmed by Holder's note, dated June 15, 1790: "Received of Robt. Craddock forty two shillings & 17 p[ence] in a credit in the Deputy Registers Office, which I promise to settle & pay to Mr. James French of Madison County for & on account of said Craddocks. John Holder"[26]

The Draper manuscripts contain several letters between Holder and Dr. James O'Fallon of Louisville. O'Fallon was an agent for the Yazoo Land Company, discussed elsewhere (Chapter 9). He wrote to Holder in September 1791.

> Sir, You will please to construct and to deliver unto Captain Philip Buckner, on his order, two Tobacco Boats, agreeable to his instructions, and at Such price as he and you shall have agreed on, which price in amount (conformable to his receipt for the Same to you given) shall have due credit given on your Bond in the hands of [*blank*].[27]

O'Fallon signed as agent of the company indicating that their interests included the tobacco shipping business. This is confirmed in another letter from O'Fallon to Holder in February 1792 directing Holder to deliver a large quantity of tobacco to Captain Buckner, "conformable to your written contract."[28] The tobacco presumably would have been in storage at Holder's Warehouse. Holder answered O'Fallon's letter immediately.

> Dear Docter
>   Capt Buckner applyed to me for Twenty Thousand pounds of Tobacco. your order I would have honored, But Capt [Simon] Spring has just aRived from Charleston with a power of attorney from Majer Snipes Revoking Yours & all othors & Requesting me to settle whot Ever whare in my hands with him. if your order had

Colonel John Holder

Com to hand Before the aRival of Spring, the Boats & Tobacco I should have paid to your orders. I am your frend & well wisher

John Holder
March 4th 1792[29]

O'Fallon then wrote to Buckner hinting that he sue Holder for not complying with his contract. Apparently, fifty hogsheads of tobacco (about 50,000 pounds) had been contracted for and Holder had delivered only thirty to O'Fallon. O'Fallon's letter to Buckner was full of plots and intrigues regarding the land company.[30] How this particular affair was resolved is unknown.

After Holder's death in 1799, his son-in-law Samuel R. Combs took over operation of the boatyard. Combs, eager to keep the business going in the upcoming spring shipping season, placed a notice in the Lexington newspaper that he was taking orders for New Orleans boats.

> The Subscriber proposes building boats for New-Orleans this season, at Holder's old landing, Clarke county, on the Kentucky river, on the most moderate terms. The advantages of a most excellent road to that place, and a commodious store-house and ferry, must render it the most advantageous place for the shipment of produce of any on the river. He can, at any time, on fifteen days notice, furnish a boat to suit the purchaser. Samuel R. Combs[31]

Although he did not state his prices, we learn that Combs could turn out a finished boat in about two week's time. Combs referred to the ferry and warehouse at "Holder's old landing," indicating that these were the same businesses previously run by Holder.

Ferry

The fact that Madison County built a road beginning "opposit to Holder's Boatyard" implies there was a way for travelers on the Madison side to cross the river to the boatyard. And indeed there was. Prior to the ferry operation, the mouth of Lower Howard's Creek was a noted crossing place on the Kentucky River during the dry season. Known as Blackfish Ford, it took its name from the Shawnee chief who passed here with his army on the way to the great siege of Boonesborough.[32] The ford was at the shoal on the downstream side of the mouth, where rock washed out of the creek valley and deposited in the river.

Business Enterprises

In high water, however, a ferry was needed to make the Kentucky River crossing. There was already a ferry nearby, just over a mile upstream at Boonesborough. Residents living on the west (downstream) side of Lower Howard's Creek could not conveniently cross the river at the Boonesborough Ferry, because the gorge of Howard's Creek presented such an obstacle to travel. More importantly, residents of Madison County could not easily access Holder's warehouse and boatyard with their produce for the same reason. Holder solved that problem by locating his ferry on the west side of Lower Howard's Creek.

The year Holder's Ferry began operation is uncertain, but one expects it would have been close to the time the boatyard started up. Clark County court issued no ferry permit to Holder, so it must have been in operation prior to 1793. Before that year, he would have sought permission for the ferry from Fayette County court, and their records prior to 1803 were lost in a fire.[b]

The ferry was first mentioned by name in a 1795 petition by residents living near the river requesting the Clark County court to open a passage way from opposite Boonesborough to the mouth of Lower Howard's Creek. The petitioners asked for a horse path "to be opened from Boonsborough Ferry Down the River to Holders Road that Leads from said Holders Ferry to Lexington."[33]

Samuel R. Combs placed a notice in the *Kentucky Gazette* in 1802 advertising land for sale, including "the Ferry & Ware House known by Holder's landing." A number of area landmarks carried Holder's name long after his death. The ferry location was still called "Holder's Landing" as late as 1807.[34]

The ferry remained at this location for many years and became popularly known as Combs' Ferry, for Holder's son-in-law, Samuel R. Combs. After Combs' death in 1833, his estate was divided and a survey map was made showing his widow's dower land. On the plat, the "ferry house" is shown on the west side of the creek near the river.

In 1858, James T. Woodward and Daniel Bently moved the ferry about three-quarters of a mile downstream, near the end of present day Amster Grove Road. The ferry remained in operation at that location until after the mid twentieth century, and the ferry landing is still visible on both sides of the river — on Amster Grove Road on the north side and on the Colonel

---

[b] Pioneer George Bryan left a statement that mentions Holder keeping a ferry at the mouth of Boone Creek. "Eli Cleveland lived in the bend of the river, just below mouth of Boon's creek at what is called Cleveland's bend. Holder lived at the place, afterwards & kept ferry." The last sentence does not fit the known evidence. Holder did have a survey in near Boone Creek that he sold to Cleveland, but there is no evidence that he ever lived there or kept a ferry there. Draper MSS 22C 16(20).

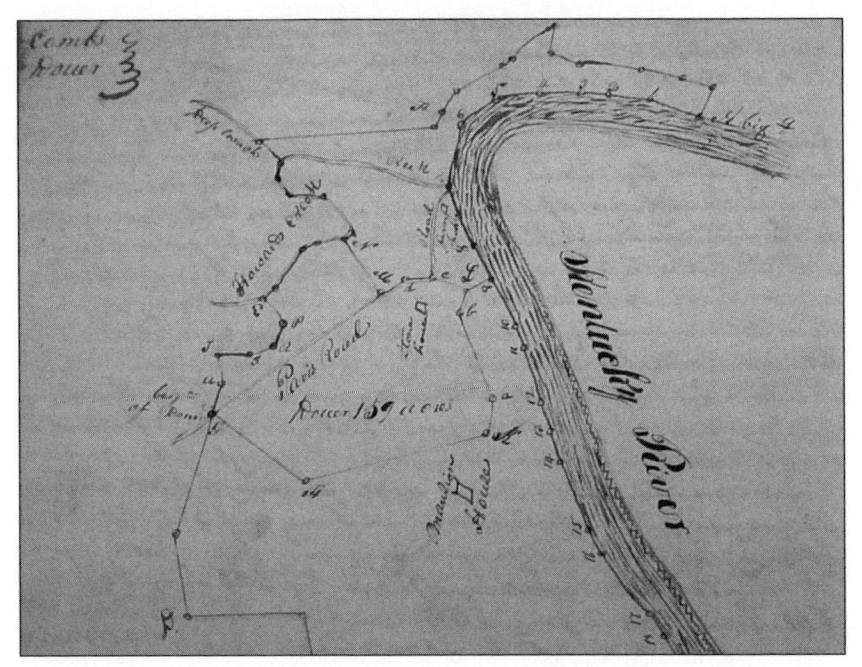

Plat for the Division of Samuel R. Combs' Estate, 1834. Shows a "Mansion House," a "Stone house" on widow Combs' dower land and a "ferry house" at the mouth of "Howards Creek."[86]

David J. Williams Firing Range on the south. There is still a Combs Ferry Road in Clark County and one in Madison County also.[35]

Warehouse

With the opening of New Orleans as a market for Kentucky goods and products, the rush was on to get in the shipping business. With perhaps slight exaggeration, a gentleman wrote from New Orleans in April 1789, "the Mississippi has been covered with fleets of boats from Cumberland, Kentucke, &c floating down great quantities of provision, flour, plank, &c."[37] Virginia law provided for the establishment of inspection warehouses at important shipping points to ensure that the market was not flooded with inferior goods produced and/or shipped by dishonest individuals. The most important inspections were for tobacco and flour, but laws also covered hemp, salt beef and salt pork.

The stated purpose of the tobacco inspection law was "for the more effectual preventing the exportation of trash, bad, unsound, and unmerchantable tobacco." The General Assembly made it unlawful to export any tobacco from the state by water "except only such tobacco as hath been or shall be reviewed and inspected [at] one of the publick warehouses." The

Business Enterprises

Survey Plat of Samuel R. Combs' Estate. Shown on original: 1, ferry house; 2, Mansion House; 3, Stone house.

legislature authorized the erection of warehouses, which were required to be "strong, close, and substantial houses, secured with strong doors hung on iron hinges, and with strong locks or bolts" and were to be provided with "a good and sufficient pair of scales with weights."

Warehouses were public buildings built on private land, and the proprietors received rent, usually four shillings for each hogshead "received, inspected and delivered." The inspectors were appointed by the governor and were considered public employees. They were paid out of fees. Their duties included grading the tobacco, packing it into hogsheads, weighing and marking the containers, and keeping detailed records. They were expected to be at the warehouse six days a week from October 1 through August 10. Inspectors had to make an annual report to the county court on the condition of the warehouse and the quantity of tobacco inspected and shipped. After paying all applicable fees, the owner of inspected tobacco was issued a receipt for his goods. These "tobacco notes" were often traded or sold and could even be used to pay taxes. Virginia had analogous statutes for the regulation of flour.[38]

Virginia established several warehouses on the Kentucky River. The one closest to Clark County was at Boonesborough on the Madison side of the river. In 1789, Fayette County sent a petition to the General Assembly requesting that new warehouses be constructed on the north side of the

Colonel John Holder

river on William Bush's land across from Boonesborough and on John Holder's land at the mouth of Lower Howard's Creek.

> To The Honourable The General Assembly Of Virginia
>
> The Petition of a number of Inhabitants of the County of Fayette Humbly sheweth
>
> That whereas a very Great Expence and Inconvenience attends the Ferriage of Tobacco over the River Kentucky to the Town of Boonsborough the greater part of which Expences and Inconveniances might be obviated by appointing Inspections on the North side of the said River at Two Distinct places to be attended by one appointment of Inspectors, as *the Precipices of Howards will not admit of a waggon Road*, we therefore pray your Honorable Body to take the same into serious consideration and should your Wisdom think our prayer reasonable that you appoint the Two following places, the one nearly opposite Boonsborough on William Bushes Land and the other *on the west side of Howards Creek* on John Holders Land and we as in Duty Bound shall ever pray &c[39] (*emphasis added*)

Attached to the petition was a signed statement by county justice Robert Todd certifying that the following notice had been posted "at the door of the court house" in Lexington for two court days:

> Notice is hereby given, that a Petition will be presented to the next General Assembly, praying that an Inspection be established for the Reception of Tobacco, on Colonel John Holder's land on the Kentucky River, below the mouth of lower Howard's Creek, at the place called Holder's landing, also another Inspection on the land of Captain William Bush, on the Kentucky River, above lower Howard's Creek, and nearly opposite to the Town of Boonsborough, to be included under one Inspection.[40]

An inspection at Bush's was desired by residents to avoid having to pay to ferry their tobacco across the river to the established warehouse at Boonesborough. However, an inspection was needed at Holder's to overcome the severe hardship placed on farmers living between Boone Creek and Lower Howard's Creek, who were forced to undertake an arduous journey to get their tobacco inspected. They had to travel to Winchester first, then to the Boonesborough ferry and the warehouse on the Madison

Business Enterprises

side of the river. Nevertheless, the petition was rejected by the General Assembly.

Signatures on the above petition provide a partial list of area residents at the time. This was part of Fayette County then but is now in Clark. Many of the individuals listed were members of the Lower Howard's Creek (Providence) Baptist Church. The surnames — Baber, Bush, Daniel, Elkin, Embry, Eubank, Haggard, Hampton, Jackson, Lisle, Martin, Quisenberry, Parrish, Ragland, Reed, Stephens, Wills — are still common in Clark County today.

A warehouse at the mouth of Lower Howard's Creek was finally authorized by the Kentucky General Assembly after separation from Virginia. In December 1792, the legislature established an inspection of tobacco "at Holder's Landing" and "at Bush's Landing." It was mandated that Bush's and Holder's "shall be in one inspection," meaning that the same set of inspectors would work at each location. In December 1795, an inspection of flour and hemp was added "at Holder's boat yard in the county of Clarke."[41]

Holder's and Bush's warehouses must have been completed soon after they were authorized, because in December 1792, Governor Isaac Shelby appointed Nicholas George, John Ellis and John Sharpe the first inspectors. In January 1794, Clark County court appointed Philip Bush, inspector, to replace Ellis who had died. "Philip Bush, Gentleman, produced in court a commission from his Eccellency the Governor appointing him Inspector of Tobacco at Holders and Bushes ware houses bearing date the 24th day of January 1794 who qualified thereto as the Law directs." William Bush signed a bond for £1,000 as his security.[42] Philip Bush served in this position for many years.

A rare report in Clark County records lists the shipments of tobacco from Holder's and Bush's landings for the year 1798:[43]

Kentucky River

An account of Tobacco inspected and delivered at Bushes & Holders landing for the year 1798.

March 16th shipped on board the boat *Enterprize* Ten Hogsheads Tobacco for the use of William Orear bound to the Port of New Orleans marked thus —

LD	No.	17	1541	130	1411
ST		7	1121	169	952
"		8	1281	150	1131
JJ		5	1237	125	1107

Colonel John Holder

"	6	1200	130	1070	Bush's
SW	14	1127	130	997	landing
"	15	1010	125	885	
WB	11	1308	125	1183	
"	12	1351	127	1224	
"	13	1435	130	1305	

April 3rd shipped for the use of John Hunt 3 Hogsheads Tobacco bound to the Port new Orleans marked Thus—

TE No.	9	1006	115	891	
"	10	1256	110	1146	Bush's
WK	16	1516	115	1401	landing
"	19	1265	125	1140	

18 April shipped on board the *Nancy & Mary* Eight Hogsheads Tobacco for the use of Robert Clarke ~~junior~~ Esquire Jerry Strode & Green[?] commanders bound to the Port of new Orleans marked Thus—

RD No.	3	1401	200	1201	Holder's
"	4	1398	201	1197	landing

FB	18	1308	122	1216	
WK	19	1265	125	1140	
DC	20	1355	120	1235	Bush's
JH	21	1286	160	1126	landing
TE	22	1338	115	1123	
JH	23	1325	125	1200	

April 29 shipped on the boat *Belfred* Two Hogsheads Tobacco for the use of Hart and company Jesse Bell commander bound to the Port of new Orleans marked Thus—

TS No.	24	1035	115	920	Bush's
"	25	1122	116	1006	landing

May 6th Shipped on the boat *liberty* Two Hogsheads Tobacco for the use of Sitez & Long Samuel West master bound to the Port of New Orleanes marked Thus—

SH No.	1	1388	105	1283	Holders
"	2	1444	100	1344	landing

Nicholas George
Philip Bush, Inspectors

At a court held for Clarke County the 17th day of November 1798 This return of a list of Tobacco inspected and Shipped at Bush's and Holders landing was produced in court and admitted to record. D. Bullock CCC

Business Enterprises

The initials before each hogshead represent the original tobacco owner, the person who paid the fees and received "tobacco notes" from the inspectors. We might speculate that JH and WB were for John Holder and William Bush. The last three numbers above (from left to right) are the tare weight, cask weight and net weight of tobacco in pounds. The difference between the tare weight and cask weight equals the weight of tobacco. The law called for at least 1,000 pounds of tobacco in each hogshead; several on the list are short, one by more than 100 pounds.

The report, taken out of the record books kept at the warehouses, lists the name of the boat, the owner, the commander, the shipping port and the destination port. The boat owner generally purchased the tobacco notes for all the tobacco on board, so he stood to keep the whole profit from the sale at New Orleans. We can identify five individuals or companies—William Orear, John Hunt, Robert Clark, Hart & Company, and Seitz & Lauman—shipping goods down river. Holder would be involved later in a lawsuit with Seitz & Lauman. The boats listed in the report—*Enterprize, Nancy & Mary, Belfred, Liberty* and one unnamed—may have been built at Holder's Boatyard.

The boats would have been carrying other cargo besides tobacco. Regulated commodities such as flour and hemp could have been included; their inspection reports, if submitted, do not appear in county records. The boats also could have carried whiskey, hams and other products that did not require inspection. A newspaper article from that period listed the following products recently shipped to New Orleans from Central Kentucky: apples, potatoes, whiskey, beer, cider and port, salted beef, salted pork, hams and bacon, lard, butter, corn, corn meal, flour, flax seed oil, lead, soap, manufactured tobacco (e.g., snuff), loose tobacco, hemp products, and plank boards.[44]

A much abbreviated version of the reports at Bush's and Holder's was filed by the inspectors for the year 1800. The following items appeared under the heading "Tobacco Inspected":

Kentucky River Bushs Warehouse
   Actual Quantity and Number of Hogsheads Tobacco Inspected at the above mentioned warehouse from the 7th of January 1800 untill April 22nd is 211 Hogsheads. 207 Hogsheads shipped on board Different boats bound to the Port New Orleans. the warehouse not complete.
Kentucky River Holders Landing
   Inspected at the above Landing 24 Hogsheads Tobacco shipped

Colonel John Holder

on board Different boats bound to the Port New Orleans. no warehouse.

The whole amount is 235 Hogsheads. 4 Hogsheads remaining in Bushs Warehouse.[45]

The same inspectors, Philip Bush and Nicholas George, were on the job. Bush's Warehouse was located across from Boonesborough on William Bush's land. The inspectors reported the number of casks of tobacco shipped from Holder's Landing and stated there was no warehouse at Holder's. The warehouse at Bush's was not complete. This could indicate that the warehouses had washed out in a flood; Bush's had been partly rebuilt, Holder's had not been started. Combs advertised his "commodious storehouse and ferry" in November 1799, so the warehouses may have washed away that winter.[46]

The state faced such a huge demand for warehouses along the Kentucky River that the government could no longer afford to build and maintain them. A law enacted in 1803 describes how new warehouses were to be constructed by their owners.

> No warehouse hereafter erected shall be deemed lawful unless the body shall be of brick or stone or scantling, enclosed with strong boards or planks well nailed on, or logs so close as to keep safely and prevent any injury by the weather, all produce that may be stored therein; to be floored with plank or timber and a good roof, shingles or plank, well nailed on. It shall be the duty of the proprietor or owner of every warehouse or the land on which any warehouse may be established by this act, his or her guardian, husband, attorney or agent (as the case may be) to build new houses agreeably to this act within twelve months from the passage thereof; and on failure every such inspection shall be discontinued and deemed unlawful, until such buildings and repairs shall be made.[47]

The law required warehouse inspectors to submit annual reports to the county court. They were to summarize the quantity of tobacco inspected and shipped and inform the court of the warehouse condition. If these reports were prepared, no record of them can be found before 1810. That year inspectors Whitson George and Ambrose Christy stated that 593 hogsheads of tobacco had been inspected at "Holders warehouse," of which 94 were still in storage on October 22. The warehouse was large enough to hold 400 hogsheads at one time. Inspectors noted that "the House are not

Business Enterprises

provided with Locks and boalts...also the scales and weights are in need of repair." The condition was as good or better than the other warehouses in the county. Business was up significantly for Combs in 1817, when 1,517 hogsheads of tobacco were inspected. Locks and bolts were still missing, scales and weights were still out of repair.[48]

The 1817 inspection of Bush's Warehouse, just up the river from Holder's, indicates there were continuing problems with the structures: "the roofs are good but the gable ends are open and require weatherboarding to prevent the rain from driving in. There is an excellent Set of weights but the Scale kneeds some repairing." The report then described the working conditions and problems the inspectors faced.

> There is no fireplace nor counting room, which since business has become more extensive puts the Inspectors to great inconveniencyes, in so much that in a croud of business and cold windy weather Masters of Boats as well as planters have been frequently been detained a considerable time until the Inspectors had an opportunity to leave the Warehous and go to some house where there was fire, where their best chance to Settle their Shiping accounts, make out Manifests and issue Tobacco notes has commonly been in a publick room where there was a croud of men drinking and carousing.[49]

We can imagine a scene from earlier years, when Philip Bush would have been attending business at Holder's Warehouse on a cold January day. With his hands nearly frozen from working in the unheated warehouse, Bush would have retired to the warmth at Holder's nearby tavern to do his paperwork. Here amid the "drinking and carousing," he would prepare tobacco notes for farmers, manifests for boat captains, and updates to the warehouse records.

For the convenience of loading produce onto boats, warehouses were usually built in the floodplain along the river. Periodic flooding of the Kentucky would have taken a toll on these structures. In some years, a particularly bad flood destroyed large numbers of warehouses which had to be rebuilt. One of the most disastrous overflows occurred in 1817, "when many valuable warehouses were washed away." Poorly constructed warehouses also had to be replaced from time to time. Holder's (Combs') Warehouse was probably still in the floodplain in 1800 when the court established a new section of road leading "to the Kentucky river at Combs Ware house."[50]

Colonel John Holder

At some point, Samuel R. Combs rebuilt Holder's Warehouse in stone. He extolled its virtues in a newspaper advertisement in 1810. The new building was "a large and commodious Stone Warehouse, 141 feet by 30, for the reception of Tobacco, Flour, Hemp, &c." Combs said the road to the place had been lately "placed in complete order" rendering it more convenient "as a general deposit for produce" than any other location on that part of the river.

A map submitted with an old road report shows the warehouse was standing near the mouth of Lower Howard's Creek. There is some hatching along the road to the warehouse to indicate the Kentucky River cliffs. Judging from this drawing the warehouse was down the hill below the cliffs in the floodplain. This is confirmed by an elevation view (not shown) that has the warehouse near river level. The "present road," shown on the map as A to C, was referred to elsewhere as the "old dirt road" that ran down the hill to the warehouse and terminated at the ferry landing.[51]

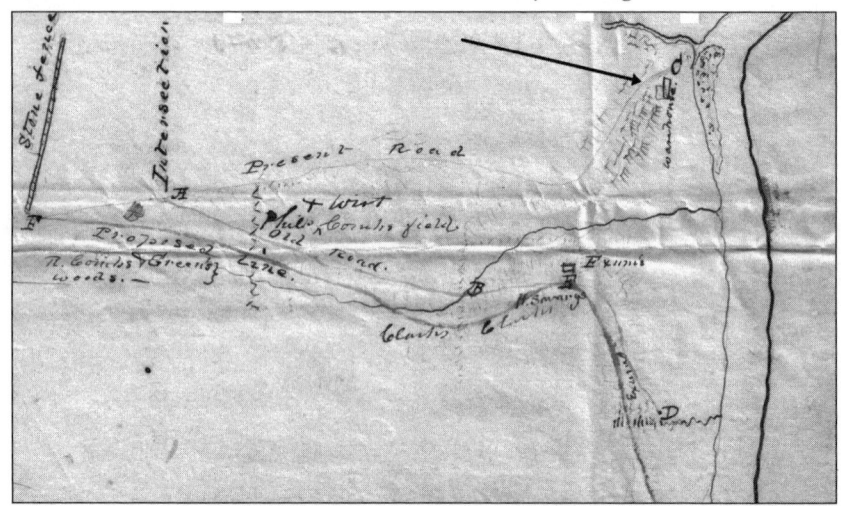

Map attached to a Clark County road report.[52] Arrow points to the "warehouse." North is to the left side of the picture.

We cannot close this discussion on Holder's Warehouse without pointing out other features on this most informative map. For example, at the mouth of Lower Howard's Creek the artist has drawn a shoal in the river. This was at the noted low water crossing of the river known as Blackfish Ford. The "Present Road" on the map is the remnant road still visible in the Lower Howard's Creek Nature and Heritage Preserve. This road ran parallel to the stone fence along the parking area and is traceable for some distance down

Business Enterprises

the hill. This was the early route of Holder's Road, which began at Holder's Landing and ran to the Bourbon County line. It was also called the Bourbon Road, a name used interchangeably with Holder's Road.

The map also shows the "Proposed Line," depicted as F to G, which the petitioners wished to open in 1844. The portion of this route near the river in now known as Amster Grove Road. When James T. Woodward and Daniel Bently moved Holder's/Combs' Ferry about three-quarters of a mile downstream, Amster Grove Road became part of the highway connecting Paris and Richmond. The road to the new ferry location is clearly shown on the historic Clark County maps of 1861 and 1877. Near the new ferry, Henry Calmes Jr. and Lewis Adams established a steam powered sawmill and gristmill. The mill, later owned by John W. Martin, was still in operation in 1880.[53]

Gristmill

John Holder owned a mill on Lower Howard's Creek, some distance removed from his enterprises on the river. The mill site is about .7 miles upstream from the mouth of the creek. The beginnings of Holder's Mill are nearly lost in the mists of time. One of the early millers, Ambrose Coffee, who operated John Holder's mill, made a statement in a lawsuit that provides the only information we have concerning the origin of the mill. Coffee was born in Dublin, Ireland, and came to America as a young man. He served out his time as an indentured servant then came to Kentucky,

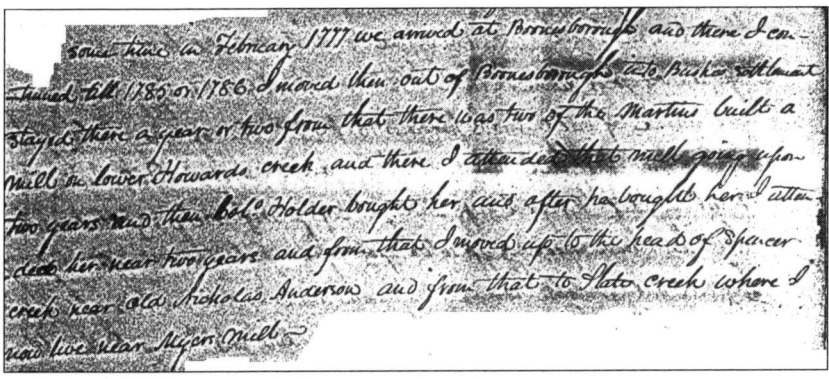

. . . some time in February 1777 we arrived at Boonesborough and there I continued till 1785 or 1786 I moved then out of Boonesborough into Bushes settlement stayed there a year or two from that there was two of the Martins built a mill on lower Howards creek and there I attended that mill going upon two years and then Colo. Holder bought her and after he bought her I attended her near two years and from that I moved up to the head of spencer creek near old Nicholas Anderson and from that to Slate creek where I now live near Myers mill[54]

165

Colonel John Holder

where he found employment as a miller. He may have been one of the men recruited by John Holder.

Coffee's statement lacks punctuation and is somewhat difficult to understand. (I inserted spaces in the transcription where new sentences are presumed to begin.) Several incorrect transcriptions have appeared previously in articles and books, including "John Martin built a mill" and "two John Martins built a mill." The deposition does not mention the name "John Martin." Given that Coffee left Boonesborough in 1785 or 1786 and stayed at the Bush Settlement one or two years, he could have come to the mill sometime between 1786 and 1788. This would have been the timeframe in which the Martins finished building the mill, if Coffee was the first miller (we do not know that he was). The mill could have been built somewhat earlier than 1786-1788 if Coffee was not the first miller. Also, Coffee does not state whether the Martins built a gristmill or sawmill. The usual source of data—county order books—for early mills is not available for the mill built by the Martins. Virginia law required permission from the county court prior to erecting a mill dam. Lower Howard's Creek was in Fayette County at that time, and the county records prior to 1803 were destroyed in a fire.

The 1786-1788 dates coincide with the arrival of the Martins in Clark County. William, Orson, John Jr. and Valentine Martin came out in 1786. Their parents, John Martin Sr. and his wife Rachel, probably arrived from Fluvanna County, Virginia, the following year, 1787, when they were accepted as members in the Howard's Creek Baptist Church.[55]

The statement "two of the Martins built a mill" implies that the Martins actually built the structure themselves. John Martin and his son Orson were both blacksmiths by occupation. Since blacksmiths were often skilled mechanics, the construction of a mill would have been within the Martins' capabilities. Orson later had his own sawmill and gristmill, which his brothers Valentine and Jobe helped him build. The evidence for this is found in an 1802 statement of moneys owed to Valentine by his brother Orson. In it we find several charges for sawing wood indicating that Valentine may have been operating Orson's sawmill during the period. Valentine was also building Orson's mill and house.

> Orson Martin Dr to Valentine Martin:
> For Work Done & Cash lent December 15, 1800 (9.15.6)
> From the old Book (1.0.0)
> To Sawing Done (12.4.0)
> To lincy 6½ yards at 6 Shillings per yard (1.19.0)

Business Enterprises

    To building the Mill walls (27.12.6)
    To the hole amount of sawing, 1801 (17.18.0)
    To sawing 1700 feet of weather boarding & scantling (1.2.6)
    To Building Chimney & House plastered (6.0.0)
    To pointing a House & Arching a tale Race (5.9.0)
    To water & Cogg pitts & Laid block walls (3.12.0)
    To by Jobe Martin (2.13.0)
    To one day work (0.6.0)
    To Cash Lent (3.12.0)
    To sawing in the year 1802, 26,900 feet (13.13.0)
    To work Done at sundry Times (0.17.0)[56]

The ruins of a 3½ story, water powered, stone gristmill located in the Lower Howard's Creek Nature and Heritage Preserve has been referred to, by local tradition, as the Martin-Holder-Bush Mill, so named for its successive owners. Several issues need to be addressed before these ruins can be equated with the mill the Martins built. A brief description of early milling in Kentucky may be helpful in providing context for this discussion.

When settlers came to Kentucky the first crop they always grew was corn which, even years later, continued to be a staple of their diet. When corn passed the roasting ear stage, it had to be crushed into meal to make it edible. In the beginning, corn was pounded in hollow stumps or ground in hand mills. Benjamin Allen described the laborious task of cranking the hand mill at Stephen Boyle's station near Winchester. As a boy, to make the mill easier to turn, he and his brother set the grinding stones farther apart which made a coarse, unsatisfactory cornmeal. He stated that he frequently had to prepare "a little corn in the hand mill. Just took the corn in our hats. We got to understand it, and would set it high, so that it would come out faster, and that made it coarser, and then mother would scold."[57]

Pioneers anxiously awaited and actively pursued the construction of mechanically powered mills in their neighborhoods. The first water mills in Kentucky were small affairs built to grind corn for personal use of the settlers. A person brought his corn to the mill to have it ground, and the miller kept a small share of the meal as payment for the service. Small quantities of corn—usually a sack or two—were taken to the mill on each trip, since the cornmeal tended to spoil and could not be stored for a long time. The miller had few opportunities to sell meal, so he often used his share to make whiskey.

Nathaniel Hart Jr., whose father was killed by Indians, lived at Boonesborough and later on Lower Howard's Creek. He stated in a deposition

Colonel John Holder

that he frequently had taken corn "to Morgans Mill on Boons Creek, where the people of Boonsborough got the first grinding done that was done in that part of the country at a water mill."[58] Charles Morgan's gristmill was in operation by the summer of 1784 and was shown on John Filson's "Map of Kentucke." Morgan built a tub mill, one of the simplest types to construct and operate. The tub mill had a small paddlewheel attached to the bottom of a vertical shaft. A stream of falling water was directed so as to turn the paddlewheel and the rotating shaft turned a millstone. The top millstone (called the "runner stone") was turned by the rotating shaft; the bottom millstone (called the "bed stone") was fixed. As described in a treatise on water power, the tub mill's great merit was "its simplicity and low cost of construction." The vertical shaft was in direct connection with the upper millstone; therefore no cogs or gears were required.

The author explained why tub mills were often the first type built on the frontier:

Diagram of a Tub Mill

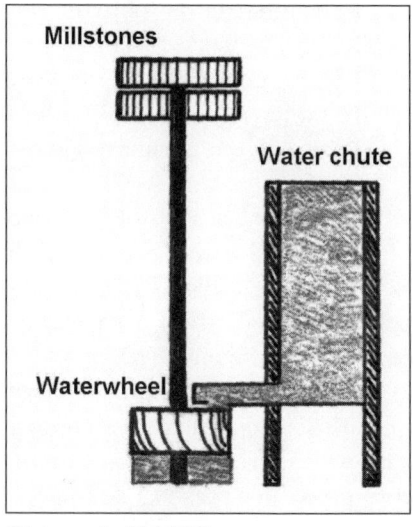

"This mill and its small waterwheel represented mechanical power in its most 'democratic,' that is to say, egalitarian, form.... The multitude of small streams afforded numerous sites where the slope and volume of flow were seasonally quite adequate to local needs. The mechanical equipment and the structures of such mills are neither large nor complicated. They are made today as in the past largely of wood. For craftsmen skilled in their building, tub mills evidently required no more than one or two weeks of labor, depending on size, and an outlay of perhaps no more than several dollars to

Diagram of an Overshot Mill

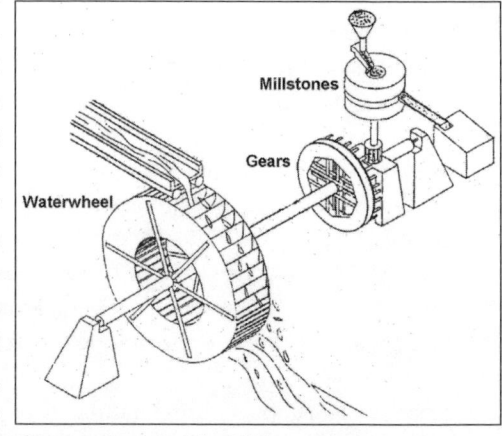

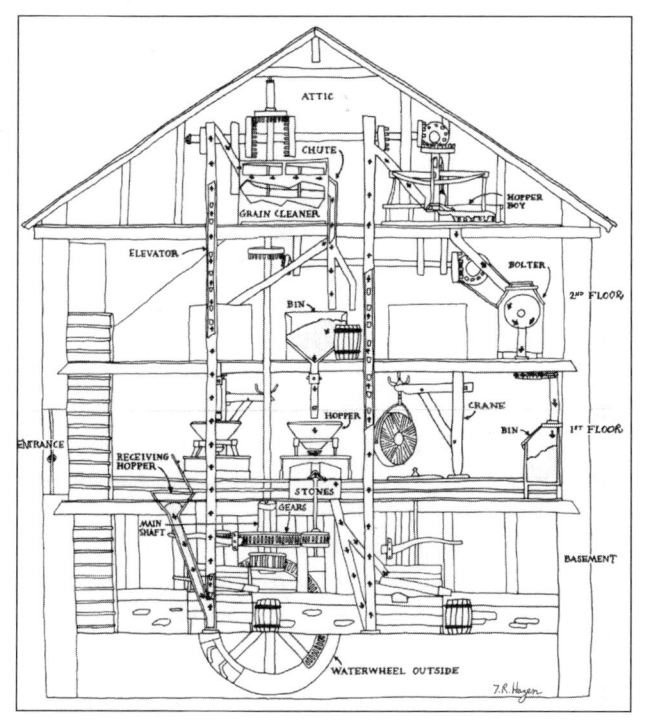

Diagram of an Automated Mill. Drawing by Theodore R. Hazen.

obtain the iron or ironwork required, and a similar amount for millstones if bought rather than made."[59]

Tub mills could be constructed without the expertise and expense of an experienced millwright. These mills continued to be made and used in Appalachia well into the twentieth century. One of the Foxfire books gives detailed instructions for making a tub wheel.[60]

Another advantage was that tub mills could be operated with a low water head, the difference in height between the top and bottom of the falling stream of water. Thus, these mills usually did not require the construction of a tall dam or lengthy mill race. The mills were usually housed in a small, one or two story structure.

Tub mills were often replaced with a more advanced design that employed a large waterwheel mounted on a horizontal shaft. A complex set of gears and cogs was required to redirect the power of the horizontal shaft to a vertical shaft, which turned the millstone. They were characterized by their waterwheels: overshot, undershot or breast wheels. With an overshot waterwheel, a stream of water was directed to the top of the wheel where it was released; the water fell into buckets built into the wheel. The force of

Colonel John Holder

the water striking the bucket and the weight of the water caused the wheel to turn. Construction of the waterwheel and gears required considerably more expertise than a tub mill, and the mill dam and race were much more important.

The earliest of these mills were typically two stories with two working levels. The gearing was located in the basement and the millstones were on the first floor. Grain and product could be stored on either level. A major advantage of these mills was their suitability for grinding a variety of grains (e.g., corn, wheat and rye). With a pair of imported French buhr millstones, a good miller could produce a high quality flour.

The stone flour mill that was housed in the ruins at the Preserve was of a highly sophisticated design—known as an automated flour mill—first developed in the late 1700s by Oliver Evans and not widely adopted until around the turn of the century. These mills required at least four working levels to accommodate all of the mechanical equipment associated with the automated processes. It is improbable that the stone flour mill, a structure based on Oliver Evans' principles, could have been erected by the Martins in the 1786-1788 timeframe. Evans did not build his first model until 1785. He was awarded U.S. Patent No. 3 for his automatic gristmill in 1791.[61]

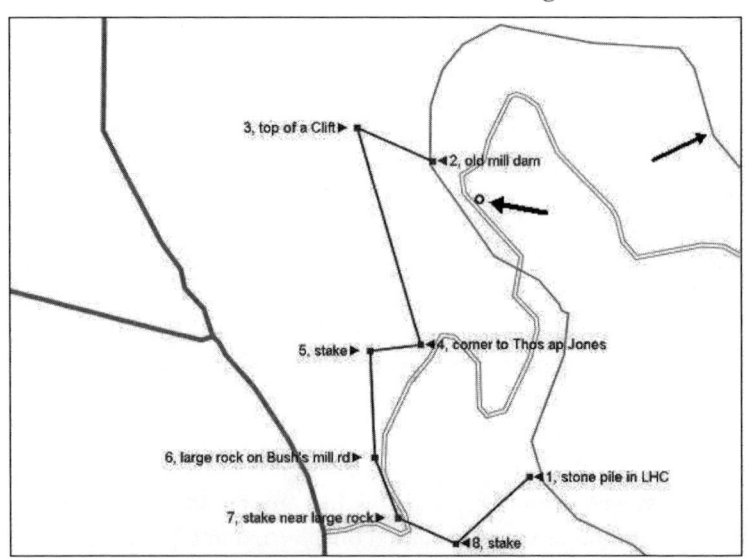

1829 Survey Showing the "Old Mill Dam." The "old mill dam" on Lower Howard's Creek was located at corner #2 of the survey. The thick arrow points to the stone flour mill ruins (circle). The double line is the Bush Mill Road that begins at present day Athens-Boonesboro Road, crosses Lower Howard's Creek, then goes by the mill ruins and the "John Martin House" (not shown). The thin arrow points to Jonathan Bush's mill dam. LHC, Lower Howard's Creek. See the text for an explanation of the tract of land and its corners.[62]

Business Enterprises

What type of mill did the Martins build in 1786-1788? A likely answer is that they built a small corn grinding mill. There would have been no reason for the Martins to erect a large and costly stone structure just to grind corn, and the technology did not exist at that time to build an automated flour mill. Nor was there a wagon road at that time to get to the mill. Nor was there a flour inspection warehouse to take the product. Nor was there even a market for the flour at that time. A much more modest structure would have been capable of providing valley residents with a place to get their corn ground, as well as supplying a small distillery with grain. This implies that the Martins' mill may have preceded the stone flour mill.

There is evidence for an earlier mill near the site. In 1829, Samuel R. Combs sold Jonathan Bush 32 acres on the west side of Lower Howard's Creek. A map of the tract (see 1829 Survey Showing the "Old Mill Dam") shows one of the corners located at the site of an earlier mill and dam."[63] No information was given in the deed concerning whose mill it was or what type it had been. The mill could have been an early gristmill or sawmill. The location of the dam indicates that it was in John Holder's original patent boundary. This could have been the dam for the mill the Martins built. Due to the dam's location, it could not have supplied water for the four level, stone flour mill, which stood at a higher elevation than the dam. The earlier mill was probably in the floodplain, in which case the mill and dam would have been destroyed eventually by the creek flooding. No remnants of the mill or dam have been found.[c]

We encounter a problem when trying to place the Martins' mill in historical context. The numerous surveys made for John Holder indicate that the Martins built their mill on land located within Holder's patent. The Martins—John, William and Orson—did own land nearby on Lower Howard's Creek, but they purchased from William Bush.[64] No deed has been found of any Martin buying land from Holder. The official record of this sale would have been recorded in the Fayette County deed books. These were damaged by fire in 1803 but have been partly restored. It is possible that a Martin-Holder deed could have been lost. However, the simplest conclusion seems to be that the Martins built their mill on Holder's land. If

---

[c] We cannot rule out the possibility that the Martins built a sawmill rather than (or in addition to) a gristmill. By that time, 1786-1788, settlers were clearing the creek valley and building homes. This would have provided a source of saw logs and a market for the mill's output. By the time Holder bought the mill, he may have started his boatyard. He would have needed timbers and planking to construct his flatboats. By 1796, Orson Martin was operating a sawmill of his own about two miles upstream. That year he petitioned the county court for permission to erect a water powered gristmill "on his own Land on Howards creek near his Saw Mill." Clark County Order Book 2:113.

Colonel John Holder

they did so, it must have been with some kind of agreement with Holder for the long term use of his land. This could have been a lease, a partnership or some other kind of arrangement.

The evidence presented above suggests that the Martins probably did not build the stone flour mill associated with the ruins in the Lower Howard's Creek Nature and Heritage Preserve. These mill ruins are the vestiges of a complex automated flour mill, while the mill the Martins built was probably much smaller, simpler and may have been in a different but nearby location.

Since the Martins built the mill on Holder's land, Holder must have had some involvement in the enterprise from the beginning. And Holder eventually acquired the Martins' interest. Recalling Ambrose Coffee's deposition, he stated that he "attended that mill going upon two years and then Colo. Holder bought her and after he bought her I attended her near two years...."[65] From the range of dates Coffee supplied, he came to the Martins' mill in 1786-1788, ran it for nearly two years, and then Holder bought the mill in 1788-1790. No deed has been found of Martin selling land or mill to Holder.[d] Presumably, when Holder bought the Martins' mill, he terminated whatever agreement they had had. The evidence then pairs the Martins' and Holder's ownership with the early mill operated by Ambrose Coffee.

In summary, the evidence suggests the following sequence of events. Two Martins, possibly John Sr. and his son Orson, built a mill on John Holder's land (1786-1788). Holder bought the mill (1788-1790) and Ambrose Coffee ran it until 1790-1792. This mill, which may be referred to as the Martin-Holder Mill, may have ground corn for settlers in the creek valley and perhaps also for distillers. The Martin-Holder Mill may have been located at a site near the "old mill dam" on Lower Howard's Creek, not far from where the stone flour mill was later erected.

Ambrose Coffee left Holder's Mill in about 1790-1792. Holder was still proprietor of the mill in mid 1798, as evidenced in county road orders.

---

[d] Some have suggested that a later lawsuit, *Martin v. Holder's heirs*, resulted from the sale of John Martin's mill to Holder. This seems unlikely. The suit was initiated in 1802 by John Martin Jr. for a broken covenant. He had an agreement signed by John Holder in 1793; Holder was to make Martin a deed for 100 acres out of Holder's land on Upper Howard's Creek, Lulbegrud or Red River. He died without making the deed. In 1807, the court ruled against Holder's heirs and ordered them to pay Martin damages of £300. Several years later Martin had to sue again when the heirs still had not paid. The court found for Martin again. *John Martin v. John Holder's heirs*, 1807, *John Martin Jr. v. John Holder's heirs*, 1811, Clark County Circuit Court case files. The numerous entries in the Circuit Court Order Books always refer to the plaintiff as John Martin Jr.

Business Enterprises

Orson Martin appointed Overseer of the new road from the Stone Meeting House on Howard's Creek to Taylor's Mill. William Taylor appointed Overseer of the road from Taylor's Mill to Holder's Mill.[66]

And Holder still owned the mill when he died in 1799. In June of that year, William Taylor, "living on Howards Creek," was indicted by the grand jury

for not clearing the road leading from his own Mill to Holders Mill by the information of Jonathan Baker of Winchester and William Trimble living on the waters of Howards Creek.[67]

The period Holder owned the mill, c.1790-1799, would have been an ideal time frame to modernize the milling operation and get into the flouring business. With the opening of the Mississippi River and the market at New Orleans, merchant mills that specialized in making flour began to be erected on a much larger production scale than the early corn grinding mills. The *Kentucky Gazette*, Lexington's newspaper that began in 1787, carried frequent news about mills and advertisements for mills. The first mention of flour mills in the paper occurred in the early 1790s: Tolliver Craig's Mill on North Elkhorn Creek (1792), John Cock's Mill in Lexington (1793), Thomas Lewis' Mill on Town Branch near Lexington (1794) and Eli Cleveland's Mill on Boone Creek (1795).

In 1795, the emerging importance of merchant flour mills and the export market led the Kentucky General Assembly to enact laws to regulate this enterprise. These acts established a series of flour inspection warehouses, where "all boulted [sifted] wheat flour and every cask thereof brought for exportation" could be examined. Inspectors were appointed by the governor. "Casks," or barrels, had to be constructed in accordance with strict standards. They were to be made of seasoned wood with staves 27 inches long and heads 17½ inches in diameter, tightened with 10 hoops, using 4 nails in each "chime hoop" and 3 nails in each "bilge hoop." The miller was to brand each barrel with his name and the tare and net weights. Each barrel was to contain 196 pounds of flour. The grade of flour—superfine, fine, or condemned—was to be branded on the barrel by the inspector.

Any flour remaining in a warehouse for more than nine months was to be sold at public auction. It was unlawful to export any flour not inspected, to export "condemned" flour, or to alter a brand. This system of warehouses and inspectors was designed to discourage a fairly obvious list of unscrupulous practices. It was meant to help Kentucky's merchant flour

Colonel John Holder

mills compete in the growing export market by forcing manufacturers to supply a uniform commodity.[68]

In December 1795, the General Assembly authorized an inspection of flour to be added at Holder's Warehouse, located "at Holder's boat yard in the county of Clarke."[69] This suggests that someone in the Lower Howard's Creek neighborhood was already making flour at that time or anticipated making flour soon.

The Martin-Holder Mill may have been capable of producing flour, though on a much smaller scale than the later stone flour mill. At some point, Holder may have installed a set of French buhr millstones to produce small quantities of flour for export. This flour would have been packed in barrels, inspected at Holder's Warehouse and loaded at Holder's Landing onto flatboats built at Holder's Boatyard.

Sometime after Oliver Evans' work became widely known in the mid-1790s, the Martin-Holder Mill was replaced with an automated flour mill—the 3½ story stone mill represented by the historic ruins in the Preserve. Holder could have had the stone flour mill built during this period, but we can find no evidence to prove it.[e]

---

[e] Several observations, when taken together, tend to suggest Holder did not build the stone flour mill: There was no convenient road from Holder's Mill to the warehouse on the river, and Holder did not petition the county to open one. A road to access the warehouse, called "Bush's Mill Road," was not established until 1809. (Clark County Order Book 4:321) Holder did not own the land where the dam for the stone flour mill was located, nor did he own all of the land on which the mill race was situated. Jonathan Bush purchased that land from Matthew Patton's heirs and Charles Morgan. (Clark County Deed Book 7:423, 9:47) Holder's heirs allowed the mill to be sold at public auction, where it brought only £75, indicating that the mill was not one of Holder's major enterprises. And the 3 acres of land that went with Holder's mill could not have included the entire millrace for the stone flour mill. Matthew Patton and Robert Clark Jr. purchased the mill at auction, then had the deed issued to Jonathan Bush in 1806. (Clark County Deed Book 7:283)

Chapter 11
Roads Lead to Holder's

Holder's plantation at the mouth of Lower Howard's Creek was the terminus of a number of roads. This was partly a matter of geography and partly a result of Holder's business establishments being located there. His seat on the county court put Holder in a position to influence road building decisions affecting his enterprises.

Roads could be built at county expense for the convenience of traveling to the county courthouse or to any public warehouse, river landing, ferry, mill, iron- or lead-works. The process began with the county court appointing three or more viewers to find the most convenient route for the road. Roads established on private lands required the owner's permission or the owner had to be paid damages. In practice, owners had much influence over the routing of roads. Once the court established the road, surveyors were appointed to open and maintain the roads. The surveyor, also called the overseer, was responsible for calling out the hands and superintending the work. Males over age 15 were subject to call for this heavy work, which typically involved clearing trees and brush from a path 15 to 30 feet wide, leveling the roadbed by cutting down high places and filling in low spots, and installing bridges over small streams. In the mid 1800s, the work got even harder when roads were macadamized by spreading rock and pounding it into a smooth surface.[1]

Salt Spring Trace

The earliest road to Holder's referred to in the records was a buffalo trace. The trace ran from the Kentucky River up Lower Howard's Creek. Near the present reservoir, the trace turned and followed the North Fork to the head. From there the trace went on to Lower Blue Licks. Native Americans used the network extensively. Blackfish and his Shawnee followed it when descending Lower Howard's Creek on their way to the great siege of Boonesborough in 1778. They camped just below the reservoir the night before the siege; the place was known for years as the Indian Camp. Pioneers traveling from Boonesborough to Lower Blue Licks used the same

Colonel John Holder

trail, which they called the Salt Spring Trace.[2] William Bush described the trail in a deposition he gave in a land trial:

> I have been acquainted with the lower Salt Spring trace ever since the Spring of the year 1775 and it leads from Boonsborough to Howards creek and to the said Indian encampments and crossed the north fork about thirty or forty yards above the mouth of said north fork, thence up the north fork…and on to the said lower blue Licks.[3]

John Pleak added that the trace "crossed Howards creek three times, thence crossing a small drain and up the west side of a stoney point and crossing the ridge over to the north Fork of Howards creek."[4] According to longtime Clark County resident, Doug Oliver, the old road along the North Fork is still in place under the water of the reservoir. Doug recalls that when the old reservoir was drained to build the new dam (1984), a deeply rutted road and stone fence beside it were uncovered.

The Salt Spring Trace was just that—a trace or trail suitable for travel on foot or horseback. When Kentucky began to be more densely settled and economically developed, wagons were needed to move raw materials and goods. Wagon roads required much more expense and labor to open and required continual maintenance. Expenses were defrayed by the county levy (i.e., taxes) and labor was provided by local area residents. Thus, the opening and maintenance of roads became one of the most important and politically sensitive functions of county government.

Boonesborough to Holder's Ferry/Boatyard

Another connection important for Clark County travelers was from the area opposite Boonesborough down to Holder's ferry and boatyard. Residents filed a petition to the court to open this road in 1795.

> To The Worshipfull Court of Clark County We your petitioners humbly Request that your worships in your Clemency and wisdom would Grant an order of Court Directing a bridle way to be opened from Boonsborough Ferry Down the River to Holders Road that Leads from said Holders Ferry to Lexington and your Petitioners as in duty bound will Ever pray &c[5]

While a wagon road was not feasible on this route in early times, a horse trail was needed. The report of the viewers—William Martin, John Bush,

Roads Lead to Holder's

Francis Bush and William Parrish—was submitted to the county court in April of that year. They "marked out the nearest and best way.... Beginning in the land of William Bush, thence through said Lands and the Lands of John Holder to said Holders road (both parties agreed) and find there may be a bridle way got."[6]

This route, starting at the ferry landing on present day Ford Road, went down the north side of the Kentucky River to Athens-Boonsboro Road to the mouth of Lower Howard's Creek. The road was described as a "bridle way" or horse path. It would be many years before this route was made passable for wagons, except for the short stretch to Bush's Warehouse.

Holder's Road/Bourbon Road

The best known and longest used route to the boatyard was known as Holder's Road. This road eventually became part of the main highway from Paris to Richmond. In Clark County, the road began at the Bourbon line and terminated at Holder's landing, ferry, warehouse and boatyard. It was also called the Bourbon Road.

The Madison County section of the road predates the formation of Clark County. In 1790, they opened a road that connected "Madison courthouse" and Boonesborough with Holder's ferry and boatyard. The Madison road terminated nearly opposite the mouth of Lower Howard's Creek.[7]

In August 1793, Clark County court ordered Hubbard Taylor, John McGuire, Richard Hickman and Neil McCann to view a new road "from John Holder's Boat yard towards Bourbon Court house as far as the County line." The road was established by the court at two sessions. In January 1794, the court opened the section from the county line to near the present day intersection of Becknerville Road and McClure Road. The section running from that intersection to Holder's Boatyard was opened in January 1795.[8] When put together, the two sections were long referred to as Holder's Road.

In 1832, an interesting alteration was proposed to the road for the convenience of an influential landowner, namely, Hubbard Taylor. The change resulted in a 90 degree turn that is still there on present day Venable Road. The accompanying map shows "Holder's lane" (now Venable Road) connecting Todds Road (now Colby Road). Holder's Road originally ran on a direct line, but the alteration left it with a right angle bend to the west.

Holder's, and later Combs', ferry and warehouse were at the southern terminus of the road in Clark County. The section of road leading from the bluff down to the river must have been a challenging hill for wagons to negotiate. In 1825, the county court appointed four men to see if a better route could be located to get down the hill to Samuel R. Combs'

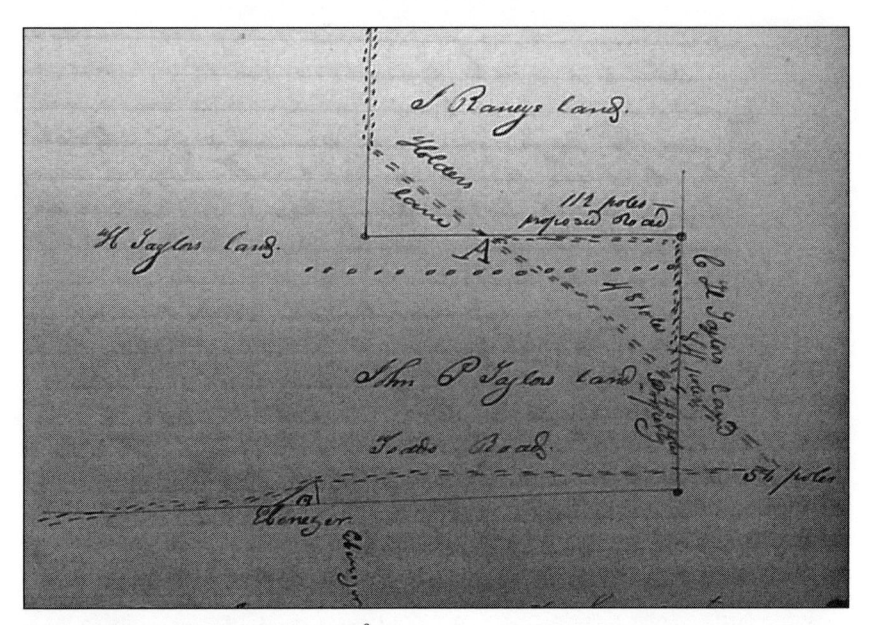

Proposed change to Holder's Road, 1832.[9]

new warehouse. Their report stated that they examined the present road and "believe it to be the nearest and best way down the clift to said new warehouse." At their November session in 1851, the court appropriated $60 for "the Improvement of the River Hill at Combs Ferry." The money was spent "to Blow out and remove Such Rock as could Not be removed by the ordinary Hands that Work Roads."[10]

The southern end of the road went through the present Lower Howard's Creek Nature and Heritage Preserve. It ran along the east side of the stone fence beside the parking lot and is traceable most of the way down the hill. In 1858, when James T. Woodward and Daniel Bently moved Combs' Ferry downstream, they opened a new road to the ferry. The ferry landing was at the west end of present day Amster Grove Road. The report to the court stated that "Mr. Woodward does not intend to deprive the public of the ford on the old Road, on the Kentucky River at the mouth of Howard's Creek." The old dirt road was left in place and a cutoff, labeled "passway" on the map (see Changes to Holder's Road, 1858), was installed between the "Pike" and the "old road." There was a gate at either end of the cutoff, one on Woodward's land on the Pike and one near Benjamin Hieronymous' house[a] on the old road. From Hieronymous' place, Woodward "let the old Road be open down the Hill to the ford." A second passway may be seen

---

a Benjamin Hieronymous died in 1859 and was buried in the graveyard near the house.

Roads Lead to Holder's

Site of Holder's Road. This shows a portion of the road crossing Lower Howard's Creek Nature and Heritage Preserve near the present parking lot.

running beside the river. The map also shows that the turnpike continued on the Madison County side of the river, and the old road there was replaced by the turnpike.

In spite of Woodward's assurance that the old road would be kept open, it was closed two years later. This was the era when turnpike companies were replacing many of the poorly maintained county roads with more convenient modern roads and charging a toll for using them. Holder's Road was now operated by the Kentucky River Turnpike Company, and the terminus of the road had been rerouted to the new ferry landing. The company applied to the county to close the old road and posted notices at the courthouse and other places in the neighborhood. The court appointed several men from the area to determine the inconvenience to the public, if any, of closing the old road. At January court in 1860, Edmund T. Taylor, James P. Lydanne and Willis Martin reported there would be no adverse effect to the public, and the court permitted closing the old road from the tollhouse (at the present intersection of Combs Ferry Road and Athens-Boonesboro Road) down the hill to the river at the mouth of Lower Howard's Creek. The old road is not shown on historic maps of Clark County published in 1861 and 1877. Out of habit no doubt, the court continued to refer to the Kentucky River Turnpike as Holder's Road for many years.[11]

Colonel John Holder

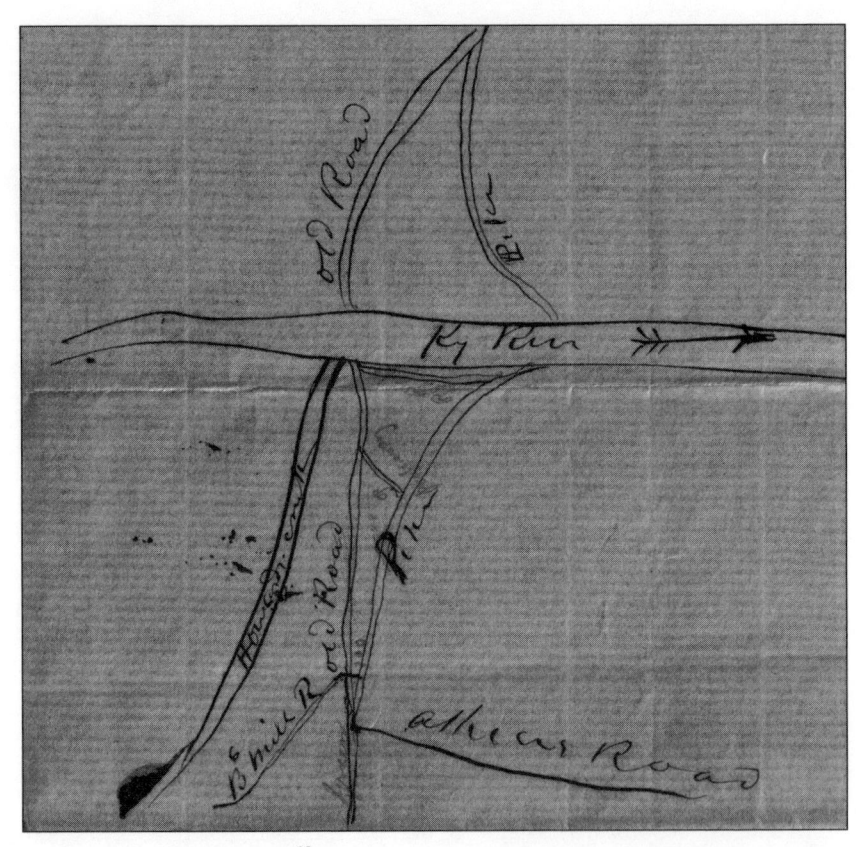

Changes to Holder's Road, 1858.[12] *Shown on the north side of the river (bottom of page): New Road ("Pike") to the Woodward-Bently Ferry; "old Road" to the Holder-Combs Ferry and ford; Bush's Mill Road; and Athens Road.*

Although stretches of the old highway have been relocated over the years, you can still drive the general route of Holder's Road. Referring to the map (Holder's Road Today), one begins at Combs Ferry on the Kentucky River (bottom of the map), then proceeds north on Athens-Boonesboro Road (Route 418), north on Combs Ferry Road (Route 3371), north on Becknerville (Route 3371), west on Colby Road (Route 1927), north on Venable Road, and north on Clintonville Road (Route 1678) to the Bourbon County line.

Winchester to Holder's Boatyard

One of the first roads called for by the newly formed Clark County court in 1793 was to run from the courthouse to Holder's Boatyard. In July of that year, John Holder, William McMillan, John Frame and James Dunlap were appointed to view

Roads Lead to Holder's

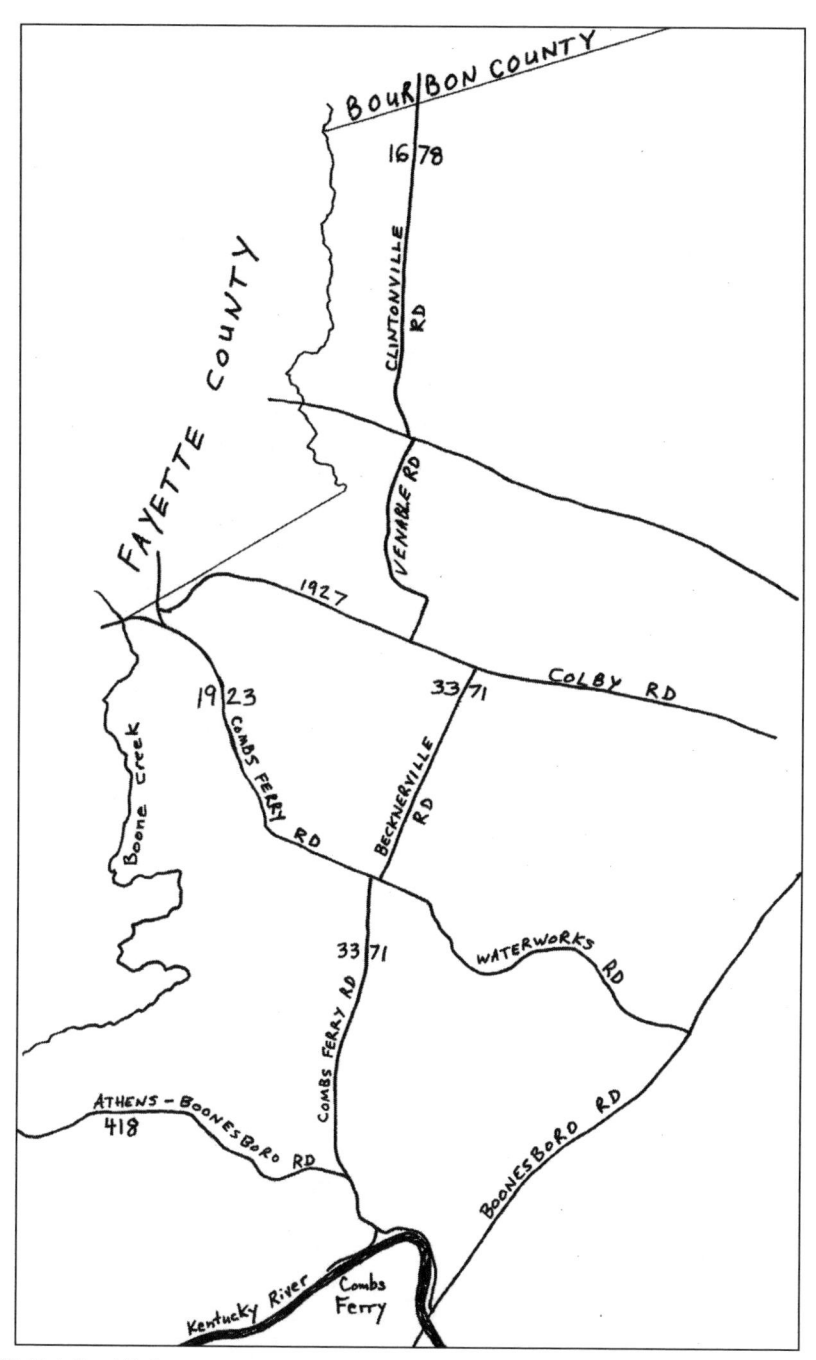

Holder's Road Today

Colonel John Holder

the nearest and best way for a road from Colonel Holder's Boatyard to the place appointed for erecting the publick buildings for this County.[13]

It would have been logical for them to use the existing trail that descended Lower Howard's Creek. Getting to the creek by the most direct route from Winchester, one would have traveled along what is now Boone Avenue and Old Boonesboro Road, striking the creek near the present reservoir. This route is confirmed by a court order calling for the road to start at the south end of Main Street. At that time, Main Street ended near Fairfax (now Lexington Avenue). From there the road was to run southwest to James McMillan's plantation, which was near the present reservoir on Lower Howard's Creek. From there to the boatyard, the road may have run along the creek following the old buffalo road-Indian trail-Salt Spring Trace.[14]

Subsequent road requests indicate that the county did not succeed in opening a functional wagon road all the way to the mouth of the creek in 1793. The road from Winchester joined the road from Strode's Station at James McMillan's plantation, then followed the meanders of Lower Howard's Creek downstream as far as the Martin-Holder Mill. The road included many creek crossings. At its lower end, the creek becomes deeply entrenched and, near the mouth, a high cliff rises on the west side. A road all the way to the mouth of the creek would of necessity end on the east side of the creek. From this point, there was only a bridle path upstream to the Boonesborough ferry and a creek crossing to get to Holder's ferry, warehouse and boatyard. For this reason, the lower end of the creek valley did not have a serviceable wagon road for many years (i.e., the 1850s). Thus, Holder's enterprises at the river had to be accessed from Clark County by way of Holder's Road or from Madison County by way of Holder's Ferry.

In 1799, Robert Clark Jr. and Matthew Patton acquired Holder's Mill. They applied that year to the county court to open a road from the mill to the Kentucky River.[15] The court appointed viewers to assess two different routes to the river:

> Ordered that John Martin Sr., Orson Martin, Richard Hickman, Edmund Hockaday and William Martin, being first sworn, review the nearest and best way for a road from Patton's mill on Howards Creek to Combs boat yard [and] viewing also a way for the same down the said Creek.[16]

While one route was to follow the creek all the way to the river, the other was go overland to the boatyard, presumably leaving the creek valley and running up the hill to Holder's Road. It was two years (1801) before the viewers returned their report to the court. They were "of opinion that a road can be made down the Creek with Less Labour and to the Greatest advantage to the Publick."[17] It was not to the greatest advantage of Matthew Patton or Samuel R. Combs, however, so the court did not establish the road at that time.

In 1806, Jonathan Bush acquired Holder's Mill.[18] From his efforts to get a road to the warehouse on the river, we surmise that Bush planned to enlarge the mill and change its operation from grinding corn for the neighborhood to manufacturing wheat flour for export. Farmers could bring sacks of corn to the mill on horseback for grinding, so a wagon road was not essential to a business on the scale of the original mill. If one is going to export flour, however, the whole scope of the business is expanded. Instead of sacks of meal, the mill would turn out barrels of flour. Wagons would be required to haul barrels of flour to the inspection warehouse on the river. Thus, in 1807 Jonathan Bush and Samuel R. Combs proposed to build a road from Bush's Mill to Combs' Warehouse. This time they specified the route and the court appointed viewers to mark out

> a road from Martins ford on Howards creek down the creek to Jonathan Bush's mill and from there to Intersect the Bourbon road leading to Holders warehouse.[19]

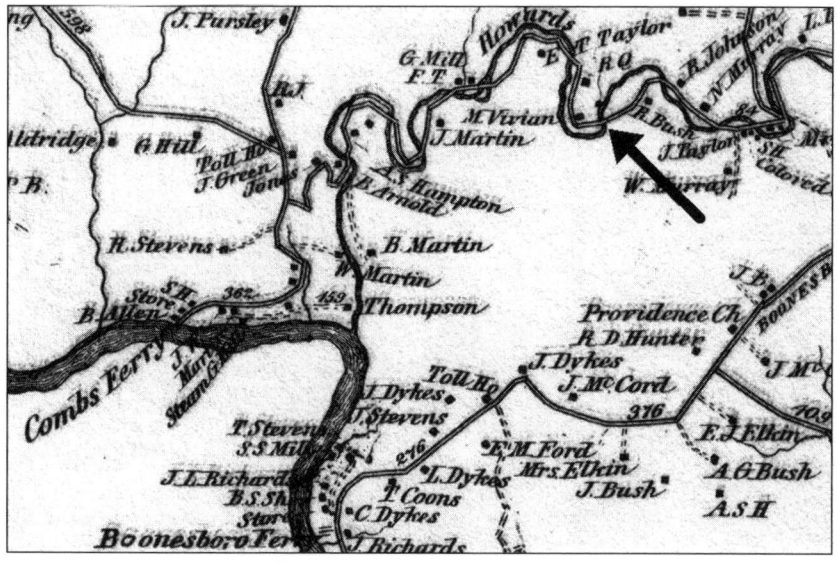

Martin's Ford (arrow), 1877 Map.

Colonel John Holder

Martin's ford was on Orson Martin's land, 25 acres where he had a mill in what used to be called "Factory Bottom." Martin's tract was upstream from the mouth of West Fork, on the north side of the creek. The exact location of the ford (see Martin's Ford, 1877 Map) was determined by plotting a deed that refers to "the old Martin ford."[20]

At the time the road was proposed, Orson Martin had a flour mill in Factory Bottom and William Taylor had a flour mill at the mouth of West Fork, so the new road to the warehouse would have benefited them as well as Bush and Combs.[21]

In May of 1809, the county court ordered the road established along the specified route:

> from Martins ford on Howards Creek down said Creek a path way already opened to Jonathan Bushes mill, from thence a path way crossing Howards Creek a little below the mill and near the foot of a hill passing through the Land of said Bush, from thence up the north side of said Hill by several windings to the top, and from thence the nearest way to Intersect the Bourbon Road near the River Hill at a Bridge on said road.[22]

The court assigned Jonathan Bush overseer of the road; Isaac Hockaday

Ford near the Old Stone Church. Joe Kendall Neel, University of Kentucky Master's Thesis, 1938.

Roads Lead to Holder's

Road down Lower Howard's Creek. This picture was taken, looking east, about one-third of a mile downstream from the Old Stone Church. Road is visible on the left (north) side of the creek. Joe Kendall Neel, University of Kentucky Master's Thesis, 1938.

and Whitson George were to allot hands to do the work.[23] With the opening of this section, one could finally take a wagon from Winchester to Lower Howard's Creek, down the creek to Bush's Mill, up the hill to Holder's Road, then down the "River Hill" by way of Holder's Road to Combs' warehouse, boatyard and ferry.

The segment running from Bush's Mill "up the north side of said Hill by several windings to the top" was long known as the "Bush Mill Road." This road is still in use today in the Lower Howard's Creek Nature and Heritage Preserve, where it serves as the entrance road to the creek valley. It begins at the trailer at the top of the hill and descends the hill "by several windings" to the creek. While hiking along this steep road, one can imagine what the trip would be like in a wagon. Going up must have been hard work for the team pulling a loaded wagon; coming down must have been a harrowing ride for the driver.

The completed road—from Winchester to the mouth of Lower Howard's Creek—has a long history. It is shown on historic Clark County maps of 1861, 1877 and 1926. The road was used throughout the nineteenth and most of the twentieth century. The road, though county maintained, was never

Colonel John Holder

paved. We have several photos showing portions of the road in 1938.

Although the section of the road that followed the creek fell out of use when the valley was depopulated in the mid 1900s, it is still easily traceable on the ground today. Portions of the road located in the Lower Howard's Creek Nature and Heritage Preserve have been restored.

Future plans call for the road to be restored throughout the length of the Preserve as funds become available.

Restored Road, 2009. The picture was taken in Lower Howard's Creek Nature and Heritage Preserve, looking north toward the creek crossing below the mill ruins.

Road to the Mouth of Lower Howard's Creek

As mentioned above, the road to the Kentucky River by way of Lower Howard's Creek proposed by the county court in 1793 was never finished. It was proposed again in 1799 but was not built then either. The road was proposed as part of a larger project in 1853. The court appointed Edmund Taylor, Richard G. Bush and Smallwood A. Elkin to view "the way for a new road" beginning at Jonathan Bush's mill, running down the creek past Benjamin Exum's sawmill to the Kentucky River, and from there to run up the river to the Winchester-Kentucky River Turnpike at the Boonesborough ferry landing.[b] The viewers did their job well and even returned to the court

---

[b] A small portion of this road—from the Boonesborough ferry landing to Bush's Warehouse—had been in place for many years.

Roads Lead to Holder's

a detailed map of the proposed road prepared by John W. Martin, the county surveyor. The original map and road report were found several years ago among old documents boxed up in the courthouse attic.[24] The viewers stated they were of opinion that

> said road is highly necessary and no inconvenience to any person on whose land said road runs, and a great convenience to the parties, neighbourhood and individuals, and also a great convenience to the public generally. The parties living between the mouth of two mile and Howards Creek are greatly benefitted by this road both in milling and traveling. And the travelling public generally, the said proposed road is giving an advantage both to the river and the Mills of Exum and Bush's. This road is comparitively more level than any other road leading to the above mentioned places, and we are of opinion that 15 feet would be width sufficient for said road.[25]

This statement was followed by the metes and bounds from the survey.

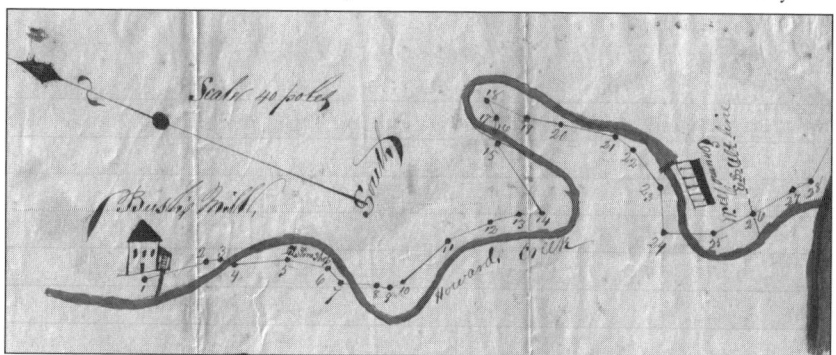

Road from Bush's Mill to the Kentucky River (top) and from there to the Turnpike (bottom), 1853. Original map found in the Clark County court loose papers

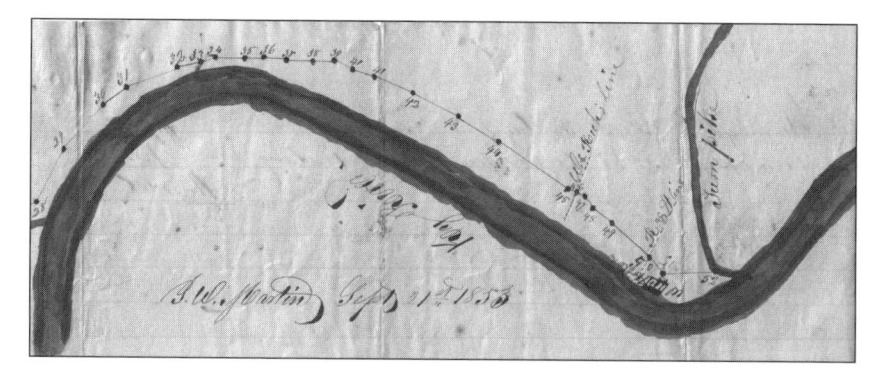

Colonel John Holder

The documents reveal several interesting features. First, the map shows the location of Jonathan Bush's flour mill and Benjamin Exum's sawmill (and dam), the four places where the road crosses the creek and one crossing (points 24-25 below Exum's Mill) where a bridge needed to be built. The survey notes running "by an old road" at point 23. This could have been a road coming down off what is known today as Thompson Ridge. The map also shows a "Stone Shop" just downstream from Bush's Mill. Today this site is enclosed by a restored stone fence on the right side of the road approaching the swinging bridge in the Preserve. The Stone Shop belonged to Richmond Arnold, whose nearby home is shown on the historic 1861 map. In the 1850 and 1860 censuses, Ricmond Arnold, stonemason, was living on Lower Howard's Creek. Finally, the survey map shows the house of William Hooten, just west of the Boonesborough ferry landing and turnpike road.

Unfortunately, Clark County's order book for this period is missing, so we do not have a record showing whether or not the road was completed according to the survey. There was no mention of the proposed road tying into a crossing at the mouth of Lower Howard's Creek where Hall's Restaurant is today. Although we take it for granted now, it would be several more years before a bridge was built there. The crossing is shown on a topographic map from 1890, but not on the historic maps of 1861 or 1877.[26]

Chapter 12

Howard's Creek Industrial Center

Holder's mill on Lower Howard's Creek and his business enterprises on the Kentucky River formed the nucleus for one of Kentucky's earliest industrial areas. The steeply falling stream bed combined with Holder's warehouse and boatyard attracted many water powered industries to the valley. Early wagon roads were built along the creek and connected to the warehouse and boatyard.

According to historian Robert S. Cotterill, this area eventually became one of the largest factory centers west of the Allegheny Mountains.

> The main road to Boonesborough was down Lower Howard's Creek. The industrial center of Winchester in 1812-14 was not in Winchester at all, but down along the aforementioned creek. Here were located factories, the fulling houses, the tanneries and the grain mills. This was one of the largest factory centers west of the Alleghenies in 1812 and had a wide reputation. The road from the now reservoir to the Kentucky river was lined with houses every hundred yards and the Howard's Creek settlements promised great developments. The ruins of some of these places are still to be seen.[1]

There is ample evidence for Cotterill's claim. Numerous factories were built in the valley and thrived until about the Civil War. They declined thereafter and died out completely around the turn of the century. The factories that have been identified are shown on the map below and described in the following sections. These include 15 mills, 4 distilleries, 2 quarries, a woolen factory, stone shop and blacksmith shop on Lower Howard's Creek and its tributary, West Fork. On John Holder's land along the Kentucky River, there was a sawmill, gristmill and blacksmith shop. There were 7 mills, 3 distilleries and a blacksmith shop in the creek valley before 1800. And to

Colonel John Holder

support Cotterill's statement above, we can identify 11 mills, 4 distilleries and a blacksmith shop on Lower Howard's Creek before 1812.

Many ruins still mark the location of these mills and factories. A continuing effort is being made to preserve them.

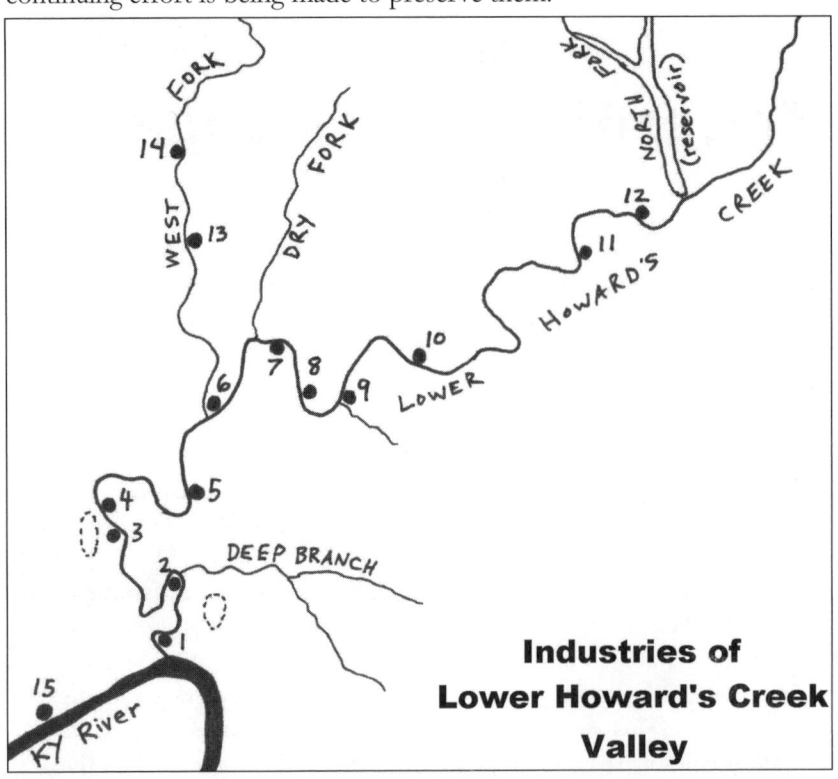

Industries of Lower Howard's Creek Valley

Filled circles:
1. Benjamin Exum Sawmill
2. Samuel R. Combs Sawmill*
3. Richmond Arnold Stone Shop
4. Martin-Holder Mill
   Jonathan Bush Flour Mill
5. William T. Bush Distillery
6. Edmund Taylor Flour Mill
7. Jonathan Bryan Gristmill
   William Taylor Fulling Mill and Distillery
8. Factory Bottom
   Orson Martin Sawmill,
      Flour Mill and Blacksmith Shop
   Isaac Hockaday Woolen Factory
9. William Trimble Distillery*
10. Smith Sawmill
11. John Rees Gristmill
12. John Wilkerson Gristmill and Sawmill
13. Robert Didlake Gristmill
14. William Wilkerson Mill*
15. Adams and Calmes Sawmill,
    Gristmill and Blacksmith Shop

Dotted ovals:
Richmond Arnold quarry (left)
and Robert Martin quarry (right)

Not located:
Edmund Hockaday Distillery

* tentative identification

Howard's Creek Industrial Center

Jonathan Bush Flour Mill

The stone flour mill in the Preserve, referred to in the previous chapter, was operated for many years by Jonathan Bush and may have been built by him. Holder's mill site was auctioned off by the sheriff in 1799 to satisfy a judgment against Holder. The purchasers were Matthew Patton and Robert Clark Jr. Holder's mill went by several names over the next few years: Clark and Patton's Mill (1799), Patton's Mill (1799), Matthew Patton Sr. Mill (1801), and Patton's Mill on Howard's Creek (1802). No deed was recorded by the sheriff during this period. Clark sold his interest to Patton, who in turn sold to Jonathan Bush. Then in 1806, Patton having died, his heirs directed that the deed for the mill property be issued in Bush's name.[2]

Painting of the Jonathan Bush Mill. Courtesy of the Clark County-Winchester Heritage Commission.

A Bush descendant later claimed that Jonathan was the builder of the stone flour mill. According to a 1923 newspaper article:

> Practically all of these old mills have passed away with the exception of the old Bush mill, near the mouth of the creek, which

Colonel John Holder

is still standing and of which two fine oil paintings have been presented to the Clark County Historical Society by Captain C. E. Bush, a grandson of the original builder of the present structure.... This old mill building is built of the Kentucky marble and bids fair to stand for centuries yet, if a proper roof is maintained upon it.[3]

Undated 20th Century Photos of the Bush Mill. Courtesy of Kathryn Owen.

Howard's Creek Industrial Center

Ownership of the mill passed to Jonathan's son William T. Bush after Jonathan died in 1857. Subsequent owners were James F. McKinney (1861), Alexander S. Hampton (1867), John W. and Joel T. Hart (1891), Green A. Parker (1905) and Hubbard L. Stevens (1906). The mill went out of operation sometime after Stevens bought it.[4]

Bush Mill undated (top) and 1938 (bottom). Courtesy of Pat Shely (top) and Joe Kendall Neel's University of Kentucky Master's Thesis (bottom).

Colonel John Holder

Bush Mill Today (2009).

Details of the mill's operation are found in the U.S. Manufacturers Census from 1850 through 1880.

Year	Owner's name	Capital invested	Bushels of grain used	Value of flour, meal, etc.
1850	Jonathan Bush	$4,000	6,000	$4,800
1860	William T. Bush	$5,000	15,000	$13,200
1870	A. S. Hampton	$4,000	8,000	$15,000
1880	A. S. Hampton	$5,000	9,300	$12,685

Unfortunately, "a proper roof" was not maintained and much of the mill structure eventually collapsed. The ruins of the old mill remain unstable. The Preserve is seeking funds to protect the structure from further damage from the elements.

William T. Bush Distillery

William T. Bush operated a distillery on land he purchased from his father Jonathan. Jonathan sold William 8 acres on Lower Howard's Creek, including "the old still house," for $350. William put the distillery, along with his flour mill, up for sale in 1858.

Howard's Creek Industrial Center

> I will also sell one-third interest in a Copper Distillery situated within a half mile of the Mill. There is sufficient apparatus connected with it to make six barrels of whiskey per day.[5]

Bush's distillery is listed in the 1860 manufacturers census. It had a capital value of $2,600, indicating that William had put up a new distillery or modernized the earlier one. Bush's distillery produced 8,300 gallons of "copper whiskey" from 3,500 bushels of corn and rye. The following year, Bush sold the distillery to John Grigsby, but the deed was not recorded until 1864. The property was described as the tract "heretofore owned by W. T. Bush and occupied by him and S. A. B. Woodford and is known as "the Still house tract."[6] Woodford descendant, John Venable, has a stencil—W. T. Bush & Co. Copper Distilled—presumably used to letter whiskey barrels.[a] The storage warehouse was on Woodford's land near the distillery. There is a story that during the Civil War, a company of Union soldiers stopped at Woodford's place and he offered them refreshments from one of his barrels. When that was gone they asked for more and Woodford refused, whereupon they either took or destroyed all the whiskey in the warehouse. There is evidence that the story is true. More than 25 years after the war, Woodford received damages from the government in compensation for the seized whiskey:

> A special from Washington says that the claim of S. A. B. Woodford, of this county, for a lot of whiskey seized during the war by the Federals under General Sturgis, has been allowed. The amount of the claim was about $8,000 and the attorney at Washington wanted $4,000 for his services, but the fifth auditor of the Treasury only allowed $900.[7]

Ruins of the distillery and springhouse are described in a survey of cultural resources near the Lower Howard's Creek Nature and Heritage Preserve. The distillery was located just north of the Preserve boundary. The spring which served the distillery was referred to as "the upper spring of Bush" in Jonathan Bush's deed to his son William.[8]

Jonathan Bryan Gristmill

In 1790, James Bryan purchased a tract of land at the junction of

---

[a] The stencil is on exhibit at the Bluegrass Heritage Museum in Winchester. John and his sister Jane Venable Brown live in the home S. A. B. Woodford built on the waters of Lower Howard's Creek. The whiskey warehouse is still standing on their farm.

William T. Bush Distillery. Stone pier of the distillery (top) and springhouse (below).

Howard's Creek Industrial Center

Lower Howard's Creek with West Fork. Three years later, his son Jonathan petitioned the Clark County court for permission to erect a water powered gristmill on the property. In 1796, a deed to a tract adjoining the Bryans was described as "beginning at a small sycamore tree standing on the Creek Barr below Briants Mill dam."[9] A few years later, James and Jonathan Bryan moved to Missouri, where they lived near Daniel Boone and his family.

Mill dam abutment (left) and mill ruins (right) at the site of Jonathan Bryan's gristmill and William Taylor's fulling mill on the south bank of Lower Howard's Creek.

James Bryan was born in Virginia, one of seven sons of Morgan and Martha (Strode) Bryan. James served in the French and Indian War, was a member of the North Carolina House of Burgesses and a justice of the peace in Rowan County. Sometime after his wife, Rebecca Enochs, died in childbirth, James came to Boonesborough. The state of Virginia awarded James a patent to 1,400 aces of land on South Elkhorn Creek for "raising a Crop of Corn in the country in the year 1776." In 1779, he helped his brothers—William, Joseph and Morgan—bring their families out from the Yadkin River valley to settle Bryan's Station. James' motherless children reportedly spent much time in the household of Daniel and Rebecca Boone. Boone's wife, Rebecca Bryan, was James' niece. James served as a private in John Holder's company at Boonesborough in 1779.[10]

Jonathan (1759-1846), born in North Carolina, was the second son of James and Rebecca Bryan. Jonathan married Mary Hughes Coshow, a widow with one son. He lived in close proximity to Daniel and Rebecca Boone all his life, first in North Carolina, then in Kentucky and finally in Missouri. James lived with his son in Missouri and died there in 1807 in consequence of falling from his horse. He was buried in the Jonathan Bryan Cemetery in present-day Marthasville. Daniel Boone and his wife were buried in the David Bryan cemetery nearby. Jonathan Bryan reportedly fashioned a rough tombstone for Boone's grave.[11]

Colonel John Holder

William Taylor Fulling Mill and Distillery

In 1797, William Taylor bought the Bryans' gristmill tract.[12] Taylor continued to operate the gristmill and added a fulling mill and distillery. Fulling mills were used for cleaning and thickening ("fulling") woolen cloth. While having financial problems in 1802, Taylor tried to sell his property, which he described in an advertisement in the *Kentucky Gazette*:

> Mills For Sale. The subscriber has for sale 196 acres of land, lying on Lower Howard's creek, in Clarke county, the former property of James Bryant. There is on it an elegant two story Dwelling House, a good country Gristmill, a good new Fulling Mill, in good repair, well established; a good Still House. The buildings all well built of Stone.[13]

Taylor's problems continued when his gristmill burned the following year. He accused Orson Martin of arson but Martin was never charged.[14]

William Taylor House (2004).

Taylor eventually paid off his debts and went on to erect a flour mill at the confluence of Lower Howard's Creek and West Fork.

William Taylor was a native of Ireland and trained as a fuller or cloth dresser in England. Taylor's first marriage—to Elizabeth Owen daughter of Clark County minister Lawrence Owen—ended in divorce, a rare occurrence in those times. He then married Hannah Hinde Kavanaugh, the daughter of Dr. Thomas Hinde and widow of the Methodist minister

Howard's Creek Industrial Center

Williams Kavanaugh. Taylor died unexpectedly in 1814, leaving two small children and no will.[15]

Edmund Taylor Flour Mill

Although this flour mill was built by William Taylor, it is usually identified with his son Edmund, who was the proprietor of the mill until his death in 1891. Edmund Taylor's and Jonathan Bush's flour mills were two of the most important manufacturing facilities in Clark County for much of the 19th century. Taylor's somewhat unusual mill was described by a contemporary:

> At the Junction of West Fork and Howard's Creek is Taylor's Mill formerly owned by Judge Ed Taylor. It was different in one respect from any other mill we ever knew. The water which turned the wheel and thus furnished the motive power was carried in a millrace dug high upon a hillside on the other side of the creek from the mill and when the water reached a point opposite the mill, it was conducted across the creek in a large trough, framed at the top of large cedar posts and fully forty feet above the bed of the creek.[16]

Edmund Taylor's Mill ruins (left) and portions of the mill dam (right) in 2004.

Based on the ruins remaining in place today, it appears that Taylor's Mill was powered by two dams, one on Lower Howard's Creek and one on West Fork. A University of Kentucky Master's thesis by Joe Kendall Neel[b] supports the notion that there were two dams for the mill:

---

[b] Neel had a biological sampling station at "the remains of the pond of Taylor's Mill" on the main stem of Howard's Creek. The pond was "70 to 120 feet wide, 700 feet long, and 1½ to almost 6 feet deep."

199

Colonel John Holder

Taylor's Mill was situated below the present [1938] home of R. L. Quisenberry. It was operated by Judge Taylor. Two ponds were constructed for this mill, one on the main stream and another on West Fork.[17]

Portions of the milldams exist today. The core of the dam on West Fork has washed away, but the abutments are still visible on both sides of the creek. Part of one stone wall of the gristmill still stands.

The 1870 manufacturers census provides additional information regarding "E. T. Taylor's Flour & Grist Mill." The waterwheel was rated at 10 horsepower, there were two sets of stones for grinding, one paid employee and the mill operated eight months out of the year. The business produced flour, meal and bran valued at $4,840 which was "ground for private owners." This was usually an indication that the products of the mill were going to a distillery for the production of whiskey, of which there were several in the area.

More detail was provided in the 1880 census. The mill had a 20-foot fall of water to power a breast wheel 4½ feet in breadth and rated at 8 horsepower. That year the mill used 3,640 bushels of wheat and 3,750 bushels of corn to produce sales of $5,845.

In time, Edmund's son William took over operation of the mill. William never married and lived at home:

> The miller was Judge Taylor's oldest son Will, who was virtually blind from birth but who knew every foot of the old mill as he knew his bed room. To the traveler passing in the night the suggestion was rather ghostly to hear the old mill running at full speed in the darkness with no light visible.[18]

We have not yet learned the exact year Taylor's Mill went out of operation. We do know that after being in the family for 117 years, the mill tract finally left the Taylor name in 1914. In a civil action styled *Maggie McMurtry &c vs. Houston Taylor &c*, the Clark circuit court ordered a public sale of the property referred to as the "Taylor Mill Tract." The master commissioner sold the tract to Robert L. Quisenberry for $2,480. After payment of the last installment, a deed was issued to Quisenberry on May 2, 1914.[19]

Orson Martin Sawmill and Blacksmith Shop

In 1796, Orson Martin purchased 25 acres of land from William Bush. That year Martin petitioned the county court for permission to erect a

Howard's Creek Industrial Center

gristmill "near his Saw Mill." Martin's tract on the north side of Lower Howard's Creek, was later the site of several other mills, and the area became known as "Factory Bottom." In 1799, county court orders mention a road that ran from "Austin Martin's Mill" to the Becknerville area. The sawmill may have been on the tract Martin sold to Daniel Orear in 1813.[20]

Orson Martin was the son of John and Rachel (Pace) Martin. Orson was a blacksmith like his father. His blacksmith shop was located near his sawmill and is mentioned in numerous documents. For example, in 1808 the county court proposed to turn the road "from Orson Martin's shop to Lexington."[21]

John Martin and his son Orson may have erected the early gristmill on John Holder's land (Martin-Holder Mill). As a young man, Orson was one of the leading entrepreneurs on Lower Howard's Creek. Unfortunately, after such early promise, his career crashed under the weight of family problems and business reversals brought on by the destructive effects of alcohol addiction.[22]

Orson Martin Flour Mill

The county court granted Orson Martin permission to erect a water powered gristmill on his Factory Bottom tract in 1796.[23] The mill was still unfinished five years later, when Martin entered into an agreement with Daniel McVicar, who agreed to help finish the mill and then lease it from Martin. The contract called for Martin "to Finish Both the Water wheels, Cog wheels and trundle Head, and everything necessary to run two pair of Stones, the Machinery excepted [and] to find the bolting Cloths & all the Iron Works, Wire for the screen, and timber for finishing the mill Compleat." McVicar agreed "to put a pair of Good four and a half feet Burr stones, a screw of the best kind, bail & Crane, one scale, Beam scales and necessary Weights for Weighing flower, also two sets of Elevators, one Hopper boy, and in fact all the Machinery necessary for Manufacturing wheat [flour] in the most Compleat manner."[24] Reference to the screw conveyor, elevators and hopper boy clearly establishes that Martin intended to construct an automated flour mill along the lines patented by Oliver Evans.

By 1810, Martin had broken contracts to manufacture flour for James Flanagan and Josiah Hart, who sued and obtained a judgment against him. When Martin failed to pay back several loans, the court ordered his tract—then called Factory Bottom—sold to pay the debts. At the sheriff's auction, James Reed bid $490 for 16¼ acres of Factory Bottom, "to include the Grist Mill and dwelling house of said Martin." Reed sold the tract to John Halyard (1813), Halyard sold it to Ambrose Christy (1829), Christy conveyed it to his son-in-law, Thomas Vivion (1838) and Vivion sold it to Edmund Hockaday (1849). Hockaday's deed stated that the property included a mill "known by the name of Vivion's mill, formerly owned by John Halyard and built by Austin Martin."[25]

Isaac Hockaday Woolen Factory

The 1850 population census for Clark County lists Edmund W. Hockaday, age 46, farmer. Residing with him was his son Isaac, age 24, who is listed as a manufacturer. The Hockadays put up a new building in Factory Bottom that was used as a woolen mill for producing various types of cloth. The 1850 manufacturers census lists Isaac H. Hockaday as the proprietor of a "wool manufactory." The factory had a capital value of $2,000, used 2,000 pounds of wool to produce 1,000 yards of "jeans and linsey" with a value of $500. The motive power was listed as water and steam. The steam engine presumably would have been used in the dry months when the flow of water was not sufficient to run the mill.

Edmund Hockaday sold the factory in 1856 to James P. Lyddane and George O. Wiggard, woolen manufacturers from Maryland. The deed conveyed all interest "to the house erected by him [Hockaday] on said land for a factory and all of the fixtures and machinery of every kind and description belonging to said factory."[26] The 1860 manufacturers census lists Lyddane and Wiggard's "woolen factory" with a capital value of $4,000, which suggests that the partners had made some improvements to the machinery. The factory used 10,700 pounds of wool to produce $10,000 worth of "Janes [Jeans] and Lindsey." At this time, the factory had four paid employees—one of whom was Patrick Fulton, a weaver from Ireland—and was powered by a ten horsepower steam engine. A fuller description of their operation is given in a notice the owners placed in the *Winchester Chronicle*:

> We are prepared to manufacture the following articles in the best style for customers, namely, Fine and Course Janes; Fulled Janes; Plain and Striped Linsey; Tweeds; Cloth; Flannel and Broad Blankets. Carding and Spining done as heretofore. Wool will be received and Goods delivered at the following places: Davis, Haggard & Co, Winchester; Oldham & Scott, Lexington; E. Pendleton's store, Pine Grove; Anthony's, Athens. Goods always on hand for sale or exchange for Wool. All accounts due when Goods are delivered. Letters addressed to Winchester, Clark county, Ky. LYDDANE & WIGGARD.[27]

Howard's Creek Industrial Center

The partners had agreed to pay Hockaday $1,900 for the factory; they paid him $1,400 in cash and signed a note for the balance. When the note went unpaid, Hockaday sued and the factory was sold at auction. The buyer was James F. McKinney, who faired little better than his predecessors. McKinney owned several other mills and was proprietor of the Cottage Furnace in Estill County. When his properties became entangled in lawsuits, the woolen factory was sold to "Robert Bush, of color." The 1874 deed referred to the tract as the "Old Factory Place," which "has several houses on it including the Mill or Factory house." No evidence has turned up to show when the factory closed down.[28]

Wiggard moved to Wheelersburg, Ohio, and went into the woolen manufacturing business there. It appears that his partner died before 1870. Neither James Lyddane nor his wife Abigail is found in the census for that year. Their daughter Alice was living with the Wiggards in Ohio, and their son Charles was living with Robert Bush in Clark County. Charles Lyddane became a noted citizen of Winchester, editor of the *Clark County Democrat* and long time superintendent of public schools.[29]

John Rees Gristmill

In 1805, John Rees petitioned the Clark County court for permission to build a gristmill and dam on Lower Howard's Creek "near his own house… at the Edge of the great road." The court granted him permission to erect a dam 5 feet high. Rees was living on land he purchased from Matthew Wills. Several years later, a court document mentioned one the corners located at "M. Willses old mill dam." The mill appears not to have been in operation long.[30]

John Wilkerson Gristmill and Sawmill

In 1811, John Wilkerson had a gristmill on Lower Howard's Creek. The mill was located just downstream from the present reservoir, on Lettie Lane. From a deposition taken in a land case, we learn that the place the Shawnee stopped on their way to besiege Boonesborough in 1778—known as the "Indian Camp"—was below the mouth of the north fork of Lower Howard's Creek "between Major John Wilkerson's Mill dam and Mill." Wilkerson sold 38 acres, including his mill, to William Tate in 1818.[31] From the deed description, we learn that the mill had an unusual configuration: There were two mill dams, one on the Main Fork of the creek and another on the North Fork. One can speculate about the purpose of the two dams. There is a waterfall on the Main Fork just before its confluence with the North Fork. (The present Reservoir Lane crosses a bridge over the falls today.) The drop

Colonel John Holder

is about 6 to 8 feet. If the dam was built below the confluence, 6 to 8 feet of vertical head would be lost. The dam on the Main Fork was above the falls and the race channeled water into the mill pond on the North Fork, thus preserving the head. The second dam also provided more water for the mill than a single dam across the North Fork could have supplied.

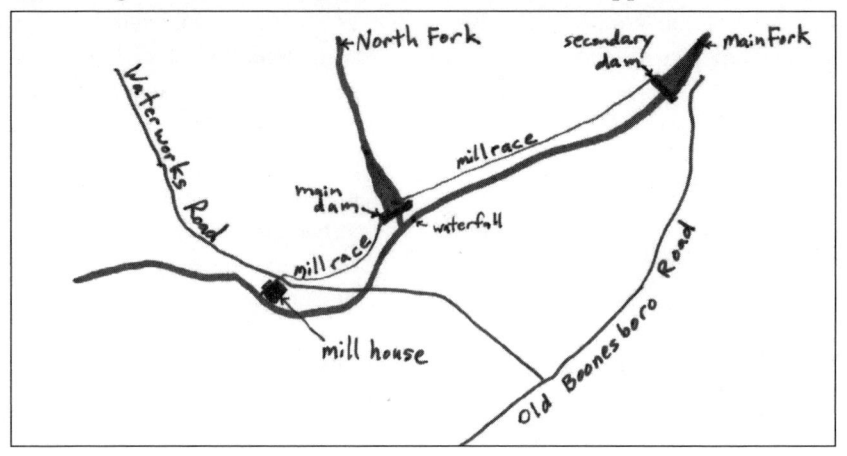

Site Plan for the Wilkerson-Tate Mill.

The deed to Tate describes one of the corners as "a black walnut & white walnut just below the mills." The plural "mills" suggest that Wilkerson and Tate operated a gristmill and sawmill. After William died, the mill was run by his son Zachariah Tate. It was still going in 1861 when it was mentioned in the local newspaper, the *National Union*. By 1870 Zachariah had converted the gristmill to run by horse power.[32] It is not known when Tate's Mill went out of operation.

Robert Didlake Gristmill

Samuel Smith received a permit for a dam across the West Fork of Lower Howard's Creek in 1796; however, there is no indication that he ever completed a mill there. In 1806, Robert Didlake acquired a permit for a dam on West Fork "at or near a Mill Seat formerly condemned for Samuel Smith." Didlake's tract and his mill were on the east side of the creek. When the adjoining tract on the west side of the creek was sold in 1864, it mentioned the "Mill House," the "Mill Dam" and the "Old Mill Road."[33] The location taken from the deeds match the ruins of a mill and dam ruins located on West Fork, north of the Lower Howard's Creek Nature and Heritage Preserve. The old mill road, running parallel to West Fork, is still plainly visible.

Howard's Creek Industrial Center

Millstone fragment (left) and mill wall (right) at Didlake's Mill.

It is possible that this mill was later operated under the name of Webb's Mill. Charles Lyddane, in his history of Lower Howard's Creek, wrote

> A short distance up West Fork was Webb's Mill. This was limited in capacity and the water power was uncertain, hence it did not amount to much.[34]

Richard Webb owned a large tract on West Fork, on the opposite side of the creek from Didlake, which he purchased from Edmund W. Hockaday in 1864.[35]

William Wilkerson Mill

William Wilkerson's mill was mentioned in a road order in Clark County which is the only reference to it. In 1822, Samuel R. Combs requested the county court to open a road "from William Wilkersons mill on the west fork of Howards creek to John McCalls mill on boons creek."[36] There is an unknown mill ruins on West Fork, that may have been Wilkerson's mill. It was about a quarter of a mile upstream from Didlake's Mill. The dam site, mill race and mill foundation are still visible on the west side of the creek. Nothing else is known about this mill.

Smith's Sawmill

The only mention of Smith's sawmill is an 1829 deed from the heirs of William Bush. The deed describes a tract of land beginning "on howards creek opposite Smiths Saw mill, thence with Philip Bush and Robert Clark."[37] This places the mill on the north side of Lower Howard's Creek, about a quarter of a mile downstream from the Old Stone Church.

Samuel R. Combs Sawmill

In 1823, Samuel R. Combs applied to the county court for permission

Colonel John Holder

to erect "a water Grist and saw mill on Howards Lower creek" on his land and to condemn 1 acre of Jonathan Bush's land for a dam abutment. The following year he asked the court to open a road from the mouth of the creek then "up the same to Combs mill." It is uncertain if he finished the gristmill, but his sawmill was built and may have furnished timbers and lumber for his boatyard. Combs' estate appraisal listed one "Lott of plank and Scantling at mill & elsewhere, $50."[38]

The sawmill was mentioned in an 1877 deed as being downstream from the mouth of Deep Branch. A reference in the deed to "a point near where Combs old saw mill stood" indicates that the mill was gone but not forgotten.[39] This would place the mill somewhere along the base of Thompson's Ridge in the Lower Howard's Creek Nature and Heritage Preserve. A visual reconnaissance of this area by preserve manager, Clare Sipple, and the author turned up a possible dam abutment on the east side of the creek. No sign of the sawmill was found.

Benjamin Exum Sawmill

Benjamin Exum and Edmund W. Hockaday went to the county court to obtain permission to build a sawmill on Lower Howard's Creek in the year 1845. After the mill was built, it was referred to only as Exum's Mill. The sawmill is shown on road survey made in 1853.

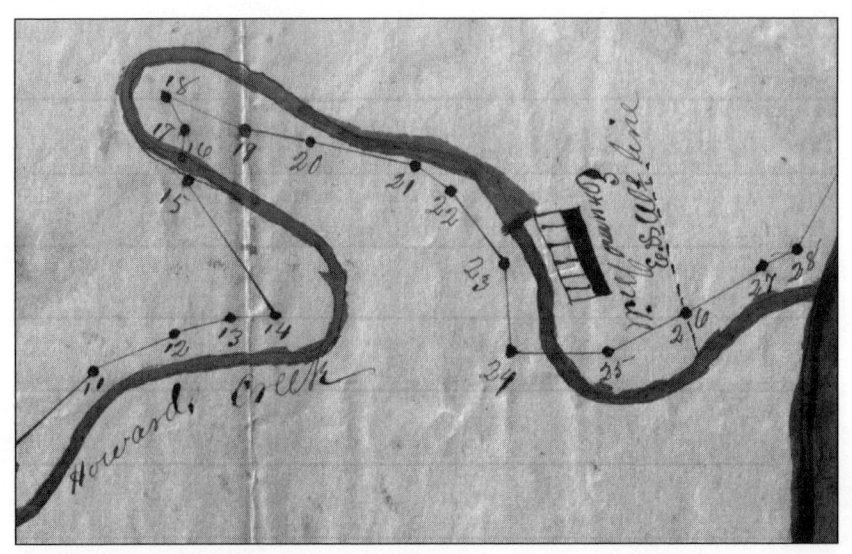

Exum's Sawmill near the mouth of Lower Howard's Creek[40] *This mill stood on the east side of the creek, just north of the parking lot at Hall's Restaurant. The drawing suggests that the mill was situated very close to the dam. No sign of the mill or dam can be seen today.*

Howard's Creek Industrial Center

William Trimble Distillery
Edmund Hockaday Distillery

One of the first revenue measures adopted by the newly formed United States government was a tax imposed on the manufacture of whiskey. The tax was greatly resisted in the western districts and resulted in open revolt in Pennsylvania. This insurrection—called the "Whiskey Rebellion—had to be put down by armed troops. Kentucky also opposed the tax but, rather than revolting, many of the distillers here simply refused to pay the tax.[41]

Although he was sympathetic to the distillers, Kentucky's federal judge, Harry Innes of the U.S. Court for the District of Kentucky, set out to enforce payment of the whiskey tax. In 1796, he fined William Trimble $25.38 for failure to pay the tax on his still. Trimble was fined again in 1799, this time for $250. The location of his distillery is unknown but was probably on Lower Howard's Creek where he owned 1,400 acres of land. A possible location is at the spring known from early times as Trimble's Spring Branch. This small stream, just north of Factory Bottom, enters the main creek from the east side.[42]

In 1798, Edmund Hockaday was fined $200 for failure to pay the tax on his still. This was the grandfather of Edmund W. Hockaday. Edmund Sr. owned land on the West Fork of Lower Howard's Creek and it seems reasonable to suppose that his distillery was located there.[43]

Calmes and Adams Sawmill, Gristmill and Blacksmith Shop

Henry Calmes Jr. and Lewis Adams erected a large lumber mill on the Kentucky River, on land that had been owned by John Holder. The site of this establishment—sawmill, gristmill and blacksmith shop—was the river bottom along present day Amster Grove Road. The mills, shown on the 1861 Hewitt map, were run by steam engines rather than water power. In 1864, the partners sold their mills and blacksmith shop to Willis F. and John W. Martin. The mills turned out 250,000 board feet of lumber in 1870 and 75,000 board feet in 1880.[44] The owners provided a description of their mills in a newspaper notice in 1877:

> Martin, Atkerson & Co. have added to their saw mill at Combs' Ferry a shingle machine with which they are making from twelve to fifteen thousand shingles per day. They are also erecting a flour and grist mill about sixty feet from the saw mill. A large boiler in the saw mill building furnishes steam for the two mills, the flouring mill having a separate engine and the steam being carried from the boiler through underground pipes. The saw mill has an average

Colonel John Holder

capacity of 8,000 feet per day, although not long since a run of over 18,000 feet was made.[45]

John W. Martin kept a lumber yard in Winchester, near his residence on Lexington Avenue.

Quarries

The ledges of rock on Lower Howard's Creek provided an exceptional building stone that was used not only in the valley but throughout the county. The two most noted formations were the Oregon, also called "Kentucky River Marble," a tan to grayish dolomite containing variable amounts of limestone, and the Tyrone, a whitish-colored stone known as birdseye limestone, sometimes called "Tyrone Limestone."[46]

Numerous old quarry sites have been found in the Lower Howard's Creek Nature and Heritage Preserve. Most were hillside quarries where rock was cut out of ledges, but there is evidence that even the creek bed itself was mined for stone. Only two of the known quarry sites are shown on the map at the beginning of this chapter.

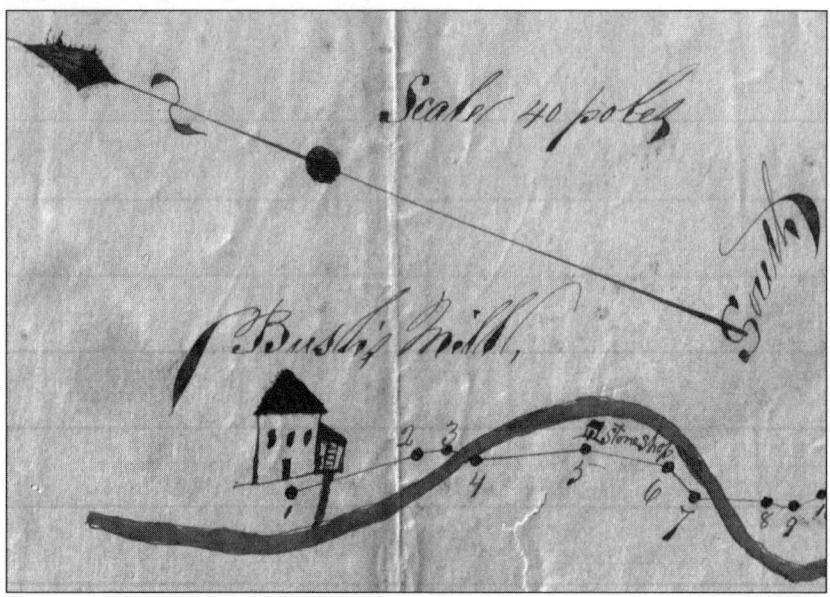

Stone Shop (at 5) near Bush's Mill.

In 1850, the U.S. census began listing the occupation of each resident. We find among the people living on Lower Howard's Creek a number of men who gave their profession as stonemason or stonecutter:

Howard's Creek Industrial Center

1850	1860	1870
Richard Arnold	Richard Arnold	Michael Dunn
John Deacon	Robert Martin	Charles Devine
Robert Martin	John Coons	Selid Johnson (B)
Edwin Combs	Patrick Burk	Dick James (B)
John A. Brink		Jerry McKinzie (B)
Joseph Deacon		Dennis Burnes
James Connell		Benjamin Boone
		Michael Styles
		Gransond Hill
		Albert Hill

Richmond Arnold Quarry and Stone Shop
Robert Martin Quarry

The most prominent stonemasons in 1850 and 1860 were Richmond "Richard" Arnold and Robert Martin, who were related by marriage. Both men had quarries within the present Preserve boundaries. An 1853 road survey shows a "Stone Shop" just downstream from the Bush Mill. This site, on the west side of the creek, is currently enclosed by a magnificent edge laid stone fence, which was recently restored with a Transportation Enhancement grant from the Kentucky Transportation Cabinet. On the 1861 Hewitt map, Richmond Arnold is shown living here and it is logical to presume that he operated the stone shop. Drawing a parallel with blacksmith shops, we speculate that a stone shop was where stone was tooled, shaped and finished into products with a local market, such as lintels, dimension stone for construction and gravestones. Arnold's quarry was on the hillside above his stone shop and house.

In 1870, Arnold and Martin listed their occupations as farming, which suggests a possible decline in quarrying within the creek valley. This trend is supported by the decline in the number of stone workers living on the creek from 1850 to 1860. Although the number reported in 1870 is larger, the list includes all the stone workers living in Precinct 4—roughly, the area between Twomile Creek and Boone Creek. (The census taker did not go down the creek as in previous years, and it is not possible to identify who was living in the valley.) Many of the workers listed in 1870 may have been employed building stone fences using field stone rather than quarried stone. The other notable trend is the appearance of African-American (indicated by "B" in the chart) stone workers in 1870.

In the census of 1880, Richmond Martin, age 67, again gave his occupation as stonemason. His son Henry, 29, was still living at home and was also a

Colonel John Holder

Site of the Richmond Arnold Stone Shop. The shop was enclosed by the edge laid stone fence on the right side of the road (Bush's Mill Road). Arnold's quarry was up the hill on the left side of the picture.

stonemason. Robert Martin, 60, gave his occupation as stonemason and a note written beside it states, "works in Rock quarry."

End of an Era

The large gristmills in the valley were thriving enterprises up until the Civil War. During the war, the federal government shut down Kentucky's access to southern markets, where most of her exported goods had been shipped. Development of the railroads during the post-war period sparked an economic boom in Winchester, which became a hub for four different lines. Rail transportation largely displaced the annual migration of flatboats on the Kentucky River during the spring tides. With improvements in the technology of steam engines, industries came to rely less on water power, which could seldom be counted on more than nine or ten months out of the year. Also during this period, newly developed roller mills began to replace the traditional stone grinding techniques for producing wheat flour. Roller mills had a much higher output and could produce a more consistent product at a lower cost. Essentially all of the small distilleries in the county shut down after the government began taxing whiskey while it was aging in warehouses. Sawmills went out of business after nearby forests were cleared. These factors, along with the rapid expansion of turnpike roads in Clark County, resulted in a gradual extinction of industry in the Lower Howard's Creek valley. One by one, the factories closed their doors. The abandonment of two landmark flour mills—Stevens' (formerly Bush's) Mill and Taylor's Mill—around the beginning of the 20th century signaled the end of an era. As Charles Lyddane wrote in 1916, "The above will give a slight idea of the business activity which formerly permeated this region. Alas! It all belongs to the past."[47]

Holder as Visionary

The brief survey in this chapter should not be considered an exhaustive listing of all the industries located in the valley of Lower Howard's Creek. A number of mills, distilleries, factories and shops may have been missed. No attempt was made to locate other industries, such as tanneries, that were present in the valley. As it stands, however, the list seems impressive enough to justify Robert Cotterill's statement that Lower Howard's Creek "was one of the largest factory centers west of the Alleghenies in 1812."

Col. John Holder played a leading role in this development. He settled the land at the mouth of the creek, built a fortified station and recruited talented people to construct and operate his enterprises: boatyard, warehouse, ferry and tavern. Holder also led the way in the use of water power in the valley. He engaged the Martins to build a mill on his land in the late 1780s. This was the first of the many mills later erected along the creek. Other businesses followed. Soon the valley was teeming with the manufacture of flour, whiskey, woolen cloth, lumber and other goods. Holder's warehouse and boatyard offered the means to get these products inspected, stored and shipped off to market.

While we can hardly claim that Holder foresaw all of this when he placed his first entry on this land in 1782, we should certainly credit his accomplishments. When opportunity knocked, he stepped in boldly to take advantage. He saw a need and made things happen. As Dr. Clifton "Pete" Smith wrote in his book *Lower Howards Creek*, "Lieutenant Colonel Holder, the visionary, acted!" He surely did.

Chapter 13
Public Service and Local Affairs

Kentucky became a state in 1792, and there immediately ensued a controversy over where to locate the capital. John Holder was among a group of citizens from Clark and Madison who submitted a petition offering the state 18,550 acres of land and £2,630 English Sterling to locate the seat of government at Boonesborough. John Holder made the largest cash offer, £300, and Green Clay offered the most land, 10,000 acres. Other Clark County men on the list included Robert Clark Jr. and Sr., William Orear, James and Robert McMillan, Edmund Ragland, Bennett Clark, William and Philip Bush, Achilles Eubank, Robert Elkin, Edmund Hockaday and David Bullock. Their bid failed, however, as the legislature voted to make Frankfort the capital.[1]

Clark County was formed from parts of Fayette and Bourbon in December 1792. In addition to his numerous business and military activities, John Holder found time to serve in the new county government. While one might argue that his service advanced his own interests, this was not always the case. There were instances where it caused problems for him and in one case nearly resulted in his financial ruin.

Kentucky Militia

The Kentucky Militia was also organized in 1792, the same year Kentucky became a state. The 17th Regiment, a new unit in Kentucky's 2d Brigade, was established in newly formed Clark County. On December 22, 1792, Governor Isaac Shelby appointed the following officers in the 17th Regiment: John Holder, lieutenant colonel and commandant; Richard Hickman, first major; and Robert McMillan, second major. Holder was still serving in this capacity at the time of his death in 1799.[2]

There is no indication that Holder participated in the disastrous military expeditions against the Northwest Indians led by General Josiah Harmar (1790) or Arthur St. Clair (1791). Nor has he been mentioned in connection

Public Service and Local Affairs

with the successful expedition of General "Mad Anthony" Wayne, which ended with the American victory at the Battle of Fallen Timbers in 1794. During the latter campaign, Governor Shelby ordered the state militia to protect the back parts of the settlements. Holder received the following instructions from the governor, dated June 13, 1794:

> In Order to Secure protection to the most exposed Settlers on the frontier of Clark County The Governor in Consequence thereof Ordered Col. John Holder to employ two Spyes for two months at the expence of the General Government.[3]

In October of that year, Holder sent recommendations to the governor for additional officers, which were appointed by Shelby.

> On the report of John Holder, Lieutenant Colonel, Commandant of the 17th Regiment the following Officers were Commissioned Viz. Captain, John Morton; Lieutenants, William Tinsley, John Ray, Martin Johnston; Ensigns, James Browning, John Dale, Jeremiah Strode & Jesse Robertson.[4]

Following General Wayne's victory, the raids into central Kentucky essentially ended, and the militia had less responsibility for defense against the Indians. The legislature then assigned them duties as "patrollers," who were to monitor the activities of slaves within the county, especially during the nighttime hours. Creation of the patrollers resulted in part from a general fear throughout the South of slave uprisings. Patrollers were directed to spend twelve hours each month going through their districts where they were to "visit negro quarters and other suspected places of unlawful assemblies of slaves."[5] Anyone caught without a pass from their master could be severely punished.

John Holder, as overall commander of the 17th Regiment, was in charge of the Clark County patrollers. The copy of Captain James Stevens' patroller report was found among the loose papers at the Clark County courthouse. Stevens requested payment to James Duncan, John Gaines, John Williams and Thomas Burrus for patrolling from July to October 1796, and Holder signed the report.[6]

County Justice

On December 21, 1792, Governor Isaac Shelby named the first justices for Clark County. John Holder was among those appointed.

Colonel John Holder

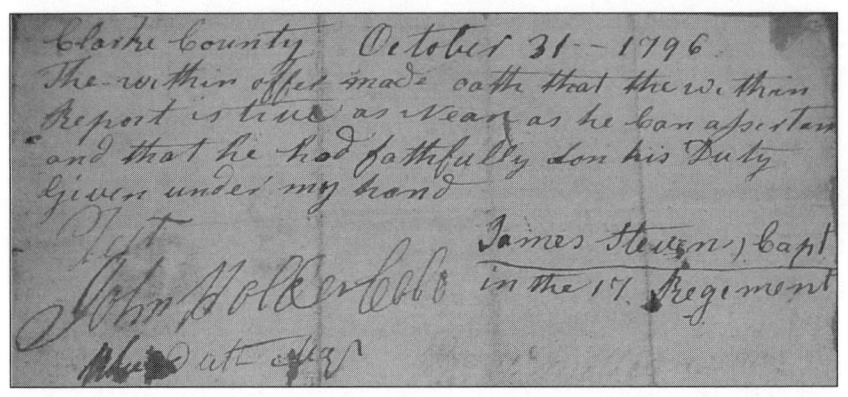

Clarke County October 31 - - 1796
The within offi[ce]r made oath that the within Report is true as Near as he Can assertan and that he had fathfully don his Duty
Given under my hand

Test.
John Holder Colo.

James Stevens, Capt.
in the 17 Regiment

    The Governor nominated & by and with the advice & consent of the Senate appointed Robert Clarke, Hubbard Taylor, John McGuire, James McMillion, John Holder, Enoch Smith, John Baker, Jilson Payne, William Suddith, Abijah Brooks, Gentlemen, Justices of the Peace for the County of Clarke, the first three to act as Justices of the Court of Quarter Sessions & the remaining seven as Justices of the County Court.[7]

    The court of quarter sessions was Kentucky's first court system for trying civil and criminal cases. Robert Clark, Hubbard Taylor and John McGuire were the first justices of that court. The court met four times a year until the system was revised in 1803, when the court of quarter sessions was replaced by the circuit court.

    The remaining justices, including John Holder, constituted the "county court," which formed the most vital part of state government. Most Kentuckians dealt regularly with their county court, seldom with state government and rarely, if ever, with the federal level. County court was similar to our present fiscal court, though the former was much more powerful, having broad executive, legislative and judicial authority. "So comprehensive and pervasive were the powers and responsibilities of the courts that sooner or later almost everyone in the county, from white adults to slaves, had business with them. County court day attracted many hundreds each month.

Public Service and Local Affairs

Court day was also the occasion for politicking and merrymaking, gossiping, and sometimes brawling." Members of the county court, known as justices of the peace, were among the most influential men of their communities. The court's most significant jurisdiction included wills and estates, the poor and the vagrant, guardians and apprentices, ferries, milldams, bastardy, emancipation, Negro felonies, the fining of officers, appeals from magistrates, roads, taxes, appropriations, towns, and patronage.[8]

The first session of the county court met at John Strode's house at Strode's Station on March 26, 1793. Holder and the other justices produced their commissions from the governor and took the prescribed oath of office. The minutes of the meeting were duly recorded, and the original document is preserved in Order Book 1 at the Clark County clerk's office. The court continued to meet at Strode's until November when they moved to John Baker's place in what is now Winchester.[9]

Court sessions at that time were unlike anything we are familiar with today. One of the pioneers, Benjamin Allen, described what it was like on court day before the first courthouse was built.

> In the first settling of Winchester, this John Baker had a little half faced camp of red oak logs down where [Mrs.] Lingingfelter's house is now in the hollow, little tother side of the hollow from hers. His family in one end and a barrel of whiskey in the other and a couple of red oak poles run along at the lower end, where the barrel was, for a bar room—only of court days though. Put his half face there in the winter [1793], and the Court House was put there in the spring. Had me there for a tapster that first Barrel. I was the first man that ever sold a pint or half pint of whiskey there.[10]

This hollow where court was held is on the west side of Maple Street between Washington and Broadway. Baker's place was just north of where Beverly White Tower stands today on the former site of the public spring. John Bruner later ran a tanyard there, which he sold to Valentine Lingenfelter. A "half face camp" is a cabin with three walls, open on one side, and a shed roof. Allen describes whiskey being dispensed "only of court days." The court met there until May 1794 when the first courthouse was ready. For the use of his cabin, John Baker received £5 from the county levy.[11]

John Holder had an excellent attendance record in 1793 and was active in the court's affairs. In March the court appointed Holder and Jilson Payne to serve as judges "to superintend the ensuing Election of representatives." Clark County was entitled to two representatives in the Kentucky General

Colonel John Holder

Assembly. James McMillan and Richard Hickman were elected. In May, Holder and Robert Clark were securities for David Bullock, the first county clerk. In July, the court voted "to erect the publick buildings for this county …on the land of John Baker." The justices present at the balloting were John Holder, Jilson Payne, James McMillan, Enoch Smith, William Sudduth and John Baker.[12] These six men formed a committee to locate "the particular spot of ground" for building the courthouse.

Winchester pioneer Benjamin Allen mentioned three different sites that were considered in voting for the county seat.

> Only lost the county seat's being fixed at Bob McMullen's Big Spring—on Howard's Lower Creek, 3 miles from Winchester—by one vote. Strode's was also in nomination, but it was too nigh the Fayette line.[13]

John Holder was one of three justices present at the court session that laid out plans for the first courthouse. They ordered the sheriff to let to the low bidder "the building of a cabbin with two rooms, one 20 feet square and the other ten by Twenty, one story high, for the purpose of holding court therein, of good Oak or Ash logs, the Flowers to be laid with good sound puncheons and the floors above to be laid with good sound plank loose laid down." The court of quarter sessions was the first to use the new building for their meeting on May 2, 1794. The county court met there for the first time in July. Benjamin Allen[a] said the courthouse "was of open round logs on the hill" above Baker's half faced camp; it had "a cabin roof and a log partition for a jury room." He said it cost $16 to build.[14]

In July 1794, the court voted to lay out a new road from the courthouse to Holder's Boatyard, the first of several county roads to his place on the Kentucky River. In August, Holder was the security for William Harris, who was appointed constable. And the court, ordered a road from Holder's Boatyard "toward Bourbon Court House as far as the county line." In November, the court granted Holder a tavern license. His attendance at court was good the following year, and he continued to be involved in locating and constructing the public buildings (courthouse and jail). In November 1794, upon the recommendation of Enoch Smith, Clark County surveyor, Holder was sworn in as one of the deputy county surveyors.[15]

The duties of justices extended outside of the courtroom. One task was

---

a The following description of the first courthouse comes from another pioneer: "Winchester, about 1793, had a court house like a Tobacco house, of open round logs in the midst of the cane." Shane interview with James M. Stevenson, Draper MSS 11CC 51.

Public Service and Local Affairs

> *John Holder was recommended by Enoch Smith Gent. Surveyor of this County as a fit and proper to act as a deputy who took the oath of a Surveyor and thereupon he is admitted to officiate as such in this County*

to certify an applicant's petition for the bounty on wolves. Holder routinely performed this function and issued a voucher such as the one below with his prominent signature. Because wolves were such a problem in Kentucky at that time, the court was authorized to pay 8 shillings for each wolf's head or scalp produced.

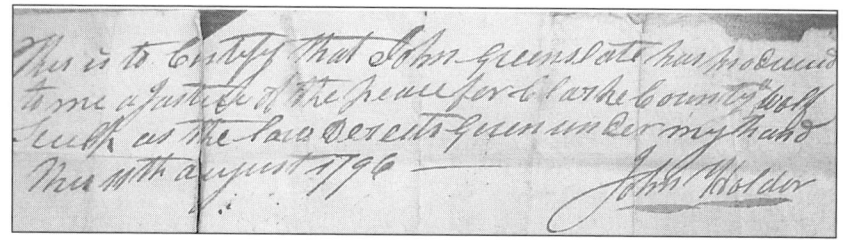

This is to Certify that John Greenslate has produced to me a Justice of the peace for Clarke County a Wolf Scalp as the law Derects Given under my hand this 11th august 1796 John Holder[16]

Holder continued to serve as a justice until his death in 1799. There is no indication he ever sought elected office and, indeed, it is hard to imagine where he would have found the time. His attendance as a justice fell off in 1796, when he missed court five months out of eight. The September court minutes state that Holder "was summoned to appear here this day to shew ...why he failed to give in a list of his Taxable property for the present year." The court fined him one penny and the Commonwealth's costs of 22 shillings 11 pence. Robert Clark Jr. and fellow justice James McMillan were fined that day for the same offense. Holder submitted his property list to the tax commissioner on the 24th of that month. He reported owning 24,000 acres of land, 27 slaves, 10 horses and 50 head of cattle.[17]

The following year, 1797, Holder's attendance slipped further; he missed court six out of eight months. There were other justices who attended as poorly as he did. As the number of justices increased over the years, attendance became much less of a necessity. Around that time, there were at least fourteen justices for Clark County. Holder failed to submit his taxable property list for 1797 and was again cited by the court.[18]

Colonel John Holder

Holder's Attendance at County Court[19]

Year	Sessions Holder Attended	Total Court Sessions
1793	5	7
1794	6	8
1795	4	8
1796	3	8
1797	2	8
1798	2	8
1799	Holder did not attend	

John Holder was one of the most active members of the county court in its formative years, 1793-1795. The following two years, he attended court less often and was less involved in county business. The last session he attended was in July 1798.

* * *

There have been consistent reports that John Holder was one of the first trustees of Winchester. (For example, the historic highway marker for Capt. John Holder.) The General Assembly appointed the original trustees: Richard Hickman, David Bullock, Josiah Bullock, William Bush, Josiah Hart, John Elliott, Benjamin Combs and John Strode. Trustee resignations and new appointments were recorded in the minutes of trustee meetings; John Holder's name does not appear in the minutes.[20]

The Higgins Fiasco

John Holder provided security for numerous individuals with business before the court, a practice that cost him dearly in the case of Robert Higgins. Higgins served as a deputy sheriff under John Martin, and then in 1795 he ran for sheriff and was elected. The day Higgins was sworn into office his securities—John Holder, William Higgins, James McMillan, William Craig and Francis Price—signed a penalty bond for $3,000.[21] The following year Sheriff Robert Higgins

> came personally into Court and who together with John Holder & William Higgins his securities entered into and acknowledged their bond in the penalty of £10,000 conditioned as the law directs for the collection of the Tax of 1796.[22]

Public Service and Local Affairs

It is difficult imagine that men in those times agreed to bonds of such staggering sums but they did. These bonds for Higgins came back to haunt Holder and, after his death, his heirs.

The first hint of a problem came when John Baker, William Sudduth and Robert McKinney were appointed by the court to settle accounts with the sheriff for the 1795 and 1796 taxes. In March 1798, Sheriff Higgins was fined 20 shillings for "neglect of duty" and the first of a series of suits was filed against Higgins and his securities. Clark County clerk, David Bullock, sued the sheriff for £87 plus costs. Higgins "acknowledged the plaintiffs notice and confessed judgment."[23]

Dillard Collins was elected sheriff in May 1798 and took the oath of office in July. In August the court ordered John Baker, William Sudduth and Robert Clark Jr. to prepare a report on the collection of the county levies for 1795, 1796 and 1797; the report was submitted and approved in November. In January, the commonwealth attorney Levi Todd[b] sued Higgins and his securities for £122, a portion of the missing 1796 levy.[24]

Part of the explanation of what happened may be inferred from a directive the court issued to Levi Todd: "Ordered that the Attorney for the County make a Statement of the erronious Taxation imposed on the people thereof by misconstruction of the Revenue Law and the practicle part thereof and transmit the same to the Attorney General of the Commonwealth." County tax commissioners attempted to collect the missing revenue but shortfalls were the responsibility of Higgins and his securities. Court documents issued in an effort to collect from Higgins were marked "no effects." That meant he was insolvent and had no money and no property to attach. Higgins, however, was apparently not charged with a crime. He continued to reside in the county after serving out his term as sheriff and had regular business before the court.[c] It appears that he merely bungled the tax collection, which left his securities responsible for the deficit.[25]

The suits against Higgins' securities multiplied in 1798. Holder and the others found themselves having to make up for the taxes Higgins failed to collect.[26] After an execution was issued to sell some of Holder's property, he petitioned the state to release him from the obligation. He may have

---

[b] Levi Todd was an early settler and one of the founders of Lexington. He was the first clerk of the Fayette County court and a general in the Kentucky militia. He served for a time as the deputy states attorney (also called the commonwealth attorney) for Clark County. When he resigned in 1801, Henry Clay was appointed in his stead. Kleber, *Kentucky Encyclopedia*, p. 888; Clark County Court of Quarter Sessions Order Book 3:61.

[c] Robert Higgins later moved to Floyd County, Kentucky, where he was residing in 1802. Clark County Court of Quarter Sessions Order Book 3:184.

Colonel John Holder

requested assistance from one or more of Clark County's legislators—Representatives Richard Hickman or Robert Clark Jr. or Senator Hubbard Taylor. On December 13, 1798, the General Assembly passed an "Act for the Relief of John Holder."

> Holder was security for Robert Higgins, sheriff of Clarke. An execution, obtained by the commonwealth against Higgins and his securities, had been levied on Holder's property, on a suggestion that Higgins had [no] property. This act authorises a suspension of the proceedings against Holder; that the sheriff should return the execution staid by this act, but that the lien should be preserved, and other executions might go out against Higgins, or his estate. Holder's property to be sold by *venditioni exponas*, if the debt should not otherwise be discharged.[27]

The act provided minimal relief for Holder. The following year, the Commonwealth issued an execution against Higgins' securities, and 106 acres of Holder's land on the Kentucky River near Jouett Creek were exposed for sale. The tract was purchased by John Morton for $44.27.

Following his death, Holder's land continued to be sold off to satisfy executions against Higgins' securities. Robert Higgins owed £23.15.7 to Thomas Arnold, county clerk of Bourbon, for tax revenues due to that county. To pay Higgins' debt, the Clark County sheriff sold 100 acres of Holder's land to George Rout for £30. Holder's heirs lost the Lower Howard's Creek mill tract, which sold for £75. The sheriff of Madison County auctioned 1,400 acres on Silver Creek that Holder had acquired from John Hall; the tract sold for £172. *Benjamin Hallock v. John Holder* was one of the more unusual cases. Hallock, of Bourbon County, obtained a judgment against Andrew Hood in Clark. Hallock sued "in consequence of Higgins's returning the Execution satisfyed & not paying me the money." In other words, Sheriff Higgins collected the money from Hood but never gave it to Hallock. Holder, on the hook as security, had 677 acres of his land sold to satisfy this debt.[28]

Holder's heirs applied to the legislature for relief from Higgins' debts. In 1812 the General Assembly approved "An act for the relief of John Holder's heirs and others."

> The persons relieved by this act were the heirs of the security of an insolvent sheriff of Clarke, and the securities of an insolvent sheriff of Bourbon. The relief given was a remission of the

Public Service and Local Affairs

damages and interest, and an acceptance, on the part of the state, of the principal debt.[29]

One of Holder's contemporaries stated that "Colonel James McMillan …with Colonel Holder and Bob Higgins' father lost all their property going security for Bob Higgins, sheriff of Clarke County."[30] The implication, which other writers have picked up on, is that Holder died bankrupt. The Higgins fiasco damaged but did not bankrupt Holder. A search of records in Bourbon, Clark and Madison, where most of his property was located, identified about 3,000 acres sold to satisfy Higgins' debts, a small percentage of Holder's total acreage.[31] As mentioned previously, Holder reported ownership of 24,000 acres on the 1796 tax rolls, along with 27 slaves. He also still had the boatyard, ferry, mill and warehouse.

Lawsuits

Robert Higgins' debts were actually a minor problem for John Holder compared to the myriad other claimants who sued him for various reasons. While Holder displayed great vision in acquiring land and pursuing his business interests, he suffered from a lack of attention to detail and a failure to follow through on his obligations in a timely manner.

Early Kentucky residents were often in court defending the titles to their land. Others with large land holdings, being short of ready cash, were often sued for debt. And, then as now, many men got overextended in business or simply spent beyond their means. John Holder was involved in numerous suits in his lifetime, most often as a defendant. A number of his suits proved to be complex drawn out affairs. Listing and describing them all would require a book of its own. Therefore, only a few representative cases are discussed in this section.

John Jouett

In 1787, John Holder gave a note to John Jouett of Mercer County promising to pay him "One Hundred Silver Dollars."[d] Four months later, Holder was called before the Virginia Supreme Court for the District of Kentucky to answer Jouett's action against him for debt. Francis Holder signed a bond as his brother's security. The case was eventually assigned to the Clark County court but no record of final judgment could be found.[32]

The most important lawsuit John Holder faced during his lifetime was initiated by John Jouett in 1793. Jouett attempted to establish his brother's claim to 1,000 acres at the mouth of Lower Howard's Creek, essentially the

---

d Court documents stated that 100 silver dollars was equivalent to "£30 current money of Virginia."

Colonel John Holder

same tract that Holder patented and lived on. The suit, discussed in detail in another chapter ("In Search of Land"), was not settled in Holder's favor until 1830.

Thomas Mount

In a case nearly matching John Jouett's for length and futility, Thomas Mount of Prince William County, Virginia, sued to obtain title to 6,055¼ acres which he had purchased from Holder in 1789.[e] Instead of having a deed drawn up, Holder gave Mount a penalty bond for £1,500, which would only be invoked if Holder failed to deliver a good title to the land. A witness later stated that the agreement was signed at Charles Smith's house in Frederick County, Virginia. Holder died without ever giving Mount a deed, and he sued Holder's heirs for the land in Fayette circuit court. The case dragged on for years. Mount died in Shelby County in 1818, and his heirs carried on the suit. The family won a judgment for the land in 1825, and a tract was laid off by Clark County surveyor, Thomas Hart. But then the case was overturned on appeal and sent back to Fayette. In 1835, the Mounts won a final judgment; however, when they went to take possession of their land, they found it occupied by tenants who held under another title. Rather than start over in court with a suit of ejectment, the Mounts gave up their quest.[33]

John Hall

Kentucky pioneer Robert Tate claimed a 400 acre settlement and 1,000 acre preemption on Silver Creek, in present day Madison County, by virtue of raising a crop of corn there in the year 1775. Tate assigned his claim to John Hall, who in turn sold it to John Holder in 1782 in exchange for three slaves. Holder secured a patent to the land in 1783.[34] The transaction between Hall and Holder was not straightforward. Holder took possession of the property but gave Hall a bond promising to deliver the slaves by an appointed date. The date came and went, years passed, and finally in 1791 Hall sued Holder for breach of their agreement. Eventually the case appeared in Clark County court with noted attorneys on each side, James Brown[f] for Hall and Levi Todd for Holder.

---

[e] In another suit, *Mary Mounts v. John Holder*, the Virginia Supreme Court for the District of Kentucky found against Holder and awarded damages to Mary of £21.11.6. Thomas Mount married Mary Clayton, so the Mary in this suit may be his spouse. Michael L. Cook, *Virginia Supreme Court District of Kentucky Order Books, 1783-1792* (Evansville, IN, 1988), p. 248.

[f] James Brown was a brother of Doctor Samuel Brown and Senator John Brown, was secretary to Governor Shelby, and after removing to Louisiana was elected several times to the U.S. Senate. Charles R. Staples, *History of Pioneer Lexington, Kentucky 1779-1806* (Lexington, 1939), p. 293.

Public Service and Local Affairs

Hall filed a complaint seeking to recover the £1,000 penalty for noncompliance that Holder had agreed to as a condition of his bond. The details were much more complicated. As it turns out, the bond had been sold to Captain Simon Spring. Attorney Brown stated that "the suit of Hall v. Holder was commenced by me at the Instance of Simon Spring." Captain Spring was one of the agents of the Yazoo Company. At the first hearing of the case in Clark County, Holder "saith that he hath performed the conditions in the declaration [bond]." The bond was produced and the following statement was found on the back of it:

> Received September 15th 1790 of Colonel John Holder on Account of the above Bond for Captain Spring, as his Attorney in fact, One Hundred and twenty two Pounds, 14 [shillings], 2 [pence]. Ebenezer S. Platt

Enter Ebenezer S. Platt, a notorious yet fascinating rogue who appeared briefly on the scene in Kentucky. Born on Long Island, Platt moved to Savannah where he entered business as a shipping merchant. At the outset of the American Revolution, Platt was captured by the British while transporting munitions to Georgia rebels. He was taken to England in chains and thrown into Newgate Prison. He was eventually released through the intercession of Patience Lovell Wright with King George III. Platt married Wright's daughter, but later abandoned her and removed to Kentucky. He was appointed captain of a cavalry company in Holder's Yazoo Regiment. Platt resided briefly in Clark County then left the state owing large sums of money. One of his victims was Daniel Boone. Boone's son recalled, "My father gave security for Captain Ebenezer S. Platt for £500 which he had to pay off. He never recovered but a moiety of it. Yet he was so confiding that he loaned this man a Negro, a horse, a saddle, and a bridle, supposedly to go to Louisville on business, but he never heard of him but once afterwards. Captain Platt was in New Orleans, so my father never got his property or its worth again."[35]

Platt's endorsement on the bond to Hall proved useful to Holder. Holder also produced a receipt from Platt for this payment, dated August 1792 at Lexington, stating that this satisfied the condition of the bond. The plaintiffs disputed Holder's claim and the case was continued in order to take Platt's deposition. According to James Brown, the case "was sent for trial to Clark County where it remained on the Dockett 5 or six years and at last was dismissed for want of Testimony on the part of the Plaintiff. Ebenezer Platt was the witness. He was frequently summoned but never attended and at length left the State." Hall finally gave up and the suit was discontinued in February 1798.[36]

Holder's heirs later lost the land Holder had acquired from Hall. It was sold to pay debts incurred by Sheriff Robert Higgins that fell to Holder as his security.[37]

John Martin Jr.

Another damaging suit against John Holder resulted in a judgment in favor of John Martin Jr. This may have been the son of John Martin Sr., Holder's Lower Howard's Creek neighbor. The root cause of the suit was a practice repeated over and over by Holder, namely, the sale of land with the promise to make a deed at a later time. In August 1793, Holder signed a covenant to give Martin 100 acres of land out of the large holdings he had on Upper Howard's Creek, Lulbegrud or Red River.

> This shall oblije me my heirs &c to John Martin his heirs or assigns to make or cause to be made a good & Sufficent Deed with a general warrantee Title to one hundred acres of land out of aney of my land that lies on Howards upper Creek Lulbergrud or Red river that is not previously Sold; the one hunded acres to be of the first quallity or as much land of the Best we can get & as will make up the worth of the hunded acres of the first quallity to be ajudged to by Jacob Dooling; the Deed to be made By the twenty fifth of December one Thousand seven hunded & ninty three. Given under my hand & Seal this 6th of august 1793
>
> John Holder
>
> Test
> John Martin Sr
> Joseph x Brandenburg

The deed was to be made by December 25 of that year. Many Christmases came and went with no deed. After Holder's death, Martin was unable to get a deed from the heirs, so he brought suit in Clark County. Robert Trimble, later justice of the U.S. Supreme Court, served as Martin's attorney. The heirs, responding through their attorney, George Webb, stated that "they Have not any Lands & tenements by Hederatory descent of John Holder In fee simple."

The case was continued until July 1807, when a jury found against the heirs and awarded Martin $450 damages for the lost acreage plus his costs to defend the case.[38]

Public Service and Local Affairs

In order to satisfy the judgment, David Hampton, the Clark County sheriff, exposed for sale Holder's remaining share of his 50,612½ acre survey. This land was situated along Red River mostly in present day Powell County. Holder located the tract, had it surveyed by Justinian Cartwright in 1785, then assigned one-fourth of it to John Cape, one-fourth to Daniel Gano and one-fourth to Ebenezer Platt (Platt assigned his share to Andrew Holmes). Holder sold 6,000 acres of his share to George Nicholas and John Breckinridge, which left him—and subsequently his heirs—with an interest of approximately 6,650 acres.

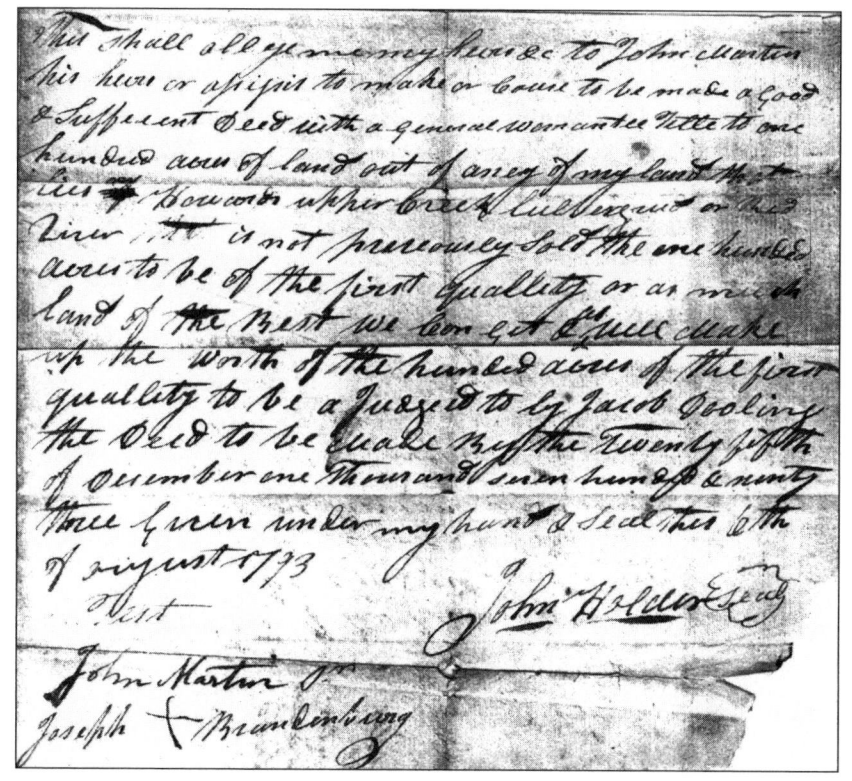

Holder's Bond to John Martin Jr.

The auction of the remaining property took place "at the house formerly occupied by Tillman Bush opposite red river Ironworks," and the buyer was James Sympson of Winchester. In 1815, the sheriff made a deed to Sympson's heirs, William Sympson and Chilton Allan.[39] The loss suffered by Holder's heirs may not have been as harmful as we might expect judging from the amount of acreage involved. The tract probably included overlapping claims made by others. Holder had made no effort to extinguish the other claims, so it is uncertain how much land Sympson and Allan ended up with.

Green Clay

This case demonstrates the difficulties faced when doing business in an economy short of cash money. John Holder held a promissory note from Amos Ogden for £200. Owing a debt to Green Clay, Holder assigned this note to Clay in 1786. When he attempted to collect, Clay learned that Ogden had been in prison for other debts in Maryland and was bankrupt. Clay then sued Holder for the debt before the Virginia Supreme Court. The court found for Clay and ordered the Fayette County sheriff to attach Holder's goods to satisfy the judgment. Only one brass candlestick was collected. After separation of Kentucky and formation of Clark County, the case came before the court of quarter sessions. It was continued a number of times before being dissolved in 1794 owing to "the plaintiff failing further to prosecute his Suit."[40]

Samuel Smith

Samuel Smith was a Winchester merchant who together with Robert Clark Jr. built the second iron furnace in Kentucky—the Red River Ironworks at present day Clay City—in about 1805. Following Clark's death, Smith partnered with Porter Clay, Henry Clay's brother, in a sawmill and boat building business at the ironworks.[41] The parties involved in *Samuel Smith v. John Holder* include Laurence Thompson (Revolutionary War veteran and Nathaniel Hart's son-in-law) Green Clay (wealthy landowner of Madison County), Robert Craddock (Danville land speculator), William "Captain Billy" Bush (Clark County) and others. The claims and counterclaims were so numerous and confusing that only the principal thread of the case will be followed here.

The suit arose from a promissory note John Holder gave Laurence Thompson for the sum of £38.7.7.

> Received June 14th 1787 of R[obert] Craddock thirty Eight pounds seven shillings & seven pence, which sum I promis to pay Capt. L. Thompson for said Craddock towards the first payment due on and assignment dated October 7th 1786.
> Teste   John Holder
> Laurence Thompson

Thompson assigned (i.e., sold) the note to William Bush, who in turn assigned it to Samuel Smith. Smith sued in 1793 and at a trial held the

Public Service and Local Affairs

following year, the jury found in his favor. Holder immediately appealed and filed for an injunction, which was granted. For his defense, he claimed he gave a receipt to Laurence Thompson which Thompson fraudulently altered to make it to look like a promissory note. Holder said Thompson passed off the fake note to William Bush and it finally ended up in the hands of Samuel Smith.

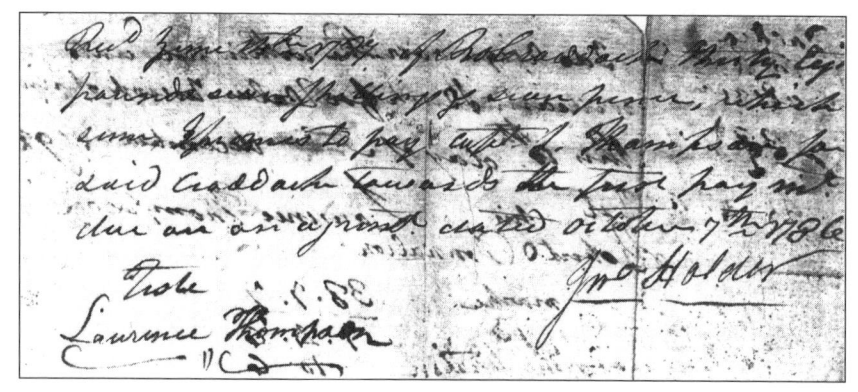

Holder's Promissory Note to Thompson. Although the note is hard to read and has writing bleeding through from the back, there is no obvious indication that it was altered. Holder's unusual defense failed to persuade the jury. They ordered him to pay the note plus the plaintiff's costs and court costs.[42]

Seitz and Lauman

With money coming in from his enterprises, Holder made liberal use of credit with Winchester and Lexington merchants. He ran up a large tab at the store of Seitz and Lauman purchasing items such as tumblers, hats, wool, hinges and knee buckles. John A. Seitz and Frederick Lauman were Lexington merchants who had a successful business selling general merchandise at their store on Main Street.[g] The company engaged in the New Orleans trade in the 1790s: "New Orleans. The subscribers will engage a number of Able Bodied Men to conduct their Boats to New Orleans. Liberal wages will be given. Apply to Seitz & Lauman. A generous price will be given for clean Wheat, Hemp and Tallow, in Merchandise."[43]

By early 1796, Holder was indebted to the store more than £300 for purchases beginning the previous September. Seitz and Lauman sued Holder for payment in the Clark County court of quarter sessions, and

---

[g] "Frederick Lauman & John Seitz were merchants in Lexington from 1793 or 1794 to 1800 and John A. Seitz alone to about 1803 or 4. Mr. Seitz's store was on N.E. corner Main & Mill street, the old stone store; he removed to Natchez. He was German or Dutch, and a public spirited citizen." William Leavy, "A Memoir of Lexington and Its Vicinity," *Register of the Kentucky Historical Society* (1943) 41:107-137.

Colonel John Holder

the court ordered Holder to pay the debt plus costs. Holder then filed for an injunction to prevent execution of the court's judgment. As frequently happens in litigation, the issues become very cloudy after we hear both sides. The case of *Holder v. Seitz & Lauman* was filed in October 1797. Holder told his story first.

> To the Worshipful Court of Clarke County now in chancery sitting humbly complaining, sheweth to your worships your Orator John Holder that a Judgment was obtained against him in Clarke court... for the sum of about 300£ by Seitz & Lauman of Lexington, now, so it is, may it please your worships that your Orator [is] conscious that accounts subsisted between your Orator and the said Seitz & Lauman; that he was indebted to them; that they would also allow all just credits which your Orator could produce against them or justly had against them. [your Orator] did not even defend the suit and therefore had judgment for the sum above mentioned given against him.
>
> Now may it please your worships, your Orator declares that by punctual agreement your Orator was to have built five boats for the said Defendants, to be paid for them at the current price; that he completed these boats for the said Defendants; that they refused to take only three; a principal part of the work was done on the [other] two boats which they refused to take; the reason your Orator did not entirely complete the remaining 2 was that they were by contract to give him 10 days notice before they took them and as the Defendants never gave this notice to your Orator, he apprehended a noncompliance with their contract with respect to your Orator, and therefore he did not entirely complete them; your [Orator] states that credit should have been given and discount made at the time the judgment was obtained against your Orator by said Defendants for the work which your Orator done for them on the two remaining boats and that the Defendants never did it.
>
> Your Orator further states that he was overcharged in the price of the goods which he purchased of them and for which suit was commenced against your Orator; that he was charged more than by punctual agreement he was to have had the goods at; all which actings and doings of the said Defendants are contrary to equity and good conscience and tend to the manifest injury and oppression of your Orator. . . .

Public Service and Local Affairs

May it please your Worships, the premises considered, to grant to your Orator the Commonwealth writ of injunction to enjoin the said defendants and all others from any further proceedings on the judgment or execution aforesaid untill the matter can be fully heard in equity. . . .[44]

The court agreed to look into the equity matter and issued an injunction.

Seitz and Lauman promptly answered Holder's charges. They stated that "intending to send produce to New Orleans, they contracted with the Complainant for the making and delivery of four good Kentucky Boats for which they were to allow him the customary price out of the amount which was then due from the Complainant to the Defendants." Contradicting Holder, they said that they gave him ten days notice when they were ready for the first boat, but when they arrived at the boatyard they found "that she was not ready." Seitz and Lauman said that they were then "under the necessity of sending five of their own hands to assist for ten days in finishing her, by which the Defendants were delayed in their journey about 14 days, by which means the Defendants are informed they lost about 2000 Dollars in consequence of flour falling in that time from 20 to 12 Dollars per Barrell, besides the other expenses of the delay. They added that "the Complainant failing to have the next Boat ready by the [appointed] day, these Defendants [were] obliged to give Cash to Elisha Winter[b] for a Boat to carry their produce." Seitz and Lauman acknowledged that they received two other boats from Holder. They said that after the court issued its judgment, they met with Holder and agreed to a settlement of how much he was due for delivery of three boats. They submitted a copy of their agreement, signed by Holder, giving Holder credit for £36 per boat, for a total of £108 to be credited to his account.

They also produced a deposition from William Jones stating that he was present when the agreement was reached. Jones volunteered that Holder asked Seitz to sell some boats for him, and Seitz replied that "he would if he could." This could have been the same William Jones who married Margaret Drake and was living then in the Lower Howard's Creek neighborhood.

Seitz and Lauman denied Holder's contention that he was overcharged for the goods he purchased and stated that Holder "never threw out any insinuation of the kind that these Defendants ever heard until he wished to obtain an Injunction." They claimed they were ready to prove that Holder

---

[b] Elisha Winter was a prominent early merchant of Fayette County. He had a business complex on the Kentucky River at the mouth of Tates Creek. There, in addition to building boats, he had a store, gristmill and distillery. *Kentucky Gazette*, October 24, 1805.

Colonel John Holder

"has often declared that the goods were purchased on reasonable terms and that he had been honorably dealt with by these Defendants."

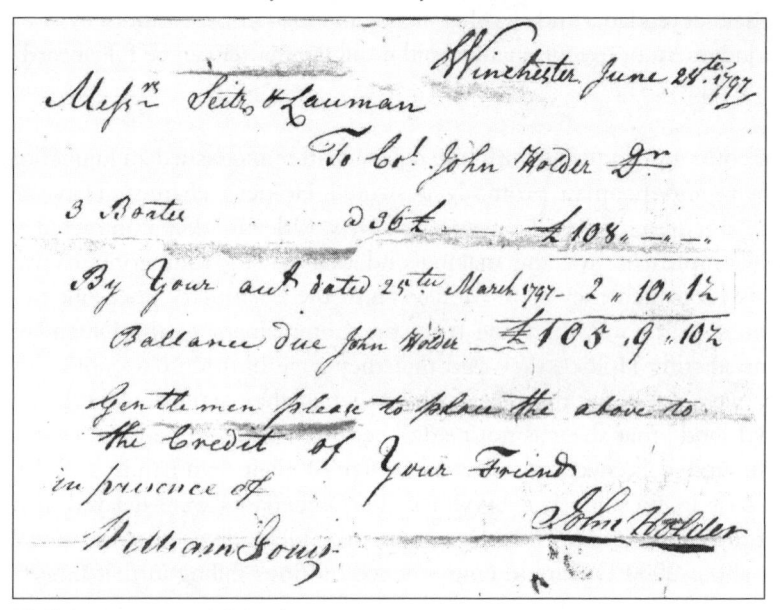

Holder's Agreement with Seitz & Lauman.

The issue was resolved in February 1798, when the court dissolved the injunction and ordered Seitz and Lauman's judgment against Holder to stand.[45]

Somewhat surprisingly, the merchants continued to buy boats from Holder, and he continued to buy goods from Seitz and Lauman. In fact, they sued him again in Clark County. Henry Clay served as Holder's attorney and a hometown jury heard the case, but it didn't help. They found in favor of Seitz and Lauman again. The court ordered Holder to pay £5 plus court costs. The judgment was issued in February 1799.[46] Holder died the following month.

Sharshall Jordan

Sharshall Jordan (1748-1813) served as an officer in the Revolutionary War from Culpeper County, Virginia. He came to Clark County in about 1795 and lived on Indian Creek, a tributary of the Kentucky River.[47] Jordan purchased his 200 acre plantation from John Holder and settled on the land. Holder gave Jordan a penalty bond for £1,000 promising a clear title to the land before December 25, 1798; Francis Holder was a witness to the bond.

Public Service and Local Affairs

Jordan stated that he "often applyed to the said John Holder to comply with the conditions of the bond, but he never coud get a deed." Holder died before executing a deed for the tract. John Haggard and James French, who claimed the same land, entered a suit of ejectment against Jordan in an effort to evict him from his homeplace. Jordan's application to Holder's heirs for a deed was unsuccessful, so he sued them in Clark County court and won a judgment for the value of the land, £330, plus damages. Rather than pay Jordan, the heirs allowed the sheriff to sell six tracts of land totaling 1,140 acres in order to satisfy the judgment.[48] In a similar suit about the same time, George Johnson sued Holder's heirs and won a judgment against them for the value of the land, £272, plus damages. The sheriff sold three tracts of Holder land totaling 801 acres to satisfy the judgment.[49]

* * *

These eight examples are representative of the forty plus suits filed against Holder or his heirs in Clark County. Most numerous were the suits by individuals and merchants for debts. This was certainly not uncommon in Kentucky's cash strapped economy of the late 1700s. Many well to do citizens with large landholdings had trouble paying their debts due to lack of ready cash. However, Holder had an advantage over others, owning several businesses that produced a regular income. The suits brought against him by merchants suggest that Holder purchased store goods freely, perhaps extravagantly. When sued for not paying his debts, he usually had an explanation, excuse or difference of opinion, but his arguments seldom persuaded juries.

The other common trend in Holder's suits was his failure to provide a deed after he sold someone land. One explanation could be that he himself had problems gaining undisputed title to the land. Some of his grants were delayed for years. The large tract he claimed with John Taylor was not granted until 1811, twelve years after his death.[50] In instances where he had an undivided interest in land, he could not give a deed until the land was divided. In some instances, Holder delayed recording his own deeds. For example, Holder earned a locator's fee for the large tract patented to Richard Graham. Graham gave him a deed for his share of the tract in 1791, but Holder never had the deed recorded. It was not until 1802 that the deed was produced in Clark County court by his heirs, witnessed and recorded in the deed books.[51] Giving a bond instead of a deed would also be understandable if the property had not been surveyed at the time of sale. In the case of the bond to Sharshall Jordan, however, Holder included the

Colonel John Holder

metes and bounds of the land in the bond he signed.[52] Whatever the various reasons for delay, there is no question that Holder was far from diligent in attending to the details of his land business.

The only case out of the ordinary was a suit against Holder for slander filed by Thomas Stevens. The case was dismissed soon after it was filed, indicating that Holder reached some agreement with Stevens out of court.[53]

It is perhaps significant that Holder does not appear as plaintiff in any of these Clark County cases. The only exception was when he appealed cases before the local tribunal. For example, after he lost the judgment to Seitz and Lauman, he sued them seeking first an injunction and then a reversal of the judgment. There must have been any number of people who owed him money. He may have been too engaged in other matters to attend to this important aspect of his business.

Near the end of his life, Holder recognized that the claims against him had reached the crisis stage. He took several steps to raise the money he needed to pay off his debts. He sold Gregory Glasscock of Fayette County 1,000 acres of land for £2,000 "in hand paid." Holder then sold most of his slaves to his brother-in-law Richard Callaway for £1,500 "in hand paid."[54] Holder then took the drastic measure of appointing three trustees to handle his affairs. They placed the following notice, dated March 22, 1799, in the *Kentucky Gazette*:

> Notice, That col. John Holder, of Clarke county, has conveyed to the subscribers, all his estate real and personal, of whatever description in trust for paying his debt, and complying with his contracts &c. All those, therefore who have any demands upon the said Holder, are requested to make them known to John Patrick, at Richmond, Madison county, who is properly authorized by the Trustees to adjust and liquidate the same, and to make such arrangement for payment as the situation of the estate will permit.
>
> Those who may be indebted to the said Holder are likewise requested to pay to the said Patrick, their respective debts, as no indulgence can hereafter be given.
>
> James French
John Patrick
Richard Callaway[55]

These influential individuals were related to Holder through his wife. James French was the first county surveyor of Madison and was married to Keziah Callaway, Fanny's half sister. Richard Callaway, son of Colonel

Public Service and Local Affairs

Richard Callaway, served several terms in the General Assembly. John Patrick, who married a granddaughter of Colonel Callaway, was heavily involved in local politics.[56]

It was not uncommon to appoint a trustee or trustees to manage one's affairs in instances of mental or physical incapacity or illness. Whether this was the situation with Holder or not is unknown, but he died soon after on March 30. There is no indication that the trustees ever settled any of Holder's debts.

Chapter 14
Journey's End

John Holder died in the spring of 1799. The exact date of his death comes from a letter written by James Stonestreet to Lyman Draper:

> I have seen Mrs. [Rhoda] Vaughn. She says her father Colonel Holder died on the 30th of March 1799. She fixed the date by the birth of her oldest son.[1]

Stonestreet was a wealthy Clark County farmer. He is listed in the 1850 census as 62 years of age and worth $20,000. He married Lucy Fishback and lived in the Pine Grove area. He visited Rhoda and wrote to Draper in 1853. Rhoda's recollection should be accurate, as she reports her first son was born on the same day Holder died. She had married Eli Vaughn in June 1797.

The cause of Holder's death is unknown. Goff Bedford wrote that Holder had been ill for several years before he died, but he gave no source for this information. One family legend has it that John Holder was killed by Indians. There is no contemporary evidence to support this, and none of the Holder family members who corresponded with Lyman Draper ever mentioned it.[2] It is unthinkable that such an event would not be reported by at least one of the many people who spoke of Holder in interviews and letters. The numerous lawsuits against his heirs stated that Holder had died, none said he had been killed.

Family tradition puts Holder's death in the winter of 1797-98, so we have a conflict. We have already learned that contemporaries of Holder gave much more accurate information about him than his family was able to provide. However, there is additional evidence to support the date given by Rhoda Vaughn. Holder was living in July 1798, when he was one of the justices present at county court and was the security for Benjamin Dod Wheeler, who was sworn in as coroner. Holder signed a deed selling 21 slaves to his brother-in-law in October 1798. He was still among the living in February 1799, when the county court returned a judgment against him.

Journey's End

Had Holder been dead, the plaintiffs would have been required to refile the case against his heirs. Finally, in March 1799, Holder appointed three trustees to handle his financial affairs.[3]

Another piece of evidence points to March 1799 as the correct month. Holder was appointed colonel of the 17th Regiment of the Kentucky militia when it was first formed in 1793 and served as its commander until his death. Shortly afterwards, on April 12, 1799, Richard Hickman received his appointment as the second commander of the battalion.[4] A statement of William Sudduth confirms that Holder was still serving as regiment commander when he died. He said that Holder "was appointed a Colonel of Militia, which he retained untill his death."[5]

Holder's Estate

John Holder did not leave a will, and the county court was unusually silent regarding his estate. No one was appointed to list and appraise his slaves and personal goods. No widow's dower was awarded to Fanny. This may reflect the fact that the court knew Holder's affairs were in a mess. It was probably common knowledge. In one of the lawsuits, the plaintiff stated that Holder had "departed this life…leaving a considerable estate. That no person has qualified as his administrator, nor is any person likely so to do."[6] It is surprising, however, to find that several years passed before the court appointed guardians for his minor children. Although their mother was living, the law required a guardian to be named whenever the father died leaving infant children.

In May 1801, Richard Hickman was assigned guardian to Holder's heirs specifically "for the purpose of dividing a tract of land on the Kentucky river in this County between Josiah Jackson and the heirs aforesaid." In July, the order was rescinded and Samuel R. Combs was appointed guardian of "the Infant heirs of John Holder." The heirs were not named in either order. Another order, in April 1802, appointed James French guardian for the purpose of dividing another tract of land. The infant[a] heirs were named as "John, Sophiah, Caleb, Richard, Lidda, Fanny and Kitty Holder." Richard, Caleb and Frances had guardians appointed by the Madison County court in 1804.[7]

In June 1802, Fanny gave a quitclaim deed for a tract of land to Samuel R. Combs in consideration of "Motherly love" and "one Dollar." She released any interest she had to 382 acres where "said Combs now lives." This was the property on Lower Howard's Creek and Kentucky River where

---

[a] Males and females were considered infants until age 21. Those listed must have been born after April 1781.

Colonel John Holder

Holder's ferry, warehouse, boatyard and other enterprises were located. Fanny retained rights to 200 acres on Jouett Creek where she was living. Her place was mentioned in a petition to build a gristmill submitted by Harry Hieronymous in February of that year. He applied to the court "to condemn a mill seat across duetts creek, near the road leading across said creek from my House to Mrs. Fanny Holders."[8]

Fanny remained a widow for nearly three years then married John McGuire in December 1802. McGuire was an early resident and hunter at McGee's Station on Jouett Creek. He was a captain in the militia and was appointed one of the first justices of Clark County along with John Holder. John McGuire was listed on the 1806 Clark County tax roll with 157 acres on Howard's Creek and 3 horses.[9] Fanny and McGuire had one daughter named Betsy. Fanny died not long after Betsy was born.

In November 1803, Fanny made a will, which was probated in February 1804. Fanny directed that "the land whereon she now resides in Clark County, on Jouits Creek, 200 acres," was to be divided equally among her children "when they become of age or marry." Her "three Negroes and their increase" were to be dispersed in the same manner.[b] Fanny's will lists the names of eight of her children: Sophia, John, Caleb, Richard, Lydia, Fanny, Kitty and Betsy. Her eldest daughter, Theodosia Combs, signed the will as a witness. The same list of children, including Theodosia but excluding Betsy, appears repeatedly in lawsuits as the heirs of John Holder.[10]

Holder Graveyard

John and Fanny Holder's graves cannot be found today. They were probably buried on his farm overlooking the Kentucky River and Lower Howard's Creek. There is evidence to suggest that they lie in unmarked graves in what is now called the Hieronymous Cemetery.

Richard G. Williams, who married Holder's daughter Catherine, wrote to Draper in 1851 describing a visit to their burial place:

> I have been at their graves, but there is no stone to tell when or where born, or when they died. They were buried on their farm about 2 miles below Boonsboro.[11]

---

[b] In 1809, Henry Clay purchased two of the slaves named in Fanny's will. The bill of sale read, "Know all men by these presents that I John Hart of Fayette County, Trustee for the benefit of the heirs of John Holder deceased, have this day sold and delivered to Henry Clay esquire a negro woman called Ede & her son Giles, the former about forty years of age & the latter about nine, for and in consideration of the Sum of five hundred dollars." After Fanny died, John Hart of Lexington was the guardian for Sophia Holder. James F. Hopkins, editor, *Papers of Henry Clay, Vol. 1, The Rising Statesman, 1797-1814* (Lexington, 1959), p. 395.

Journey's End

Williams' daughter, Jessie Williams Hart, described her family's attempts to locate the grave.

> Nor have the descendants as yet found the graves of John and Frances (Callaway) Holder. Some time prior to 1839, probably about 1835, my father [Jesse Williams] visited these graves. He stated they were buried side by side, near the center of the old farm, at the mouth of Howard's Creek, two miles from Boonesborough. He recalled that the graves were surrounded by a stone wall about three feet high. . . .
>
> In the summer of 1923 a descendant, Judge O. W. Williams, made search for the two graves. He found an old circular walled stone grave yard about thirty to forty feet in diameter, with graves stones hidden in a thicket of young trees and vines, at the top of the bluff on the northwest side of Howard's creek, near the road from Boonesborough to Lexington, and not far from the mouth of the creek. This was known to the neighbors as the Hieronymous burying ground. The Clark county records show that some years after the death of John Holder a Hieronymus became the owner of a part of the old Holder domain.
>
> Within the old walled enclosure Judge Williams found perhaps twenty graves in evidence, some fallen stones, some partly buried and possibly some entirely hidden. Only a few stones were still standing, and the most modern of these bore the name Hieronymus, born 1772, died 1859.[12]

The Hieronymous referred to was Benjamin (1772-1859). Mrs. Hart later gave another account of the search for the graves with some additional details:

> My father visited the graves of John and Frances Holder, on their farm, at the mouth of Howard's creek, a few miles from Boonesborough. His visit was made in 1839 or 1840 and he said the graves were marked, but ten years later my grandfather, Richard Gott Williams, wrote to Dr. Draper that they were unmarked. So if there had been a marker, it had been of lumber and quickly decayed.[13]

Mrs. Hart's identification of the Hieronymous Cemetery as the burial place of John and Frances Holder led the Clark County Historical Society to place a marker there for these two noted pioneers. A gravesite dedication

Colonel John Holder

Graveside Dedication Service. Photos, top to bottom: John and Frances Holder marker; Robert Coney at the podium, Dr. C. R. "Pete" Smith seated on his right and members of the Holder family; rifle salute by the Brigade of the American Revolution. Photos by Paula Coney.

Journey's End

service was held on October 17, 1998, nearly two hundred years after Holder's death. A number of Holder descendants, accompanied by historical society members and Revolutionary War reenactors, attended the ceremony.

Children of John Holder and Fanny Callaway

John and Fanny Holder had eight children, all born in Fayette County/Clark County, with the possible exception of Theodocia. Their names are listed in various records, including marriage consents, Fanny's will, guardian appointments and lawsuits against Holder's heirs. One of the most extensive studies of the Callaway and Holder families was published in 1929 by Jessie Williams Hart, a granddaughter of John Holder's daughter Catherine. She provided the following information about John and Fanny's children, not all of which was documented:[14]

1. Theodocia, born about 1782, married Samuel R. Combs in 1797
2. Sophia, born 1784, died 1806 of tuberculosis
3. John Walton, born about January 1786, married Catharine Penn in Virginia in 1808, died near Winchester, Tennessee, in 1842 [gravestone says born November 6, 1785, died September 21, 1841]
4. Caleb, born about 1788, married in Georgia and soon died
5. Richard Callaway, born about 1790, married his brother Caleb's widow, died in Chickasaw County, Mississippi
6. Lydia, married Thomas G. Jones in 1812 when about age 20
7. Frances Walton, born about 1795, married Edward McGuire, and died in Aberdeen, Mississippi
8. Catharine, born 1797, married Richard G. Williams in 1812

Additional information about the children and their families is summarized below.

Theodocia Holder and Samuel R. Combs

Theodocia may have been the first child born to John Holder and Fanny Callaway. She was named after Fanny's younger sister. Theodocia married S. R. Combs in Clark County on October 9, 1797. John Holder gave his consent, so she was not yet 21. Samuel Richardson Combs (c.1771-1833) was the son of Clark County pioneers Benjamin Combs and Mary Richardson. They are buried near their homeplace on present day Becknerville Road. Samuel's brother was Gen. Leslie Combs, a hero of the War of 1812 and later a noted attorney in Fayette County. Samuel and Theodosia lived on Holder's place, and Samuel took over many of his business ventures on

Colonel John Holder

Lower Howard's Creek after Holder's untimely death in 1799. Combs Ferry was one of these.[15]

Samuel R. Combs served as an officer in the militia and commanded a cavalry company in Richard M. Johnson's regiment during the War of 1812. Combs built a sawmill and gristmill on Lower Howard's Creek and still had the sawmill when he died. He was also involved in the political affairs of the county. In a letter dated 1907, Dr. Glenmore Combs wrote, "Capt. Samuel Combs perhaps had more native ability than any of the four sons, although Gen. Leslie Combs was more widely known. Samuel Combs was a Captain in the War of 1812 and represented this county several times in the State Legislature."[16] The record of S. R. Combs' service in the legislature has not been found.

There is evidence that Combs had a temper and was inclined to violence. In 1815, he was indicted for stabbing Elijah G. Browning, a Winchester merchant. No further details are available except that Combs was found not guilty following a jury trial.[17] In October 1833, Samuel R. Combs was murdered in front of the Clark County courthouse. The *Kentucky Gazette* carried a brief obituary:

> We learn that Capt. Samuel Combs of Clarke county was killed a day or two since in a rencontre with a man in the streets of Winchester, the county seat. Capt. C. was an early and respected citizen of this State. He migrated here in times that tried the settler's courage and bore a conspicuous part.[18]

A little more detail was provided in the *Lexington Observer & Reporter*:

> To the Editors, dated
> Winchester, October 1
> This morning about 8 o'clock, an unfortunate rencounter took place before the Court House door, between Samuel R. Combs and sons against two of the Bushes, sons of Ambrose, which terminated in the death of Samuel R. Combs, sen. His head was nearly separated from his body, the main artery being entirely separated. Combs had shot a man named Nelson the day previous with a pistol and was in custody of the Sheriff, and the Bushes were summoned as a guard. He died in about 30 minutes or less after he received the cut.[19]

This is supplemented by the following undocumented report:

Journey's End

On October 1, 1833, Samuel R. Combs was brutally murdered by a young member of the neighboring Bush family. After his "throat had been cut from ear to ear, he called bystanders to come and see a brave man die. He lived only a few minutes, but long enough to dictate his will by holding his severed windpipe with his own hand."[20]

While it makes a great story, the account of Combs dictating his will cannot be verified. If he did so, it was not probated in court. Oral wills ("nuncupative wills") were legal in Kentucky if given in the presence of witnesses.

From these accounts, we may summarize the events as follows: On September 30, 1833, Combs shot a man named Nelson with a pistol. Nelson was not further identified and it was not stated whether or not he died. The next morning, Combs was escorted to the courthouse by two sons of Ambrose Bush Jr. From later indictments we know they were James and Lamentation Bush. At the courthouse door, a confrontation occurred between Combs and his sons and the Bushes. Two of Combs' sons were later indicted, John Holder Combs and Aaron Burr Combs, along with their neighbor Benjamin Hieronymous. In the melee, Samuel had his throat cut by Lamentation Bush, who was subsequently charged with murder. Combs died several minutes later due to loss of blood from a severed artery.

Samuel R. Combs lived on John Holder's old place on the Kentucky River, on land between Lower Howard's Creek and Jouett Creek. Two of Ambrose Bush's sons, James and Lamentation, lived nearby on Jouett Creek. If there had been any previous bad blood between Combs and the Bushes, it has not yet come to light. Combs did have a history with the Nelson family, which will be examined in the next section. The last section will review the court proceedings that resulted from Combs' murder.

Combs-Nelson Connection From the county tax lists, we know there were several Nelson families living in Clark County in 1833. They include Edward, William, Joel, Julius, James, Jefferson, James B., George and Reuben Nelson. Only James B. Nelson is shown owning property. He was taxed for 164 acres on the waters of Boone Creek, on land patented by Richard Hickman. This places him, and probably other Nelsons as well, in the general area of Jouett Creek.

The Nelson who was shot by Combs has not been identified, but there is a Combs-Nelson connection that almost certainly played a role in this matter. In January 1832, Sabrina Nelson sued Samuel R. Combs in Clark circuit court for slander and sought $1,000 in damages. She called as witnesses

Colonel John Holder

Edward Nelson, Benjamin J. Miller, Elliott Holliday, Joseph Holliday, Waller Holliday, James Holliday, Manuel Wyatt, George Wyatt, Fleming Wyatt, Thomas Wyatt, and Thomas Hatton. Their testimony has not been found.

The following excerpts are taken from the brief prepared by her attorney, Samuel Hanson:

> Sabrina Nelson…is and from her nativity hath been a chaste woman and hath been so accounted by her neighbors & acquaintances. Nevertheless, the defendant…intending to injure and defame the said Sabrina, in a certain conversation which the defendant had with divers good citizens of this Commonwealth of and concerning the said Sabrina…did with a loud voice falsly & maliciously utter and publish of and concerning the Plaintiff the following false, scandalous and malicious words, towit:
> "She is a whore."
> "I carnally knew her."
> "She went off with a bean in her belly."
> "She went off with a pumpkin seed in her belly.
> "I had to do with her fifty times."
> "I have been as intimate with her as I have been with my own wife."
> "She is an unchaste woman."
> "She was pregnant with child."
> "She is now pregnant with child."
> By means of speaking of which several false scandalous and malicious words, the Plaintiff saith she hath sustained damage to the amount of $1,000. Wherefore she brings suit &c.[21]

The suit was dismissed in March. The agreement signed by Sabrina Nelson (by her mark) and S. R. Combs states that the defendant was to pay her attorney fees and court costs, an indication that Combs admitted culpability and paid Sabrina to settle out of court.

It seems likely that Combs' shooting of Nelson a year and a half later was related to this unfortunate episode. Edward is the only Nelson mentioned by name in Sabrina's suit. Whether he was the man shot is not known. After searching newspapers, court records and family histories for a follow up on these events, no other details were discovered.

Sabrina Nelson was mentioned one more time in Clark County records. In 1841, Allen Carter charged the county $5.00 for "Making Coffin for Sabrina Nelsons Sun." The county paid him $2.50 in 1846.[22]

Journey's End

Aftermath of Combs' Murder Following the gruesome and very public murder of Samuel R. Combs, Lamentation Bush was indicted in Clark circuit court for the crime. His brother James was also indicted, although on lesser charges. Lamentation and James were grandsons of Ambrose Bush Sr. Ambrose Sr. was one of five Bush brothers who settled in Clark County.[23]

Ambrose's son, Ambrose Jr., lived on the west side of Jouett Creek on land he acquired from John Holder at a sheriff's auction. The little valley there is still known as Bush Hollow. In 1824, Samuel R. Combs sold 117 acres to James and Lamentation Bush, and then in 1830 Combs sold James Bush another 5 acres.[24] Both of these tracts were on Jouett Creek.[c]

Details of the criminal case against Lamentation and James could not be located, as the court papers appear to have been misplaced.[25] One of the court record books contains summaries of actions taken by the court in 1834 and 1835, which are summarized below.

The record in *Commonwealth v. Lamentation Bush* indicates that Bush was tried for Combs' murder in October 1833 before two of the county justices. As this was a capital offense, they turned the matter over to the commonwealth attorney. Lamentation Bush appeared at a court held on March 24, 1834, Judge Richard French presiding, "to answer to a charge of murder exhibited against him." In the court's language, on the motion of Bush and by the consent of his securities, he was "bound in recognizance." The case of *Commonwealth v. Bush* was presented to the grand jury the next day. Asa K. Lewis was their foreman. After hearing the evidence against Bush, the grand jury returned the indictment "not a True Bill." Judge French then declared, "Nothing further appearing or being alledged against said Bush, It is ordered that he be discharged."[26]

When the commonwealth attorney indicts someone for murder, he presents his evidence to a grand jury. If twelve members of the grand jury do not find probable cause for the charge, the indictment is returned as "not a true bill." This finding means the Commonwealth cannot prosecute the accused on that charge.

The witnesses called in the case are known, as they requested payment for attending court to testify. The list includes William Taylor, Edward Green, Samuel Blackburn, Hudson Martin, Craven Barkley, John C. Martin, John S. Jenkins, George W. Merritt, Leslie C. Bostic, John H. Combs, Henry

---

c Ambrose Bush Jr. married Jane Quisenberry, a daughter of Rev. James Quisenberry and Jane Burrus. Lamentation Bush married first Betham Peddicord, daughter of William Peddicord, in 1827; he married second Sarah H. Martin in 1836. Lamentation was one of the Clark County patrollers in November 1827. James Bush was born in 1800 in Clark County. He married Nancy Poindexter in 1822. He died in 1887 and was buried in the Winchester Cemetery. Ann Poindexter Couey, *The Family of James Bush and Wife Nancy Poindexter* (Winchester, 1979).

Kohlhass, William H. McCauley, James McCauley, Thomas N. Burgess, Alfred Bowren, Wyatt Ousley, Lindsey Coleman, William Hernden and Joseph H. January. Some of these men lived in Winchester and others lived in the Jouett Creek-Lower Howard's Creek area.[27]

Immediately after the grand jury declined to prosecute Lamentation Bush for murder, the commonwealth attorney entered indictments against "John H. Combs and other Defendants." Although the charges were not specified in the court record, one suspects they were related to the fracas that occurred at the courthouse when Combs was murdered. At the June term of court, the commonwealth attorney entered a motion to drop the charges against Aaron Burr Combs and Benjamin Hieronymous. *Commonwealth v. John H. Combs, James Bush, and Lamentation Bush* was then continued for several terms.[28]

Finally in March of 1835, the case was heard in court. The defendants, by their attorneys, pleaded not guilty and the sheriff was ordered to empanel a jury. The record shows Judge French "Ordered that said Jury to be discharged," probably because they could not reach a verdict. The case was continued again at the April and June terms.[29] The order book for the remainder of 1835 (Book X) is missing, so the final verdict in the case, if any, is not known.

* * *

Samuel R. Combs and Theodocia Holder had 11 children that can be proven (there may have been others):[30]

1. Sarah Sophia Combs, married first cousin Richard P. Holder
2. Elizabeth Combs, married Benjamin F. Combs
3. Mary Ann Combs, married Leslie C. Bostick
4. Samuel Richardson Combs Jr., married Margaret Van Antwerp
5. Marquis Combs
6. Aaron Burr Combs
7. Owen Combs
8. Elliott Combs
9. Rufus K. Combs, married Sarah L. Chism
10. John Holder Combs
11. Frances Maria Combs, married Dr. John Stout

Theodocia died in 1822. Samuel R. Combs married Margaret W. Thompson on April 30, 1826. Samuel and Margaret had one son, Werter.[31]

Journey's End

Sophia W. Holder

Sophia is listed as the second child by most Holder family researchers. Little is known of her. After Fanny died she went to live in Lexington with her guardian, John Hart. She died, unmarried, in Fayette County in 1806. Sophia W. Holder made a will in August of that year, and it was probated in Fayette County court in October. She must have been 21 years of age or the court could not have accepted her will. Sophia left her property to her sisters Lydia, Fanny and Kitty. The will was witnessed by her brother John W. Holder and guardian John Hart, who were also named as executors.[32]

John W. Holder

John Walton is the name most researchers assign to the eldest son of the family. The birth date carved on his gravestone by his children is November 6, 1786. John married his first cousin, Catherine Penn, in Amherst County, Virginia. She was the daughter of Gabriel Penn and Sarah Callaway, who was the oldest daughter of Col. Richard Callaway. Gabriel fought in the Revolutionary War and became a wealthy planter in Amherst County. Gabriel's will, probated in 1798, left his daughter Catherine, "besides the four negroes" given her by deed, "a good feather bed and furniture, a riding horse and saddle, two cows and calves and such pewter as has been usually given to my other daughters." John W. Holder married Catherine on July 20, 1808, in Amherst County.[33]

John and Catherine returned to live in Clark County, where he began a prosperous farming career. He is listed in the 1810 census with three daughters and thirteen slaves. He may have left the county soon after the census was taken, since he appears on the tax list for that year, with the added notation that he was "Gone." John and Catherine moved to Franklin County, Tennessee, where he shows up on the tax list for 1812.

Franklin County is celebrated as the home of Sewanee, The University of the South; birth place of Diana Shore; final resting place of Confederate General E. Kirby Smith; and one time residence of Davy Crockett. (In 1835 John W.'s brother Richard ran against Crockett for a seat in the Tennessee House of Representatives.) The county seat was named in honor Gen. James Winchester, a noted soldier of the Revolutionary War and the Indian Wars. Many settlers in Franklin County came from Kentucky.[34]

John W. Holder lived near an enclave of family connections that included his step-father John McGuire and half-sister Betsy, Richard Callaway Jr., Ephraim Drake, Samuel and Betsey (Callaway) Henderson, Margaret Drake

Colonel John Holder

Jones, Margaret's half brother, William P. Anderson,[d] and others.[e] John must have been on close terms with Margaret, as he witnessed the power of attorney she had drawn up for her son-in-law Presley Anderson. John continued to increase his slave holdings; the 1840 census lists him with 88. He had one of the first cotton gins in the Cowan neighborhood of Franklin County and was a justice of the county court.[35]

John died on September 21, 1841, in Franklin County and is buried in the Holder Cemetery. His wife Catharine died May 3, 1852, and was buried beside her husband. John's will lists the following children:[36]

1. Frances Henrietta Holder, married Peter S. Decherd
2. Sophia Holder, married James A. Snowden
3. Louisa Holder, married Holman A. Huddleston
4. Elizabeth Holder, married Andrew Mathews
5. Virginia Holder, married John Hart
6. Richard P. Holder, married his first cousin, Sarah Sophia Combs, daughter of Samuel R. and Theodocia (Holder) Combs

Caleb H. Holder

After his mother died, Caleb went to live in Madison County with his uncle, Richard Callaway Jr., whom he chose as his guardian in 1804. In September 1806, Col. Richard Callaway's daughter, Nancy, of Amherst County, Virginia, conveyed to Caleb Holder all her interest in her father's lands "in consideration of ten shillings" and "more especially the natural love and affection which she hath and beareth toward the said Caleb." Nancy was Caleb's spinster aunt. Somehow the two became acquainted, and she developed a strong affection for him. She may have come to Kentucky to visit family, or Caleb may have gone back to Virginia for that purpose. These are just a few examples of the strong and continuing ties the Holder children had to the Callaway family. Caleb Holder was still residing in Madison County in 1811, when he sold a tract of land for his Aunt Nancy to John Patrick, who was married to a granddaughter of Colonel Callaway.[37]

Much of what we know about Caleb comes from his service in the War of 1812. He was appointed a lieutenant in the Kentucky militia and was with the American army that marched north to engage the British at the

---

    d After John Buchanan died, his widow, Margaret Patton Buchanan, married William Anderson. They had a son William P. Anderson.

    e There was another group of Holders living in Franklin County, Tennessee, in 1812. This group was headed by John Holder, born in Prince William County, Virginia, 1749. He married Agnes Bledsoe and moved to North Carolina. The 1812 tax roll for Franklin County lists the following Holders in this group: John, Moses, Bledsoe, Tassy, Martin, and Solomon. Bill Holder's homepage.

Journey's End

River Raisin, near Lake Erie in northern Ohio. Caleb fought in the battle at Frenchtown and was taken prisoner on January 22, 1813. Many of the prisoners were slaughtered on the spot by the Indians, which led to the famous battle cry, "Remember the Raisin!" Caleb survived and after his release, he was promoted to captain. He then headed an infantry company in Col. John Miller's regiment.[38]

When he came back from the war, Caleb resided in Lexington for a time. While there in 1814, he sold his interest in his father's estate to brother Richard C. Holder for $500. In 1816, Caleb went to Georgia, where he married Harriett Jane Dunbar. He died about a year later and left no children.[39]

Richard Callaway Holder

After Fanny Holder died, William Irvine was appointed guardian of Richard C. Holder by the Madison County court in 1804 and, presumably, Richard went to live with him. William was the brother of Christopher Irvine, who had married Fanny's sister Lydia. Richard later served as deputy circuit court clerk for Madison.[40]

Richard volunteered for the war in August 1812. He was appointed first-sergeant of Capt. William Kerley's Company in the 1st Rifle Regiment. When his tour was up, he enlisted again after Governor Shelby put out a call for 1,500 volunteers in August 1813. Richard was appointed captain of the 7th Company in Col. William Williams' Regiment of the Kentucky Light Dragoons. Richard's unit marched with Shelby's army of Kentuckians to Lake Erie. They arrived following Perry's victory and took up pursuit of the British commander Colonel Henry Proctor and Tecumseh. The two armies met in battle at the River Thames on October 5. Tecumseh was killed and the Americans were victorious.[41]

Following the war, Richard returned to Madison County. He got into the manufacturing business for a time (1817-18) when he was owner of Holder & Co. Wool & Cotton Factory. Family tradition says he went to Georgia to take care of his deceased brother Caleb's estate and there fell in love with and married Caleb's widow. Richard did marry the widow Harriett Jane, who apparently came from a wealthy family (she held 18 slaves in her own name when she married Caleb). Returning to Madison, Richard got into the horse trading business. He was listed for several years (1820-22) with one stud horse and 10 horses or mules, then the number increased to 20 horses or mules (1823-25). Following his marriage to Harriett Jane, the slaves he reported increased from two in 1818 to 21 in 1819. By 1825, their number had increased to 32.[42]

In about 1825, Richard moved to Salem in Franklin County, Tennessee.

Colonel John Holder

He kept his house and lot in Richmond for a few years, then cut his ties to Kentucky in 1828 when he gave Howard Williams a power of attorney to sell his Madison County property.[43] Richard got into the cotton business in Franklin County. A county history states that

> Peter Simmons, John R. Patrick and Dick Holder, early merchants of Salem, used to ship large quantities of cotton on 'flats' from the mouth of Bean Creek to New Orleans, and then walk back through the Chickasaw and Choctaw Indian nations.[44]

The same history reports that Franklin County "at that early day was one of the leading cotton-producing counties of the State. The cotton was shipped out of the Elk River on flat-boats, and thence by way of the Tennessee and Mississippi Rivers to New Orleans, where it was sold for from 1¾ to 2¼ cents per pound."[45]

Richard later moved to Mississippi and died there. His biography in that state has information provided by his son William:

"Richard Calloway Holder...engaged in raising and dealing in horses [in Madison], building up quite a trade in Georgia and South Carolina. He was married to Miss Dunbar in Georgia, after which he removed to Tennessee and settled in Franklin county. Two daughters—Sarah S. and Fanny L.—and one son, William Dunbar, were the issue. The mother died when the son was only a few weeks old. Her mother, surviving and being a member of the family, took care of and reared the infant. In 1839, the family, consisting of grandmother, father and three children, removed to Mississippi, the grandmother dying in 1844 and the father previously in 1842. Meanwhile the sisters had married; the son [William D.] settled temporarily in 1841 with his father near Houston, Mississippi. His father dying there, the son soon thereafter moved to Pontoloc, Mississippi. . . ."[46]

William D. Holder, grandson of Col. John Holder, fought in the Civil War and rose through the ranks to Major-General of the Mississippi Division.

The children of Richard and Harriett Jane were[47]

1. Sarah S. Holder, married (1) Osborne D. Herndon and (2) Rev. William McQuiston
2. Frances "Fanny" Holder, married Gabriel Ragsdale
3. William Dunbar Holder, married Catharine Bowles

Lydia Holder

After Fanny died, the court appointed Richard Hickman to be Lydia

Journey's End

Holder's guardian. Hickman was married to Fanny's sister.*f* At some point, Lydia may have been taken in by her older sister Theodocia. There is a female, aged 16-26, in Samuel and Theodocia's household in the 1810 census. Lydia married Thomas G. Jones in November 1812. Samuel R. Combs, gave his consent as Lydia's guardian. This was probably the same Thomas G. Jones who served a two month tour in Capt. William Kerley's rifle company (August 15-October 14, 1812). Thomas was listed as the 4th Corporal. This was the same company in which Richard C. Holder was 1st Sergeant.[48]

Thomas G. Jones was recorded in the 1820 census for Clark County. In addition to Thomas and Lydia, the household included two males under 10, one male 16-18, two males 26-46, and 13 slaves. Thomas died two year later. The Lexington paper carried a notice for "Thomas G. Jones of Winchester," who died in December 1822. Lydia may have died in Lexington in 1833. The Lexington newspaper carried a list of cholera deaths that June and July. Mrs. Lydia Jones, widow, Mill Street, was one of the victims.[49]

Thomas and Lydia reportedly had three children:[50]

1. Thomas Jones
2. Caleb Holder Jones (died in the Mexican War)
3. Mary Frances Jones

Frances W. Holder

Frances was named after her mother and was also called "Fanny" by her family. When her mother died, Frances was taken into the home of Robert Caldwell, her court appointed guardian, in Madison County. Caldwell was a well to do merchant and tavern keeper in Madison. He served as a county justice and sheriff. He was also the son-in-law of Lydia Callaway, Fanny Holder's sister. Caldwell was still guardian for Frances in 1814, when he gave his consent for her marriage to Edward McGuire.[51]

Edward McGuire was a son of John McGuire by his first marriage. John's second wife was the widow of John Holder.*g* Edward was named executor in his father's will and was to receive one-third of all his lands and tenements. Edward served in the War of 1812 as a sergeant in William Garrard's company. One of the family biographers wrote, "In 1812 a [news] paper published at Winchester, Ky., stated that Mrs. Elizabeth Callaway had

---

f Richard Hickman married Lydia Callaway after her first husband, Christopher Irvine, died. Hickman and wife Lydia are buried at Caveland in Clark County.

g There is no indication that John McGuire kept any of Fanny's children in his household after she died. The Callaway family seems to have stepped forward to see to the children's upbringing and well being.

Colonel John Holder

sent a pair of sox (doubtless of her own knitting) to Edward McGuire; also she had sent three pair of sox, one pair of pantaloons and one coat to be used by Kentucky Volunteers."[52] Another Winchester newspaper printed an advertisement in 1814 for Edward's store in Winchester:

> Will pay cash for tobacco, hides, and whiskey, bacon, tallow, tow linen and feathers. Edward McGuire & Co.[53]

Frances was mentioned in several letters the family wrote to Lyman Draper. William D. Holder, John Holder's grandson, wrote, "None of Colonel Holder's children survive but the two youngest, to wit, Mrs. Frances W. McGuire, now of Aberdeen [Mississippi] & Mrs. Catherine Williams of Rockcastle County, Kentucky, Mt. Vernon P.O., the former aged about 53 & the latter 51 years."[54] The letter was written in 1849, which would give a birth year for Francis of about 1796 (and about 1798 for Catherine).

Holder's letter went on to state, "Mrs. McGuire recollects to have heard repeatedly the anecdote of her Mother & Aunt—Mrs. John Holder & Mrs. Samuel Henderson—their maiden names were Frances & Elizabeth Callaway, moulding bullets at the Fort at Boonsboro whilst the men were discharging them at the Indians. The young ladies themselves repeatedly fired at the Indians themselves from the fort. This is all the information I have been able to obtain from Mrs. McGuire except the following named person from whom she supposed you may be able to gather Some facts which may be useful for you. If there are any old papers left by Col. John Holder, they are most probably in possession of Peter S. Deckerd, Esq., Winchester, Tennessee."[55] Decherd married John W. Holder's daughter Frances Henrietta.

Draper did write to Decherd, who responded as follows, "I have conversed frequently with Mrs. McGuire about the early times in Kentucky & she knows but little, being very young when her Father died. She often mentioned that her Aunt, a Mrs. [Lydia] Hickman, who was one of the elder Miss Callaways, was at the Big siege of Boonsboro & remembered all about it."[56]

Edward McGuire is said to have died at Cape Girardeau, Missouri, and Frances at Aberdeen, Mississippi; the following children were reported:[57]

1. John E. McGuire
2. Edward McGuire Jr.

Catherine Holder

Catherine Holder was called "Kitty" by her family. Catherine's descendants

Journey's End

give her birth date as April 12, 1797. After Fanny died, Catherine's guardian, reportedly, was John Hart of Lexington, who was also guardian for Sophia Holder. No guardian appointment for him is found in the records of Fayette County, where he lived. Hart, a son of Nathaniel Hart of Boonesborough, married Mary Irvine, a daughter of Lydia Callaway Irvine (Fanny Holder's sister). A few years later Catherine was transferred to another relation, Thomas Howard, in Richmond.[58]

Catherine married Richard Gott Williams in Madison County on December 23, 1812. We have a published biography for Richard:

> Richard G. Williams was born in Culpeper County, Va., in 1787; he came to Kentucky in 1808 and first settled in Madison County, where he lived a number of years, and then moved to Rockcastle County. He was a saddler and harness-maker by trade, which he followed for many years in Mount Vernon. His wife, Katherine (Holder) Williams, was born at Boonesboro, Clark County, Ky, and was a daughter of Capt. John Holder, who was a Revolutionary soldier and one of the earliest settlers of Kentucky. Mr. and Mrs. Richard G. Williams were the parents of eleven children.[59]

Richard Williams corresponded with Draper on several occasions. In his first letter he wrote, "I learn from my wife that her Mother died when she was six years of age, and she has heared that her father died when she was only one year old. My wife is now in her 55th year."[60] He followed up Draper's queries with another letter stating, "Not having the family record, I am unable to give the precise date of the deaths of Col. John and Mrs. Holder but have no doubt from my wifes recollection the dates given are correct."[61]

Catherine died in 1884, aged 87 years old. She was the last survivor of the Holder children. Richard and Catherine had 13 children. The list below was provided by Catherine's granddaughter and biographer, Jessie Williams Hart:[62]

1. John Holder Williams, M.D., married Cornelia Dupree
2. Frances Holder Williams, married Charles K. V. Martin
3. Eliza Williams, married John D. Matlock
4. Jesse Caleb Williams, married Mary A. Collier
5. Sophia Williams, married William H. Wilson
6. Rachel Amelia Williams
7. Mary Catherine Williams, married M. Williamson Boulware

Colonel John Holder

8. Jacob John Williams, married Elizabeth Miller
9. Oscar Waldo Williams
10. Susan Maria Virginia Williams, married James Wilson
11. William H. Williams, married Eliza Wilson
12. David Napoleon Williams, married Mary Haley
13. Harriet Eloisa Williams, married (1) James Boulware and (2) a Van Winkle

Journey's End

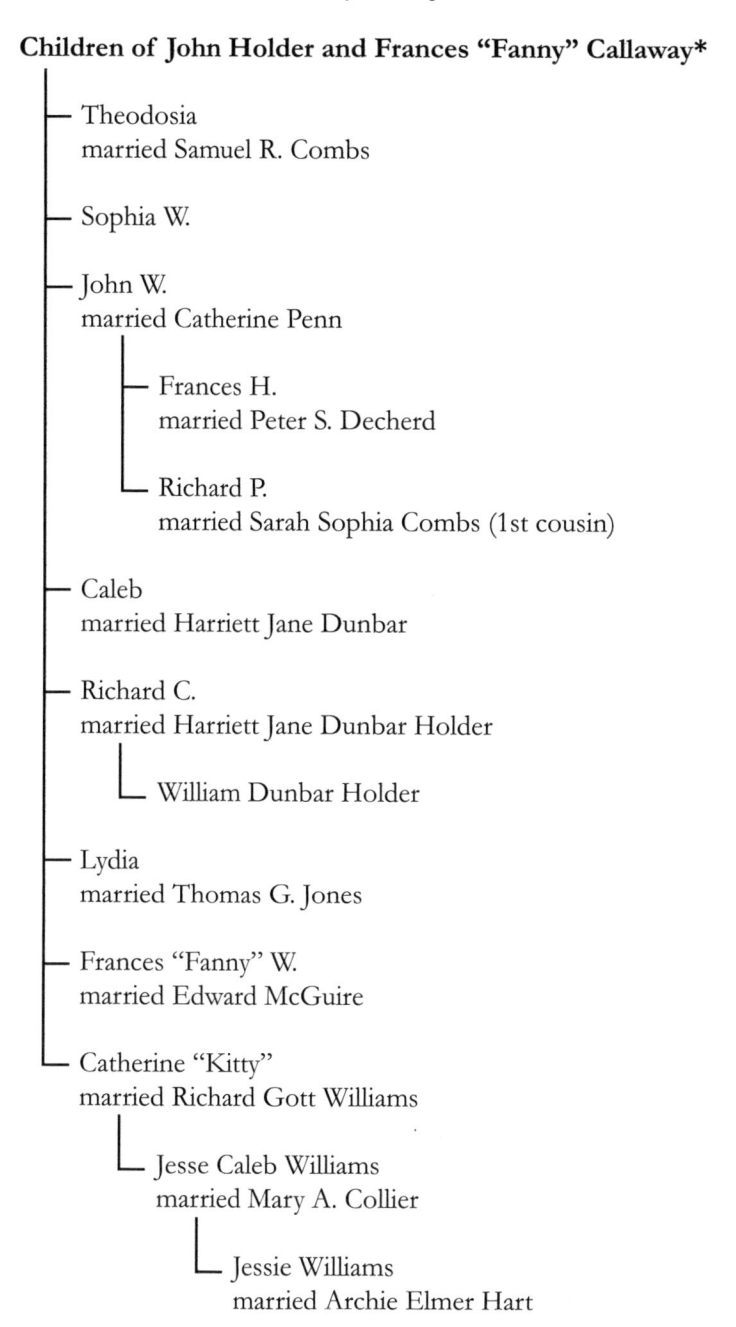

Children of John Holder and Frances "Fanny" Callaway*

- Theodosia
  married Samuel R. Combs

- Sophia W.

- John W.
  married Catherine Penn
  - Frances H.
    married Peter S. Decherd
  - Richard P.
    married Sarah Sophia Combs (1st cousin)

- Caleb
  married Harriett Jane Dunbar

- Richard C.
  married Harriett Jane Dunbar Holder
  - William Dunbar Holder

- Lydia
  married Thomas G. Jones

- Frances "Fanny" W.
  married Edward McGuire

- Catherine "Kitty"
  married Richard Gott Williams
  - Jesse Caleb Williams
    married Mary A. Collier
    - Jessie Williams
      married Archie Elmer Hart

* Not all of John and Fanny's grandchildren and great-grandchildren are shown on this chart.

Afterword

John Holder has been a challenging and fascinating figure to research and write about. We know little about Holder before he arrived in Kentucky but from that point on, we have discovered, his was a life filled with adventure and marked by accomplishments. He seems to have been a courageous leader in battle, and he participated in most of the campaigns to subdue the Indians who menaced the frontier. Although he must have come to Kentucky with but few assets, Holder plunged into the land business with such fervor that he managed to patent over 100,000 acres in his own name or in partnership with others. He established a noted station near Boonesborough and used the location to launch some of the most important business enterprises of early Kentucky. His contemporaries described him as a man of commanding appearance and great energy of character. He died in the prime of his life at about the age of 45.

A highway marker in Clark County pays tribute to some of Holder's accomplishments, though several errors (at least four) mark the text. Another marker, in Nicholas County, commemorates his company's defeat at the Upper Blue Licks (also includes several errors, including the date of the battle). He deserves better.

Captain John Holder

An outstanding pioneer at Fort Boonesborough, 1776-1781. Among the rescuers of Calloway and Boone girls captured by Indians. Named colonel of militia, 1779. Engaged in expeditions against Indians. In 1781 built Holder's Station and operated boatyard at the mouth of Howard's Creek. Led in the Battle of Upper Blue Licks, 1782. Trustee of Winchester, justice Co. Court.

Upper Blue Licks

Aug. 12, 1782, Capt. John Holder and 17 militiamen overtook band of Wyandotte on Great Salt Creek (Licking River) six miles N.E. The Indians had captured two boys, Jones Hoy and Jack Calloway, near Boonesborough. In skirmish that took place Holder lost four men, and being outnumbered he withdrew without the boys. Hoy held captive seven years, Calloway not so long.

Though his name is not attached to it, part of John Holder's original plantation is included in the Lower Howard's Creek Nature and Heritage Preserve. This land, owned by the Clark County Fiscal Court, has been set aside for the permanent protection of native plants and wildlife as well as the cultural landmarks within the Preserve boundaries. The property includes a portion of Holder's Road and the site of Holder's Mill. According to Preserve manager, Clare Sipple, additional acquisitions in the future could include other sites associated with Holder.

Lower Howard's Creek Nature and Heritage Preserve. Entrance to the Preserve on Holder's plantation.

John Holder was such a dominant force in his time it is surprising how little known he is today in his adopted land. While he was living, Holder's name was attached to numerous sites in the area. The following are examples:

Holder's Creek	Holder's Ferry
Holder's Road	Holder's Tavern
Holder's Boatyard	Holder's Landing
Holder's Station	Holder's Plantation
Holder's Mill	Holder's Warehouse
Holder's Store	Holder's Preemption

Some of these names, like Holder's Road and Holder's Warehouse, lived on long after he was gone. But today in Clark County there is not a place or feature bearing his name, nary a road, creek or hill. Well, there is a Holder's

Tavern inside Hall's Restaurant, a well known eating establishment at the mouth of Lower Howard's Creek. While that is most fitting, no doubt, it does not provide the recognition that he deserves. Maybe at some future date John Holder will have a more fitting Clark County landmark named in his honor.

A Note on Sources

Several historic maps of Clark County are mentioned repeatedly in the text by date only and refer to the following:

1861
E. A. and G. W. Hewitt, "Topographical Map of the Counties of Bourbon, Fayette, Clark, Jessamine and Woodford, Kentucky from Actual Surveys," Smith, Gallup and Co., New York, 1861

1877
Atlas of Bourbon, Clark, Fayette, Jessamine and Woodford Counties, Ky., D. G. Beers and Co., Philadelphia, 1877

1926
C. D. Hunter, "Map of Clark County, Kentucky," Kentucky Geological Survey, Frankfort, 1926

The following sources are cited in the endnotes in a shortened form as follows:

Bill Holder's homepage:
http://home.earthlink.net/~bgholder/

Certificate Book
Kentucky Historical Society, *Certificate Book of the Virginia Land Commission, 1779-1780* (Frankfort, 1981)

Chalkley, *Chronicles of the Scotch-Irish*
Lyman Chalkley, *Chronicles of the Scotch-Irish Settlement in Virginia Extracted from the Original Court Records of Augusta County, 1745-1800*, 2 volumes (Rosslyn, VA, 1912)

Clark County Court loose papers
Early papers of the Clark County court, discovered in disarray in the

courthouse attic, were flattened, cleaned and arranged into folders by date; many of these papers are currently being stored at the Bluegrass Heritage Museum in Winchester

Clift, *Cornstalk Militia*
G. Glenn Clift, *"Cornstalk" Militia of Kentucky, 1792-1811* (Frankfort, 1957)

Collins, *History of Kentucky*
Richard H. Collins, *History of Kentucky, 2 volumes* (Covington, 1874)

Crabb, *Siege of Boonesboro*
Anne Crabb, *And the Battle Began Like Claps of Thunder, The Siege of Boonesboro, 1778, As Told by the Pioneers* (Richmond, 1998)

Doyle, *Marriage Bonds*
George F. Doyle, *Marriage Bonds of Clark County, Kentucky* (Winchester, 1933)

Doyle, *Marriage Records*
George F. Doyle, *Marriage Records of Clark County, Kentucky, from 1793 to 1800, Inclusive* (Winchester, 1933)

Draper, *Life of Daniel Boone*
Lyman C. Draper, *Life of Daniel Boone*, Ted Franklin Belue, editor (Mechanicsburg, PA, 1998)

Draper MSS
Lyman C. Draper manuscripts at the Library of the Wisconsin Historical Society (accessed on microfilm at the M. I. King Library, University of Kentucky); in citing (e.g., 1A 69), the first number is the volume, the letter is the collection (A is the Bedinger Papers), and the last number is the page

Enoch, *Where in the World*
Harry G. Enoch, *Where in the World? Historic Places in Clark County, Kentucky* (Winchester, 2007)

Faragher, *Daniel Boone*
John Mack Faragher, *Daniel Boone, The Life and Legend of an American Pioneer* (New York, 1992)

GRC Papers
George Rogers Clark Papers, Illinois Regiment, Virginia State Library and Archives, 13 microfilm rolls

Hammon, *My Father, Daniel Boone*
Neal O. Hammon, *My Father, Daniel Boone* (Lexington, 1999)

Hammon and Taylor, *Virginia's Western War*
Neal O. Hammon and Richard Taylor, *Virginia's Western War, 1775-1786* (Mechanicsburg, PA, 2002)

Harding, *George Rogers Clark and His Men*
Margery H. Harding, *George Rogers Clark and His Men, Military Records, 1778-1784* (Frankfort, 1981)

Hart, *Callaway Family*
Jessie Williams Hart, *Callaway Family of Virginia and Some Kentucky Descendants* (n.p., 1929)

Hening, *Statutes at Large*
William W. Hening, *Statutes at Large, Being a Collection of all the Laws of Virginia, 13 volumes* (New York, Philadelphia, Richmond, 1819-1823)

James, *George Rogers Clark Papers*
James Alton James, editor, *George Rogers Clark Papers, 1781-1784* (Springfield, IL, 1912)

Kentucky Land Trials
These lawsuits appear in the records of the Fayette County Circuit Court and are cited by book and page number; abstracts of the records are available in Michael L. Cook and Bettie A. C. Cook, *Fayette County Kentucky Records, Volume 1* (Evansville, IN, 1985)

Kleber, *Kentucky Encyclopedia*
John Kleber, editor, *Kentucky Encyclopedia* (Lexington, 1992)

Littell, *Statute Law of Kentucky*
William Littell, *Digest of the Statute Law of Kentucky, 5 volumes* (Frankfort, 1809-1819)

Mastin, *Lexington 1779*
Bettye Lee Mastin, *Lexington 1779, Pioneer Kentucky as Described by Early Settlers* (Lexington, 1979)

Old Kentucky Surveys and Grants
Old Virginia Surveys and Grants
Surveys and grants are cited by book and page number taken from the following indexes and copied from microfilm at the Kentucky Historical Society or University of Kentucky; Joan Brookes-Smith, *Index for Old Kentucky Surveys & Grants* (Frankfort, 1975); Joan Brookes-Smith, *Master Index, Virginia Surveys and Grants, 1774-1791* (Frankfort, 1976); copies of these surveys and grants are now easily obtained on the Internet at the Kentucky Land Office, http://sos.ky.gov/land/

Parish, "Intrigues of Doctor James O'Fallon"
John C. Parish, "Intrigues of Doctor James O'Fallon," *Mississippi Valley Historical Review* (1930) 17:230-240

Ranck, *Boonesborough*
George W. Ranck, *Boonesborough* (Louisville, 1901)

Robertson, *Petitions of the Early Inhabitants of Kentucky*
James R. Robertson, *Petitions of the Early Inhabitants of Kentucky to the General Assembly of Virginia, 1769 to 1792* (Louisville, 1914)

Verhoeff, *Kentucky River Navigation*
Mary Verhoeff, *Kentucky River Navigation* (Louisville, 1917)

Young, *Narrative of Daniel Trabue*
Chester Raymond Young, editor, *Westward into Kentucky, The Narrative of Daniel Trabue* (Lexington, 1981)

Endnotes

Introduction
1 Draper MSS 28C 10. In his collection, in a series known as Draper's Notes (Draper MSS 33S), there is an "Index to Notebook M." The index shows entries for John Holder on pages 1, 11-12, and 71-87. Unfortunately, Notebook M cannot be found.
2 Faragher, *Daniel Boone*, pp. 133, 139; Robert Morgan, *Boone, A Biography* (Chapel Hill, NC, 2007), pp. 202-213.

Virginia Beginnings
1 Frederick County (VA) Deed Book 16:127; Shane interview with Paul Evans, Draper MSS 11CC 79 ("Colonel Holder's sister, Mrs. Peggy Bevan, is dead."). A good entry point to Holder family genealogy is Bill Holder's homepage (see Note on Sources).
2 John P. Alcock, *Fauquier Families, 1759-1799* (Athens, GA, 1994), p. 174.
3 Harry C. Groome, *Fauquier During the Proprietorship* (Richmond, VA, 1927), p. 84; Joshua Fry and Peter Jefferson, "Map of the most inhabitated part of Virginia. . ." (London, England, 1755); Stafford County (VA) Will Book O:488; Fauquier County (VA) Deed Book 7:381; Fauquier County (VA) Minute Book 1764-1768, p. 380.
4 Peggy Shomo Joyner, *Abstracts of Virginia's Northern Neck Warrants and Surveys, 1653-1781, Vol. 5* (Portsmouth, VA, 1995), p. 41.
5 Ruth and Sam Sparacio, *Fauquier County Minute Book 1759-1762* (McLean, VA, 1993), p. 2; Bill Holder's homepage.
6 Harry C. Groome, *Fauquier During the Proprietorship* (Richmond, VA, 1927), p. 104.
7 Northern Neck (VA) Grant Book E:455, 491.
8 Fauquier County (VA) Minute Book 1759-1762, p. 138.
9 Kleber, *Louisville Encyclopedia*, p. 141.
10 Fauquier County (VA) Minute Book 1764-1765, pp. 73, 103; Fauquier County (VA) Minute Book 1766-1767, pp. 188-189.
11 Fauquier County (VA) Minute Book 1759-1762, pp. 199, 200, 204, 304; Fauquier County (VA) Minute Book 1763-1764, pp. 149, 151, 153; Fauquier County (VA) Minute Book 1764-1768, pp. 378, 380, 385, 401; Fauquier County (VA) Minute Book 1768-1773, pp. 16-17.
12 John T. Phillips, *Historian's Guide to Loudoun County, Virginia, Vol. 1* (Leesburg and Middleburg, VA, 1996); History of Loudoun County, Virginia, at http://www.loudounhistory.org/history-loudoun.htm.
13 Joan W. Peters, *Tax lists from the Fauquier County Court Clerk's Loose Papers, 1759-1782* (Westminister, MD, 1999); Marty Hiatt and Craig R. Scott, *Loudoun County, Virginia, Tithables, 1758-1786* (Athens, GA; 1994).
14 J. Christian Kolbe, Archives Research Services, Library of Virginia, "Colonial Tithables, Research Notes Number 17," http://www.lva.lib.va.us.
15 Holder deposition in Bourbon County Order Book B:628; Bedinger Papers, Draper

MSS 1A 69; Shane interview with Daniel Bryan, Draper MSS 22C 9(10); William Sudduth to Draper, Draper MSS 14U 110; Shane interview with John Rankins, Draper MSS 11CC 82; Ranck, *Boonesborough*, p. 108; Richard P. Holder to Draper, Draper MSS 24C 29; W. D. Holder biographical sketch in The National Historic Society, Confederate Veterans, 1896, transcription on Bill Holder's homepage; Mrs. E. A. (Jessie) Hart letter to S. J. Conkwright, copy at the Clark County Public Library, Winchester; an undated genealogy, Bill Holder's homepage.

16 Frederick County (VA) Deed Book 16:127.
17 Loudoun County (VA) Deed Book G:270.
18 Leigh Ann Boucher, "Atchison Family, mid 1700s/1800s," laboucher@earthlink.net.
19 Virginia Conservation Commission, Colonial Highway Marker.
20 Frederick County (VA) Deed Book 18:366.
21 Loudoun County (VA) Deed Book E:297; Prince William County (VA) Deed Book 1749-1752, p. 145.
22 Shane interview with John Rankins, Draper MSS 11CC 82.
23 See for example, Bill Holder's homepage. There are two other Holders—Jesse and Benjamin—listed on Revolutionary War muster rolls for Virginia. Jesse was a member of the 5th Virginia Regiment, Benjamin served in the 6th Virginia Regiment. A James Holder enlisted in Monongalia County, Virginia, and received a Revolutionary War pension. Original muster rolls, http://www.footnote.com; James Holder, Revolutionary War pension file, S. 8736, VA.
24 Kleber, *Kentucky Encyclopedia*, p. 571.
25 Old Virginia Grants 12:346, 14:308.
26 Lloyd D. Bockstruck, *Virginia's Colonial Soldiers* (Baltimore, 1988), p. 141; family histories, deed research and maps in Cecil O'Dell, *Pioneers of Old Frederick County, Virginia* (Marceline, MO, 1995), pp. 196, 211, 215, 220; Chalkley, *Chronicles of the Scotch-Irish*, Vol. 2, pp. 132-133.
27 "At a Meeting of the several Commissioners appointed to settle the Accounts of the Militia in actual service in the late Expedition against the Indians under Lord Dunmore held at Romney," Virginia Public Service Claims, Romney and Winchester, 1775, http://www.lva.virginia.gov/.
28 Dixon and Hunter's, *Virginia Gazette*, December 16, 1775.
29 Purdie's *Virginia Gazette*, December 15, 1775.
30 Pinkney's *Virginia Gazette*, December 30, 1775.
31 Philip Regan, Revolutionary War pension file, S. 22462, VA.
32 Louis L. Guy Jr., "Norfolk's Worst Nightmare" at http://www.norfolkhistorical.org/; Purdie's *Virginia Gazette*, July 12 and 19, 1776.
33 U.S. Congress, *Resolutions, Laws and Ordinances Relating to the Pay, Half Pay, Commutation of Half Pay, Bounty Lands, and Other Promises Made by Congress to the Officers and Soldiers of the Revolution* (Washington, DC, 1838), pp. 492-494; Horace E. Hayden, *Virginia Genealogies; A Genealogy of the Glassell Family of Scotland and Virginia* (Wilkes-Barre, PA, 1891), pp. 41-42.
34 Thomas Jones, Revolutionary War pension file, S. 46053, VA.
35 Revolutionary War pension files of Philip Regan, S. 22462, VA; John Malone, S. 36076, VA; Soloman Bishop, S. 30863, VA; and Marquis Calmes, S. 12674, VA.
36 J. E. Norris, editor, *History of the Lower Shenandoah Valley Counties of Frederick, Berkeley, Jefferson and Clarke* (Chicago, 1890), pp. 590-594; T. K. Cartmell, *Shenandoah Valley Pioneers and Their Descendants* (Winchester, VA, 1909), p. 19; National Register Nomination Form, Old Chapel (Cunningham's Chapel), Millwood, Clark County, Virginia, 1972; Cecil O'Dell,

Pioneers of Old Frederick County, Virginia (Marceline, MO, 1995), pp. 226-228.

37   Marquis Calmes, Revolutionary War pension file, S. 12674, VA.; Old Virginia Grants 4:261; Clift, *Cornstalk Militia*, p. 155; *Kentucky Observer Reporter*, March 6, 1834.

38   Frederick County (VA) Order Book 15:365.

39   Virginia Public Service Claims, Revolutionary War, Commissioner's Book 2, p. 186, http://www.lva.virginia.gov/; Virginia Revolutionary War Public Service Claims, Library of Virginia, http://www.lva.virginia.gov/.

40   Richard P. Holder to Draper, October 6, 1850, Draper MSS 24C 29.

Rescue of the Boone-Callaway Girls

1   Draper, *Life of Daniel Boone*, pp. 411-421.

2   For one example, Faragher, *Daniel Boone*, p. 139.

3   Lyman Draper to Richard French, January 10, 1843, Draper MSS 12CC 207.

4   Boone's account is found in John Filson, *Discovery, Settlement and Present State of Kentucke* (Wilmington, DE, 1784), p. 60; Floyd's account is copied in Ranck, *Boonesborough*, p. 249; Smith's account was published as "Adventure with the Indians," *Western Review* (January 1820) 1:352; Reid's account in Draper MSS 10NN 150-153, 177-183.

5   Draper, *Life of Daniel Boone*, p. 429.

6   John Gass to Draper, August 3, 1845, Draper MSS 24C 77; Draper interview with John Gass, November 14, 1845, Draper MSS 24C 75(1).

7   Draper MSS 24C 47, 31C 2(33-34); Joseph Martin to William Martin, 1844, Draper MSS 24C 41(2).

8   Draper MSS 31C 2(38-39).

9   Draper interview with George Bryan, Draper MSS 22C 16(13).

10   Draper interview with Mrs. Elizabeth Thomas, Draper MSS 12C 26-29

11   Draper interview with Nathan Boone in Hammon, *My Father, Daniel Boone*, pp. 49-51.

12   Shane interview with Richard French, Draper MSS 12CC 201-210.

13   Richard French to Draper, April 30, 1844, Draper MSS 24C 25.

14   Kentucky Land Office, Secretary of State, Commonwealth of Kentucky at http://apps.sos.ky.gov/land/nonmilitary/settlements/.

15   Shane interview with Septimus Scholl, Draper MSS 11CC 51-53.

16   Richard P. Holder to Draper, October 6, 1850, Draper MSS 24C 29.

17   William M. Bransford, "The Capture and Rescue, A Tale of the 'Dark and Bloody Ground,'" *Southern Lady's Companion*, November and December 1848, copied in Draper MSS 24C 48-48(10).

18   William M. Bransford to Draper, March 1, 1852.

19   Draper from William D. Holder, P. S. Decherd, Richard P. Holder, R. G. Williams, Draper MSS 24C 27-30, 43-46; Norman E. Gillis, *Goodspeed's Biographical and Historical Memoirs of Mississippi, Vol. 1* (Chicago, 1891), p. 939.

20   Draper from Richard French, Samuel H. Dixon, Eudocia Estill, Alfred Henderson, Draper MSS 24C 30-32, 38; Shane interview with Richard French, Draper MSS 12CC 204-205.

21   Collins, *History of Kentucky, Vol. 2*, p. 526; Ranck, *Boonesborough*, p. 51; R. S. Cotterill, *History of Pioneer Kentucky* (Cincinnati, 1917), p. 105; John Bakeless, *Daniel Boone, Master of the Wilderness* (New York, 1939), pp. 138-139; Thomas D. Clark, *The Kentucky* (Lexington, 1942), p. 53; G. Goff Bedford, *Land of Our Fathers, History of Clark County, Kentucky* (Winchester, 1958), pp. 45-46; Faragher, *Daniel Boone*, pp. 133, 139.

Kentucky Frontier
1 Hammon and Taylor, *Virginia's Western War*, pp. 49-66; Draper, *Life of Daniel Boone*, pp. 435-452.
2 Draper MSS 4B 125; Hammon and Taylor, *Virginia's Western War*, pp. 61-62.
3 Draper, *Life of Daniel Boone*, p. 525.
4 Smith was the informant for an article in Hunt's Western Review: "Adventure with the Indians," *Western Review and Miscellaneous Magazine* (1820) 1:353.
5 Draper, *Life of Daniel Boone*, p. 525; Draper MSS 37J 14, 44J 4-6, 17, 22, 23, 24.
6 Draper interview with Daniel Bryan, Draper MSS 22C 9(10).
7 Daniel Bryan, Revolutionary War pension file, S. 1172, NC.
8 Samuel Bryan's Revolutionary War pension file, W. 9366, NC and VA.
9 Shane interview with Daniel Bryan, Draper MSS 22C 14(15).
10 Clark's "Diary," December 25, 1776 to March 30, 1778, in James, *George Rogers Clark Papers*, p. 23; Draper, *Life of Daniel Boone*, p. 418.
11 Petition No. 6, Robertson, *Petitions of the Early Inhabitants of Kentucky*, pp. 43-44.
12 Ibid. p. 44.
13 Kentucky Land Office, http://apps.sos.ky.gov/land/nonmilitary/settlements/.
14 Mann Butler, *Valley of the Ohio*, G. Glenn Clift and Hambleton Tapp, editors (Frankfort, 1971), pp. 107-110.
15 Ibid., p. 110; Smith to Clark, Draper MSS 48J 19, 20, transcribed in "George Rogers Clark and the Kaskaskia Campaign, 1777-1778," *American Historical Review* (1903) 8:495-497.
16 Moses Nelson, Revolutionary War pension file, R. 7585, VA/NC.
17 John Hamlin, Revolutionary War pension file, S. 15443, NC.
18 Ibid.
19 Ibid.
20 James McCullough, Revolutionary War pension file, S. 30570, NC.
21 Samuel Estill, Revolutionary War pension file, S. 12876, VA.
22 Little Page Proctor, Revolutionary War pension file, W. 576, VA.
23 Moses Nelson, Revolutionary War pension file, R. 7585, VA/NC.
24 Josiah Collins, Revolutionary War pension file, S. 30336, VA.
25 Crabb, *Siege of Boonesboro*; Hammon and Taylor, *Virginia's Western War*, pp. 67-94; Draper, *Life of Daniel Boone*, pp. 459-494.
26 Draper, *Life of Daniel Boone*, pp. 498-500; Collins, *History of Kentucky*, Vol. 2, pp. 664-665; Crabb, *Siege of Boonesboro*, pp. 7-10.
27 Draper interview with John Gass, Draper MSS 24C 73.
28 Shane interview with Daniel Bryan, Draper MSS 22C 14(12).
29 Bedinger Papers, Draper MSS 1A 69.
30 Draper, *Life of Daniel Boone*, p. 500; Ranck, *Boonesborough*, pp. 72-73; Hammon and Taylor, *Virginia's Western War*, pp. 82-84.
31 Enoch, *Where in the World*, p. 27.
32 Ibid., p. 151.
33 Shane interview with George Bryan, Draper MSS 22C 16(19).
34 Crabb, *Siege of Boonesboro*, pp. 59-69.
35 Ibid., pp. 15-28.
36 Draper interview with John Gass, Draper MSS 24C 73(10-11).
37 Shane interview with John Gass, Draper MSS 11CC 13.
38 Ted Belue's Note "p." in Draper, *Life of Daniel Boone*, p. 540.
39 Young, *Narrative of Daniel Trabue*, p. 59.
40 Draper, *Life of Daniel Boone*, p. 513.

In Command at Boonesborough

1 Young, *Narrative of Daniel Trabue*, p. 63-64, 172; Draper, *Life of Daniel Boone*, pp. 520-521; Hammon, *My Father, Daniel Boone*, p. 70.
2 Bedinger Papers, Draper MSS 1A 12-13.
3 Shane interview with Josiah Collins, in Mastin, *Lexington 1779*, pp. 50-52.
4 Collins, *History of Kentucky*, Vol. 2, p. 137.
5 Josiah Collins, Revolutionary War pension file, S. 30336, VA.
6 Shane interview with Josiah Collins, in Mastin, *Lexington 1779*, p. 51, 76-77.
7 Young, *Narrative of Daniel Trabue*, p. 56.
8 GRC Papers, 1:427.
9 GRC Papers, 1:304.
10 Josiah Collins, Revolutionary War pension file, S. 30336, VA.
11 Young, *Narrative of Daniel Trabue*, p. 56.
12 Bedinger Papers, Draper MSS 1A 13.
13 Bedinger Papers, Draper MSS 1A 14-15.
14 William D. Brown, "A Visit to Boonesborough in 1779, The Recollections of Pioneer George M. Bedinger," *Register of the Kentucky Historical Society* (1988) 86:320.
15 Bedinger Papers, Draper MSS 1A 47-48.
16 Ralph Morgan deposition, 1815, in Draper MSS 14DD 108.
17 Bedinger Papers, Draper MSS 1A 69.
18 Bedinger Papers, Draper MSS 1A 15-16.
19 Ibid., Draper MSS 1A 4.
20 Ibid., Draper MSS 1A 4. Virginia Land Law allowed a preemption claim of up to 1,000 acres of land for growing a crop of corn in Kentucky. Hening, *Statutes at Large*, 10:40.
21 Bedinger Papers, Draper MSS 1A 4.
22 Ibid., Draper MSS 1A 4.
23 Young, *Westward into Kentucky*, pp. 69-70, 174.
24 Shane interview with Elijah Foley, Draper MSS 11CC 135.
25 Charles G. Talbert, "Kentucky Invades Ohio, 1779," *Register of the Kentucky Historical Society* (1953) 51:228-230; Draper MSS 17J 26.
26 Bedinger Papers, Draper MSS 1A 19.
27 Collins, *History of Kentucky*, Vol. 2, p. 179.
28 Deposition of Levi Todd in *Helm v. Watson et al.*, 1808, Kentucky Land Trials B:513.
29 Hammon and Taylor, *Virginia's Western War*, pp. 105-106; Charles C. Talbert, "Kentucky Invades Ohio, 1780," *Register of the Kentucky Historical Society* (1954) 52:295.
30 Bedinger Papers, Draper MSS 1A 20-21.
31 Quoted in Temple Bodley, *History of Kentucky* (Chicago, 1928), p. 202.
32 Shane interview with Josiah Collins, in Mastin, *Lexington 1779*, p. 52.
33 Bedinger Papers, Draper MSS 1A 20.
34 Bedinger Papers, Draper MSS 1A 22-23; Louise P. Kellogg, *Frontier Advance on the Upper Ohio, 1778-1779* (Madison, WI, 1916), p. 365.
35 Shane interview with Josiah Collins, in Mastin, *Lexington 1779*, p. 92.
36 Bedinger Papers, Draper MSS 1A 20-31.
37 Quoted in Temple Bodley, *History of Kentucky* (Chicago, 1928), p. 202.
38 Dixon and Nicolson's *Virginia Gazette*, July 10, 1779; Charles G. Talbert, *Benjamin Logan, Kentucky Frontiersman* (Lexington, 1962), pp. 78-79.
39 Shane interview with Josiah Collins, in Mastin, *Lexington 1779*, p. 54.

40   Ibid., p. 54.
41   Talbert, *Benjamin Logan,* pp. 80-81.
42   Dixon and Nicolson's *Virginia Gazette,* July 10, 1779.
43   Edward Hall, Revolutionary War pension file, W. 3017, VA. Neither Nathaniel Bullock nor Little Page Proctor is listed on Holder's pay roll for the expedition. However, Little Page Proctor stated in his pension application that he served five years under Holder and was on Bowman's expedition. Little Page Proctor, Revolutionary War pension file, W. 576, VA.
44   Bedinger Papers, Draper MSS 1A 22-23; Draper MSS 17J 26; Shane interview with Josiah Collins, in Mastin, *Lexington 1779,* p. 51; Elisha Collins, Revolutionary War pension file, S. 10463, VA.
45   Draper MSS 17J 30.
46   Draper MSS 17J 29-30.
47   Petition No. 10, Robertson, *Petitions of the Early Inhabitants of Kentucky,* p. 53; Hening, *Statutes at Large,* 10:196.
48   Draper, *Life of Daniel Boone,* p. 558.
49   Ibid.; Shane interview with John Gass, Draper MSS 11CC 15; February 1781, Lincoln County Order Book 1:4A.
50   Bowman to Broadhead, Draper MSS 16S 5-8, transcribed in Louise P. Kellogg, *Frontier Retreat on the Upper Ohio, 1779-1781* (Madison, WI, 1917), pp. 184-186.
51   Hammon and Taylor, *Virginia's Western War,* p. 127.
52   Little Page Proctor, Revolutionary War pension file, W. 576, VA.
53   Hammon and Taylor, *Virginia's Western War,* pp. 128-130; Chinn, pp. 235-238; Revolutionary War pension files, Samuel Estill, S. 12876, VA, and Jesse Hodges, S. 31143, VA.
54   GRC Papers, 5:404.
55   "A Pay Roll of Capt. John Holders Company of Militia under the Command of Col. Benjamin Logan Commencing the 12th [July] and ending 25th August, 1780," Harding, *George Rogers Clark and His Men,* pp. 58-59; Draper MSS 60J 112.
56   Samuel Estill, Revolutionary War pension file, S. 12876, VA. Also in Draper MSS 60J 112.
57   Harding, *George Rogers Clark and His Men,* p. 59.
58   GRC Papers, 12:134.
59   GRC Papers, 4:842, 844.
60   GRC Papers, 4:447.
61   Hammon and Taylor, *Virginia's Western War,* p. 139.
62   GRC Papers, 4:759.
63   Shane interview with William Clinkenbeard, Draper MSS 11CC 63.
64   "An act for establishing three new counties upon the western waters, May 1780," Virginia General Assembly in Henning, *Statutes at Large,* 10:315.
65   William Chenault, "Early History of Madison County," *Register of the Kentucky State Historical Society* (1932) 30:138.
66   Shane interview with Daniel Sphar, Draper MSS 11CC 107.
67   Ibid., Draper MSS 11CC 107.
68   Shane interview with William Clinkenbeard, Draper MSS 11CC 56.

Domestic Relations
1   F. B. Kegley, *Kegley's Virginia Frontier* (Roanoke; VA, 1938), pp. 368-371. Contains a brief biography of John Buchanan and family.

2   Patricia Givens Johnson, *James Patton and the Appalachian Colonists* (Pulaski, VA, 1983), p. 216; letter from George Washington to Gov. Robert Dinwiddie, October 10, 1756, in W. W. Abbot, editor, *Papers of George Washington, Colonial Series, Vol. 3* (Charlottesville, VA, 1984), pp. 430, 434.

3   *John Drake v. John Campbell, 1807*, quoted in Chalkey, *Chronicles of the Scotch-Irish, Vol. 2*, p. 172; Kegley, *Virginia Frontier*, pp. 369-370; Patricia Givens Johnson, *William Preston and the Allegheny Patriots* (Blacksburg, VA, 1976), pp. 101, 107, 118.

4   Collins, *History of Kentucky, Vol. 2*, pp. 417-418; Harriette Simpson Arnow, *Seedtime on the Cumberland* (Lincoln, NE, 1995 edition), pp. 158-163; Gordon Aronhime, "Joseph Drake, 18th Century Frontier Bad Boy," *Bristol (TN) Herald Courier*, April 28, 1963; Col. James Dysart deposition in Chalkley, *Chronicles of the Scotch-Irish, Vol. 2*, p. 172.

5   Collins, *History of Kentucky, Vol. 2*, p. 512; Draper MSS 3B 50-65.

6   Draper, *Life of Daniel Boone*, p. 269.

7   Chalkley, *Chronicles of the Scotch-Irish, Vol. 2*, p. 172; Aronhime, "Joseph Drake, 18th Century Frontier Bad Boy"; Fincastle County (VA) Record of Surveys, Plot Book A, p. 93; Fincastle County (VA) Order Book 1:4, 7, 85, 130, 138, Book 2:6, 11, 24, 38, 56, 76, 105. Fincastle County records abstracted in Michael L. Cook and Bettie C. Cook, *Fincastle and Kentucky County, Virginia-Kentucky Records and History* (Evansville, IN, 1987).

8   William Christian to William Preston, July 9, 1774, in Reuben G. Thwaites and Louise P. Kellogg, *Documentary History of Dunmore's War, 1774* (Madison, WI, 1905), pp. 75-78.

9   Neal Hammon and James R. Harris, "Letters of Col. John Floyd, 1774-1783," *Register of the Kentucky Historical Society* (1985), 83:205-209; Johnson, *William Preston*, p. 107.

10   Mary B. Kegley, *Soldiers of Fincastle County, Virginia, 1774* (Wytheville, VA, 1974), p. 39; John Floyd to William Preston, October 16, 1774, in Thwaites and Kellogg, *Dunmore's War, 1774*, pp. 266-269.

11   Richard Henderson, "Judge Richard Henderson's Journal of a Trip to "Cantuckey" and of Events at Boonesborough in 1775," in Ranck, *Boonesborough*, p. 174.

12   Depositions of James Thompson, Robert Craig and James Dysart, in *John Drake v. John Campbell et al.*, Augusta County (VA) Court records; Aronhime, "Joseph Drake, 18th Century Frontier Bad Boy."

13   Statement of John Gass, Draper MSS 24C 92(1), 100.

14   Deposition of William B. Jones (1843), in *Stovall and Marshall v. Sims et al.*, Chancery Court Minute Book, 1815-1844, Franklin County, Tennessee, p. 472.

15   *Certificate Book*, p. 225; Old Kentucky Grants 7:304.

16   Deposition of William Buchanan in Petition No. 7, Robertson, *Petitions of the Early Inhabitants of Kentucky*, p. 45; Shane interview with James Wade, Draper MSS 11CC 29-30; R. S. Cotterill, "Battle of Upper Blue Licks," *Filson Club Historical Quarterly* (1927) 2:29-33.

17   Answer of John Campbell, in *John Drake v. John Campbell et al.*, Augusta County (VA) Court records.

18   State of Virginia, Journal of the House of Delegates, May 5, 1775-December 19, 1778, p. 77.

19   Ibid., p. 78.

20   *Certificate Book*, p. 101; Kentucky Land Office, Secretary of State, Commonwealth of Kentucky at http://apps.sos.ky.gov/land/nonmilitary/settlements/; Old Virginia Surveys 7:379; Old Virginia Grants 13:424.

21   Clark County Order Book 4:506, 516, 526.

22   Eli Vaughn answer in *John D. Stovall, administrator of the estate of Joseph Drake, deceased v. Eli Vaughn*, 1826, Clark Circuit Court Record Book, pp. 38-42, and loose papers in the case at the Kentucky Department of Libraries and Archives in Frankfort.

23 Deed from Margaret Jones to John Drake, copied in *John Drake v. John Campbell et al.*, Augusta County (VA) Court records.

24 Madison County Deed Book I:252, K:563; William S. Bryan and Robert Rose, *A History of the Pioneer Families of Missouri* (St. Louis, MO, 1876), p. 238; U.S. Census, Montgomery County, MO, 1850.

25 Franklin County (TN) Will Records Book, 1808-1876, p. 66.

26 Deposition of Rhoda Vaughn in Daniel Hickey's Revolutionary War pension file, W. 7744, VA.

27 Stonestreet to Draper, August 24, 1853, Draper MSS 4C 66.

28 *John D. Stovall v. Eli Vaughn*, 1826, Clark Circuit Court.

29 Ibid.

30 Doyle, *Marriage Records*; Doyle, *Marriage Bonds*; Clark County Court loose papers (1797); Eli Vaughn deposition in *John Jouitt v. John Holder*, Fayette Circuit Court, 1793, copies of the court papers found in Special Collections, M. I. King Library, University of Kentucky.

31 *John D. Stovall v. Eli Vaughn*, 1826, Clark Circuit Court.

32 Fayette County Deed Book 14:54, 24:248.

33 *Lexington Observer Reporter*, July 14, 1849, cited in G. Glenn Clift, *Kentucky Obituaries, 1787-1854* (Baltimore, 1979), p. 186.

34 "The First White Woman Born in Kentucky," *The Guardian* (January 1873), 4th Series, Vol. 1, No. 4, published in Columbia, TN.

35 George W. Ranck, *History of Lexington* (Cincinnati; 1872), pp. 116-117.

36 Frances K. S. Barr, *Old Episcopal Burying Ground* (Bowie, MD, 2002), p. 14.

37 Ranck, *History of Lexington*, p. 117.

38 Collins, *History of Kentucky, Vol. 1*, p. 512.

39 Ranck, *Boonesborough*, pp. 49-53; R. S. Cotterill, *History of Pioneer Kentucky* (Cincinnati, 1917), pp. 104-105; H. Addington Bruce, (New York, 1910), pp. 155-157; Faragher, *Daniel Boone*, pp. 131-139.

40 Michael E. Drake, *The Search for the Ancestors and Descendants of Henry Brasater Drake of Coles County, Illinois* (Bowie, MD, 2002), pp. 104-108.

41 *John D. Stovall v. Eli Vaughn*, 1826, Clark Circuit Court.

42 U.S. Census, Clark County, 1820, 1830; Fayette County, Kentucky, 1840, 1850, 1860.

43 Draper, *Life of Daniel Boone*, pp. 557-559; Kleber, *Kentucky Encyclopedia*, p. 152.

44 The reference given for Fanny's birth date is the Richard Callaway Bible. An old transcription of this bible, at the Library of Virginia in Richmond, shows no date for Frances and has numerous errors. (http://www.lva.virginia.gov/) Callaway family researchers viewed the actual bible at a meeting of their Association in Louisville and were able to correct some of the information. (http://www.callawayfamily.org/) We have not been able to find a copy of the revised transcription.

45 Draper, *Life of Daniel Boone*, p. 412.

46 W. D. Holder to Lyman C. Draper, April 4, 1849, Draper MSS 24C 27; Lincoln County Order Book 1:4A. W. D. Holder got the story from Mrs. McGuire, who was John Holder's daughter.

47 Mrs. Mary Irvine Hart, Draper MSS 18S 213; Bedinger Papers, Draper MSS 1A 69.

48 Deposition of David Crews, 1811, *Banta's heirs v. Clay*, Madison County Circuit Court Complete Records Book D:283-285.

49 Shane interview with John Rankins, Draper MSS 11CC 81.

50 Draper, *Life of Daniel Boone*, p. 411; Jessie Williams Hart letter to S. J. Conkwright, June 15, 1934, Holder family folder, Clark County Public Library, Winchester.

51   *John D. Stovall v. Eli Vaughn*, 1826, Clark Circuit Court.

52   *John D. Stovall and wife Mary, Daniel Marshall and wife Nancy, administrators of the estate of John Drake v. Julius Sims and wife Jane, William Jones, and Sibby Jones, otherwise known as Sibby Holder*, Franklin County (TN) Chancery Court Book, 1815-1844, pp. 455-475, hereinafter referred to as *Stovall and Marshall v. Sims et al.*

53   Answers of Sabrina Jones (1841) and William B. Jones (1843), *Stovall and Marshall v. Sims et al.* Her name was spelled "Sabrina" and "Sebrina" almost interchangeably in original documents.

54   Answer of William B. Jones (1843), *Stovall and Marshall v. Sims et al.*

55   Answer of Sabrina Jones (1842), *Stovall and Marshall v. Sims et al.*

56   Ibid.

57   Answer of William B. Jones (1843), *Stovall and Marshall v. Sims et al.*

58   Communication from Debra Anderson, Rancho Murieta, CA, stating that Lucy Witcher Blythe had some family letters that refer to Sibby Drake Jones as the spinster sister of Euphemia.

59   William S. Bryan and Robert Rose, *A History of the Pioneer Families of Missouri* (St. Louis, 1876), p. 238.

60   Clark County Deed Book 2:40, 4:223, 10:29.

61   Shane interview with William Clinkenbeard, Draper MSS 11CC 54-66.

62   Ibid.

63   Ibid.

64   Madison County Deed Book I:252.

65   Answer of William B. Jones (1843), *Stovall and Marshall v. Sims et al.*

In Search of Land

1   Ralph Morgan deposition, Draper MSS 14DD 106.

2   "Bear Incident, Spring of 1779," Draper MSS 1A 56.

3   Thomas Swearingen's will, Clark County Will Book 6:27; deposition of John Holder, Bourbon County Order Book B:627-630; Michael L. Cook and Bettie C. Cook, *Fincastle and Kentucky County, Virginia-Kentucky Records and History* (Evansville, 1987), pp. 141-142.

4   Harry G. Enoch, *In Search of Morgan's Station and the Last Indian Raid in Kentucky* (Bowie, MD, 1997), pp. 22-24.

5   Petition No. 9, Robertson, *Petitions of the Early Inhabitants of Kentucky*, pp. 48-52.

6   Hening, *Statutes at Large*, 10:134.

7   Petition No. 8, Robertson, *Petitions of the Early Inhabitants of Kentucky*, pp. 44-48.

8   Hening, *Statutes at Large*, 10:431-432.

9   "An act for establishing a Land office, and ascertaining the terms and manner of granting waste and unappropriated lands," May 1779, Hening, *Statutes at Large*, 10:50-65.

10   Hening, *Statutes at Large*, 10:39-48.

11   Kentucky Land Office, http://apps.sos.ky.gov/land/nonmilitary/settlements/.

12   Ibid.

13   *Certificate Book*, pp. 71, 82.

14   *Certificate Book*, p. 101.

15   Young, *Narrative of Daniel Trabue*, p. 75.

16   "Colonel William Fleming's Journal of Travels in Kentucky, 1779-1780," in Newton D. Mereness, *Travels in the American Colonies* (New York, 1916), pp. 626-627.

17   "Fleming's Journal," pp. 630.

18   Young, *Narrative of Daniel Trabue*, p. 47.

19   Nancy O'Malley, *Stockading Up* (Lexington, 1987), pp. 158, 161.

20   Old Virginia Surveys 1:207. David McGee's 400 acre settlement was surveyed September 27, 1780 by John Floyd.
21   Hammon and Taylor, *Virginia's Western War*, p. 125; "Fleming's Journal," pp. 644-647.
22   May 30, 1780, Lincoln County Entry Book 1:59.
23   Willard R. Jillson, *Old Kentucky Entries and Deeds* (Louisville, 1926), p. 223.
24   *Levi Hart v. James Vallandingham et al.*, Fayette County Circuit Court, Kentucky Land Trials, Record Book G:14.
25   Lincoln County Order Book 1:4A.
26   Ibid., 1:4A, 174, 198.
27   Kentucky Court of Appeals Deed Book J:9-11.
28   Madison County Order Book A:82.
29   Ibid., A:83.
30   Lincoln County Order Book 1:13.
31   Information taken from the court papers in *John Jouitt v. John Holder* found at the Archives and Special Collections, Margaret I. King Library, University of Kentucky, Lexington.
32   Ibid.
33   Harry G. Enoch, *John Howard of Howard's Creek, Biography of a Clark County Pioneer* (Winchester, KY, 2005).
34   *Lexington Observer & Kentucky Reporter*, November 12, 1834.
35   Certificate of the Virginia Land Commission, October 30, 1779, Kentucky Land Office.
36   *Samuel R. Combs et al. v. John Jouitt*, Kentucky Court of Appeals, 1821.
37   Fayette County Entry Book 2:317.
38   Old Virginia Surveys 7:230.
39   Survey by James Darnaby, February 19, 1822, in *John Jouitt v. John Holder's heirs*.
40   Old Kentucky Surveys 7:230.
41   Old Virginia Grants 8:585.
42   Ranck, *Boonesborough*, pp. 178, 196; deposition of David McGee, June 10, 1818, in *John Jouitt v. John Holder's heirs*; Edward A. Jonas, *Matthew Harris Jouett, Kentucky Portrait Painter, 1787-1827* (Louisville, 1938), p. 10.
43   Answer of John Jouitt, October 14, 1793, *John Jouitt v. John Holder*, Court of Appeals.
44   Copies of the court papers referred to above in *John Jouitt v. John Holder* may be found at the Archives and Special Collections, Margaret I. King Library, University of Kentucky, Lexington.
45   Kleber, *Kentucky Encyclopedia*, p. 480.

Holder's Station
1   Deposition of Joseph Berry, 1807, *Peter Henry's heirs v. Daniel Sturgis et al.*, Kentucky Land Trials D:295.
2   Deposition of Joseph Proctor, June 1815, copied in Draper MSS 12CC 209.
3   Deposition of Aquilla White, 1808, *Peter Henry's heirs v. Daniel Sturgis et al.*, Kentucky Land Trials D:225.
4   Ibid., deposition of Robert McMillan, 1808, D:226-228.
5   Deposition of Nathaniel Hart Jr., July 26, 1819, *Jouitt's heirs v. Holder's heirs*, Fayette County Circuit Court.
6   Ibid., depositions of Ambrose Bush, Whitson George and Eli Vaughn, June 4, 1817.

7   Clark County Court loose papers (1844).
8   Shane interview with William Clinkenbeard, Draper MSS 11CC 54-66.
9   Henderson to Holder, March 15, 1784, Draper MSS 26C 59.
10 Draper MSS 25C 81.
11 Numerous accounts of this battle are available: Draper MSS 13C 40, 24C 73(26-29), 18S 235-237; J. J. Marshall, *Reports of Cases at Law and In Equity Argued and Decided in the Court of Appeals of the Commonwealth of Kentucky* (Frankfort, 1832), pp. 302-309; Bessie T. Conkwright, "Estill's Defeat or the Battle of Little Mountain," *Register of the Kentucky State Historical Society* (1924) 22:311; Harding, *George Rogers Clark and His Men*, pp. 113-114.
12 The number of men with Caldwell varies in different accounts; John Bradford reported over 600. Thomas D. Clark, *The Voice of the Frontier, John Bradford's Notes on Kentucky* (Lexington, 1993), p. 54.
13 Neal Hammon, *Daniel Boone and the Defeat at Blue Licks* (n.p., 2005), pp. 14-18; James Callaway to Draper, January 1857, Draper MSS 24C 67.
14 Shane interview with John Sappington, Draper MSS 12CC 188. For a detailed discussion of the raid, see Anne Crabb, "'What Shall I Do Now?' The Story of the Indian Captivities of Margaret Paulee, Jones Hoy, and Jack Callaway, 1779-ca.1789," *Filson Club History Quarterly* (1996) 70:363-404.
15 John Filson, *Discovery, Settlement and Present State of Kentucke* (Wilmington, DE, 1784), p. 74.
16 Dianne Wells, *Roadside History, A Guide to Kentucky Highway Markers* (Frankfort, 2002), p. 66.
17 Benjamin Logan to Benjamin Harrison, August 31, 1782, in James, *George Rogers Clark Papers*, p. 101.
18 Samuel Boone, Revolutionary War pension file, S. 1168, NC, SC; Draper MSS 22C 72.
19 Shane interview with Fielding Belt, Draper MSS 12CC 245.
20 Ibid.
21 Shane interview with James Wade, Draper MSS 11CC 29-30.
22 R. S. Cotterill, "Battle of Upper Blue Licks," *Filson Club Historical Quarterly* (1927) 2:29.
23 "Fleming County Was the Scene of Many Early Indian Battles," by R. S. Cotterill, 1922, in *Kentucky Explorer* (2003) 18(5):13.
24 Michael Cassidy's account according to David D. Finley, Draper MSS 21S 220; Colonel Thomas Jones' account according to his son, Francis Jones, Draper MSS 21S 229-230.
25 Draper MSS 21S 229-230.
26 Nathan Boone to Draper, discussed in Neal O. Hammon, *Daniel Boone and the Defeat at Blue Licks* (2005), pp. 49-53.
27 Michael Cassidy's account, Draper MSS 21S 220-221; Colonel Thomas Jones' account, Draper MSS 21S 229-230.
28 Maj. John H. Craig to Draper, Draper MSS 9J 114; Francis Jones to Draper, Draper MSS 21S 232.
29 Samuel Boone, Revolutionary War pension file, S. 1168, NC, SC.
30 Shane interview with Isaac Clinkenbeard, Draper MSS 11CC 15.
31 Shane interview with William Clinkenbeard, Draper MSS 11CC 63.
32 Shane interview with Josiah Collins, in Mastin, *Lexington 1779*, p. 98.
33 Shane interview with James Wade, Draper MSS 11CC 29-30.
34 William Sudduth to Draper, Draper MSS 14U 110.

35   Shane interview with Fielding Belt, Draper MSS 12CC 245, 21S 206.
36   Ibid., Draper MSS 12CC 245; Collins, *History of Kentucky, Vol. 2*, pp. 233-234.
37   Francis Cassidy to Draper, Draper MSS 21S 176; James Jones to Draper, Draper MSS 21S 171-172.
38   Levi Todd to Stephen Trigg, August 16, 1782, James, *George Rogers Clark Papers*, p. 89.
39   Hammon and Taylor, *Virginia's Western War*, p. 164.
40   James, *George Rogers Clark Papers*, pp. 341-342.
41   R. S. Cotterill, "Battle of Upper Blue Licks," *Filson Club History Quarterly* (1927) 2:29-33.
42   A list of the participants in the Battle at Lower Blue Licks and a discussion of the sources may be found in Neal O. Hammon, *Daniel Boone and the Defeat at Blue Licks* (2005), pp. 120-128.
43   Hammon and Taylor, *Virginia's Western War*, p. 167.
44   Ibid., pp. 168-170; Charles G. Talbert, "Kentucky Invades Ohio, 1782," *Register of the Kentucky Historical Society* (1955) 53:288-297.
45   Draper MSS 28C 10.
46   Shane interview with John Rankins, Draper MSS 11CC 81.
47   Shane interview with William Clinkenbeard, Draper MSS 11CC 59.
48   *Ambrose Bush v. Luke Holder*, 1799, Clark County Court of Quarter Sessions; Clark County Deed Book 3:379.
49   Clark County Deed Book 3:379; *Ambrose Bush v. Luke Holder*, 1799, Clark County Court of Quarter Sessions Order Book 2:35, 110, 170.
50   Littell, *Statute Law of Kentucky*, 2:69-72.
51   Clark County Court loose papers (1798).
52   W. D. Holder to Draper, April 4, 1849, Draper MSS 24C 27.
53   Clark County Will Book 9:49.
54   Ibid.
55   Petitions No. 47, 60, 65 and 72, Robertson, *Petitions of the Early Inhabitants of Kentucky*, pp. 107, 124, 130, 139; *Kentucky Gazette*, June 16, 1792; *Winchester Advertiser*, November 5, 1814; "A List of Levies which have moved out of my County or have no effects, returned to the Court of Claims in the year 1816, Benjamin Harrison," Clark County Court loose papers (1793).
56   Deposition of Edmund Callaway taken in *Commonwealth v. Jacob Smith*, Clark County Court loose papers (1805).
57   William S. Bryan and Robert Rose, *A History of the Pioneer Families of Missouri* (St. Louis, MO, 1876), pp. 132-134; Annette Bowen, personal communication, July 5, 2009.
58   Doyle, *Marriage Records*; Doyle, *Marriage Bonds*.
59   Littell, *Statute Law of Kentucky*, 2:67.
60   Clark County Deed Book 4:178; Clark County Court loose papers (1806). There is no record of George or Margaret Rout selling the tract on Jouett Creek.
61   Clark County Deed Book 9:202, 27:224; Clark County Order Book 6:124-125, 142; "Bivions old still house" is mentioned in the index but not in the road order itself. See Harry G. Enoch and Larry G. Meadows, *Clark County Road Book, Index to Roads, Turnpikes, Railroads, Mills & Ferries in Clark County Order Books, 1793-1876* (Clay City, 2005), p. 17.
62   Clark County Will Book 9:373, 467.
63   Clark County Order Book 11:290; Clark County Court loose papers (1844).
64   Clark County Deed Book 30:340.
65   Clark County Court loose papers (1813).
66   Clark County Court loose papers (1816, 1817, 1819); Doyle, *Marriage Bonds*.

67   Clark County Court loose papers (1818).
68   Young, *Narrative of Daniel Trabue*, p. 59.
69   Draper interview with Daniel Bryan, Draper MSS 22C 9(10).
70   Shane interview with Daniel Bryan, Draper MSS 22C 14(12).
71   Bedinger Papers, Draper MSS 1A 69.
72   Richard P. Holder to Draper, October 6, 1850, Draper MSS 24C 29.
73   R. G. Williams to Draper, September 29, 1851, Draper MSS 24C 43.
74   Draper MSS 28C 10.
75   Petition No. 25, Robertson, *Petitions of the Early Inhabitants of Kentucky*, p. 79; George M. Chinn, Kentucky, *Settlement and Statehood, 1750-1800* (Frankfort, 1975), pp. 383-387; Charles G. Talbert, "Kentucky Invades Ohio, 1786," *Register of the Historical Society* (1956) 54:203; Lowell H. Harrison, *George Rogers Clark and the War in the West* (Lexington, 1976), pp. 101-104.
76   Draper MSS 53J 51.
77   Draper MSS 53J 59-61; Mann Butler, *Valley of the Ohio* (Frankfort, 1971 edition), pp. 241-243.
78   William H. English, *Conquest of the Country Northwest of the River Ohio, 1778-1783, and Life of George Rogers Clark* (Indianapolis, 1896), p. 815; Lowell H. Harrison, *George Rogers Clark and the War in the West* (Lexington, KY, 1976), p. 104.
79   Philander D. Chase, editor, *The Papers of George Washington, Presidential Series, Vol. 11* (Charlottesville, VA, 1987), p. 195.
80   Littell, *Statute Law of Kentucky*, 3:100.
81   Petition No. 72 (dated 1789), Robertson, *Petitions of the Early Inhabitants of Kentucky*, p. 139; *Kentucky Gazette*, June 16, 1792.

Land Speculator
1   Kentucky Land Office at http://apps.sos.ky.gov/land/nonmilitary/LandOfficeVTW/.
2   Washington County Book Commission, *Washington County, Kentucky, Bicentennial History, 1792-1992* (Paducah, 1991), pp. 9-10; Clift, *Cornstalk Militia*, p. 55; Michael L. Cook and Bettie A. Cook, *Pioneer History of Washington County, Kentucky* (Utica, KY, 1980), p. 23; Orval W. Baylor, *Early Times in Washington County, Kentucky* (Cynthiana, 1942), pp. 5-9; Collins, *History of Kentucky, Vol. 1*, pp. 354-355, and *Vol. 2*, p. 749.
3   Fayette County Entry Book 1; Lincoln County Entry Book 1:337.
4   John McIntyre deposition, 1814, Kentucky Land Trials D:212.
5   Aquilla White deposition, 1814, Kentucky Land Trials D:226-228.
6   Willard R. Jillson, *Old Kentucky Entries and Deeds* (Louisville, 1926); Old Virginia Surveys and Grants; Old Kentucky Surveys and Grants.
7   B. R. "Bud" Salyer, "Early Kentucky Surveyors and Deputy Surveyors," at sos.ky.gov/land/; Justinian Cartwright, Revolutionary War pension file, S. 30316, VA.
8   Old Virginia Grants 13:118; Old Kentucky Grants 4:101, 6:219, 17:484.
9   Old Virginia Surveys 7:403, 11:76.
10   Old Virginia Surveys 10:443.
11   Cape: http://www.uky.edu/LCC/HIS/sites/capitol.html; Gano: Collins, *History of Kentucky*, Vol. 2, p. 707; Holmes: George M. Chinn, Kentucky, *Settlement and Statehood, 1750-1800* (Frankfort, 1975), pp. 494-495.
12   Fayette County District Court Deed Book B:61.
13   Old Kentucky Grants 8:92; Clark County Deed Book 5:147, 228.
14   Old Virginia Surveys 7:230; Old Virginia Grants 8:585.
15   *Caleb Embry v. John Evans et al.*, Estill Circuit Court, 1827, quoted in Ellen Rogers and Diane Rogers, *Estill County, Kentucky, Circuit Court Records* (n.p., 1984), p. 931.

16 Fayette County Entry Book 2:232.
17 Shane interview with Cuthbert Combs, Draper MSS 11CC 80.
18 Old Virginia Grants 5:42, 9:554.
19 Agreement between John Howard and John Holder, August 12, 1783, John Howard Papers, University of Kentucky Archives, M. I. King Library, Lexington.
20 Fayette County Survey Book B:131.
21 John Howard to John Holder, July 19, 1786, John Howard Papers.
22 Ibid.
23 Clark County Deed Book 1:461, 584.
24 Benjamin Howard to "Mr. Detheridge, Surveyor," November 30, 1795, Benjamin Howard Papers.
25 Survey by P. Datherage for Capt. Benjamin Howard, December 7, 1795, Benjamin Howard Papers.
26 Order on John Holder to Capt. Benjamin Howard, December 7, 1795, Benjamin Howard Papers.

Yazoo Land Company
1 Charles H. Haskins, *The Yazoo Land Companies* (New York, 1891), pp. 6-9; John F. Claiborne, *Mississippi as a Province, Territory and State, Vol. 1* (Jackson, MS, 1880), pp. 155-156; Richard A. McLemore, *History of Mississippi, Vol. 1* (Hattiesburg, MS, 1973), p. 164; Frank E. Smith, *The Yazoo River* (Jackson, MS, 1988), pp. 3-5.
2 Parish, "Intrigues of Doctor James O'Fallon," 17:238; U.S. Congress, *American State Papers, Indian Affairs, Vol. 4* (Washington, DC, 1832), p. 114; Mississippi Project-American Local History Network, "Yazoo Land Companies, 1789," www.usgennet.org/usa/ms/state/.
3 Parish, "Intrigues of Doctor James O'Fallon."
4 Ibid.
5 Ibid; *Kentucky Gazette*, February 26, 1791.
6 U.S. Congress, *American State Papers, Indian Affairs, Vol. 4* (Washington, DC, 1832), pp. 115-117; Parish, "Intrigues of Doctor James O'Fallon," 17:244.
7 O'Fallon to Washington, September 25, 1790, in U.S. Congress, *American State Papers, Indian Affairs, Vol. 4* (Washington, DC, 1832), p. 115.
8 Parish, "Intrigues of Doctor James O'Fallon."
9 *Gazette of the United States* (Philadelphia), December 11, 1790, in Draper MSS 14U 239.
10 *Kentucky Gazette*, May 14, 1791.
11 Parish, "Intrigues of Doctor James O'Fallon," 17:245-246, 249, 252-256.
12 Draper MSS 4CC 170.
13 Parish, "Intrigues of Doctor James O'Fallon," 17:257-261.
14 Draper MSS 24C 27.

Business Enterprises
1 Shane interview with William Clinkenbeard, Draper MSS 11CC 54-66.
2 Littell, *Statute Law of Kentucky*, 1:678.
3 William D. Holder to Draper, April 4, 1849, Draper MSS 24C 27.
4 Benjamin Howard to "Mr. Detheridge, Surveyor," November 30, 1795, Benjamin Howard Papers.
5 Madison County Order Book A, April 25, 1787.
6 Madison County Court of Quarter Sessions, Circuit Case Files, Box 11, *Holder v. Arthur*.

7   Madison County Order Book A, April 8, 1789.
8   Madison County Court of Quarter Sessions, Case Files, Box 15, "Proctor Receipt." Note dated May 1787.
9   Clark County Order Book 1:68; *Kentucky Gazette*, September 7, 1793.
10 Shane interview with Francis F. Jackson, Draper 15CC 9-10.
11 Verhoeff, *Kentucky River Navigation*, p. 55.
12 Ibid., pp. 53-56; Thomas D. Clark, *Clark County, Kentucky, A History* (Winchester, 1996), p. 103.
13 Shane interview with Francis F. Jackson, Draper 15CC 9-10.
14 Ibid.
15 Thomas D. Clark, *The Kentucky* (Lexington, 1969), p. 69.
16 "Boats & Boat Building," in Leland D. Baldwin, *Keelboat Age on Western Waters* (Pittsburgh, 1941), pp. 39-55.
17 Shane interview with Francis F. Jackson, Draper 15CC 9-10.
18 *Kentucky Gazette*, April 18, 1789.
19 *Kentucky Gazette*, May 11, 1793; William H. Perrin, *History of Bourbon, Scott, Harrison and Nicholas Counties, Kentucky* (Chicago, 1882), p. 180.
20 Clark County Order Book 1:46, 68; *William Harris v. John Holder*, Clark County, 1796, Drawer 3, Kentucky Department of Libraries and Archives.
21 Harry G. Enoch, *Bound for New Orleans! Original Journal of John Halley of His Trips to New Orleans Performed in the Years 1789 & 1791* (Winchester, KY, 2005).
22 Madison County Order Book A, March 2, 1790.
23 Madison County Order Book B, May 6, 1800.
24 John Holder to James French, undated, James French Papers, University of Kentucky Archives, M. I. King Library, Lexington.
25 Thomas Speed, *Political Club, Danville, Kentucky, 1786-1790* (Louisville, 1894), p. 95; Old Virginia Grants 11:490.
26 James French Papers.
27 Dr. O'Fallon to John Holder, September 3, 1791, Draper MSS 4CC 165.
28 Dr. O'Fallon to John Holder, February 14, 1792, Draper MSS 4CC 166.
29 John Holder to Dr. O'Fallon, March 4, 1792, Draper MSS 1E 98.
30 Dr. O'Fallon to Capt. Philip Buckner, undated, Draper MSS 4CC 170.
31 *Stewart's Lexington Herald*, December 31, 1799.
32 "The Indian Camp," in Enoch, *Where In The World*, p. 151.
33 Clark County Court loose papers (1795).
34 *Kentucky Gazette*, August 2, 1803; Clark County Order Book 4:195.
35 Ibid.; Clark County Order Book 13:589.
36 Clark County Will Book 8:267.
37 Verhoeff, *Kentucky River Navigation*, pp. 42-81.
38 "An act for reviving several Publick Warehouses for the Inspection of Tobacco," October 1778, Hening, *Statutes at Large*, 9:482-521; "An act to Regulate the Inspection of Flour," November 1781, Hening, *Statutes at Large*, 10:496-498.
39 Petition No. 72, Robertson, *Petitions of the Early Inhabitants of Kentucky*, p. 139.
40 Ibid.
41 An Act establishing an Inspection of Tobacco at Clevelands, Holders, Staffords and Bush's Landings, "Excerpts from Executive Journal of Gov. Isaac Shelby," *Register of the Kentucky Historical Society* (1930) 28:7; Littell, *Statute Law of Kentucky*, 1:150, 330; 2:139-140.
42 Isaac Shelby Executive Journals, 1792-1797, cited in *Kentucky Ancestor* (1993) 28(4); Clark County Order Book 1:73.

43   Clark County Deed Book 3:353-354; Clark County Order Book 2:271.
44   *Kentucky Gazette*, August 25, 1802, quoted in Charles R. Staples, *History of Pioneer Lexington, Kentucky 1779-1806* (Lexington, 1939), pp. 180-181.
45   Clark County Deed Book 4:123.
46   *Stewart's Kentucky Herald*, December 31, 1799.
47   Littell, *Statute Law of Kentucky*, 2:269.
48   "Annual Return of Holders Warehouse," October 22, 1810 and October 27, 1817, Clark County Court loose papers (1810, 1817).
49   "Annual Report of Bush's Warehouse" by inspectors Joseph George and John V. Bush, October 27, 1817, Clark County Court loose papers (1817).
50   Verhoeff, *Kentucky River Navigation*, p. 10; Clark County Order Book 2:387.
51   *Kentucky Gazette*, January 16, 1810; map and road order, Clark County Court loose papers (1844).
52   Clark County Court loose papers (1844).
53   Clark County Order Book 13:589; Clark County Deed Book 42:476; U.S. Manufacturing Census, Clark County, 1870, 1880. Order Book 13 is missing from the county clerk's office. Reference to Woodward and Bently's order is found in the county road book, transcribed in Harry G. Enoch and Larry G. Meadows, *Clark County Road Book, Index to Roads, Turnpikes, Railroads, Mills & Ferries in Clark County Order Books, 1793-1876* (Clay City, 2005), p. 39.
54   Deposition of Ambrose Coffee, 1809, in Madison County Deed Book I:95.
55   Deposition of Rachel Martin Bush in Obadiah Baber's Revolutionary War pension file, R. 347, VA; George F. Doyle, *A Transcript of the First Record Book of Providence Church, Clark County, Kentucky* (Winchester, 1924), p. 6.
56   Harry G. Enoch, *Life and Times of Orson Martin* (2004), unpublished manuscript.
57   Shane interview with Benjamin Allen, Draper MSS 11CC 69.
58   Deposition of Nathaniel Hart taken on July 26, 1819 at the office of Robert Wickliffe in Lexington in the case of *John Jouitt v. John Holder*, Fayette Circuit Court, 1793.
59   Louis C. Hunter, *A History of Industrial Power in the United States, 1780-1930, Volume One: Waterpower in the Century of the Steam Engine* (Charlottesville, 1979), pp. 71-83.
60   Eliot Wigginton, editor, *Foxfire 2* (New York, 1973), p. 142.
61   Grenville Bathe and Dorothy Bathe, *Oliver Evans, A Chronicle of Early American Engineering* (Philadelphia, 1935), pp. 11-23.
62   Map produced by plotting the metes and bounds found in Clark County Deed Book 23:463.
63   Clark County Deed Book 23:463.
64   Clark County Deed Book 1:403, 630, 2:113.
65   Deposition of Ambrose Coffee, 1809, in Madison County Deed Book I:95.
66   Clark County Order Book 2:240.
67   Clark County Court of Quarter Sessions Order Book 2:149.
68   "An act to establish Inspections of Flour and Hemp," 1795, in Littell, *Statute Law of Kentucky*, 1:443-450.
69   Littell, *Statute Law of Kentucky*, 2:139-140.

Roads Lead to Holder's
1   Littell, *Statute Law of Kentucky*, 1:371-377.
2   Clark County Circuit Court, 1812, in Complete Record Book of Clark County Land Trials, 1817-1818, pp. 459, 479.
3   Ibid., p. 477.

4   Ibid., p. 481.
5   Clark County Court loose papers (1795).
6   Clark County Order Book 1:166, 175.
7   Jackie Couture, *Madison County, Kentucky, Court Order Book A, 1787-1791* (Bowie, MD, 1996), pp. 84, 122.
8   Clark County Order Book 1:49, 76-77, 159-160.
9   Clark County Court loose papers (1832); Clark County Will Book 7:748.
10 Clark County Court loose papers (1825, 1852).
11 Clark County Order Book 14:46, 63.
12 Clark County Court loose papers (1858).
13 Clark County Order Book 1:36-37.
14 Clark County Order Book 1:59, 115.
15 Clark County Order Book 2:325.
16 Clark County Order Book 2:353.
17 Clark County Order Book 2:522.
18 Clark County Deed Book 7:282, 283.
19 Clark County Order Book 4:194.
20 Clark County Deed Book 2:113, 22:12.
21 Clark County Deed Book 4:285; *Kentucky Gazette*, July 12, 1803; Clark County Order Book 4:327.
22 Clark County Order Book 4:321.
23 Ibid.
24 Clark County Court loose papers (1853).
25 Ibid.
26 U.S. Geological Survey, Richmond, KY Quadrangle, 1:125,000, March 1897 edition from a survey in 1890, copy at the University of Kentucky Map Room, M. I. King Library, Lexington.

Yazoo Land Company
1   Robert S. Cotterill, Clark County Chronicles, *Winchester Sun*, August 16, 1923.
2   Clark County Deed Book 7:282, 283; Clark County Order Book 2:338, 353, 522, 3:116.
3   Clark County Chronicles, *Winchester Sun*, September 13, 1923.
4   Clark County Deed Book 42:310, 45:593, 58:66, 75:313, 77:122.
5   *Winchester Chronicle*, October 7, 1858; *National Union*, March 1, 1861.
6   Clark County Deed Book 38:105, 42:125.
7   Clark County newspaper clipping, dated March 6, 1888, copy provided by Roberta Newell.
8   Jennifer L. Barber, "Cultural Resource Survey of the Lower Howard's Creek Area, Clark County, Kentucky," Contract Publication Series 04-042, Cultural Resource Analysts, Inc., 2005; Clark County Deed Book 38:105.
9   Fayette County Burnt Records 3:354; Clark County Order Book 1:5, 23; Clark County Deed Book 2:113.
10 *Certificate Book*, p. 130; National Historical Co., *History of St. Charles, Montgomery and Warren Counties, Missouri* (St. Louis; 1885); Draper MSS 17J 29, 22C 6, 12, 13; William Bryan and Robert Rose, *History of the Pioneer Families of Missouri* (St. Louis; 1876), pp. 132-133; J. D. Bryan, "The Boone-Bryan History," *Register of the Kentucky Historical Society* (1930) 28:244.
11 J. D. Bryan, "The Boone-Bryan History," *Register of the Kentucky Historical Society* (1930) 28:244; Draper MSS 28CC 57; 22S 99; Lilian H. Oliver, *Some Boone Descendants and*

Kindred of the St. Charles District (n.p., 1964, copy at the Kentucky Historical Society Library, Frankfort, Kentucky), pp. 74-77.
12   Clark County Deed Book 4:487, 6:131, 304.
13   *Kentucky Gazette*, April 16, 1802.
14   Clark County Circuit Court Order Book A:167.
15   A. H. Redford, *Life and Times of H. H. Kavanaugh, D. D.* (Nashville, 1884), pp. 22-24, 40-49, 52; Clark County Order Book 5:170, 204; Clark County Will Book 3:344, 367, 4:232.
16   Charles Lyddane, "Howard's Creek," *Clark County Republican*, April 15, 1916.
17   Joe Kendall Neel, *Lower Howard's Creek, A Biological Survey* (Master's Thesis, University of Kentucky; 1938).
18   Charles Lyddane, "Howard's Creek," *Clark County Republican*, April 15, 1916.
19   Clark County Deed Book 87:147.
20   Clark County Deed Book 1:113, 9:464; Clark County Order Book 2:113; Clark County Court loose papers (1799).
21   Clark County Order Book 4:242.
22   Harry G. Enoch, "Life and Times of Orson Martin," unpublished manuscript, 2004.
23   Clark County Order Book 2:130.
24   Clark County Deed Book 4:285.
25   Clark County Circuit Court Order Book A:167, 256, 277; Clark County Deed Book 9:147, 352, 23:605, 28:468, 34:274.
26   Clark County Deed Book 38:118; Enoch, *Where in the World*, p. 129.
27   *Winchester Chronicle*, October 7, 1858.
28   Clark County Deed Book 42:369, 45:438; Enoch, *Where in the World*, p. 131.
29   Enoch, *Where in the World*, p. 131.
30   Clark County Order Book 4:5, 14; Clark County Deed Book 7:214, 216; Clark County Procession Book, p. 68.
31   Jessie Hodges deposition in Enoch, *Where in the World*, p. 153.
32   *National Union*, February 1, 1861; U.S. Manufacturers Census, Clark County, 1870.
33   Clark County Order Book 2:86, 119, 4:94, 103; Clark County Deed Book 37:25.
34   *Clark County Republican*, April 15, 1916.
35   Clark County Deed Book 37:25.
36   Clark County Order Book 6:316.
37   Clark County Deed Book 23:485.
38   Clark County Will Book 8:142-144.
39   Clark County Order Book 6:568, 674; Clark County Deed Book 46:595.
40   Clark County Court loose papers (1853).
41   Leland D. Baldwin, *Whiskey Rebels; The Story of a Frontier Uprising* (Pittsburgh, 1939).
42   Willard R. Jillson, *Early Kentucky Distillers, 1783-1800* (Louisville, 1940), pp. 44, 48.
43   Ibid., p. 46.
44   Clark County Deed Book 42:476; U.S. Manufacturers Census, Clark County, 1870 and 1880.
45   *Clark County Democrat*, February 21, 1877.
46   Arthur McFarlan, *Geology of Kentucky* (Lexington, 1943), p. 12.
47   *Clark County Republican*, April 15, 1916.

Public Service and Local Affairs
1   J. T. Dorris, "1792 Offer for the Location of the Capital of Kentucky at Boonesboro," *Register of the Kentucky Historical Society* (1933) 31:174; copy of the original petition at the Kentucky Room, Library, Eastern Kentucky University, Richmond, KY.

2   "Excerpts from Executive Journal of Gov. Isaac Shelby," *Register of the Kentucky Historical Society* (1930) 28:10.
3   Ibid., 28:143.
4   Ibid., 28:146.
5   Littell, *Statute Law of Kentucky*, 2:264.
6   Clark County Court loose papers (1796).
7   "Excerpts from Executive Journal of Gov. Isaac Shelby," *Register of the Kentucky Historical Society* (1930) 28:8.
8   Robert M. Ireland, *County Courts in Antebellum Kentucky* (Lexington, 1972), p. 4.
9   Clark County Order Book 1:1, 15, 26, 37, 52, 61.
10 Shane interview with Benjamin Allen, Draper MSS 11CC 68.
11 Clark County Deed Book 27:566; Clark County Order Book 1:147.
12 Clark County Order Book 1:10, 25, 35.
13 Shane interview with Benjamin Allen, Draper MSS 11CC 70.
14 Clark County Order Book 1:82-83, 105; Clark County Court of Quarter Sessions Order Book 1; Shane interview with Benjamin Allen, Draper MSS 11CC 68, 71.
15 Clark County Order Book 1:37, 46, 49, 68, 158.
16 Clark County Court loose papers (1796).
17 Clark County Order Book 2:65, 95.
18 Clark County Order Book 2:212.
19 Clark County Order Book 1 and 2.
20 Littell, *Statute Law of Kentucky*, 1:187; Minutes of the Winchester Trustees, copy in Winchester City Hall.
21 Clark County Order Book 1:192.
22 Clark County Order Book 2:117.
23 Clark County Order Book 2:224.
24 Clark County Order Book 2:231, 241, 250, 289.
25 Clark County Order Book 2:289-290, 296-297.
26 Clark County Court of Quarter Sessions Order Book 2:8, 19-20, 44, 268, 269, 271.
27 Littell, *Statute Law of Kentucky*, 2:195.
28 Clark County Deed Book 3:379, 4:178, 6:478, 7:283, 315, 9:105, 10:155; Madison County Deed Book L:515; *Benjamin Hallock v. John Holder*, Clark County, 1798, Drawer 11, *Thomas Arnold v. Robert Higgins*, Clark County, 1799, Drawer 14, Kentucky Department of Libraries and Archives, Frankfort.
29 Littell, *Statute Law of Kentucky*, 4:336.
30 Shane interview with Jeptha Kemper, Draper MSS 12CC 132.
31 Clark County Deed Book 4:147, 7:1, 9:105; Madison County Deed Book L:515.
32 *John Jouett v. John Holder*, Supreme Court papers transcribed by George Doyle, John Holder folder, Clark County Public Library, Winchester; *John Jouett v. John Holder*, 1795, Drawer 1, Kentucky Department of Libraries and Archives, Frankfort.
33 Information comes from Pat Mount's website at http://freepages.genealogy.rootsweb.ancestry.com/~patmount/ThomMountnotes.html.
34 *Certificate Book*, p. 78; Old Virginia Grants 2:213-215.
35 Robert S. Davis Jr., "A Georgian and a New Country: Ebenezer Platt's Imprisonment in Newgate for Treason in 'The Year of the Hangman', 1777," *Georgia Historical Quarterly* (2000) 84:106-115; Hammon, *My Father, Daniel Boone*, p. 109.
36 *John Hall v. John Holder*, Clark County, 1798, Drawer 11, Kentucky Department of Libraries and Archives, Frankfort; Clark County Court of Quarter Sessions Order Book 1:6, 22.
37 Madison County Deed Book L:515.

38 *John Martin Jr. v. John Holder*, Clark County, 1807, Drawer 70, Kentucky Department of Libraries and Archives, Frankfort.
39 Old Kentucky Surveys 1:443; Fayette County District Court Deed Book B:61; Clark County Deed Book 11:270.
40 *Green Clay v. John Holder*, in John Holder folder, Clark County Public Library, Winchester; *Green Clay v. John Holder*, 1794, Drawer 1, Kentucky Department of Libraries and Archives, Frankfort; Clark County Court of Quarter Sessions Order Book 1:37.
41 Verhoeff, *Kentucky River Navigation*, pp. 158-159, *Kentucky Gazette*, October 11, 1808.
42 *Samuel Smith v. John Holder*, Clark County, 1795, Drawer 2, *John Holder v. Samuel Smith*, 1798, Drawer 11, Kentucky Department of Libraries and Archives, Frankfort; Clark County Court of Quarter Sessions Order Book 1:9, 23.
43 *Kentucky Gazette*, January 5, 1793, March 18, 1797.
44 *John Holder v. John A. Seitz and Frederick Lauman*, Clark County, 1798, Drawer 11, Kentucky Department of Libraries and Archives, Frankfort.
45 *John A. Seitz and Frederick Lauman v. John Holder*, Clark County, 1796, Drawer 9, and; Clark County Court of Quarter Sessions Minute Book, February 28, 1798; Clark County Court of Quarter Sessions Order Book 1:211.
46 Clark County Court of Quarter Sessions Order Book 2:73.
47 Effarilla Jordan declaration for a Revolutionary War pension as the widow of Sharshall Jordan, W. 9090, Virginia.
48 *Sharshall Jordan v. John Holder's heirs*, Clark County, 1802, Drawer 31, Kentucky Department of Libraries and Archives, Frankfort; Clark County Court of Quarter Sessions Order Book 3:205.
49 *George Johnson v. John Holder's heirs*, Clark County, 1802, Drawer 31, Kentucky Department of Libraries and Archives, Frankfort; Clark County Court of Quarter Sessions Order Book 3:73.
50 Old Kentucky Grants 17:484.
51 Clark County Deed Book 4:433.
52 *Sharshall Jordan v. John Holder's heirs*, Clark County, 1802, Drawer 31, Kentucky Department of Libraries and Archives, Frankfort.
53 *Thomas Stevens v. John Holder*, Clark County, 1797, Drawer 9, Kentucky Department of Libraries and Archives, Frankfort.
54 Clark County Deed Book 3:333, 369.
55 *Kentucky Gazette*, March 28, 1799.
56 William Ellis, H. E. Everman and Richard Sears, *Madison County: 200 Years in Retrospect* (Richmond, KY, 1985), pp. 13, 79, 82; Collins, *History of Kentucky, Vol. 2*, p. 776.

Journey's End
1 Stonestreet to Draper, August 24, 1853, Draper MSS 4C 66.
2 A. Goff Bedford, *Land of Our Fathers* (Winchester, 1958), p. 105; Hart, *Callaway Family*, p. 192.
3 Clark County Order Book 2:236, 241; Clark County Deed Book 3:369; Clark County Court of Quarter Sessions Order Book 2:73; *Kentucky Gazette*, March 28, 1799.
4 Clift, *Cornstalk Militia*, pp. 17, 73.
5 William Sudduth to Lyman Draper, Draper MSS 14U 110.
6 *Sharshall Jordan v. John Holder's heirs*, Clark County, 1802, Drawer 31, Kentucky Department of Libraries and Archives.
7 Clark County Order Book 2:483, 503, 3:39; Madison County Order Book C:227, 230, 262.

8   Clark County Deed Book 4:413; Clark County Court loose papers (1802).
9   Shane interview with William Clinkenbeard, Draper MSS 11CC 65; Shane interview with Thomas Hart, Draper MSS 11CC 79; "Excerpts from Executive Journal of Gov. Isaac Shelby," *Register of the Kentucky Historical Society* (1930) 28:8.
10 Doyle, *Marriage Bonds*; Clark County Will Book 1:347.
11 R. G. Williams to Draper, September 29, 1851, Draper MSS 24C 43.
12 Jessie Williams Hart, *The Callaway Family* (n.p., c.1927), p. 80.
13 Hart, *Callaway Family*, p. 192.
14 Hart, *Callaway Family*, p. 196.
15 Kathryn Owen, *Old Graveyards of Clark County, Kentucky* (New Orleans, 1975), p. 23; *Stewart's Kentucky Herald*, December 1799; *Kentucky Gazette*, January 16, 1810.
16 G. Glenn Clift, editor, *Kentucky Soldiers of the War of 1812* (Baltimore, 1995), p. 228; Clark County Order Book 5:319, 6 (1817-1824):568; Jane Gray Buchanan, *Thomas Thompson and Ann Finney of Colonial Pennsylvania and North Carolina* (Oak Ridge, TN, 1987), p. 172.
17 Clark County Court loose papers (1815).
18 *Kentucky Gazette*, October 5, 1833.
19 *Lexington Observer & Kentucky Reporter*, October 3, 1833.
20 Buchanan, *Thomas Thompson*, pp. 172-173.
21 *Sabrina Nelson v. S. R. Combs*, 1832, Clark Circuit Court, Civil Cases, Drawer 402, Kentucky Department of Libraries and Archives, Frankfort.
22 Clark County Court loose papers (1846).
23 S. J. Conkwright and S. H. Rutledge, "Map of the Bush Settlement" (1923), Clark County Public Library, Winchester.
24 Clark County Deed Book 3:379, 21:16, 24:466.
25 The index to Clark County criminal cases at the Kentucky Department of Libraries and Archives in Frankfort shows this case and gives the box and bundle numbers. However, the papers could not be found at the Archives. The Clark County circuit clerk's office said that all papers were sent to the Archives.
26 Clark County Circuit Court Order Book W, pp. 4, 15, 17.
27 Clark County Circuit Court Order Book W, p. 88.
28 Clark County Circuit Court Order Book W, pp. 132, 213.
29 Clark County Circuit Court Order Book W, pp. 312, 343, 370.
30 Hart, *Callaway Family*, p. 203; Doyle, *Marriage Bonds*; Buchanan, *Thomas Thompson*, pp. 172-173; Clark County Deed Book 25:508, 28:68, 85, 183, 193.
31 Buchanan, *Thomas Thompson*, pp. 172-173.
32 Fayette County Will Book A:340.
33 Mary D. Ackerly, *Our Kin* (n.p., c.1930), p. 189; Amherst County (VA) Will Book 3:506; Anne Mitchell, Marriage Records from Amherst, Virginia through 1850, http://genealogy-by-anne.com/gen/history/amherst-history/amherst-marriage-records.html.
34 http://www.winchester-tn.com/home.html; *National Banner and Nashville Whig*, May 29, 1835, at http://www.genealogybank.com/gbnk/.
35 Madison County Deed Book I:252 (p-o-a); David McNeely's Revolutionary War pension file, W. 1051, VA (justice of the peace); *Goodspeed's History of Tennessee, Franklin County*, at http://freepages.history.rootsweb.ancestry.com/.
36 Franklin County (TN) Wills 1808-1876, p. 194; *Peter S. Decherd v. John W. Holder's heirs*, Franklin County (TN) Probate Court, 1843, transcribed by Annette Bowen; Doyle, *Marriage Bonds*.
37 Madison County Order Book C:230; Madison County Deed Book F:449, H:99. John Patrick married Elizabeth Callaway, a daughter of George Callaway, in 1787 in Bedford

County, Virginia. Callaway Family Association, http://www.callawayfamily.org.

38   *Kentucky Gazette*, March 24, 1812, March 16, 1813, January 31, 1814; G. Glenn Clift, *Remember the Raisin!* (Frankfort, 1961), pp. 51, 173. Caleb Holder's company roster is given in Minnie S. Wilder, editor, *Kentucky Soldiers of the War of 1812* (Baltimore, MD, 1969 edition), p. 346.

39   Madison County Deed Book K:486; Hart, *Callaway Family*, p. 209; *Garrard Alexander v. Richard C. Holder*, Madison County Circuit Court, 1827, Kentucky Department of Libraries and Archives, as transcribed by Annette Bowen.

40   Madison County Order Book C:227; *Kentucky Gazette*, February 27, 1809.

41   G. Glenn Clift, *Remember the Raisin!* (Frankfort, 1961), p. 208; Anderson C. Quisenberry, *Kentucky in the War of 1812* (Frankfort, 1915), pp. 85-110, 102-193.

42   Madison County Tax Assessment Books, 1817-1825; *Garrard Alexander v. Richard C. Holder*, Madison County Circuit Court, 1827, Kentucky Department of Libraries and Archives, Frankfort, transcribed by Annette Bowen.

43   Madison County Deed Book S:253; Frances T. Ingmire and Helen S. Swenson, *Abstracts of Franklin County, Tennessee, Wills, 1808-1875* (St. Louis, 1984), p. 23.

44   *Goodspeed's History of Tennessee, Franklin County*.

45   Ibid.

46   *Goodspeed's Biographical and Historical Memoirs of Mississippi, Vol. 1, Pt. 2* (Chicago, 1891), pp. 239-241.

47   Hart, *Callaway Family*, p. 210; *Goodspeed's Biographical and Historical Memoirs of Mississippi, Vol. 1, Pt. 2* (Chicago, 1891), p. 240; U.S. Census, Pontotoc County, MS, 1860; Herbert H. Evans to Emily Mosely, August 22, 1946, copy at the Kentucky Historical Society Library, Frankfort.

48   Clark County Order Book 3:355; Doyle, *Marriage Bonds*; G. Glenn Clift, *Remember the Raisin!* (Frankfort, 1961), p. 208.

49   G. Glenn Clift, *Kentucky Obituaries, 1787-1854* (Baltimore, 1977), p. 30; *Lexington Observer and Reporter*, August 22, 1833

50   "Ancestors of Mrs. Josephine Jones Weakley," in Jeannette T. Acklen et al., *Tennessee Records: Bible Records and Marriage Bonds* (Baltimore, 1977), p. 331.

51   Madison County Order Book C:262; William Ellis, H. E. Everman and Richard Sears, *Madison County: 200 Years in Retrospect* (Richmond, KY, 1985), pp. 17-18, 37; George Doyle, *Marriage Bonds*.

52   Clark County Will Book 2:326; G. Glenn Clift, *Remember the Raisin!* (Frankfort, 1961), p. 229; Hart, *Callaway Family*, p. 220.

53   *Winchester Advertiser*, August 19, 1814.

54   W. D. Holder to Draper, April 4, 1849, Draper MSS 24C 27.

55   Ibid.

56   Peter S. Decherd to Draper, September 21, 1850, Draper MSS 24C 28.

57   Hart, *Callaway Family*, p. 220.

58   Hart, *Callaway Family*, p. 221.

59   William H. Perrin et al., *Kentucky, A History of the State, 8th Edition* (Louisville and Chicago, 1888), p. 1012.

60   R. G. Williams to Draper, September 29, 1851, Draper MSS 24C 43.

61   R. G. Williams to Draper, January 28, 1852, Draper MSS 24C 44.

62   Hart, *Callaway Family*, pp. 238, 245-255; Mary D. Ackerly, *Our Kin* (n.p., c.1930), pp. 327-328.

Index

A
Adams, George 66
Adams, Lewis 207
Adkinson, Kandie 94
Alexander, Morgan 22, 23, 24, 25
Allan, Chilton 225
Allen, Benjamin 167, 215, 216
Amelia County, Virginia 26
Amherst County, Virginia 245, 246
Anderson, Debra 11
Anderson, Euphemia Jones 75
Anderson, John 86
Anderson, Nicholas 53, 65, 82, 98, 165
Anderson, Presla 74
Anderson, Presley 74, 75, 85, 86, 87, 246
Anderson, Presley Jr. 85, 86, 89
Anderson, William 85, 86, 246
Anthony, James 53, 64
Anthony, Jonathan 64
Antwerp, Margaret Van 244
Ark, Uriel 61
Arnold, Richmond "Richard" 188, 190, 209
Arnold, Thomas 220
Arthur, Talbot 146
Ash, Uriel 61
Ashby's Gap 19, 20
Atchison, John 20
Au Poste Vincennes 42
Augusta County, Virginia 85, 99

B
Bailey, Thomas 61
Bakeless, John 35
Baker, John 214, 215, 216, 219
Baker, Jonathan 173
Ballard, Bland 60, 61
Banta, Peter 64
Barkley, Craven 243
Barnes, James 53
Barren River 69
Barrows Run 15
Bath County, Kentucky 41
Bathe, James 53
Battle at Frenchtown 247
Battle at Old Chillicothe 56
Battle of Blue Licks 32, 108
Battle of Brandywine 102
Battle of Fallen Timbers 213
Battle of Guilford Courthouse 99
Battle of King's Mountain 130
Battle of Lower Blue Licks 109
Battle of Point Pleasant 22, 71
Battle of Saratoga 73
Battle of Upper Blue Licks 116, 254
Battle on the Little Miami River 58
Battson, James 20
Baughman, Catherine 92
Baughman, Henry 61
Baughman, John 61
Baukman [Baughman], John 53
Beasley, John 94
Beasley, William 45, 90, 94, 124
Bedford County, Virginia 55, 81
Bedford, Goff 234
Bedinger, George Michael 18, 45, 49, 52, 53, 54, 56, 57, 58, 59, 60, 61, 82, 90, 91, 125, 132
Bell, Jesse 160
Bell, Thomas 64
Belt, Fielding 110, 114, 115
Belue, Ted Franklin 258
Bennett, Joshua 131
Bently, Daniel 155, 165, 178
Berkeley County, Virginia 45, 52, 90, 132
Berry, Benjamin 25
Berry, James 53, 61, 107
Berry, Joseph 104
Bethy, Elisha 60
Big Sandy River 132
Bird, Henry 59, 62
Bishop, Solomon 25
Bivin, Peggy 123
Bivion, Bazell 123
Bivion, Betsey 123
Bivion, Charles 123
Bivion, Margaret 123
Bivion, Randolph "Randle" 122, 123
Black Beard 45
Black Hoof 45
Blackburn, Samuel 243
Blackfish Ford 46, 154
Blackfish, Chief 44, 45, 46, 56, 59, 106, 175
Blackwell, John 120
Blackwell, William 15
Bledsoe, Abraham 69
Bledsoe, Agnes 246
Bledsoe, Anthony 69
Bledsoe, Isaac 69
Boone Creek 37, 41, 94, 97, 105, 124, 131, 155, 173, 209, 241
Boone, Benjamin 209
Boone, Daniel 7, 8, 9, 11, 28, 29, 30, 31, 32, 33, 34, 35, 37, 38, 41, 44, 46, 49, 56, 70, 71, 82, 91, 106, 108, 117, 131, 136, 137, 146, 197, 223, 258
Boone, Jemima 9, 28, 31, 32, 34, 46, 68, 79, 82, 121
Boone, Lavina 32
Boone, Mary 38
Boone, Rebecca 197
Boone, Samuel 109, 113, 116
Boone, Squire 114, 116, 117
Boone, Thomas 123
Boone's Paint Creek Expedition 10
Boone's Station 49, 67, 105, 113
Bostick [Bostic], Leslie C. 243, 244
Botetourt County, Virginia 37, 69, 75, 132, 136
Boulware, James 252
Boulware, M. Williamson 251
Bourbon County, Kentucky 17, 25, 45, 63, 90, 94, 131, 139, 145, 165, 180, 212, 220, 221
Bowen, Anne 11
Bowles, Catharine 248
Bowman, John 10, 37, 55, 56, 57, 58, 59, 60, 62
Bowren, Alfred 244
Boyle, John 63
Boyle, Stephen 167
Bradley, Edward 91
Brandenburg, Joseph 224
Branham, Henry 12
Bransford, William M. 33, 34, 35
Breckinridge, John 8, 133, 225
Brewer, Mary Taylor 145
Brink, John A. 209
Bristor (Bristow/Bristoe), William 20
Broadhead, Daniel 62
Brock, Henry 127, 128
Bronaugh, William 17
Brookes-Smith, Joan 260
Brooks, Abijah 214
Brooks, Thomas 30
Brown, James 222, 223
Brown, Jane Venable 195
Brown, John 222
Brown, Samuel 222
Brown, William 150
Browning, Caleb 120
Browning, Elijah G. 240
Browning, James 213
Bruner, John 215
Bryan, Daniel 18, 38, 39, 40, 45, 124
Bryan, Elizabeth 122
Bryan, George 31, 155
Bryan, James 61, 195
Bryan, Jonathan 190, 195, 197
Bryan, Joseph 197
Bryan, Martha (Strode) 197
Bryan, Morgan 197
Bryan, Rebecca 197
Bryan, Samuel 39
Bryan, William 38, 197
Bryan's Station 38, 40, 94, 108, 109, 113, 115, 197
Bryant, James 198
Buchanan, Ann 69
Buchanan, Bill 114
Buchanan, James 98, 115, 116
Buchanan, Jane 69
Buchanan, John 68, 69, 70, 71, 75, 85, 89, 246
Buchanan, Margaret 68, 70, 89
Buchanan, Margaret Patton 246
Buchanan, William 30, 64, 70, 72, 80, 113, 115, 116
Buckhannon, William 114
Buckner, Philip 142, 153, 154
Bullitt, Alexander S. 15
Bullitt, Cuthbert 15
Bullitt's Lick 50
Bullock, David 212, 216, 218, 219
Bullock, John 64
Bullock, Josiah 218
Bullock, Nathaniel 30, 60
Bundrin, David 48
Bunton, James 60, 61
Burch, Daniel 120
Burgess, Thomas N. 244
Burk, Patrick 209
Burnes, Dennis 209
Burrus, Jane 243
Burrus, Thomas 213
Bush Hollow 243
Bush, Ambrose 105, 120
Bush, Ambrose Jr. 119, 241, 243
Bush, Ambrose Sr. 243
Bush, C.E. 192
Bush, Francis 177
Bush, Howard 100, 101
Bush, James 243, 244
Bush, John 176
Bush, Jonathan 170, 171, 174, 183, 184, 188, 190, 191, 193, 194, 195, 199, 206
Bush, Lamentation 241, 243, 244
Bush, Philip 159, 160, 162, 163, 205, 212
Bush, Robert 203
Bush, Tillman 225
Bush, William 30, 41, 54, 100, 101, 132, 158, 159, 161, 162, 171, 176, 177, 190, 193, 194, 195, 196, 200, 205, 212, 218, 226, 227
Bush's Settlement 53, 54
Butler, John 61
Butler, Peter 14

C
Caldwell, Robert 249
Caldwell, William 108
Calk, William 131, 132, 152
Callaway, Caleb 81, 98
Callaway, Doshia [Theodocia] 98
Callaway, Edmund 121

283

Callaway, Elizabeth "Betsy" 9, 28, 33, 34, 35, 46, 47, 65, 68, 74, 79, 81, 82, 249, 250
Callaway, Flanders 28, 31, 34, 35, 74, 79, 121
Callaway, Frances "Fanny" 9, 10, 11, 28, 31, 32, 33, 34, 35, 36, 39, 47, 68, 74, 78, 79, 81, 82, 83, 85, 86, 88, 97, 120, 146, 153, 232, 239, 250
Callaway, George 81
Callaway, Isham 81
Callaway, Jack 108
Callaway, John 61, 81, 98, 113
Callaway, Keziah 31, 35, 81, 98, 153, 232
Callaway, Lydia 81, 98, 249
Callaway, Mary 81
Callaway, Mildred 81
Callaway, Nancy 81, 246
Callaway, Richard 9, 28, 30, 31, 34, 35, 37, 39, 41, 44, 46, 47, 49, 55, 61, 62, 65, 68, 81, 82, 91, 97, 98, 108, 113, 146, 232, 233, 245, 246
Callaway, Richard Jr. 30, 34, 81, 245, 246
Callaway, Sarah 81, 245
Callaway, Theodosia 81
Callaway, Zachariah 81
Calloway County, Kentucky 9, 81
Calloway, Eliza 32
Calloway, Jack 83, 109, 254, 255
Calloway, John 53
Calmes Neck 25
Calmes, Henry Jr. 165, 207
Calmes, Marquis 23, 25
Campbell County, Kentucky 131
Campbell, William 71
Cape, John 133, 139, 225
Carroll E. Ecton Reservoir 45
Carter, Allen 242
Cartwright, John 53
Cartwright, Justinian "Jesse" 101, 131, 132, 136
Cartwright, Robert 53
Cassiday's Creek 32
Cassidy, Francis 115
Cassidy, Michael 110, 115, 116
Chalkley, Lyman 257
Charles County, Missouri 122
Chism, Sarah L. 244
Christian, William 70, 126
Christy, Ambrose 162, 201
Churchill, Armistead 17
Clark County, Kentucky 7, 8, 9, 10, 13, 14, 22, 45, 54, 56, 74, 75, 76, 86, 91, 95, 100, 112, 118, 119, 120, 121, 124, 128, 131, 132, 133, 134, 137, 144, 146, 147, 151, 152,

154, 155, 156, 157, 159, 164, 165, 166, 176, 177, 180, 185, 187, 188, 197, 198, 199, 202, 203, 205, 211, 212, 213, 215, 216, 217, 219, 220, 221, 222, 223, 224, 225, 226, 227, 231, 232, 234, 236, 239, 240, 243, 245, 249, 254, 255, 256
Clark County, Virginia 14, 18, 21, 26, 27, 30
Clark, Bennett 212
Clark, Frances 141
Clark, George Rogers 8, 10, 37, 38, 40, 41, 43, 50, 51, 52, 55, 59, 63, 65, 115, 117, 126, 127, 141, 143
Clark, James 8, 133
Clark, Robert 160, 161, 205, 216
Clark, Robert Jr. 174, 182, 191, 212, 217, 219, 220, 226
Clark, Robert Sr. 212
Clark, Thomas 35, 147
Clark's Wabash Expedition 125
Clarke, Robert 214
Clay, Green 8, 212, 226
Clay, Henry 91, 119, 219, 226, 236
Clay, Porter 226
Clayton, Mary 222
Clemens, William 115
Clemms, John 114
Clemons, Elizabeth 116
Clemons, John 116
Clemons, William 116
Clemons/Clements, John 116
Cleveland, Alexander 97
Cleveland, Eli 63, 97, 155, 173
Cleveland, Oliver 97
Clift, G. Glenn 258
Clinkenbeard, Isaac 113, 114, 116
Clinkenbeard, William 66, 67, 87, 106, 114, 118
Cock, John 173
Coffee, Ambrose 64, 172
Colefoot, John 64, 107
Coleman, Lindsey 244
Collier, Mary A. 251, 253
Collins, Dillard 219
Collins, Elijah 61
Collins, Elisha 59
Collins, Josiah 50, 51, 57, 58, 59, 61, 114
Collins, Richard H. 35, 79, 258
Collins, William 61
Combs, Aaron Burr 241, 244
Combs, Benjamin 25, 135, 137, 218, 239, 244
Combs, Cuthbert 25
Combs, Cuthbert Jr. 135, 136, 137
Combs, Cuthbert Sr 135
Combs, Edwin 209

Combs, Elizabeth 244
Combs, Elliott 244
Combs, Fielding 135
Combs, Frances Maria 244
Combs, Glenmore 240
Combs, John H. 241, 243, 244
Combs, Joseph 135, 136, 137
Combs, Leslie 239, 240
Combs, Marquis 244
Combs, Mary Ann 244
Combs, Owen 244
Combs, Rufus K. 244
Combs, Samuel R. 120, 123, 125, 154, 155, 156, 157, 164, 171, 177, 183, 190, 205, 235, 239, 240, 241, 242, 243, 244, 246, 249, 253
Combs, Sarah Sophia 244, 246, 253
Combs, Theodocia/ Theodosia (Holder) 236, 239, 246
Combs, Werter 244
Combs, William 61
Combs' Ferry 106, 148, 155, 177, 178, 180, 207
Coney, Paula 12, 238
Coney, Robert 11, 238
Connell, James 209
Constant, John 53, 61, 90, 112, 116
Conway, Thomas 15
Cook, Bettie A.C. 259
Cook, David 107
Cook, Michael L. 222, 259
Cooke, David 61
Coons, John 209
Copher, Jesse 64
Corbin, Hannah 123
Cornwallis, Lord 107
Coshow, Mary Hughes 197
Cotterill, Robert S. 35, 110, 111, 112, 189, 190, 211
Cowan, John 65
Cox, Isaac 127
Cozart, Peter 64
Crabb, Anne 11, 258
Craddock, Robert 153, 226
Cradlebaugh, William 30, 53, 61, 64, 107
Craduck, Robert 152
Craig, Tolliver 173
Craig, William 218
Crawford, William Jr. 16
Crews, David 82
Crews, Zachariah 64
Crockett, Davy 245
Culpeper County, Virginia 14, 18, 21, 34, 146, 230, 251
Cumberland Gap 39, 52, 69
Cumberland River 69

D

Dale, John 213
Dalton, Valentine T. 126
de Gardoqui, Don Diego 139
Deacon, John 209

Deacon, Joseph 209
Decherd [Deckerd], Peter 34, 246, 250, 253
Denton, John 60
Denton, Thomas 63
DePaul University 7
DeQuindre, Antoine Dagnieau 45
Detherage, Phillip 137
Devine, Charles 209
Dickinson, Josiah 19
Dicks River 71
Didlake, Robert 190, 204, 205
Dillard, Thomas 41
Dix River 30
Dixon, Elizabeth 35
Dixon, Samuel 35
Donaldson, Patrick 67
Doniphan, Joseph 53, 90
Donnalson, Patrick 114
Dooling, Jacob 224
Douglas/Douglass, John 113, 114, 116
Doyle, George F. 258
Drake, Anna 73
Drake, Ephraim 69, 71, 73, 245
Drake, Euphemia 68, 88
Drake, James 72
Drake, John 72, 75, 76, 88, 89
Drake, Joseph 68, 69, 70, 71, 72, 74, 75, 76, 79, 80, 83, 88, 89
Drake, Margaret 46, 68, 72, 73, 74, 75, 76, 77, 80, 81, 83, 84, 85, 86, 88, 92, 94, 115, 229
Drake, Mary 72, 76, 88, 89
Drake, Michael 12
Drake, Nancy A. 89
Drake, Rhoda 68, 75, 76, 79, 80, 81, 83, 86, 88, 89
Drake, Sabrina 68, 83, 88
Drake, Samuel 69
Drake's Creek 70
Drake's Pond 70
Draper, Lyman C. 9, 10, 27, 29, 31, 34, 35, 38, 39, 40, 47, 48, 53, 57, 60, 61, 62, 70, 82, 114, 115, 117, 124, 125, 143, 146, 234, 236, 237, 250, 258
Draper's Meadows 69
Drowning Creek 73, 74
Dumford, John 61
Dumpard, Daniel 94
Dunbar, Harriett Jane 247, 253
Dunbar, William 248
Duncan, James 53, 213
Dunlap, James 180
Dunmore, Lord 21, 23, 24
Dunn, Michael 209
Dupree, Cornelia 251
Duree, Daniel 64
Duree, Samuel 53, 90
Dysart, James 69

E

Eaton, Sally 123

284

Edwards, Harkness 96
Elk Creek 39
Elk River 248
Elkhorn Creek 54, 173
Elkin, Robert 76, 122, 212
Elliott, John 218
Ellis, John 159
Enochs, Rebecca 197
Eslinger, Ellen 7, 12
Estill County, Kentucky 73, 133, 150, 203
Estill, Eudocia 35
Estill, James 52, 53, 61, 66, 74, 91, 92, 104, 107
Estill, Samuel 43, 52, 53, 64, 92
Estill's Station 104
Eubank, Achilles 134, 212
Evans, Oliver 170, 174
Evans, Peter 152
Everman, Arthur 123
Everman, Jacob 123
Everman, James 123
Everman, John 123
Everman, Mary 123
Exum, Benjamin 188, 190, 206

F

Fairfax County, Virginia 14
Fairfax, Thomas Lord 13, 18
Fallon, James 139
Falls of the Ohio 40, 49, 55, 62, 126
Faragher, John Mack 11, 35, 258
Farrell, Mary Alice 12
Fauquier County, Virginia 13, 14, 15, 16, 21, 120
Fayette County, Kentucky 41, 49, 66, 67, 72, 74, 76, 77, 85, 91, 94, 99, 100, 101, 103, 112, 117, 118, 121, 124, 128, 130, 131, 132, 133, 144, 145, 155, 157, 159, 166, 171, 212, 219, 226, 229, 232, 236, 239, 251
Fayette County, Virginia 8
Fear, Edmund 94, 97
Filson, John 108, 168
Fincastle County, Virginia 37, 69, 70
Fish, Nancy 123
Fishback, Lucy 234
Fitzhugh, William 133
Flanagan, James 201
Fleming County, Kentucky 111, 115, 131
Fleming Creek 110
Fleming, John 110, 112, 113, 114, 115, 116, 131, 132
Fleming, William 93, 95
Fleming's Pond 113
Floyd County, Kentucky 219
Floyd, Jane 173
Floyd, John 30, 69, 70, 71, 72, 73, 115, 135
Fluvanna County, Virginia 166

Forie, Albert 64
Fort Boonesborough 11, 37, 42, 49, 60, 68, 80, 99, 254
Fort Harrodsburg 37
Fort Laurens 59
Fort Pitt 62
Fort St. Asaph 37
Fort Steuben 142
Frame, John 180
Franklin County, Tennessee 11, 74, 75, 76, 83, 84, 86, 245, 246, 247, 248
Franklin, Thomas 133
Frederick County, Virginia 10, 14, 16, 18, 19, 21, 22, 25, 26, 76, 145, 222
French, Cuzza [Keziah] 98
French, James 31, 98, 132, 152, 153, 231, 232, 235
French, Richard 29, 31, 35, 243
Frost, Isaac 22
Frost, Thomas 22
Frost, William 22
Fulton, Patrick 202
Furr, Enoch 64

G

Gaines, John 213
Gano, Daniel 133, 225
Garrard, William 249
Gary, Andy 12
Gass, David 30, 46, 52, 53, 61, 64, 65, 91, 92, 107
Gass, Jennie 107
Gass, John 30, 45, 47, 53
Gass, Sarah 46
Gear [Fear], Edward 61
George, Nicholas 159, 160, 162
George, Whitson 53, 106, 162, 185
Gillespie, Edward 120
Girty, Simon 57, 109
Glasscock, Gregory 232
Goggans, William 64
Goochland County, Virginia 99
Goodman, Daniel 37
Goose Creek 16, 20
Graham, John 137, 138
Graham, Richard 133, 231
Grayson, Benjamin 133
Great Miami River 63, 117
Great Run 13, 14, 15
Great Salt Creek 254
Green River 38, 70, 135
Green, Edward 243
Greenslate, John 217
Grigsby, John 195
Grimes, Benjamin 122
Grubbs, Higgison 64
Guess [Gass], John 31
Gwynn's Island 24

H

Haggard, John 231
Haggin, John 55
Haley, Mary 252
Hall, Edward 53, 101, 135
Hall, John 220, 222

Hall, Micajah 150
Hall, Thomas 53
Hall, William 53
Halley, John 151
Hallock, Benjamin 220
Halyard, John 201, 202
Hamilton, James 64
Hamlin, John 41, 42, 43
Hammon, Neal 108, 259
Hampton, Alexander S. 193, 194
Hampton, David 225
Hancock Creek 45
Hancock, Stephen 44, 61, 91
Hancock, William 61
Hanging Fork 30
Hanks, Nancy 15
Hanover County, Virginia 26
Harbison, John 61
Hardin, Silas 55
Harding, Margery H. 259
Hargrave, Lt. 43
Harmar, Josiah 212
Harper, James 114, 116
Harper, Jim 113
Harper, John 53, 82, 114
Harper, Peter 53
Harris, Archy 150
Harris, Billy 150
Harris, Daniel 150
Harris, John 150
Harris, Tom 150
Harris, Webber 150
Harris, William 147, 148, 150, 216
Harrison County, Kentucky 63, 145, 150
Harrison, Benjamin 109
Harrod, James 37, 49, 50
Harrod, William 51, 55, 56, 60
Hart, Archie Elmer 253
Hart, David 30
Hart, Jessie Williams 18, 237, 239, 251, 259
Hart, Joel T. 193
Hart, John 193, 236, 245, 246, 251
Hart, Josiah 201, 218
Hart, Nathaniel 53, 66, 91, 98, 226, 251
Hart, Nathaniel Jr. 30, 105, 167
Hart, Thomas 222
Hartford, Adam 145
Harveson [Harbison], John 53
Hatton, Thomas 242
Hawiston, John 61
Hays, William 61, 63
Hazen, Ted 12
Hazen, Theodore R. 169
Hedgman River 13
Hedgman, George 14, 17
Hedgman, John 15
Hedgman, Nathaniel 13
Hedgman, Nathaniel Jr. 13
Hedgman, Peter 13, 14
Henderson, Betsey (Callaway) 245

Henderson, Fanny 79
Henderson, Richard 37, 38, 48, 71, 81, 91, 106
Henderson, Samuel 28, 30, 31, 32, 33, 35, 37, 74, 79, 245, 250
Hening, William W. 259
Henry, Patrick 41, 126
Hernden, William 244
Herndon, Osborne D. 248
Hewitt, E.A. 257
Hewitt, G.W. 257
Hickman, Richard 132, 177, 182, 212, 216, 218, 220, 235, 241, 248, 249
Hickman, William 57, 60
Hieronymous, Benjamin 106, 178, 237, 241, 244
Hieronymous, Francis 18
Hieronymous, Harry 236
Hieronymous, Henry 18, 101
Hieronymous, John 18
Higgins, Robert 218, 219, 220, 221, 224
Higgins, William 218
Hill, Albert 209
Hill, Gransond 209
Hill, Lenard 120
Hinde, Thomas 198
Hinkston Creek 63
Hite, Isaac 37
Hobbs, Maxine 12
Hockaday, Edmund 182, 190, 202, 205, 206, 207, 212
Hockaday, Isaac 184, 190, 202, 203
Hodges, Jesse 30, 44, 53, 57, 61, 64, 132
Hodgkin, Will 12
Hogan, William 63
Holden/Holder, Luke 122
Holder, Agatha 16
Holder, Benjamin 17, 124
Holder, Betsy 245
Holder, Bledsoe 246
Holder, Caleb 235, 236, 239, 246, 247, 253
Holder, Catherine "Kitty" 34, 125, 235, 236, 245, 250, 251, 253
Holder, Cibella 20
Holder, Cull 17, 18
Holder, Davis 14, 16
Holder, Davis Jr 14
Holder, Edah 120, 121
Holder, Elijah 124
Holder, Elizabeth 246
Holder, Fanny 98, 235, 236, 245, 247, 248
Holder, Frances "Fanny" 34, 74, 237, 238, 248, 249, 251, 253
Holder, Frances H. 246, 250, 253
Holder, Frances W. 249
Holder, Francis 13, 17, 18, 21, 120, 122, 123, 145, 221
Holder, Gary 123, 124
Holder, Grace 17

Holder, Harriett Jane 247, 248, 253
Holder, Harry 17
Holder, James 17
Holder, John W. 74, 121, 235, 239, 245, 246, 253
Holder, Lidda 235
Holder, Louisa 246
Holder, Luke 13, 14, 15, 16, 17, 18, 19, 20, 21, 25, 120, 122, 145
Holder, Lydia 236, 245, 248, 253
Holder, Margaret "Peggy" 13, 14, 122
Holder, Martin 246
Holder, Moses 246
Holder, Richard 235, 236, 245
Holder, Richard C. 239, 247, 248, 249, 253
Holder, Richard P. 18, 27, 33, 34, 125, 244, 246, 253
Holder, Robin 17
Holder, Sarah 17, 248
Holder, Sibby 83
Holder, Solomon 246
Holder, Sophia/Sophiah 235, 236, 239, 245, 246, 253
Holder, Susannah 16
Holder, Tassy 246
Holder, Theodocia/Theodosia 244, 249, 253
Holder, Virginia 246
Holder, William 14, 18, 34, 120, 143, 146, 248, 250, 253
Holder's Boatyard 140, 148, 150, 151, 152, 154, 174, 176, 177, 180, 182, 216
Holder's Creek 91, 94
Holder's Ferry 155, 176, 177, 182
Holder's Landing 148, 151, 162, 174
Holder's Station 7, 73, 80, 83, 104, 105, 106, 109, 114, 115, 122, 128
Holliday, Elliott 242
Holliday, James 242
Holliday, Joseph 242
Holliday, Waller 242
Holmes, Andrew 133, 225
Holston River 41, 70, 71
Holt, Carol 11
Hon, Nathaniel 64
Hood, Andrew 220
Hooten, William 188
Hoover, Henry 64
Hopkins, James F. 91, 236
Horn, Jeremiah 61
Houston Creek 91, 94, 97
Howard, Benjamin 138, 146
Howard, John 99, 100, 132, 134, 135, 137, 238
Howard, Mary 99
Howard, Thomas 251
Howard's Creek 7, 83, 101
Howell, Thomas 64
Howison, Thomas 15
Hoy, Elizabeth Jones 81

Hoy, Jones 108, 109, 113, 254, 255
Hoy, William 64, 108
Hoy's Station 83, 108, 109, 110
Huddleston, Holman A. 246
Huff, Samuel 64
Huger, Isaac 139, 143
Hughs, William 64
Hundley, Anthony 146
Hunt, David 12
Hunt, John 160, 161
Hunter, C.D. 257

I

Indian Creek 134, 230
Innes, Harry 102, 207
Iron Mountain 39
Irvine, Christopher 64, 98, 247, 249
Irvine, David 134
Irvine, Lydia 98, 247
Irvine, Mary 251
Irvine, William 98, 247

J

Jackson, Con 76
Jackson, Francis 120, 121, 147, 148, 149, 150
Jackson, Josiah 120, 147, 235
James River 69
James, Dick 209
James, James Alton 259
January, Joseph H. 244
Jefferson County, Kentucky 66, 126
Jefferson, Thomas 103
Jenkins, John S. 243
Johnson Creek 45
Johnson, George 113, 116, 231
Johnson, Richard M. 240
Johnson, Selid 209
Johnson, William 53
Johnston, Martin 213
Jones, Anita 12
Jones, Caleb Holder 249
Jones, Euphemia 75, 85, 86, 87, 89
Jones, James 115
Jones, Jane 83, 85, 86, 87, 88, 89
Jones, Lydia 239
Jones, Margaret Drake 74, 75, 84, 86, 87, 245
Jones, Mary Frances 249
Jones, Richard 74
Jones, Sabrina 75, 83, 85, 86, 89
Jones, Sibby 83
Jones, Thomas 25, 112, 116, 239, 249, 253
Jones, William 68, 72, 74, 75, 83, 84, 85, 86, 87, 88, 89, 229
Jordan, Sharshall 230, 231
Jouett Creek 96, 99, 101, 102, 105, 119, 122, 123, 131, 132, 220, 236, 241, 243, 244

Jouett, John 102, 103, 221, 222
Jouett, Matthew 99, 101, 102, 103
Judy, John 67
Jump, George 23, 26

K

Kaminsky, Donna 70
Kanawha River 22
Kaskaskia 41
Kavanaugh, Hannah Hinde 198
Kavanaugh, Williams 199
Kelley, Beale 53
Kelley, John 53
Kelly, Emanuel 116
Kelly, Manuel 114
Kennedy, John 44, 63, 91
Kennedy, Thomas 140
Kenton, Simon 44
Kentucky County, Virginia 9, 37, 49, 52, 61, 64, 65, 66, 81, 96
Kentucky River 7, 8, 9, 10, 22, 28, 45, 46, 53, 55, 66, 80, 95, 98, 99, 100, 101, 102, 104, 106, 109, 110, 119, 120, 121, 122, 128, 131, 134, 135, 137, 138, 145, 147, 148, 151, 152, 154, 155, 157, 158, 159, 162, 175, 177, 178, 179, 180, 182, 186, 187, 189, 207, 210, 216, 220, 229, 230, 235, 236, 241
Kerley, William 247, 249
Kieler, Abram 64
Kincheloe's Station 116
King George County, Virginia 14
King George III 223
Kirkham, Robert 61
Kirkham, Samuel 61
Kleber, John 259
Knox, John 14
Kohlhass, Henry 243

L

Lake Erie 247
Landrum, William B. 22
Lauman, Frederick 227, 229, 230, 232
Leavy, William 227
Lee, John 61
Levin, H. 26
Lewis, Asa K. 243
Lewis, Thomas 17, 173
Licking River 55, 56, 63, 108, 109, 110, 111, 112, 113, 132, 254
Licking Run 14
Lincoln County, Kentucky 30, 62, 66, 67, 98, 126, 131
Lincoln, Abraham 15
Lindsey, Abraham 22
Lingenfelter, Valentine 215
Littell, William 259
Little Kentucky River 72
Little Miami River 56, 58, 59, 63, 117
Little, Elizabeth 12

Lockhart, Charles 53, 61, 64
Lockhart, Edward 53
Logan, Benjamin 37, 43, 55, 56, 58, 63, 64, 65, 66, 109, 117, 126
Logan, John 44, 63
Logan's Station 37, 49, 55
Long, John 116
Looney's Ferry 69
Loramie, Pierre 117
Loudoun County, Virginia 14, 16, 20, 21, 122, 145
Love, Thomas 133
Lower Blue Licks 28, 30, 40, 44, 45, 104, 112, 115, 116, 175
Lower Howard's Creek 6, 8, 9, 18, 28, 30, 45, 49, 76, 83, 86, 87, 98, 99, 101, 102, 103, 104, 105, 106, 109, 112, 123, 129, 131, 132, 134, 136, 137, 144, 145, 147, 150, 151, 152, 153, 154, 155, 158, 159, 164, 165, 166, 167, 170, 171, 172, 174, 175, 177, 179, 182, 185, 186, 188, 189, 190, 194, 195, 197, 198, 199, 201, 203, 204, 205, 206, 207, 208, 211, 221, 224, 229, 235, 236, 240, 241, 244, 256
Lower Howard's Creek Nature and Heritage Preserve 9, 145, 164, 167, 172, 178, 179, 185, 186, 195, 204, 208, 255
Lulbegrud Creek 123
Lulbegrud River 172, 224
Lydanne, James P. 179
Lyddane, Abigail 203
Lyddane, Alice 203
Lyddane, Charles 203, 205, 211
Lyddane, James 202, 203
Lynch, David 64, 107
Lynn, Edmund 93

M

Madden, George 53
Madison County, Kentucky 73, 74, 76, 87, 90, 94, 98, 113, 137, 140, 146, 152, 153, 154, 155, 156, 177, 179, 182, 212, 220, 221, 222, 226, 232, 235, 247, 248, 249, 251
Malone, John 25
Mann's Lick 50
Mansker, Kaspar 69
Marsh Run 13
Marshall, Daniel 89
Marshall, Humphrey 102
Marshall, John 15
Marshall, Thomas 17, 98
Martin, Austin 202
Martin, Charles K.V. 251
Martin, Henry 209
Martin, Hudson 243
Martin, John 30, 31, 53, 60, 74, 91, 94, 97, 166, 171, 201, 218, 224

Martin, John C. 243
Martin, John Jr. 166, 172, 224, 225
Martin, John Sr. 166, 172, 182, 224
Martin, John W. 165, 187, 207, 208
Martin, Orson 166, 171, 172, 173, 182, 184, 190, 198, 200, 201
Martin, Rachel (Pace) 166, 201
Martin, Richmond 209
Martin, Robert 190, 209, 210
Martin, Sarah H. 243
Martin, Valentine 166
Martin, William 166, 171, 176, 182
Martin, Willis 179, 207
Martin's Ford 184
Martin's Station 62, 63, 64
Mason County, Kentucky 131
Mastin, Bettye Lee 260
Mathews, Andrew 246
Matlock, John D. 251
Matthews, J.D. 78
Maxwell, Thomas 135, 136, 137
May, George 102, 107, 132
May, John 102
May, Phil 11, 29, 46, 150
May, William 99, 102
McAfee, William 63
McAfee's Station 117
McCall, John 205
McCann, Neil 177
McCauley, James 244
McCauley, William H. 244
McCollom, John 61
McCormack, Stephen 14
McCracken, William 117
McCroskey, Andrew 140, 149
McCullough, James 43
McDougal, Nancy 149
McGary, Hugh 112, 117
McGee, David 96, 102
McGee, William 61
McGee's Station 67, 95, 104, 105, 106, 113, 114, 118, 236
McGuire, Betsy 236
McGuire, Edward 239, 249, 250, 253
McGuire, Edward Jr. 250
McGuire, Frances W. 239, 250
McGuire, John 177, 214, 236, 245, 249, 250
McIntyre, John 131
McKee, Alexander 108, 117
McKinney, James F. 203
McKinney, Robert 219
McKinzie, Jerry 209
McMillan, James 132, 182, 212, 216, 217, 218, 221
McMillan, John 30
McMillan, Robert 105, 212
McMillan, William 180
McMillion, James 214

McMullen, John 31
McQuiston, William 248
McVicar, Daniel 201
Meadows, Larry 11, 147
Mercer County, Kentucky 103, 221
Merritt, George W. 243
Miller, Benjamin J. 242
Miller, Elizabeth 252
Miller, John 247
Miro, Esteban 140, 141
Mississippi River 50, 139, 147, 148, 173, 248
Mitchell, Rachel 123
Moluntha 45
Monongahela River 117
Montgomery County, Kentucky 76, 124, 133
Montgomery County, Missouri 83, 84, 85, 86
Montgomery County, Virginia 37, 69
Montgomery, Alexander 44
Montgomery, John 29
Morgan, Charles 168, 174
Morgan, Ralph 52, 53, 61, 90, 91
Morgan, Robert 11
Morgan, William 53, 90
Morris, William 61
Morrow, James 120
Morton, John 213, 220
Moss, John 18
Moss, Zealy 18, 120
Moultrie, Alexander 139, 140, 143
Mount, Pat 12
Mount, Thomas 222
Muddy Creek 90, 113
Murdoch, John 60

N

Neel, Joe Kendall 12, 151, 184, 185, 193, 199
Nelson, Edward 241, 242
Nelson, George 241
Nelson, James 241
Nelson, Jefferson 241
Nelson, Joel 241
Nelson, Julius 241
Nelson, Moses 41, 61, 94, 97
Nelson, Reuben 241
Nelson, Sabrina 241, 242
Nelson, William 241
New Chillicothe 117
New Piqua 117
New River 39, 69
Newell, Roberta "Bobbi" 12
Nicholas County, Kentucky 111, 254
Nicholas, George 8, 26, 133, 225
Nolan, Philip 142
Northern Neck 19

O

O'Fallon, James 139, 140, 141, 142, 143, 153, 154
O'Malley, Nancy 12
O'Post 42
Oder, Thomas 98

Ohio River 22, 44, 50, 51, 56, 59, 63, 71, 72, 117, 149
Old Chillicothe 56, 63, 117
Oldham, Jesse 53
Oliver, Doug 176
Orange County, Virginia 14
Orear, Daniel 201
Orear, William 159, 161, 212
Otter Creek 151
Ousley, Wyatt 244
Owen, Elizabeth 198
Owen, Kathryn 6, 11, 192
Owen, Lawrence 198

P

Parberry, James 131
Parish, John 143, 260
Parker, Green A. 193
Parrish, Moses 120
Parrish, William 177
Patrick, John 232, 233, 246, 248
Patterson, Robert 107
Patton, James 51, 69
Patton, Margaret 70, 89
Patton, Mary 70
Patton, Matthew 174, 182, 183, 191
Payne, Jilson 214, 215, 216
Peake, Jesse 53
Peddicord, Betham 243
Peddicord, William 243
Pendleton, Edmund 23
Penn, Catharine/Catherine 239, 245, 246, 253
Penn, Gabriel 245
Perry, James 61
Persley, Benjamin 152
Peyton, Timothy 131
Platt, Ebenezer 140, 223, 225
Pleak, John 64, 176
Plick, John 61
Pogue, William 31
Poindexter, Ann 243
Poindexter, Nancy 243
Point Pleasant 22
Polsgrove, Robert 12
Poor, Jeremiah 116
Poor, Jerry 112
Pope, William 29
Porter, Samuel 61
Post Vincennes 127
Post Vincent 126
Poste du Ouabache 42
Potomac River 18
Powell County, Kentucky 122, 133, 147, 225
Powell, Levin 17, 20, 91
Powell, Milly 150
Powell's Valley 69
Preston, William 69, 70, 71, 99, 115
Price, Francis 218
Prince William County, Virginia 13, 14, 15, 18, 20, 21, 38, 222, 246
Proctor, Henry 247
Proctor, Joe 113, 114
Proctor, Joseph 53, 64, 104, 107, 116

Proctor, Nicholas 53, 61, 64
Proctor, Page 43, 60, 114, 116
Proctor, Reuben 53, 60, 61, 64, 107, 146
Proctor, Richard 113

Q

Quisenberry, James 243
Quisenberry, Jane 243
Quisenberry, Robert L. 200

R

Ragland, Edmund 212
Ragsdale, Gabriel 248
Raisor, Jerry 12
Ranck, George 18, 21, 35, 42, 61, 77, 79, 260
Randolph, Beverly 101
Rankins, Benjamin 18, 75, 145
Rankins, Jane 75
Rankins, John 18, 21, 82, 83, 118
Rankins, Reuben 117
Rappahannock River 13, 14, 15, 18, 24
Raven Run Nature Sanctuary 94
Rawlings, Pemberton 44, 61, 62, 91
Ray, John 213
Red River 123, 147, 172, 224, 225
Redstone Old Fort 117, 149
Reed Creek 69, 72
Reed, James 201
Rees, John 190, 203
Regan, Philip 24, 25
Reid, Nathan 30
Richardson, Mary 239
River Raisin 247
River Thames 247
Robertson, James R. 260
Robertson, Jesse 213
Robinson, David 37
Rockcastle County, Kentucky 250
Rogers, Polly 123
Rollins, Pemberton 45
Ross, Hugh 57, 61
Rout, George 14, 122, 145, 220
Rout's Hill 14
Rowan County, North Carolina 38, 39, 41, 197
Ruddle's Station 55, 62, 64

S

Saffell, W.T.R. 26
Sap Branch 111
Sapington, John 152
Scaggs, Deidre 12
Scholl, Joseph 32
Scholl, Septimus 32, 33
Scioto River 44
Scritchfield's Ford 39
Searcy, Bartlett 61, 74, 131, 132
Searcy, Reuben 61
Seitz, John A. 227, 229, 230, 232

287

Settle, Joseph 15
Shane, John 31, 32, 33, 35, 38, 39, 47, 66, 76, 82, 110, 113, 118, 124, 216
Sharpe, John 159
Shelburne Parish 16, 17, 18, 20
Shelby County, Kentucky 222
Shelby, Isaac 8, 9, 159, 212, 213
Shelhy, Wilmit 142
Shely, Pat 193
Shenandoah River 20, 22, 26
Shenandoah Valley 25
Shore, Diana 245
Silver Creek 90, 94, 97, 220, 222
Simmons, Peter 248
Sims, Jane B. 75
Sims, Julius 75, 84, 86, 89
Sipple, Clare 12, 206, 255
Skidmore, Warren 70
Smith, C.R. "Pete" 6, 211, 238
Smith, Charles 222
Smith, E. Kirby 245
Smith, Enoch 132, 214, 216
Smith, Jacob 121
Smith, John 25
Smith, Samuel 204, 226, 227
Smith, William Bailey 10, 29, 30, 31, 37, 38, 39, 40, 41, 43, 46, 64, 132
Snicker, Edward 20, 22, 25
Snicker's Ford 26
Snicker's Gap 19, 20
Snickers Ferry 22
Snipes, William Clay 139
Snow Creek 122
Snowden, James A. 246
South Elkhorn Creek 90
South, Jack 53, 57
South, John 46, 53, 56, 60, 61, 64, 65, 91, 98, 132
South, John Jr. 61, 64, 65, 92, 98, 107
South, John Sr. 92, 98
South, Margaret 46, 48
South, Thomas 57, 60, 61
South, Tom 53
Speed, James 87
Sphar, Daniel 66
Spiker, Phyllis 12
Spohr, Jacob 67
Spring, Simon 153, 223
St. Asaph 40
St. Clair, Arthur 212
Stafford County, Virginia 14, 18, 21, 137
Stagner, Barney 61
Staples, Charles R. 222
Stapleton, John 61
Starnes, Jacob 57, 61, 64
Station, Bryant's 118
Stearns [Starnes], Jacob 53
Stevens, Hubbard L. 193
Stevens, James 213, 214
Stevens, Thomas 232
Stevenson, James M. 216
Stevenson, William 116

Stone, Uriah 69
Stoner Creek 30, 63
Stoner, Michael 37, 70
Stonestreet, James 75, 234
Stout, John 244
Stovall, Jesse 89
Stovall, John 76, 83, 89
Stovall, Mary 75
Stribling, Sigismund 22
Strode, Jeremiah 213
Strode, Jerry 160
Strode, John 53, 96, 215, 218
Strode's Creek 45
Strode's Station 66, 67, 87, 96, 104, 106, 110, 113, 118, 132, 144, 215
Strong, William 106
Stroud's Station 105
Sturgis, General 195
Styles, Michael 209
Sudduth, William 18, 114, 132, 134, 214, 216, 219, 235
Surry County, North Carolina 14
Swearingin, Benoni 53, 61, 90, 91, 132
Swearingin, Thomas 53, 90, 91, 131, 132
Sycamore Shoals 38
Sympson, James 133, 225
Sympson, William 225

T

Tate, Robert 222
Tate, William 203, 204
Tate, Zachariah 204
Tates Creek 229
Taylor, Catherine (Bushrod) 145
Taylor, Edmund 91, 179, 190, 199, 200
Taylor, Griffin 145
Taylor, Hubbard 177, 214, 220
Taylor, John 53, 64, 90, 133, 231
Taylor, Richard 259
Taylor, William 145, 173, 184, 190, 197, 198, 199, 200, 243
Tecumseh 247
Tennessee River 248
Terrell, Obediah 69
Theobalds, William 150
Thomas, Elizabeth 31
Thompson, James 70
Thompson, Laurence 53, 226, 227
Thompson, Margaret W. 244
Thruston, Charles Minn 91
Tin Pot Run 13
Tinsley, William 213
Todd, John 9, 37, 115
Todd, Levi 55, 56, 63, 115, 219, 222
Todd, Robert 128, 158
Trabue, Daniel 48, 51, 55, 95, 124
Treaty of Watauga 38

Trigg, Stephen 93, 115
Trimble, Robert 8
Trimble, William 173, 190, 207
Triplett, William 131
Turkey Run 14
Twomile Creek 22, 209

U

Upper Blue Licks 73, 108, 109, 110, 115, 116, 254
Upper Howard's Creek 99, 134, 135, 136, 137, 138, 172, 224

V

Vallandingham, Benoni 61
Vaughn, Edward M. 77
Vaughn, Elijah "Eli" 68, 74, 75, 76, 77, 80, 89, 106, 120, 123, 234
Vaughn, Enis 120
Vaughn, Rhoda Drake 75, 76, 77, 78, 79, 80, 234
Venable, John 195
Verhoeff, Mary 260
Vicksburg 10
Vincennes 41, 42, 55, 126, 127
Virginia Land Commission 31, 40, 73, 93, 96, 99, 100, 102, 132
Virginia Land Law 92, 93
Vivion, Thomas 202

W

Wabash River 42, 126
Wade, James 110, 114
Wade, Richard 30
Wallace, Caleb 102
Wallings Bottom 39
Walnut Hills 10
Walton, Frances 81, 98
Walton, George 130
Walton, Matthew 8, 98, 130, 131, 132
Walton, Richard 81
Walton, Sherwood 130
Wancopin Creek 20
Wankopin Branch 20
Washington County, Virginia 37, 70, 74, 130
Washington, George 26, 40, 69, 107, 127, 140, 141
Washington, Thomas 143
Wayne, Anthony 142, 213
Webb, George 224
Webb, Richard 205
Weber, John 61
West Fork 198
West, Samuel 160
Wheeler, Benjamin Dod 119, 120, 234
White, Aquilla 53, 104, 116, 146
White, Benjamin 53, 64
Whitley's Station 55
Wickliffe, Robert 99
Wiggard, George O. 202
Wilcoxen, Daniel 61
Wilderness Trail 51
Wilkerson, John 190, 203

Wilkerson, William 190, 205
Wilkinson, James 140, 141, 142, 143, 147, 148, 149, 150, 152
Williams, Catharine/ Catherine 239, 250
Williams, David Napoleon 252
Williams, Edward 53, 82
Williams, Eliza 251
Williams, Frances Holder 251
Williams, Harriet Eloisa 252
Williams, Howard 248
Williams, Jacob John 252
Williams, Jesse Caleb 251, 253
Williams, Jessie 253
Williams, John 213, 251
Williams, John Jr. 93
Williams, Mary Catherine 251
Williams, Oscar Waldo 237, 252
Williams, Rachel Amelia 251
Williams, Richard G. 34, 125, 236, 237, 239, 251, 253
Williams, Samuel 74
Williams, Sophia 251
Williams, Susan Maria Virginia 252
Williams, William 247, 252
Wilson, Eliza 252
Wilson, James 252
Wilson, John 112, 116
Wilson, Judy 11
Wilson, Moses 61
Wilson, William H. 251
Wilson's Station 96
Winchester, James 245
Winter, Elisha 229
Wood, James 123
Woodford County, Kentucky 26, 103
Woodford, S.A.B. 195
Woodford, William 23
Woodward, James T. 155, 165, 178
Woolsey, Thomas 70
Wright, Patience Lovell 223
Wyatt, Fleming 242
Wyatt, George 242
Wyatt, Manuel 242
Wyatt, Thomas 242

Y

Yadkin River 10, 37, 38, 39, 42, 197
Yazoo River 139
York River 23, 24
Young, Chester Raymond 260
Young, Jacob 72
Young, William 120